PRAISE FOR *MADELINE KAHN*

"Madeline Kahn is remembered for her roles in *Blazing Saddles, Paper Moon*, and *Young Frankenstein*, and in his groundbreaking and definitive new biography, William V. Madison captures the complex and rich life of an artist striving for more in the glamorous, hard-knocks world of show business. Madison proves a gifted and sensitive biographer, and *Madeline Kahn: Being the Music* is an addictive read. A riveting and unforgettable portrait."

—CHRISTINA HAAG

actress and *New York Times* bestselling author of *Come to the Edge: A Love Story*

"Despite the great brio of her iconic comic roles, there was always something poignant and enigmatic about Madeline Kahn. In his wonderfully researched and sensitive biography, William V. Madison examines the threads that made her so fascinating and gives her a well-deserved place in the history of great comic actresses."

—CHARLES BUSCH

actor and playwright, *The Tale of the Allergist's Wife* and *The Divine Sister*

"With the devotion of an ardent fan and the astute thoroughness of a scholar, William V. Madison charts the star-crossed life and career of one of the greatest comedic actresses of the twentieth century. This is a marvelous book that I will love reading again and again."

—WENDY LAWLESS

New York Times bestselling author of *Chanel Bonfire*

"A lot of us have been waiting a long, long time to find out the real story of this precious, unique talent who left us far too soon. William Madison's biography of Madeline Kahn comes as a kind of gift. With great sensitivity, he captures the poignancy and the humor that went hand-in-hand in creating one of the great comic personas of the late twentieth century."

—ERIC MYERS

author of *Uncle Mame: The Life of Patrick Dennis*

"Madeline Kahn balked at attempts to biographize her in her lifetime, so she might not even read William V. Madison's haunting new book were she alive today. But for everyone else who followed her career, and for everyone who found her an enigmatic delight on stages and screens, the book is a resonant must-read, evoking its subject and the golden age of theater and film in which she lived. Madison manages to combine scholarship, a critical eye, and just enough gossip to make this a book worthy of its subject—appropriately entertaining and profoundly incisive at the same time."

—TOM SHALES
Pulitzer Prize–winning television critic

"A fine biography, worthy of Madeline's unique talent and contribution."

—ROBERT KLEIN
New Faces of 1968, The Sisters Rosensweig, and Mixed Nuts

"Madeline Kahn is the best comic or best dramatic actress, the best singer—serious or comic—and the best I've worked with, or known in my life."

—GENE WILDER
Blazing Saddles, Young Frankenstein, and The Adventures of Sherlock Holmes' Smarter Brother

"Madeline was bright, committed, thoughtful, and one of the most remarkable actresses I have ever worked with. Her work was character driven, not just for laughs, which made her unique on stage and on film. William V. Madison's biography captures Madeline's complexity and finely documents her career and personal life."

—JANE ALEXANDER
actress, author, former chairman of the National Endowment for the Arts, and wildlife conservationist

"Bids to become the surprise biography of the year. A great untold story intriguingly revealed. Superbly researched, digs deep into the life and times of its subject and captures her essence. Madison also expertly weaves in one sensitive analysis after another of what has happened to acting and actors; to American film, theater, television, and comedy the last half-century plus—and why."

—DAN RATHER
journalist and author

MADELINE KAHN

HOLLYWOOD LEGENDS SERIES
CARL ROLLYSON, GENERAL EDITOR

MADELINE KAHN

BEING THE MUSIC • A LIFE

WILLIAM V. MADISON

University Press of Mississippi • Jackson

www.upress.state.ms.us

Designed by Peter D. Halverson

The University Press of Mississippi is a member of the Association of
American University Presses.

First printing 2015
∞
Library of Congress Cataloging-in-Publication Data

Madison, William V.
Madeline Kahn : being the music, a life / William V. Madison.
pages cm. — (Hollywood legends series)
Includes bibliographical references and index.
ISBN 978-1-61703-761-0 (cloth : alk. paper) — ISBN 978-1-61703-762-7
(ebook) 1. Kahn, Madeline. 2. Actors—United States—Biography. I. Title.
PN2287.K15M34 2015
791.4302'8092—dc23
[B]
2014042232

British Library Cataloging-in-Publication Data available

CONTENTS

PART III: THE 1980s

-173-

PART IV: THE 1990s
-243-

MADELINE KAHN

Introduction

"ARE YOU LEAVING BECAUSE I'M UGLY?" AS AN ADULT, MADELINE KAHN couldn't remember whether she had measles or chicken pox or mumps the night her father walked out. All she knew was that her daddy was leaving, that she was "ugly," and that these things must be linked. That her parents' breakup might have nothing to do with her—and quite a lot to do with her mother—didn't occur to a little girl not yet three years old. She never fully came to terms with what happened that night, and she shared the story with very few friends.

Little Madeline would grow up to be one of the top comic actresses of her generation, so much a fixture in American popular culture that it's hard for some to grasp that she's gone. A decade after her death, one of her colleagues asked whether I'd spoken to her recently, and asked that I give Madi her love. Though Madeline's professional career spanned thirty-five years on film, stage, and television, her enduring reputation rests almost exclusively on a few movies, particularly *What's Up, Doc?*, *Paper Moon*, *Blazing Saddles*, and *Young Frankenstein*, all released between 1972 and 1974. They earned her two consecutive Oscar nominations for Best Supporting Actress and, especially among college boys, a pin-up status she loathed. She was nothing like the bawdy characters she played in Mel Brooks's movies, she complained, and she worried that fans who approached her would be disappointed to discover the reserved, refined, and intensely private woman she really was.

More than funny, she was (most of the time) a highly disciplined professional. She earned a degree in speech therapy from Hofstra University and sought work as a teacher, but as she took on ever-greater responsibility for her erratic, extravagant mother, she recognized the importance of money. She quickly learned that show business paid better than the

New York City schools could. A fiercely independent career woman, she nevertheless relied on two men, Peter Bogdanovich and Mel Brooks, for the roles that defined her, and without them she floundered. Gifted with shrewd intelligence and profound intuition, she seemed unsure of her talents. She was nobody's fool—except when it came to her mother, who manipulated her in every area of her life. Madeline was a popular star who fretted that she'd never work again, and she nearly ended her career herself with her disastrous experience in *On the Twentieth Century* on Broadway in 1978. In the 1980s, as Bernadette Peters and Bette Midler eclipsed her on Broadway and in Hollywood, Madeline asked her brother to let her live on his farm in Virginia, so certain was she that her career was finished. Then, only a few years later, she staged an inspiring comeback and maintained a steady momentum that continued until her death.

There was never any real question of *not* working, but Madeline often took jobs she didn't want, in projects that weren't to her taste. Like many actors, she struggled with typecasting, beginning when she was still in college. Like many other comedians, she yearned to play dramatic roles that, with rare exceptions, simply weren't forthcoming. The challenge, then, was to find the drama in comedy, to take seriously the most ludicrous characters and situations. Yet Madeline never fully emerged from the pigeonholes in which others placed her. At various points and to various people, she was *just* a comedian, *just* a singer, *just* a TV personality, *just* a movie star, *just* a character actor—presumptions that had important consequences for the roles she was offered and the working relationships she established.

Her career led her to work with some of the most important creative talents of her time: from Jerry Lewis to Bill Cosby, from Carol Burnett to Lily Tomlin, from Neil Simon to Charles Ludlam, from Leonard Bernstein to the Muppets. While the vast majority of her collaborators liked and admired her, she clashed with others, notably Danny Kaye, Harold Prince, and Lucille Ball. Her own anxieties succeeded in alienating some colleagues as well as directors such as Peter Bogdanovich and even, briefly, Gene Wilder. Tensions sometimes arose because of her habit of developing crushes (several of them reciprocal) on her leading men. But starting with the moment her father walked out, she remained wary of men and insecure about her looks, with ramifications for her professional as well as her personal life. After her parents divorced, her mother married and divorced once more, and her father married, divorced, and married again. For the rest of Madeline's adult life, she would maintain a doubtful opposition to marriage in general. Though she had several long-term boyfriends, she never lived with any of them, preferring to preserve her independence. Only in 1999, weeks before her death from ovarian cancer, did she marry the man she'd dated for the previous decade, John Hansbury.

Madeline had scant interest in sharing her life story, and she'd have fought to stop anyone else from publishing it. What mattered most to her was that she be taken seriously as an artist. When one does so, one returns, again and again, to the importance of music in her work. Inherited from both parents, her musical aptitude was first developed by her mother, a piano teacher and aspiring opera singer. Thus Madeline's gifts carried a significant liability: They were associated with a fraught relationship and with childhood memories of her mother pushing her to perform for friends and neighbors. Writing in her private notebook, Madeline described the way she learned to sing as *"not* to find 'my' voice," but based instead on "fear of retaliation."[1] A fundamental discomfort remained with her all her life despite her talent and success.

Because Madeline filmed only a few musicals, and sang only isolated snippets in other movies (including *Young Frankenstein* and *Clue*), movie audiences may not realize how central singing was to her rise as a performer. Yet Madeline owed all of her earliest opportunities and successes to her ability to sing, and it gave her an advantage at auditions. She landed a role in *Two by Two*, not least because the show's composer and producer, Richard Rodgers, knew she could sing coloratura, whereas other actresses could not. Though she sang only one professional operatic engagement, in 1970, as late as the mid–1980s Madeline continued to consider invitations from American opera companies.

Even when she wasn't singing, Madeline treated every script as if it were a score. She interpreted words as notes, establishing rhythm, accents, tonal coloring—and of course tempo, wherein lay the secret of her comic timing, as Mel Brooks observes. Improvising with her, Bill Cosby says, was like playing jazz. Hearing her high-pitched, somewhat nasal speaking voice and careful diction, audiences might be inclined to laugh anyway, but she exerted a formidable control over the responses she got, even when she had no other control over the material she played or the directors and actors who surrounded her.

During a break in the filming of Marshall Brickman's *Simon* (1980), Alan Arkin asked Madeline which of her many talents she considered her foremost. She was unable to answer him. "Well, what was the first thing you thought of doing?" he asked. "There had to be something."

Again she tried to thread her way back to her childhood ambitions. "I used to listen to a lot of music." She paused, trying to find the words for what she was thinking. "And that's what I wanted to be," she finally said.

"I don't know what you mean," I said.

She answered, and it sounded as if she'd never formulated this thought before, as if it was news to herself.

"I wanted to be the music," she said.[2]

PART I

1942–69

Childhood

MADELINE GAIL WOLFSON WAS BORN SEPTEMBER 29, 1942, AT MEMORIAL Hospital in Chelsea, Massachusetts, across the Mystic River from Boston. Her parents lived in nearby Revere at the time. Bernard P. Wolfson was twenty years old, and his wife, née Freda Goldberg, just eighteen. The couple had been married barely a year and had known each other only a little longer. Theirs wasn't entirely a stereotypical whirlwind wartime romance, and Bernie didn't join the US Army until after becoming a father. But a whirlwind it was—spurred on, no doubt, by a physical attraction that would have been strong, maybe irresistible, even if the world had not been at war. Both of Madeline's parents were strikingly good-looking: Bernie was lean, dark, and brooding; Freda red-haired and voluptuous. She passed on to her daughter the "bone structure" about which Trixie Delight would boast in *Paper Moon* (1973).

Both Freda and Bernie were fashion plates (Bernie went on to work in the garment industry), and each had a good sense of humor. Their daughter grew up to reflect and appreciate these qualities. Above all, both Freda and Bernie loved music. Years later, Madeline vividly recalled playing the "Dance of the Hours" from Ponchielli's opera *La Gioconda*, which she'd discovered through Disney's *Fantasia*. "I suppose we all had one [moment] when we said, 'Ooh, that's what I want to do,'" she told the graduating class of the American Academy of Dramatic Arts in 1989. "And my first moment was pre-speech—I could run and walk, but I couldn't carry on a conversation." Playing the record, "I just went 'Aaow!' you know, inside. And I wanted to play it again, hear that go again. It took me to that resting place, and then—Whoa! Fury! I just became *fevered*." She described "[an] awareness that there is some kind of journey you can take, without going anywhere, which transports you, utterly. And the moment I became aware of that, I just was forever different. From that point on, I wanted to sing and dance, and do things, or anything like that—*alone*. Not in front of *people*—utterly terrible idea."[1]

Bernie was an amateur who sang purely for pleasure. Freda had studied voice, and for most of her long life, she harbored ambitions for a professional career as a performer. In both training and tone, Madeline's voice was her mother's. Even in old age, Freda sounded much like her famous daughter when she spoke—the same sweet timbre, the lilting inflections.

Seeing Madeline's early affinity for music, Freda taught her to sing and play piano while she was still a toddler, and as late as the 1970s, she was still coaching her daughter. Among friends, Madeline made fun of her mother's lessons. Some can still imitate the exaggerated facial expressions she used to produce vowel sounds, and Madeline's younger brother remembers that his sister's sparkling high notes were achieved by evoking those times when he forgot to empty the cat's litter-box. Yet Freda's lessons provided a solid foundation on which Madeline would build as an adult with the help of professional coaches, including Beverley Peck Johnson and Marlena Malas. In short, Freda must have done something right, and music remained an important bond between her and her daughter. Moreover, Madeline's success using her mother's techniques suggests that Freda herself might have succeeded, if only she'd worked as hard as her daughter did.

Freda spent the end of her life in a nursing home in Virginia. I spoke with her in 2008, when her senile dementia had set in. She demurred when I asked for a singing lesson, and she could tell me little of Madeline. Her memory was bad, she said. In any case, it was easier to forget many parts of her life. Freda was a less than perfect mother, and Bernie was only one of the men who abandoned her.

When her own mother, Rose, became an invalid sometime in the 1930s, Freda's father, Samuel Goldberg, left the responsibility of her younger siblings (a sister, Mindy, and a brother, Ted) to Freda. Then, when Rose Goldberg died in 1945, Sam remarried. Pressured by his second wife (also named Rose), he quit his children altogether, and he stopped providing Freda with financial support, complaining that she only spent the money on singing lessons. With Bernie still deployed in the war, Freda was now saddled with the teenaged Ted, who was by his own account a hellion. (She did manage, though, to rope him into baby-sitting young Madeline). Furious with her father, Freda took Sam to court—and lost.

Around that time, not long after the end of the war, Bernie Wolfson came home. Almost immediately it became clear that he and Freda were incompatible. Bernie laid the blame for their divorce squarely on Freda's ambition: She wanted to move to New York, whether he wanted to go or not. She spun the story her own way, suggesting that Bernie was a womanizer and that the divorce was his fault. For most of her life, Madeline believed Freda's account. But Jeffrey Kahn, Freda's son from her second marriage, was more skeptical. "It's my impression that Mother was difficult, and that he was a very decent, nice guy," he says. "It was my mother's eccentricities and desire to pursue a career that tore things apart."

Other family members interpreted the break-up differently. "Your dad came home from the Army and HE LEFT HER," Madeline's uncle Ted wrote to her many years later. Ted had waited until he graduated high school, in 1945, then lied about his age in order to join the army, using the birth certificate of a brother who'd died in infancy. "I just wanted to run away and that was the only [way] to get out. I didn't think of Freda, either. I LEFT HER. Just now, as I wrote this paragraph, I fully realize the tragedy, pain and despair she must have been going through in just those short months. EVERYBODY in her family LEFT! At 22, a single mother with no money, no craft, and alone."[2]

Ted Barry, who changed his name shortly after the war, wrote that letter in 1998, as it became clear to Madeline and Jef Kahn that Freda was mentally unstable and incapable of caring for herself. When Madeline contacted her uncle, she'd heard only her mother's side of the story. For decades Freda had done her utmost to keep her brother at odds with the rest of her family, and she went so far as to tell many people that Ted was in the Mafia, he remembered. The hard knocks Freda endured don't altogether explain her behavior, especially her sense of entitlement, her unshakable belief that stardom was her destiny— one that didn't require much actual effort on her part.

Freda's unraveling in 1997–98 reminded both her children that many of her destructive attitudes had been present for a long, long time. This realization in turn prompted Madeline to reconsider her own past. She was overwhelmed by the evidence that her parents' break-up had been more Freda's fault than Bernie's. If Freda had misled her about that, in what other ways had she been less than honest?

In his letter, Ted Barry neglected to mention that all those who abandoned Freda effectively abandoned Madeline as well. And not long after Bernie Wolfson walked out in 1945, Freda would abandon her, too.

A Shoeshine and a Smile

Bernie Wolfson

FREDA WAS RIGHT ABOUT THIS MUCH: BERNIE WAS A LADIES' MAN. HIS
niece, Gerri Bohn Gerson, remembers, "He was smart, he was very good-
looking, he had a great sense of humor. Lots of women thought he was
wonderful." Robyn Wolfson, Bernie's daughter from his second marriage, says, "He did like women, and women did like him, and he liked
the attention. He was gorgeous; he had a great sense of humor." And
though Robyn, too, adores him still, she concedes, "My father could be
difficult to live with."

Lending credence to Freda's depiction of events, Bernie remarried
shortly after divorcing her and leaving the army. "He kind of disappointed Madeline," says Gerson, "because I think she thought that he should
come and save her." Bernie and his second wife, Shirley Feinstein Wolfson, had Robyn in 1951. The family moved several times, with a long
stay in Chicago. Only in 1959, when Madeline first came to visit them
there, did Robyn learn she had a half-sister. Madeline was sixteen or
seventeen. Robyn was eight.

When the Wolfsons returned to the Boston area a short time later,
Gerson's mother, Lilyan Wolfson Bohn (Bernie's only sibling), and Shirley determined that Bernie needed to see more of Madeline. Bernie's
mother, Bertha, a powerful influence who doted on him, was indiffer-
ent to all her grandchildren and didn't join the campaign to bring father
and daughter together. Bernie's father, Louis, avoided the discussion.
But Bernie had a predilection for strong-willed women, and his wife's
and sister's encouragement led to more frequent visits from Madeline. It
had always suited Freda's purposes to keep her daughter apart from the
Wolfsons, but by now Madeline was old enough to travel by herself, and
she made the trip to Boston many times.

In the long run the Wolfsons didn't spend much time with Madeline, and yet they did influence her. Before and after Robyn's birth, both Bernie and Shirley were traveling salespeople for garment companies, a line of work that lent itself to Bernie's skills as a joke-teller and to Shirley's desire to keep up an immaculate appearance and make a good impression. To a degree, Madeline grew up in both their images, making her way in the world as a comedian, carefully dressed and intensely concerned about other people's opinions of her.

Robyn also describes Shirley Wolfson as a perfectionist who loved to entertain and for whom family was very important, descriptions that don't apply to Bernie. "If it wasn't for my mom," Robyn says, "he never would have gotten in touch with Madeline. That's awful to say about a parent, but that's just my gut feeling." According to Gerri, Shirley would have welcomed Madeline into the family when they moved back to Boston, although both Gerri and Robyn doubt that Shirley and Bernie ever considered outright adoption. Madeline was by then a legal adult. "Shirley was happy to have Madeline," Gerri says, "but there was no way Freda was going to do that! Ever!"

The Manumit School (1948–53)

NOT LONG AFTER HER DIVORCE, FREDA MOVED TO NEW YORK TO PUR-
sue a singing career, her daughter in tow. This move guaranteed that her
authority over Madeline would trump Bernie's, but her principal conscious motivation was her own ambition. Backwater Boston had never
appreciated her talent, she believed, remembering how at the age of sixteen she was—almost simultaneously—passed over for lead soprano in
the school choir (an insulting blow to an aspiring opera star) and designated "Second Prettiest" in a Junior League beauty contest. New York,
the center of sophistication, the home of the Metropolitan Opera and
Carnegie Hall, surely would reward her.

The move was so abrupt that her daughter later speculated it might
have been a "first episode," an early indication of Freda's mental insta-
bility, and it made a profound impact on young Madeline. Soon, Freda
found it impossible to focus on her music while holding down a clerical
job and caring for a small child. And so, in 1948, when Madeline was not
yet six years old, Freda put her in a boarding school, Manumit, in the
borough of Bristol in Bucks County, Pennsylvania.

That decision may seem impossible to justify. Standards have changed,
though, and even in those days most institutional facilities for young
children were a long way from *Nicholas Nickleby*. John Kramer, who
attended Manumit for most of his primary and secondary schooling
(which included the years Madeline spent there), also enrolled at the
age of six. Both his parents were living, not even divorced, but they
were classic Greenwich Village bohemians who lived in the back of his
father's jewelry studio. "There just wasn't room for three of us, so I was
sent to school." Neither Kramer nor Madeline was the only young child
at Manumit.

The school enjoyed an excellent if somewhat eccentric reputation that appealed to Freda, who was active in left-wing causes in the 1940s. Founded in Pauling, New York, by the Rev. William Fincke in 1924, Manumit took as its model Britain's progressive Summerhill School. For a time, Fincke called Manumit "The Workers' Children's School," a kind of sobriquet, and he encouraged students not only to follow their own inclinations in their studies, but also to perform all sorts of chores. Both the Pauling campus and the Bristol campus (to which Manumit relocated in 1944, after a fire in 1943) incorporated working farms. The school's leftward tilt can be detected in the name Manumit itself: Derived from the Latin, it means "release from slavery." Rev. Fincke died in 1927 and was replaced by his son, Bill, who assumed full control in 1944 after a period of illness and interregnum. Kramer says that Bill Fincke resisted a takeover by communist sympathizers or labor-union leadership, but that he continued to pursue progressive policies. The student body included special-needs students, European–Jewish refugees, and African–American children—to the consternation of neighbors in Bucks County. Under pressure from the community, state and local authorities scrutinized Manumit closely, finding fault with everything from the physical plant to the secondary curriculum. Despite administrators' efforts to comply, the school closed in 1958.

When Kramer arrived, about a year before Madeline, the Manumit curriculum was loosely structured, "a sort of classical progressive education." The way Madeline spelled her name at the time, "Madalin," seems to reflect this disposition. But Freda was the bohemian and the activist in the family. Ultimately Manumit was a better place for her than for her daughter.

As an adult, Madeline seldom talked about Manumit. She gave friends the impression that she was lonely and not terribly popular there. "She missed her mother," says her widower, John Hansbury, noting that Madeline described herself as "hiding in the bushes" there. When Kramer and another alumnus, Aulay Carson, asked their Manumit classmates to share stories of Madalin Wolfson for this book, no one remembered her. Yet when Madeline's uncle and aunt, Ted and Jean Barry, visited the school around 1952, they found her in a beautiful dormitory (a former mansion), happily surrounded by friends. She was eager to show them around the campus, and she gossiped about the other students. She and her friends liked to spy on the high schoolers' make-out sessions. However, it's clear that Madeline was putting up a front for the Barrys, and she was already a good enough actress to persuade them.

Theater was fundamental to the Manumit curriculum, and even the youngest students participated in "creative plays," in which the children expressed their ideas and feelings about circumstances or events. There were no scripts, and Kramer (who also went into acting as an adult) describes a very loose process, involving a good deal of giggling and goofing around, under the typically laidback supervision of a teacher. But there was a stage and an audience. For a shy little girl in unfamiliar surroundings, in circumstances she hadn't chosen, among strangers who might not be interested in what she had to say, the license to speak up and be heard meant a great deal. The idea of theater as a means of self-expression took hold.

The craft of acting changed radically in the years after World War II, and Manumit gave Madeline a head start in her career. Actors would rely less and less on the externalized, presentational style of acting that—especially because of the influence of film—had come to seem artificial and old-fashioned. Inspired by teachers and directors such as Constantin Stanislavsky and Lee Strasberg, actors' preparation came to include internalized work, psychological analysis, and the use of "sense memory," experiences in one's own life that might correspond to a character's circumstances. Meanwhile, teachers such as Paul Sills and Viola Spolin recommended improvisation or "theater games"—very much like what Madeline and her classmates did in their "creative plays"—as a means of finding a character, rather than merely portraying one. Madeline's interest in these methods allied her squarely with such future colleagues as Robert Klein, Alan Arkin, and Lily Tomlin, although her approach also put her on the wrong side of what amounts to a generational split with the more traditional methods of Lucille Ball, Harold Prince, and George Rose. Only during her years at Manumit would Madeline use improvisation to express herself, rather than working within the framework of a script or a character that (in most cases) scarcely resembled her. Looking back, Madeline told another Manumit alumna, the New York City television anchor Sue Simmons, "Every artistic bone in my body was formed at Manumit."

4

Life with Stepfather

Hiller Kahn (1949–58)

"I WASN'T ONE OF THOSE KIDS WHO TAP-DANCED ALL OVER THE neighborhood," Madeline told *After Dark* magazine in 1973. "I liked to perform, but not in front of company."[3] In her personal notebook, Madeline wrote, "[M]y original desires to perform were fantasies which I enjoyed creating in my mind rather than a desire to become a 'star'"—which was Freda's goal, not hers. "I lived in my mind, my fantasies, and the opportunity to make them alive [and] real is what turns me on . . . ."[4] Outside the safe confines of "creative plays" at Manumit, young Madeline still considered performing in front of other people an "utterly terrible idea," but her reluctance didn't deter Freda. Whenever Madeline came home to New York, Freda pushed her to sing and dance for friends and neighbors. Freda was still Madeline's primary music teacher (instruments were too expensive for Manumit's budget), and as such she considered recitals par for the course. Madeline saw things differently. "You know, my mother noticed that I was amusing, or whatnot, and would like me to show someone," Madeline said in 1989, "and I found this an infuriating suggestion that made no sense whatsoever. And this sort of went on for most of my life."[5]

Around 1949, Freda even pushed her daughter in front of television cameras for the first time. Madeline and a friend, Jimmy, were picked to appear on Horn & Hardart's *Children's Hour*. After singing "Cool Water," they were invited back. Madeline recalled, "The second time, I got nervous. I saw all these kids in the wings, little savages, kicking and pushing each other out of the way. I got scared and started to cry, right there on camera. Needless to say, they never invited us on again."[6]

Television producers might be put off, but Freda wasn't, and Madeline's informal performances at home began to earn her "limited fame," drawing audiences of a dozen people or so, her stepfather, Hiller Kahn, later recalled. He first met Madeline and Freda at one such performance in 1949. Freda had taken a secretarial job, and Hiller was dating her supervisor, who suggested one afternoon that they drop by Freda's apartment to hear little Madeline. When they got to West 60th Street, the pair found Madeline singing and dancing on a tabletop while Freda played piano. Hiller enjoyed the little show and found Madeline "endearing," but initially Freda didn't make much of an impression on him. Hiller continued to date her supervisor, although he and Freda socialized together frequently. Then, Hiller and Freda "got to like each other more and more as time went on," he said. "I dropped my relationship with the girl that had introduced us in the first place, and started dating Freda. I fell in love. I don't know if Freda did or not, but I did."

It's striking how many of the Kahn family dynamics were already in play at that first meeting. Hiller and Freda "didn't hit it off right away," as he put it, and as things turned out, they really weren't meant to be together. While Freda harbored dreams of stardom, her daughter was already the main attraction. And starting perhaps with Hiller, good things often came to Freda because of Madeline.

Born and reared in Pennsylvania, Hiller had grown up somewhat in the shadow of his brother, Ernest ("Ernie"), the intellectual of the family and the pride of the boys' father, Albert, an attorney. Family members believe Hiller, who had difficulty writing, may have had a learning disability, such as dysgraphia (which his granddaughter, Eliza, has), though he was never diagnosed. He was at any rate a disappointment to his father, and after high school, he entered the military rather than attending college, while Ernie went to Harvard and later taught psychiatry at Harvard Medical School.

Hiller's sense of humor reinforced the lesson that young Madeline had learned from Freda and Bernie: A joke was a way to make a good impression, to endure an otherwise difficult situation, or to keep your cool. Ernie's ex-wife, Virginia Lewisohn Kahn, describes Hiller as "a lot of fun," adding, "I imagine Madeline picked up on a lot of this." In June 1952, Hiller and Freda brought Madeline to Ernie and Ginny's wedding in Westchester County, New York. Ginny remembers young Madeline as chubby, "very bright . . . and good company even then." Later, young Madeline came to visit Ernie and Ginny in Washington, DC, and Ginny was surprised that any little girl could be so captivated by a trip to Mount Vernon.

Not long after his brother's wedding, Hiller proposed marriage to Freda, and at the same time suggested they take Madeline out of Manumit and bring her to live with them. "I felt it was grossly unfair to have her in boarding school," he said. "I wanted her to be part of the family." Looking back, Hiller described the appeal of his paternal relationship with Madeline as much of the reason he married Freda. "She was the only little girl I've ever been very, very close to," he said. He especially enjoyed taking her to the movies on Saturday afternoons. "She loved movies, and I loved being with her. She was fun to be with." She seldom gave him any cause to worry about her, perhaps a conscious choice on her part. He recalled a little girl eager to make a good impression. "I always had a feeling that she was a little affected in the way she spoke, as though there were someone who told her that she should be very careful about choosing her words and the way she formed sentences."

Madeline's fans will recognize in this the carefully enunciated sophistication for which she strove, with pointed vocabulary and seldom so much as a hint of her Queens (or, for that matter, Boston) origins. Her distinctive manner of speaking was one of the principal elements of her performing career, constituting the basis of her characters in *High Anxiety* and *Clue*, and it's not unlike the flawless penmanship, grammar, spelling, and punctuation that characterize her writing, even in her appointment books. While it might be supposed that some of this polish derived from Madeline's college years, when she studied speech therapy, Hiller's recollection suggests that Madeline was already on this track when she was a very young girl, striving to be irreproachable.

Shortly after marrying Freda in Mexico in 1953, Hiller legally adopted Madeline, and she kept his surname for the rest of her life. The Kahns moved to an apartment in Jackson Heights, Queens, and Madeline enrolled at P.S. 135. "[E]ven tho' public school was less than adequate, it seemed easy or easier in a way to follow rules," Madeline remembered. Manumit had given her at least some preparation for life, "which is chaos."[7]

Hiller remembered the early years warmly, but there were danger signs from the start. Perhaps because she'd been living on her own for eight years, Freda's ambitions had changed by the time she married Hiller. Where once she craved stardom alone, now she also craved the perks that stardom often brings: money, and the things that money can buy. She wasn't inclined to wait for fame, or even to wait for much income, before she grabbed the cash—and spent it.

Growing up during the Depression, Freda had learned "that you do what you have to do, to get what you need," her son, Jeffrey, explained. She also learned through mishaps great and small that life isn't fair. For example, most people would agree that Freda shouldn't have needed to sue her father for child support, and that after she did sue him, she should have won. She should have won the soprano lead in the school choir. She should have won the Junior League beauty contest, and so on. If life wasn't fair, Freda seems to have reasoned, then there was no point in playing fair.

Shortly after she married Hiller, Freda carried out one of her more daring schemes. She borrowed $400, a considerable sum, from her sister-in-law, Jean Barry, on behalf of Hiller. At the same time, she went to Hiller and borrowed another $400 on behalf of Ted Barry—who, she said, needed the money *right away*, because the Mafia was after him. Freda then took all the money for herself. Neither Hiller nor Ted knew there were two loans, and each man believed he'd lent the money to the other man. Neither of them felt comfortable asking the other to repay the supposed debt. Over the years, animosity built up between Hiller and Ted, which suited Freda's purposes, but the bitterness effectively poisoned her children's relationships with her brother. It took Ted nearly half a century to figure out how Freda had conned them all.

No matter where she got the money—and sometimes when she didn't get it at all—Freda spent lavishly. To a degree, she merely hearkened to the tenor of the times: the economic boom of the 1950s in America, the rise of the middle class, and the blossoming of consumerism. But Freda went farther. She acquired grandiose tastes, and years later, both Hiller and Ted were able to quote the prices of her extravagant purchases and redecorating schemes. Her new kitchen cabinets cost a whopping seven thousand dollars, and according to family lore, she had her bedroom re-wallpapered twice in one week. Though Freda augmented the household income by giving music lessons (even charging Madeline for them), she'd quit working outside the home and didn't earn nearly enough to cover her expenses.

At first, Hiller paid, though grudgingly and with warnings that Freda must start to economize. He'd just started an automotive-supply business. "We were doing well," he remembered, "but there are limits to how much money you can spend when you're just getting underway." There was a new mouth to feed, too. Jeffrey was born on October 28, 1953, and the family moved into a house at 19904 Romeo Court in Holliswood, Queens. One-and-a-half stories built in Cape Cod style with an attached garage, the house sat on a wooded lot on a quiet street. It would remain Madeline's home base well into adulthood.

Madeline adored her baby brother, and Jef recalls her loving care more warmly than he does his mother's. His first memories are of Madeline carrying him, playing with him, and sometimes teasing him "in a very loving way," Jef says. Most of the time, however, Jef was the troublemaker. "Jef wouldn't listen to his mother, but he would listen to Madeline," Ginny says. With a background in social work and education, she was already critical of Freda's handling of both children.

Only once, when she was fourteen or fifteen, did Madeline get into serious trouble. At that age, her cousin Gerri Gerson says, they both were boy-crazy, and when Madeline came to Boston to visit, they liked to throw parties where Madeline could meet boys her age. One evening in Queens, when Hiller and Freda had gone to the movies, Madeline called a few boys, told them her parents were out, and invited them over to the house. But this wasn't like one of Gerri's parties in Boston, and things got out of hand. When Hiller and Freda came home, the boys fled. They found Madeline crying in the basement. While it was unclear exactly what happened, Hiller and Freda understood that the boys "had taken advantage of Madeline." They called the police, who questioned the girl and determined she hadn't been raped. The police then rounded up the boys and their parents, who came to Romeo Court to apologize. After Hiller and Freda calmed Madeline down, he believed "the whole incident was over. I don't think I've thought of it since then." As he looked back more than fifty years later, this was the only instance of poor judgment on Madeline's part that he could remember. As he saw it, Madeline shouldn't have spread the word that she was home alone. "I think [the boys] probably scared the hell out of her," Hiller said. This fear marked her more than he knew. A few years later, when she was an undergraduate at Hofstra, she stood out among her classmates because she showed no interest in sex.

Hiller and Freda's marriage showed strains early on. Jean and Ted Barry visited New York not long after Jef was born, but Freda called to ask them not to come to Queens. Hiller had moved out, she said, and she didn't want company. A day or so later, Madeline phoned and begged Jean and Ted to come to the house. She'd persuaded Hiller to come back, and everything was all right. Once Jean and Ted arrived at Romeo Court, they found a relaxed, evidently happy couple.

"No, we didn't fight. No, never," Hiller said. "We may have had an angry word once in a while, but we didn't fight. We had two children

in the house, and we controlled ourselves pretty well." But Freda's manipulative behavior and out-of-control spending got progressively worse,
and by 1957, they drove Hiller to leave her. Moving to the 63rd Street
YMCA in Manhattan, he took a second job and borrowed money to pay
off Freda's debts. She phoned him constantly, but he had no intention of
reconciling with her. In 1958, they obtained a divorce, although a formal
Mexican divorce wasn't handed down until 1963.

Citing cruel and inhuman treatment (a common legal tactic in such
cases and virtually a necessity under divorce law at the time), Freda sued
for alimony and child support for both Madeline and Jef. However, the
Domestic Relations Court of the City of New York found, contrary to Freda's claim, that there had been no such "cruel and inhuman" behavior
on Hiller's part. Moreover, the court found Freda, not Hiller, "responsible
for the separation." Although she apparently concealed from the court
the money she earned from music lessons ("the Petitioner has an income
of no dollars"), Freda failed to persuade the judge that she had no earning capacity. After all, she'd earned her living for eight years before marrying Hiller, and she gave no reason to suppose that she couldn't return
to clerical work. The court turned down Freda's demand for alimony (a
highly unusual decision in those days), ordered Hiller to pay her sixty-
five dollars per week for the children, and told Freda to get a job.[8]

Freda made it clear that she'd put up a fight if Hiller exercised visitation rights with Madeline, and he resigned himself to this situation, a
decision he later regretted. However, he insisted on his visitation rights
with Jef, particularly regular Saturday outings to Manhattan. At first,
Freda resisted this, too, and one day when Jef was five, she tried to prevent Hiller from taking him out of the house. A shouting match ensued,
and the police were called. Jef ran upstairs to his bedroom, and Madeline
hurried to comfort him. He remembers that with exceptional sensitivity,
"she explained that, while we were the only people in the neighborhood
to be a family of divorce, that did not make us freaks or bad people."

From that point on, Hiller's visits to Romeo Court would be marked
by Freda's gleefully handing him fresh stacks of bills to be paid, and by
his desire to make a quick getaway with his son. Generally, he recalled,
Madeline lingered in the background, laughing along with Freda; he had
the impression that Freda expected her daughter to behave this way.
"Madeline was loyal to her mother," he said simply, but he and Madeline
grew apart. In later years they made efforts to bridge the distance, usually at Jef's instigation, but their encounters were correct and not much
more.

Madeline made more of an effort with Bernie Wolfson, but their relationship followed a similar course, Robyn Wolfson says. After Hiller and Freda divorced, Madeline began to see more of her father. On those visits, their interactions were merely "amicable," Robyn observed, and she speculated that Madeline's real father–daughter relationship was with Hiller. In truth, Madeline didn't have one.

• • •

Jef's Saturdays with his father meant the boy got away from his mother on a regular basis, while Madeline was left to fend for herself. Years later, Jef sensed that his sister harbored a degree of wistfulness or resentment. After all, he says, "I've got a sane parent, and she doesn't." Though he now works in a mental health facility, he hesitates to diagnose his mother. Some of her behavior struck him as manic, he says, and at times he wondered whether she was a borderline personality.

She could be charming and highly persuasive, never more so than when she silenced or banished those who disputed her perspective or questioned her influence. Growing up, Madeline believed that neither of her fathers could be trusted, and therefore security must come from Freda and her insistence that "[t]he universe will provide," as Jef puts it. At the same time, Freda exploited the sense of responsibility that her husbands' abandonment had helped to instill in Madeline, the sense that she needed to protect and support her mother. That's a terrible burden for a teenager, and it persisted, informing not only Madeline's personal life, but also her career choices, as "support" took on financial meaning, too. Making a commercial for Light beer or Diet Coke might not befit an Oscar- and Tony-nominated star, but it's what a working single woman has to do to provide for a loved one. "Of course I have" taken jobs just for the money, she once told an interviewer. "I hope people can tell which ones those are."[9]

"It's clear that a lot of Madi's motivation in life was to please her mother," Jef Kahn says. "She did such a good job that she actually made her jealous."

The wreck of Freda's marriages continued to affect Madeline profoundly and in several ways. Like Bernie before him, Hiller walked out on Freda and Madeline at a time when the girl's appearance made her feel vulnerable. In adolescence she was chubbier than at any other point in her life. Jef says that other women in the family have gone through teenage weight-gain and wound up perfectly slender as adults, but young Madeline, cut off from so many relatives, didn't have that long-range perspective.

The principal lesson of Madeline's childhood was: *People will leave.* People may *not* leave so long as you're pretty and charming and entertaining, and so long as you do absolutely nothing wrong. Her singing brought Hiller into her family, and so she sang; the little girl who was "almost *too* polite and well-behaved" was determined not to scare him away. But he left anyway, and on a day when she was fat.

As an adult, Madeline was often wary of people, and not just in the expected way of a star concerned that others will try to exploit her celebrity. Even with close friends, she could remain guarded, and her romantic relationships were marked by varying degrees of mistrust. She balked at the idea of marriage, almost to the end of her days. Freda's frequent disparaging of Bernie and Hiller suggested that marriage was something to pursue only with partners one disliked. During Madeline's first long-term affair, Bernie and Shirley divorced, confirming her belief that marriage was a risky, improbable venture. She wasn't always able to prevent her insecurities from coloring her professional relationships, either, and if her personal history made it easier to play fragile or neurotic characters so memorably, they sometimes made her a difficult collaborator.

5

Hofstra (1960–64)

AT JUNIOR HIGH SCHOOL 109 AND AT MARTIN VAN BUREN HIGH School, Madeline made good grades. Eventually graduating third in her class at Van Buren, she expected to attend City College of New York, a public institution that had the advantage of being free (the "Poor Man's Harvard"). She intended to become a teacher, and she would never have taken a drama course if it hadn't been required. "[T]he idea of making [acting] an *occupation* never occurred to me," she said. "I was not the type at all." When the drama teacher suggested she audition for a drama scholarship to Hofstra College, Madeline recalled, "I thought it was a ridiculous idea." Nevertheless she went to the school library and prepared two monologues, one dramatic, one comic.[10] She performed the serious piece first, but it was her second monologue that made the difference. From the back of the darkened theater, she heard the professors laughing—and she won a full scholarship to Hofstra.

In the short term, this meant that Hiller wouldn't have to pay for her college education, which was a relief to them both and a source of pride to him. He was still bragging about her achievement five decades later. To a young woman of limited means but exceptional intelligence, the scholarship was invaluable. She had never before realized that "this ability to elicit laughter . . . could bring me something," but here was proof.

For her humorous monologue, she had chosen the work of an important influence on her aesthetics, the writer–actress Ruth Draper.[11] Born into an upper-class New York City family in 1884, Draper performed "monodramas," playing a variety of roles with only minimal props and a shawl, artfully rearranged to distinguish a variety of characters, even several at once. Draper's deft satire of her own class recalls that of the writer Edith Wharton, who admired her. Draper pursued a stage career to international acclaim, and she was just breaking through in recordings, radio, and television when she died in 1956. Draper's characters ranged beyond Mrs. Astor's ballroom to embrace European peasants and Midwestern housewives. Portraying them required skills that, through singing lessons, Madeline had already been developing: notably, familiarity with foreign languages. Throughout Draper's work, she manifested the kind of sophistication to which young Madeline aspired, and which she would soon make her own.

The day she auditioned for Hofstra, Madeline's career began to fall into place, not least because she aimed for a drama scholarship rather than a music scholarship. No matter what monologue she performed that day, she wasn't singing. In a sense, she was declaring independence from her mother. Yet she retained one talent even as she developed the other: The tension between the lyric soprano and the comic actor had begun. While most young performers would be thrilled to have both options at the ready, Madeline's experiences at Hofstra would exacerbate this tension, which dominated her professional life for at least the next dozen years.

• • •

When Madeline matriculated, Hofstra College was on the cusp of becoming a university. (It was accredited in 1963, while Madeline was a student there.) A private institution and formerly a branch of New York University, located in Hempstead, Long Island, Hofstra "was a local school, almost like a community college," says filmmaker David Hoffman, class of 1963. He played oboe and had won a full music scholarship, which in his case included not only tuition and books, but also money for food, a car, and an apartment. "Those scholarships don't exist any more," he says, but they and others like them at one time attracted an exceptional student body from the middle- and lower-middle classes. School administrators viewed the arts as a draw, one cheaper to develop than the sciences. When Madeline arrived, the radio and television department was new, and the school boasted enviable resources for music and theater. Even student productions might involve a full orchestra, and through the school's connections, student musicians could obtain professional gigs in New York City. For future directors like Hoffman, Francis Ford Coppola (class of '59), and Charles Ludlam (class of '64), the school provided opportunities to explore and experiment, and to showcase student performers.

At first, Madeline *didn't* perform. From time to time, she wandered to the theater to see what plays were auditioning, "and I saw those actors hanging around there in bare feet and smoking cigarettes, ooh—I got out of there so fast! I mean, I didn't feel like one of them at all, you know, and I just didn't even have the courage to look at the callboard anyway. So, I didn't." Still unconvinced of her own potential, she chose to study practical subjects that could lead to steady, regular employment: She majored in speech therapy, with a minor in education. Any current or former college student with artistic inclinations will recognize these fields of study as precisely the sort that nervous parents recommend to their children (or foist upon them) as "something to fall back on." There's no indication, however, that Madeline's parents pushed her toward speech therapy. The extent of their influence may simply have been her own clear-eyed recognition that, some day soon, she would have to support herself.

Arriving at the start of the second semester, Madeline continued to live at home, and she worked off-campus in her spare time. She did well in her courses and gave little thought to theater. A drama scholarship didn't require her to major in drama, after all, but in the fall of 1960, she discovered that the school had previously failed to inform her that her scholarship did require that she take part in productions. Now her scholarship was about to be revoked. She scurried back to the callboard, where she learned that the next play to be produced would be Elmer Rice's *The Adding Machine*. "I said to myself, 'What can I get in this play?'" Madeline remembered. "[N]ot what part do I *want*, but, 'What part do I think I can get?'" She won a role, and her scholarship was secure. But her troubles with the Hofstra drama department were just beginning.

The drama faculty at the time included Bernard Beckerman, a recognized Shakespeare scholar who provided the impetus behind Hofstra's Shakespeare festival, performed annually on a replica of the Globe Theatre stage. His colleague Miriam Tulin specialized in scene work. An aspiring actress who'd given up her career when she married, Tulin "was brilliant, very gifted, very ar-ti-cu-late," recalls Madeline's classmate, Susan Carlson, an actress who took the professional name Black-Eyed Susan. According to legend, Tulin inspired one of Madeline's most memorable characters, the actor–director Mavis Danton, featured in a sketch on *The Carol Burnett Show* in 1976. Mavis's trademark exhortation to concentrate is, "In our circles, in our circles!" and Tulin, who died in 2008, "*really* wanted us to concentrate," Black-Eyed Susan says.

In *The Adding Machine*, Tulin cast Madeline as Judy O'Grady, a prostitute, and thereafter she was typecast, playing saucy wenches and servants in one department production after another. Offstage, however,

Madeline led a very different life. David Hoffman recalls, "I never saw her with a guy." He remembers her being "totally non-sexual," unlike other young women on campus at the time. "There was a certain way of flirting, and she didn't flirt." Student productions often were musicals, and Madeline sometimes got lead roles in these. Hoffman directed her a few times, and while he found her attractive, he observed, "She never played her looks into anything. Her talent was the issue. She had a ridiculously funny voice and a ridiculously good singing voice."

Leading roles in student productions didn't translate to leading roles in theater department productions. Those went to classmates like Susan Sullivan, who went on have to a long career in television. "Madeline Kahn was a different kind of person," Black-Eyed Susan says. When their mutual friend, the budding playwright–director Charles Ludlam, introduced them, "I think he was kind of in awe of her, actually. I looked at her, and she was very sophisticated-looking, and I wasn't. Her hair was in an updo, a sweep, but it was all *big*. It was sort of like, 'Wow, she'll probably be a star. She'll get major roles.'"

Madeline probably met Ludlam in Beckerman's production of *Love's Labour's Lost*. They fascinated each other, but it was Black-Eyed Susan who became Ludlam's ally, and she remained so for the rest of his life. While Madeline and other actors tried out for more conventional shows, Ludlam delved into obscure and avant-garde playwrights, meeting with substantial resistance from the faculty. And he took Black-Eyed Susan with him—all the way to New York. Madeline, for her part, continued to struggle in the pigeonhole where the faculty had put her.

Near the end of her second year, she was ready for change. Tulin was directing Giraudoux's *The Madwoman of Chaillot*, and Madeline wanted to audition for one of the madwomen. Tulin wanted her to play the Flower Girl instead, but when Madeline allowed that she'd rather concentrate on her studies and wait for the next play, hoping for a more challenging role, "They told me that if I *didn't* do the Flower Girl, my scholarship would be revoked. That was my first big blow, and it was very difficult, very deflating, scary and discouraging . . . ." Madeline felt she'd already missed any opportunity to negotiate with the theater department. Her options now, she believed, were either to submit to typecasting or give up her scholarship, which would mean transferring—probably to City College—with no assurance that she could keep her credits.

She turned to Albert Tepper, the music faculty's advisor for student theater and director of the madrigal group with which Madeline had been singing on Saturday afternoons. When Tepper told her the music department would offer her a scholarship to cover the remaining two years of her Hofstra education, Madeline promptly cut her ties to the theater department. To satisfy the requirements of the music scholarship, her principal performing experience now came from one-act operas, oratorios, and concerts.[12] With the madrigal group, she also played Isabella in Orazio Vecchi's opera *L'Amfiparnaso*. Her acting style had developed already. If one didn't know better, one would think production photos showed a present-day college student imitating the famous movie star Madeline Kahn. At Freda's insistence, Madeline also joined a professional opera workshop, which required further study and afforded her greater freedom than the theater faculty had, enabling her to play "parts I wanted to do—mature women. I got to do scenes from Mozart and Puccini, and roles like Manon Lescaut, womanly and dramatic."[13] All of this activity fueled Freda's ambitions for Madeline's career in opera.

Madeline continued to perform in student theatricals, as well, and in 1962, she was cast as the frustrated girlfriend of Nathan Detroit in *Guys and Dolls*. "A person can develop a cold," Miss Adelaide laments in her signature number—but in Madeline's case, it was measles. Her friends remained hopeful that she might recover in time to do the show, and though they cast another student as a backup, Madeline lay in bed and rehearsed by herself, mentally preparing every entrance, costume change, gesture, and note. (The experience proved useful later in life, she said, when she arrived on movie sets and started to shoot a scene with no more preparation than what she'd done on her own, at home.) At last she felt well enough to take part in a few rehearsals with the rest of the cast.

She was still unsure of herself until opening night, when "the audience response was so enormous that I thought I was on a roller coaster," she remembered. "It was such a surprise to me that what I had prepared so earnestly and diligently by myself, not to please anyone, but just to do what I felt was the right thing—I mean, the laughter, and so on. I had to stop." For the first time, she began to think of pursuing a career in theater.

Guys and Dolls was reviewed in the student newspaper, and the faculty weighed in with its judgments, too. When one professor told her "that I stood out and that I didn't blend into the production, that I seemed to be doing some show of my own," she took the criticism to heart. "I spent the next several years trying to blend into every possible place I could." However, colleagues insist she *didn't* blend in, and some years later, she wrote, "I don't 'hide'[;] I choose to stand out and *up* for myself at the same time [and] so set an example for others to do so."[14] Only later in life did she realize that the professor who criticized her was simply wrong. Speaking at the American Academy of Dramatic Arts, Madeline tried to share the lessons of her own experience. "If you look at [reviews] to find out who you are, you're in big trouble," she told her young audience, adding that "authority figures" aren't always right.

Much of her experience at Hofstra confirmed this last insight. The theater faculty made her feel "like an outcast," she said. Another class-mate, Charlotte Forbes, described the faculty as "very narrow-minded . . . whenever any real talent showed up, they shot it down." Forbes told Ludlam's biographer, David Kaufman, "[T]he theater department felt so threatened by Madeline Kahn that they literally threw her out . . . ."[15] The abrupt change from theater to music "was very painful, very diffi-cult, and very interesting—I mean, *looking back*," Madeline said. "Look-ing back, I can now say, 'Well, thank you for that, because this was great training for the outside world.'"[16]

In the evenings and on weekends, Madeline took jobs as a dirndl-decked singing waitress at German restaurants on Long Island. Sum-mers, she lived and worked at the Bavarian Manor, a Catskills resort in Purling, New York. Looking back, she counted that gig among the dues she'd paid in a hard life (her words), though she kept her sense of hu-mor. When dogs wandered into the performing area, they'd howl along with her singing, to the amusement of the customers. "I would conclude that there was something wonderful in the sound of my voice which set animals going," she wrote years later.[17] Figuring that Kahn was too Jew-ish a name for such a setting, she adopted a stage name, Madeline Gail, for the only time in her career. Her sheet music dating from those days survives: lots of Friml and Romberg, with "Madi Gail" written in graceful cursive on each cover, and less dignified pencil markings inside.

"I sang musical-comedy numbers during show time, and *Student Prince*-type things," she remembered in 1985, during an intermission feature of a television broadcast of Verdi's *Aida* from the Metropolitan Opera. "There was a big important customer, an Italian man, and he shouted out, 'Sing *Madame Butterfly*!' And of course he didn't mean the whole opera, he meant that one very popular aria—'Un bel dì.' So if I was to come back the next summer and earn more money to get through my next year [of college], I'd better come back knowing that aria. And I didn't know anything about it. So I just learned that one aria, and a few others, and then one thing led to another. You know, I studied it, and I discovered I could sing that, sort of, that way."[18]

While Madeline never did possess the chutzpah to boast of her own talent in the middle of Leontyne Price's farewell to the stage, this modest account doesn't square with what we know about Freda's training and ambition for her daughter. On occasion Madeline clarified: The discovery she made at the Bavarian Manor was the potential *size* of her voice. As she began studying with teachers other than her mother, she built on her skills in the opera club and got plenty of experience in light classical singing for a paying audience at restaurants. Whether this kind of music would do her any good was another question. The "British Invasion" was underway, Bob Dylan would soon inform America that "The Times, They Are A-Changing," and already the Bavarian Manor's repertory was dated. Romberg's *The Student Prince* opened on Broadway in 1924, and even the Mario Lanza film version had debuted nearly a decade before Madi Gail began to warble "Deep in My Heart, Dear."

Madeline graduated in 1964 with a degree in speech therapy and experience as a student teacher, as well as an impressive array of less "practical" credentials. She was a member of two theater groups—the Spectrum Players (of which she was secretary) and the Gadfly Players—and two singing groups, the Hofstra Singers and the Opera Workshop. Taking the Drama Achievement Award and the Music Achievement Award, she was also on the dean's list. She had developed a taste for foreign films, and in one yearbook picture she bears a striking resemblance to the young Jeanne Moreau. Was that intentional? "I would never underestimate her," Jef Kahn says with a laugh.

6

The Graduate

Green Mansions (1964) and Upstairs at the Downstairs (1965–66)

AT THE START, MADELINE'S TRAINING AT HOFSTRA HAD LITTLE DIRECT impact on her performing career. She found her niche not in plays or in opera, but in cabaret and revues. Shortly after graduation, she got a job at Green Mansions, a theater colony founded in the 1930s by members of the Group Theatre near Warrensburg, New York. Still operating as an Adirondacks resort property, Green Mansions boasted a barn where young performers staged shows four nights a week. They were housed in conditions hardly distinguishable from those of a vacation camp. Green Mansions was more prestigious than the Bavarian Manor, though, and Madeline's acting skills were more frequently called on here.

Arriving at the colony, she met the man who would become her most important musical adviser, after her mother: Michael Cohen. A little older than Madeline, he had already spent a summer at Green Mansions as rehearsal pianist and accompanist. The troupe was looking for opera singers, and from the moment she started her audition piece, Musetta's waltz from *La Bohème*, Michael loved Madeline's voice. Before the summer was out, he'd written "Vocalise for Soprano and Piano," which was "dedicated to Miss Kahn." They performed this piece at a classical concert, at which Madeline also sang Schubert's coloratura Lied "Der Hirt auf dem Felsen," and the aria "Steal Me, Sweet Thief" from Menotti's *The Old Maid and the Thief*.

"We became fast friends because of the musical connections," he says. "But then it turned out during all of our work sessions she was extremely funny, too." Cohen recalls that not all their time was spent making music. Cast members met in the Green Mansions barn to work on improvisations almost every day, and as a result, Madeline's status changed. "Miss Kahn was hired as the company opera singer, but she soon became the company comedian," *Newsday* noted in 1969.[19] Offstage, she could be prankish, Cohen says: "She used to burn my T-shirts ironing them—on purpose."

Working closely with her on music, Cohen discovered that "Madeline always had a subtext when she sang. She had to know who this person was, why she was singing these notes and not some other notes, analyzing what she was singing. Especially if you take a song out of context, she would find something in it to make it relevant. She'd get the technical challenges out of the way first, then interpret." Like Madeline, Cohen had been classically trained; he would go on to write operas and several music-theater pieces. He found Madeline's approach an excellent match for his own.

When Green Mansions presented an evening of Kurt Weill songs (an appropriate choice, since Weill worked with the Group Theatre), Madeline and Michael came fully prepared. Like many New York liberals of their generation, both developed an early affinity for Weill's music. The revival of his *Threepenny Opera*, starring his widow, Lotte Lenya, had opened at the Theatre de Lys in Greenwich Village in 1954, and over its seven-year run pretty much established the concept of Off Broadway. A social satire by Bertolt Brecht, *Threepenny* seemed an oasis during the McCarthy era, and its cast included many blacklisted actors. Three decades after *Threepenny*'s premiere in Berlin, Weill's German songs became rallying cries for members of a new liberal intelligentsia whose parents knew him only as the composer of "September Song."

For Madeline, Michael Cohen composed "Das Chicago Song," a parody pastiche of easily recognizable Weill themes from *Threepenny* and *Happy End*. Tony Geiss's lyrics take particular aim at "Surabaya Johnny" and "Bilbao Song" as the singer recalls her affair with Max, who broke her heart and stole her lunch while they "tangoed the night away . . . in old Chicago, by the sea." Rhapsodic recollections are punctuated by disgusted outbursts ("Ptui!"), and the song culminates in the plaintive cry, "Max, come back! You forgot your whip!"[20]

"Das Chicago Song" would be Madeline's ticket to Broadway in 1968, and it was one of her audition numbers for Mel Brooks in 1973. She was still singing it in the 1990s. To listen to her imitation of Lenya is to confirm her claim that Marlene Dietrich wasn't the only Weimar star she was mimicking in *Blazing Saddles*. Though the accents are different (Lenya was Viennese, Dietrich Berlinerin), the attitudes are comparable, and Brecht's "alienation effect"—the sense that the performer is standing outside the drama—likewise informed Madeline's work in Brooks's films. At the American Academy of Dramatic Arts, Madeline said, "Everything I've ever done in the movies, I've drawn from my work on the stage, whether it has been in plays, or in opera, or concerts, or anything like that. Even *Blazing Saddles*, I based entirely on my knowledge of Kurt Weill, really, more than anything else. I mean, I looked at a Marlene Dietrich movie or two because Mel wanted me to. But really, *my* contribution had to do with *my* feelings about Kurt Weill."[21]

At the end of the summer, Madeline returned to live with her mother in Queens and took part-time jobs: temporary office work, babysitting, and singing three nights per week at a restaurant on Long Island. Gradually she earned enough money to afford a place of her own, an apartment on East 63rd Street in Manhattan, and she applied to the New York City school system for work as an elementary-school teacher of "speech improvement," either full-time or as a substitute, putting her Hofstra degree to use. Her application, dated March 29, 1965, reveals intriguing details, including her omission of any mention of the Manumit School. Her decision was at least in part pragmatic, since Manumit had closed, and its records were destroyed. There was no way for anyone to check them, and that in itself might appear suspicious. Moreover, the application, very much a product of its time, required Madeline to state whether she'd ever been a member of the Socialist, Communist, or Fascist Party, and while little Madalin Wolfson wasn't a card-carrying member of any political organization, Manumit did have a leftist reputation, as did Freda. Better to mention only P.S. 135. Beyond such considerations, however, the application proves that Madeline's longtime reluctance to talk about Manumit had begun already.

She did refer in interviews throughout her life to her experience as a teacher. She filed her application for employment in the coming school year, 1965–66. Records don't indicate further action, such as assignment to a particular school or employment either as a full-time or substitute teacher. She'd been a teacher's aide at Van Buren High, and she did engage in student teaching as part of her course work at Hofstra, but her teaching career ended with her application. She had hardly submitted it to the board of education before she took off in a different direction altogether. As a young adult in the big city—but also as Freda's daughter—Madeline craved independence, and she understood she'd need an income in order to get and keep it. Surprisingly, perhaps, she discovered that show business could provide steadier employment than teaching.

• • •

Shortly after applying to the board of education, Madeline auditioned for and won a spot in the chorus of a limited-run revival of Cole Porter's *Kiss Me, Kate*, featuring the original star, Patricia Morison, under the aegis of the New York City Center Light Opera Company. This was an Equity production, making Madeline eligible for her union card and opening up new professional possibilities.[22]

One of these was a Manhattan cabaret, Upstairs at the Downstairs, where Michael Cohen was musical director. Recently relocated to a townhouse at 37 West 56th Street (the former home of department store magnate John Wannamaker), the club had begun at 51st Street and Sixth Avenue, where the success of the Downstairs Room led to expansion to the second floor, the first Upstairs at the Downstairs. While the golden age of nightclubs was drawing to a close, these venues still offered the promise of an almost unmatchable sophistication, and they proved a breeding ground for generations of talent: singers who breathed new life into pop standards, comedians who set the tone for American humor. Those who didn't know already learned how to work an audience, how to put over a joke or a lyric, and how to hold a listener's attention despite the distractions of clinking cocktails and handsome busboys. Producers, casting agents, and other performers regularly came by to check out new talent, and New York nightclubs could still provide a springboard to national attention via television (notably *The Ed Sullivan Show*). As Madeline told writer James Gavin, her hope was always that the Upstairs would lead to something bigger.[23]

Downstairs at the Upstairs generally featured solo acts, and when Madeline wasn't working, she could hear performers like singer Mabel Mercer and comedian Joan Rivers. In the Upstairs room, Madeline and other young unknowns romped through a series of topical sketches and humorous songs, periodically updated and retitled. In the course of three revues—*Just for Openers, Mixed Doubles,* and *Below the Belt*—she worked with such soon-to-be-stars as Fannie Flagg (*Fried Green Tomatoes at the Whistle Stop Café*), Betty Aberlin (*Mister Rogers' Neighborhood*), Judy Graubart (*The Electric Company, Simon*), and Jenna Carter, who went on to achieve fame under her first name, Dixie, on TV's *Designing Women*. For *Below the Belt*, Madeline recommended a young comic she'd recently seen, and thus Lily Tomlin was hired for her first gig in New York. Among the men in these shows, none became a household name, but it's a measure of the talent pool at the time that the Upstairs managed to field superior performers despite low pay and a demanding schedule of two shows per night, six nights per week.

They performed in eveningwear, tuxedoes for the men and long black gowns for the women. The dress code relaxed somewhat in summer, when the women wore shorter skirts and traded in their black pumps for white ones, "to make our legs look longer," Tomlin says, recalling going shoe-shopping with Madeline. Formal dress was meant to reinforce visually the sophistication of the material, and it's one reason patrons, including Madeline's family members, recall the Upstairs as elegant. But cast members say the room was narrow, the performing space cramped, the dressing rooms mostly a state of mind rather than a physical reality.

Under producer Julius Monk, the Upstairs revues won acclaim (and thriving business), but by the time Madeline got there, Monk had decamped to start his own club at the Plaza Hotel. Many critics, and Madeline herself, considered the material in the Upstairs revues produced by Monk's successor, Rod Warren, to be inconsistent at best, and business fell off—a fact owner Irving Haber reminded Warren about continuously. As Haber saw it, only revenue from the Downstairs kept the Upstairs running.

"When I entered that job, I did not know what a revue was," Madeline told Gavin. But she soon developed reservations about the material, which she found "arch," "sarcastic," and often "effete," aimed at the club's largely gay clientele. "I had to be very smart in picking from the material Rod presented at the beginning of the season. You had to make these things work, and it was hard. At first I did whatever he asked me to. But then I got more savvy and realized, be sure you have a very good solo, be sure the other material is stuff you really feel you can make work. Rod gave his opinions, but it was basically up to you."

Though Flagg and Tomlin wrote some of their own sketches, Warren wrote much of the material himself and took contributions from freelancers, as well. He got away with paying writers even less than performers, as the market for comedy writing was limited (the few alternatives included supplying jokes to television comedians and sketches to other revues). Political humor and social commentary aimed gentle barbs at figures such as President Lyndon Johnson and California gubernatorial candidate Ronald Reagan. In *Just for Openers*, Madeline impersonated Lady Bird Johnson, mocking her "beautification" of American highways: "I go seeking buttercups, dear little buttercups, though I find practically none." But the same show included a less-gentle tirade by Flagg as a bigoted Southern waitress, and a prescient sketch in which Madeline and Aberlin played bored operators at "Dial-a-Deviate." As Aberlin observes, phone-sex lines hadn't been invented yet.

Listening now to the recordings of Madeline's three revues, it's easy to pick out the material aimed at gay audiences. In *Just for Openers*, the three women sing a proto-*Forbidden Broadway* number called "The 'Dolly' Sisters," spoofing three stars of *Hello, Dolly!* (Ginger Rogers "can't sing," Mary Martin "can't dance," and Carol Channing "can't act"). *Mixed Doubles* featured an entire song about the Spoleto Festival, and *Below the Belt* offered a song called "Camp," in which Madeline, Carter, and Tomlin learn from antique dealers and fans of Bette Davis. "After a while, I didn't feel very feminine," Madeline told Gavin. "I started to feel that parts of me were not seen or regarded highly at all."[24]

Madeline's "very good solo" in her second revue was "Das Chicago Song," and it earned her praise in the *New York Times* review of the show, at the same time stealing some of the spotlight from Janie Sell, who replaced Flagg (the *Times* critic loved Sell, though Madeline found Flagg more impressive).[25] But in her third revue, Madeline was dismayed to discover that the big comic solo—"Love's Labour Lost," about a bride's use of then-controversial contraceptives—went to another classically trained lyric soprano, Dixie Carter. In another number, "The Great Society Waltz," Carter again took the operatic chores, notably a vocalise on the Kermesse from Gounod's *Faust*. And in "Suburbia Square Dance," about wife swapping, Carter sang quotations from *West Side Story* and took all the highest notes.

Years later, Carter told Gavin that she found Madeline intimidating and that the two didn't hit it off. What's clear is that Madeline found Carter equally intimidating. For the first time, she'd found someone who could sing what she could sing and get just as many laughs. The newcomer was slimmer and arguably better looking than Madeline, too. Meanwhile, Carter's fiancé, businessman Arthur L. Carter, was trying (successfully) to steer her away from show business. Surveying the company of *Below the Belt*, he told her, "None of these people are going to make it." Those words would haunt Dixie when she sat at home watching Madeline and Tomlin on television a few years later.

Madeline formed lifelong friendships with Aberlin and Tomlin. In the mid-1960s, many people found Tomlin's comedy utterly mystifying. Already her characters included Lucille the Rubber Freak and the Very Tasteful Lady, which were unlike anything else and invested with specific, sharply observed and convincing detail. Even Madeline didn't quite understand what Tomlin was doing, but she liked it, appreciating the influence of Ruth Draper on Tomlin's work. Tomlin, in turn, admired Madeline's talent. "Everything seemed to spring from her natural comedic center," Tomlin says. "Everything about her gestures—she was inherently comedic—I can't say anything more. If she wanted the material to be comedic in her hands, it would be. Just tipping the attitude one way or the other. Even on a talk show, she's comedic, just talking, because she has that kind of musicality to her voice—her inflections." One of the world's most gifted mimics, Tomlin continues, "I can't possibly imitate it. It was the way she might ruminate over something while she's talking."

Madeline's approach to character was subtle, Tomlin says. "She didn't have to lay something on or find another voice for it, I never thought"—though she does cite a Santa Claus song from *Below the Belt*, in which Madeline used a little-girl voice. (With variations, the voice would resurface on *Saturday Night Live* and *Oh Madeline*, and in *Young Frankenstein*.) Several of her friends have observed that whether in conversation or onstage, Madeline might use an accent or alter the tone of her voice, and only later would they realize that she had just taken on a different identity, as specific in her mind as any of Tomlin's characters.

Aberlin bonded with Madeline in part because both were Jewish New Yorkers, and both their fathers walked out on them. Onstage, there was no competition, Aberlin says, not least because in numbers like "The 'Dolly' Sisters," each had her own business—though she does feel that, because she trained as a dancer, not a singer, Michael Cohen gave Madeline better songs in *Just for Openers*. She and Madeline remained close over the years, sometimes going to dinner together with Cohen, and Aberlin was among the few permitted to see Madeline at the end of her life. She describes Madeline as "a *neshuma*, a precious soul."

Aberlin has fond memories of going out with cast members and friends after *Just for Openers* finished for the night. They'd play girl-group songs on the jukebox and sing harmony. This kind of socializing had important benefits for Madeline, since the Upstairs shows attracted other talented performers who wanted to see their prospective colleagues (or rivals) performing current material. Among the connections Madeline made at this time were George Coe and Robert Klein, with each of whom she would work many times, and Jim Catusi, a comic who waited tables at the Upstairs, with whom she began an affair.

By the time Madeline started seeing Catusi in 1967, she'd gone back to live with her mother in Queens. Freda had taken secretarial jobs, first at a company called 21 Brands, then at Actors Equity. She hadn't given up her theatrical ambitions, though she had given up her first name (on the advice of a numerologist, she later said). She was now Paula Kahn, and she had headshots and résumés printed up, listing many credits—some honest, some exaggerated, and some entirely fabricated. When Paula ran low on money, Madeline demonstrated her sense of responsibility, relinquishing her independence and her apartment in Manhattan to move back to Romeo Court and help support her mother. Jef Kahn remembers that he had taken the larger of the children's bedrooms during Madeline's absence, and when she returned, she allowed him to keep it.

Living with Paula complicated Madeline's love life. Jim Catusi complained to his friend Brandon Maggart that after a bender, he'd call up Madeline at five o'clock in the morning only to spend the next hour talking to Paula. Maggart remembers that for a while Madeline moved in with Catusi. If so, it was the only time she lived with a boyfriend. But his alcoholism "was not her thing," Robert Klein says, and the relationship couldn't survive.[26] Catusi was "the only person I ever knew that was funnier drunk than sober," Maggart says. "Usually, it's the other way around: a drunk person thinks they're funny and they're not. But he was unfortunately not at his best when he had a few drinks under his belt." (Both men later went into recovery.) In 1969, the two joined a revue at the Upstairs, where producer Jon Stone spotted them and signed them for a series of vaudeville-style sketches on a new children's show, *Sesame Street*. As "Buddy and Jim," they taught kids how *not* to get through a door with an ironing board, and how *not* to hang a picture.

Catusi and Maggart—like Aberlin and Graubart—found a berth in children's television, as did many other veterans of New York's nightclub revues, and their sensibilities informed the shows in which they appeared. On the straitlaced *Mister Rogers' Neighborhood*, Aberlin sang frequently, but her comedic gifts found few outlets. *Sesame Street* and *The Electric Company*, however, took a zanier approach. Had Madeline not pursued her other options so avidly, then she, too, might have wound up on children's television in the 1970s as a regular, not as a guest star. Such a gig could have translated into steady work and the enduring affection of a generation or more of children, but the tradeoff was typecasting, as both Aberlin and Graubart would discover. In 1997, Graubart even lost a plum role in the film *Judy Berlin* to a better-known actor, her former Upstairs co-star, Madeline Kahn.

• • •

Upstairs at the Downstairs provided Madeline with an extraordinary showcase. The shows there garnered raves from Judith Crist (first at the *New York Herald Tribune*, then at the *Times*), the two record albums, and a few television appearances, including those on *The Today Show* and *The*

Ed Sullivan Show. But Madeline never saw the revues as a permanent or even lasting gig, and as soon as Aberlin and Flagg left *Just for Openers*, she began looking for other options.

One came from David Hoffman, her friend from Hofstra. Already a budding filmmaker in college, Hoffman would go on to make award-winning documentaries. In 1967, he'd been hired to co-direct an industrial film for Metropolitan Life Insurance. Intended for insurance agents, medical professionals, and patients, *A Song of Arthur, or How Arthur Changed His Tune and Solved a Weighty Problem* addressed the diet of a suburban father. To keep things lively, it was through-composed, with every line of dialogue sung to music and lyrics by Stan Freeman. The role of Arthur's wife isn't large, but it involves some comedy, and Hoffman considered the score "operatic." He immediately thought of Madeline.

They shot on Long Island in winter, 1967. On the set, Hoffman found Madeline easy to work with. He still considered her extremely attractive, though she seemed no more interested in men than she had seemed at Hofstra. On screen, she looks quite chubby, and her character, like Arthur, goes on a diet. Despite Madeline's persistent concerns about her appearance, she recognized the movie's value as a promotional tool. For the next few years, she used it to demonstrate her proficiency both as a screen actor and as a singer.[27]

Her next break came not from *A Song of Arthur*, but at the Upstairs several months later. "What you hoped for in those shows," she told James Gavin, "was that [Broadway producer] David Merrick would come in and say, 'Have I got a part for you!' And that's exactly what happened." As New York's cabaret scene faltered, unable to compete with television, rock'n'roll, and turbulent social change, "It was the right time to leave," she said. "I had gotten in right under the wire. I felt, 'This is gonna end soon.' I didn't miss it."

7

Pink-Slipped

How Now, Dow Jones (1967)

MADELINE'S REMARKABLY BAD LUCK IN BROADWAY MUSICALS STARTED with her first. A swinging, topical farce, *How Now, Dow Jones* featured a book by Max Shulman (best known for *Dobie Gillis*), lyrics by Carolyn Leigh (*Wildcat, Little Me*, and many of Frank Sinatra's best-known songs), and music by Elmer Bernstein (fresh from his Oscar for the score to *Thoroughly Modern Millie*). The plot, which Leigh suggested, focuses on a young woman who works on Wall Street and whose boyfriend refuses to marry her until the Dow Jones average tops one thousand; naturally, she winds up with someone else. Produced by David Merrick and bound for Broadway, *How Now* stopped first in Boston.

Brenda Vaccaro played the lead, "and I played this extraneous nurse," Madeline told an interviewer in 1973. "I really didn't know why they needed me. I had nothing to do. But David Merrick kept saying I was great and that he would build the part up. So I relaxed and did my job." But after the last performance at the Colonial Theatre, Madeline was handed an envelope. "I jokingly said: 'What's this—a pink slip?' And that's what it was. It was pink and it was a slip saying, 'Services no longer required.' I couldn't speak. My heart stopped."[28]

Vaccaro and another cast member, George Coe, offer more details. Director Arthur Penn hired Madeline to play a character called Miss Whipple; she was also Vaccaro's understudy. Madeline "was just funny, if you can picture her as a young woman, in a nurse's costume," says Coe. An Upstairs veteran who would figure several more times in Madeline's career, he remembers a solo number for Miss Whipple called "Rich Is Better." The song isn't listed in a playbill from later in the Boston run. At that point, Madeline sang in three ensemble numbers and the finale, and her role was shrinking underneath her. While Penn seemed to appreciate

41

Madeline, Merrick "just couldn't understand her comic genius," Vaccaro says. "He wasn't on the same page with her as a comedienne; he didn't realize what a talent she was, and he couldn't relate to her at all, which was his shortcoming."

Merrick didn't seem to understand Penn, either, though the director had guided Anne Bancroft in her Broadway debut in *Two for the Seesaw*, and enjoyed tremendous success with *The Miracle Worker*, both on Broadway and onscreen. The year before *How Now*, he'd revolutionized American cinema with *Bonnie and Clyde*. But when *How Now* ran into trouble during Boston tryouts, Merrick fired Penn, "which he did with great aplomb, as he always did," Vaccaro observes tartly. To replace the director, Merrick brought in George Abbott. Madeline had lost her champion, although she didn't realize it.

Abbott, who began his directorial career in the 1920s, was an odd choice for a new musical trying hard to be up-to-the-minute, but he'd guided such classics as *On the Town*, *Pajama Game*, and *Damn Yankees*, and he was a renowned show doctor whom Merrick trusted. Coe describes Abbott as "abusive to actors," and the director's old-fashioned, by-the-numbers approach conflicted with Madeline's exploration of her characters' inner lives. She "was just in a long line of really extraordinary talent that was fired on that musical," Vaccaro says, "because everybody had a sort of milk haze over their eyes about what to do about it." Coe deliberately got out of the show, and he wound up with Madeline on the train back to New York. "I was probably more upset about them pushing her out of the show than she was," he says, though Madeline remembered crying for days after she got home.

In the mid-1960s, with smash musical comedies like *Gypsy*, *Oliver!*, and *Hello, Dolly!* to his credit, Merrick was at the height of his power, as much a star as almost any actor in New York, and he wore the nickname "The Abominable Showman" proudly. Improbably, an Internet rumor holds that the very next season Madeline won a role in another Merrick show and got fired again during out-of-town tryouts. However, there's no substance to the rumor that she appeared in *Promises, Promises*, and the show's star, Donna McKechnie, confirms that Madeline wasn't around. In fact, Madeline lost little time making her Broadway debut. The loss of *How Now* effectively freed her to accept an offer from producer Leonard Sillman, whose *New Faces* revues had introduced a number of future stars. But her debut didn't do much to improve her luck.

8

We've Never Seen You

New Faces of 1968

BY SIGNING ON FOR *NEW FACES OF 1968*, MADELINE JOINED THE roster of Leonard Sillman's other "discoveries," which began with a 1933 edition in Los Angeles and featured Tyrone Power, Kay Thompson, and Eve Arden. Even a partial roll call from Sillman's New York *New Faces* revues is impressive: Imogene Coca, Henry Fonda, Alice Pearce, Alice Ghostley, Carol Lawrence, Paul Lynde, Jane Connell, Inga Swenson, Eartha Kitt, and Maggie Smith. However, as the *Times*'s Clive Barnes pointed out in his review of the 1968 edition, the concept of "new faces" was relative: The performers were new only to people who never went to nightclubs or watched television.[29] Several cast members, including Robert Klein and Dorothy Danner (under the name Dottie Frank), had made their Broadway debuts in other shows, and much of the material and cast in the 1968 show was recycled from the touring *New Faces of 1966*, which any New Yorker with access to Connecticut might have seen.

In *New Faces*, Madeline took part in several sketches, including a beauty pageant sketch ("Missed America") written by her friends Gail Parent and Kenny Solms. In "Luncheon Ballad," she joined Suzanne Astor, Marilyn Child, and Nancie Phillips in poking fun at society ladies involved in so many charities that they can't keep them straight. Both numbers were recycled from *New Faces of 1966*. Remarkably, in Danner's copy of the 1968 rehearsal script, Madeline's big solo, "Das Chicago Song," doesn't appear, suggesting that it was a late addition. Toward the end of the show, Madeline and Klein joined Brandon Maggart and George Ormiston in another sketch from the 1966 edition, "Die Zusammenfügung, or the Connection," a pastiche "opera by Wolfgang Amadeus Mozart" that concerns a purloined stash of marijuana. Composed by Sam Pottle, with lyrics by David Axelrod, the number took advantage of

Klein's enthusiastic baritone and Madeline's lyric coloratura. With pinpoint precision and sparkling roulades, she informs her father (Klein), that she's found a mysterious new ingredient for her soup. Sampling it, he realizes that "The pot is in the soup."

Marian Mercer took Madeline's part in the 1966 edition of "Zusammenfügung," and the resulting comparison, coupled with Madeline's Lenya impression, led Danner to consider her "a brilliant mimic," but less accomplished as an actress. Though Madeline's later performances won her over, Danner says, "At that point, it seemed like sometimes she was doing an imitation rather than investing herself." Maggart considered Madeline a great talent already, though it seems she'd set aside her Hofstra professor's demand that she blend in. Maggart says, "If you want to know how it was to work with her onstage, you might as well not *be* onstage. She had no sense of focus as to the material and what to put over in the sketch. All the eyes went to Madeline, because the motor was always running. Even when she was still, quietly observing, everybody's eye went to Madeline. She had star quality."

New Faces of 1968 attempted to replicate the feel of one of Sillman's famous, almost continual backers' auditions, where excerpts from forthcoming shows would be presented to potential investors ("My longest run in show business," says Maggart). Sillman held these auditions in his living room, which the set design evoked, and on Broadway he played the master of ceremonies, just as he did in his home. Maggart remembers that the "gypsy run-through" (a performance open only to other Broadway performers) "blew the roof off the house," and the show got a good response in previews. But on opening night, the backers dominated the audience, and they'd heard all the jokes before. "I've done thousands and thousands of shows," Maggart says, "but only one other was that silent on an opening night."

In those days, critics still reviewed opening night performances, rather than previews. There wasn't much good news in the papers for the cast, and there was even less for Sillman. Klein, Maggart, and Michael K. Allen earned favorable notices in the *Times*, and Clive Barnes singled out Madeline, too. She "had a strong voice and an incisive personality and was at her best in a Kurt Weill parody." However, he didn't mention any other cast member by name, and his overall take on the show was grim: "But perhaps the time for the Broadway revue is over. For there is no real satirical bite here—it is all far too prim and cosy. No one could possibly be offended—no one, that is, who is not offended by intrinsic mediocrity."[30]

Klein and Maggart agree with that assessment. With the Vietnam War raging, with the assassinations of Dr. Martin Luther King Jr. (during previews) and of Robert F. Kennedy (after the show opened), Klein says, "[W]e're doing a show, [singing] 'You've never seen us before, and we've never seen you before!' Hello?" "We seemed rather frivolous," Maggart agrees.

Musically, *New Faces* was old-fashioned (the first notes of the overture are glissandi on harp), while Broadway audiences wanted more for their money than a handful of satirical sketches that were, frankly, smarter than they were hip. At the same time, Danner points out, a more radical change was in the works on Broadway. *New Faces* opened at the Booth Theatre on May 2, just three days after *Hair* (which had been a hit at the Public Theater downtown in the fall of 1967) arrived at the Biltmore Theatre, two blocks away. Though *Hair* itself is a kind of revue, the contrast between the shows could hardly be greater. One cast of young performers was in formalwear and the other in tie-dye and blue jeans (and birthday suits). One show featured opera parodies and the other rock. One show focused on sassy topicality, while the other issued a call for social change. *New Faces* made youth a selling point; *Hair* made youth an instrument of revolution.

An actors' strike gave *New Faces* a dignified excuse to close. Though Maggart insists that the show's failure wasn't predetermined or intended, Klein doesn't dispel the widespread legend that Sillman was a model for the flop-happy Max Bialystock in Mel Brooks's *The Producers*. Sillman, like Bialystock, shared an affinity for widowed investors, and like his fictitious counterpart, Sillman produced many Broadway productions that lasted only a few performances.[31] Klein calls Sillman "an amateur" and a con man who, as a patient of Max Jacobson, the legendary "Dr. Feelgood," was "dealing with a loaded deck." Regular treatment with "miracle tissue regenerator shots" (the ingredients of which included B vitamins, amphetamines, and painkillers) affected Sillman's decision-making, prompting his insistence on "more ping" and sped-up tempos on the cast album, Klein says.

Sillman was a skillful enough promoter to land a feature in the fashion section of the *New York Times* just as *New Faces* began previews. In an account of the producer's efforts to find appropriate designer gowns for each woman in the cast, Sillman told the *Times* that he didn't want Madeline "to fall into the clichés of what is happening in fashion." Her "effective but unadorned" "puritan look" can be seen in the accompanying photo of all eight *New Faces* women, including Elaine Giftos (later of

The Partridge Family) and Gloria Bleezarde, who wears the only miniskirt in the company—though she's posed so as not to reveal that the dress is backless, a calculated titillation that Sillman exploited during the show.[32] For an aspiring actor, this sort of free publicity is welcome, even when the show doesn't run. Another benefit was Madeline's first commercial recording. Anticipating another success along the lines of *New Faces of 1952*, Warner Bros. produced an original cast album. In the liner notes, musical theater historian Miles Kreuger opines optimistically that "in 10 years, there will probably be a big Robert Klein film festival . . . there will be a Madeline Kahn–Brandon Maggart Comedy Hour on 3-D color television . . . ."[33]

Members of the cast—"a mixed jar of pickles," Danner says—didn't have time to get to know each other well, though Danner did get a glimpse of the "real" Madeline, calling Paula for a voice lesson over the phone. But Klein and Madeline had known each other for about two years, and they already socialized together often. She introduced him to Brenda Vaccaro, whom he dated for a while. And once, when he and Vaccaro weren't seeing each other, he slept with Madeline. In the 1960s, he says, "you just did not have that long a relationship between two young, single, attractive people without finding out what it was like." The interlude was brief, however, and they resumed their platonic friendship. "It was one of those things that goes against the books: it did not affect our relationship one iota. We were not to be partners, you know, but [it] was dignified and great. Somehow I have a big smile about it." *New Faces* marked the beginning of their professional collaboration, one of the most important in Madeline's career. It would endure for the rest of her life.

9

Cigars and Lavaliers

De Düva and *Candide* (1968)

THROUGHOUT HER CAREER, MADELINE RESPONDED TO SETBACKS BY lining up other jobs as quickly as possible. She didn't wallow in disappointment; she needed work. After *New Faces* closed, she returned to the Philadelphia area in the summer of 1968 for a production of Peter Shaffer's *Black Comedy*, which starred Hollywood luminary Sylvia Sidney. Playing a featured role, Madeline figured prominently on the cover of the playbill, standing in front of Sidney and co-star John Horn. In her program biography, she made no mention of Manumit or of her ties to the area, and in later years she made no mention of *Black Comedy*. She did keep a copy of the playbill, though.

More auspicious was her first professional movie credit, *De Düva*, also known as *The Dove*. A parody of Ingmar Bergman's *Wild Strawberries* and *The Seventh Seal*, *De Düva* grew out of a sketch on George Coe and Sidney Davis's radio program, *It's Your World and You Can Have It*. Presented as if it were the soundtrack to a Bergman film, the sketch consisted of Davis pretending to speak Swedish, along with Coe's English "translation." Response to the radio sketch inspired them both to collaborate with Anthony Lover to film *De Düva*, shot in evocative black-and-white and performed entirely in fake Swedish (what Davis called "English with party hats on"), with English subtitles that serve less as translation than as counterpoint.[34]

The film centers on Prof. Viktor Lundkvist (Coe), an elderly man who, in flashbacks, remembers his beautiful sister, Inga (Pamela Burrell) and the day that Death (Davis) came to claim her. Rather than surrender, Viktor challenges Death to a game of badminton. Following the intervention of the titular bird, brother and sister are free to pursue their innocent yet *very* passionate relationship. For the role of Sigfrid, a cigar-smoking

47

lesbian who has an eye for Inga, Coe suggested Madeline. Forty-five years would pass before he learned she was a lifelong Bergman fan. Offering Inga a cigar, she intones, "Phalliken symbol?" using an accent derived from many viewings of the master's movies.

But for Madeline, this labor of love was also an important career step. Coe had already served on the board of the Screen Actors Guild in New York, and he later served on the union's national board. He insured that *De Düva* observed SAG rules. The actors were paid scale, and those, like Madeline, who didn't have union cards, became eligible to join. *De Düva* wound up an Oscar nominee for best live action short at the forty-first Academy Awards, a credit that Madeline played up in her subsequent playbill biographies. However, Coe says, once the nominations were announced, the team knew they couldn't beat the documentary *Robert Kennedy Remembered*—and they didn't.

Even apart from the nomination, *De Düva* met with success that no one anticipated, and it surely helped to raise Madeline's profile. For years to come, repertory cinemas and film societies would run the short before screening real Bergman movies, and the picture is still hilarious. Blurry copies enjoy a cult following on the Internet, though the film has never been released commercially for home viewing. By now, the enduring popularity of *De Düva* owes at least as much to Madeline's fans as it does to Bergman's.

Madeline is entirely comfortable on camera in *De Düva*, and though her role is tiny, she devours it. Looking back, it seems obvious that she would go on to pursue a career in movies, and that she would stick to comedy. It's not surprising, either, that she'd excel in film parodies. She'd been going to the movies since she was a little girl, and watching closely. But it would be four years before she made another film, and for now movie stardom seemed a remote possibility. Other career paths would open up instead, leading almost anywhere but Hollywood—and the next path led to the opera house.

• • •

Madeline's second major project after *New Faces* was more in keeping with Paula's expectations. As part of a fiftieth-birthday celebration for Leonard Bernstein, plans were underway to revive his operetta *Candide*, beginning with a gala concert with the New York Philharmonic. Madeline was cast as the heroine, Cunegonde. Originally produced on Broadway in 1956, *Candide* ran only briefly, though the cast album is still prized for the beauty of its score and for the freshness of its performances, particularly that of Barbara Cook as Cunegonde. Since then, it hadn't been performed in its entirety on a New York stage.

Bernstein hoped to change that state of affairs, and the birthday concert became the springboard for a three-year plan that would take *Candide* on the road, fully staged. First the show would travel to San Francisco, then to Los Angeles, then to Washington's Kennedy Center (which Bernstein was scheduled to inaugurate in 1971, with the world premiere of his *Mass*), and finally arrive in triumph on Broadway. The road trip would amount to an extended workshop for a newly revised book, since Lillian Hellman's original, unfunny adaptation contributed to the show's failure, and she later forbade further use of her work. When Sheldon Patinkin, a young director in Chicago, submitted a concert narration for *Candide*, Bernstein immediately "suggested" that they meet (a suggestion from the composer was in reality a summons). Bernstein approved the narration and proposed that Patinkin craft an entirely new script, incorporating all the original songs, to premiere at the birthday gala at Lincoln Center.

In every one of its many incarnations, *Candide* follows, yet streamlines Voltaire's tale of a wide-eyed innocent forced to test his teacher's philosophy, "Everything is for the best in this best of all possible worlds." He and his childhood sweetheart, his cousin Cunegonde, are subjected to every kind of ordeal, caroming from catastrophe to catastrophe and country to country, before concluding that since the world is *not* such a nice place after all, the best we can do is to "Make Our Garden Grow." As Patinkin observes, "The essential problem is, the show doesn't have an arc." Instead, it's a string of episodes capped off by a change of heart. The more music one includes, the more dramatic impact one loses. But *Candide* boasts one of Bernstein's most captivating—and easily his most "classical"—scores for the theater, and the challenge of fixing it, making it stage worthy, and helping it to find new audiences would nettle him almost to the end of his life.

An original member of the Second City troupe, Patinkin directed the gala. (He went on to a distinguished career as a stage director and teacher at Columbia College Chicago and the University of Chicago, and as a consultant to Second City and the Steppenwolf Theater.) For the gala, Bernstein entrusted the score to one of his former assistant conductors from the Philharmonic, Maurice Peress, but he laid out a number of requirements. One of these was that Cunegonde must have a high E-flat, so that her music wouldn't be transposed. Patinkin remembers that Barbara Cook came in to audition but no longer had the note.

With the original Cunegonde out of the running, Madeline recognized a high-profile opportunity to jump-start her New York career, and she was determined to seize it. She and Michael Cohen coached her audition piece, Cunegonde's "Glitter and Be Gay." Both a direct descendant and a parody of Marguerite's "Jewel Song" from Gounod's *Faust*, the aria describes Cunegonde's fall from aristocratic virgin to high-class courtesan, even as she takes solace in the jewels with which her sugar daddies have rewarded her. Wailing lamentations alternate with giddy laughter—*staccati in alt*. This coloratura tour-de-force has become both a calling card and a challenge for big-name sopranos such as June Anderson, Renée Fleming, Natalie Dessay, and Diana Damrau. Broadway's Kristin Chenoweth sings it, too, drawing on her classical training. Yet Madeline's rendition, heard on a pirate recording made during the concert in 1968, is possibly the greatest of them all, musically accurate and comically sublime.

Much of this polish she brought directly to her audition. She and Cohen had worked out every note and every bit of business in advance. "She was not foolin' around," Patinkin remembers. "She wanted the role." Having demonstrated that she had the requisite high E-flat, Madeline read a scene with Alan Arkin, who was to play the Narrator, Dr. Pangloss, and Martin. She instantly found the comedy in the script and won the part. The cast also included the original Old Lady, Irra Petina, and as the Governor, tenor William Lewis, an alumnus of Sid Caesar's *Your Show of Shows*, soon to become a leading exponent of Richard Strauss's operas.

Peress, who was at the helm of the Corpus Christi Symphony at the time, now declares Madeline a standout among the artists he's worked with. Bernstein was so thrilled by her performance at the orchestra-dress rehearsal that he rushed onstage and knelt before her. But in conversation with Patinkin and Arkin, Madeline seemed unsure of herself, always discussing opera in terms of Paula's aspirations and influence. Madeline "was interested, but she wasn't sure," Patinkin says.

The cast rehearsed in Peress's apartment, but there weren't many rehearsals with the full orchestra. By opening night, Lewis says, "We were thinking, 'We're about to go out and sing for everybody who is anybody in the musical world.'" But then Madeline broke the tension, crawling under the piano and shrieking, "Oh, my God, I'm so scared, I've got to get out of here!" After a few minutes, she popped up again: "Okay, I'm ready." (Ten years later, Madeline's panic attacks before—and during—shows would be no joke.)

The pirate recording remains a fascinating document of Madeline's interpretive skills. For example, there's the line, "Bracelets! Lavaliers! Can they dry my tears?" Most Cunegondes wail the line melodramatically, but Madeline varies her reading and fairly growls the word "bracelets" in disgust—and the audience roars with laughter. Tellingly, perhaps, "Glitter and Be Gay" is the rare number with almost no glitches: Madeline's singing is utterly secure, and the orchestra plays smoothly despite lack of rehearsal. Listening, one misses much of the comedy in her performance, Peress says. "She juggled her breasts! It was amazing. She was outrageous. Onstage, you'd just let her out of her cage." The "topper," he says, was the moment when Madeline put the last of her jewels, a big ruby, in her bellybutton.

A benefit performance, the *Candide* concert seems to have gone unreviewed by the New York papers, but its success encouraged Bernstein to pursue his plans for the stage revival. Peress brought most of the company to Corpus Christi for another concert performance, replacing Alan Arkin with Robert Klein, who had worked with Patinkin at Second City and who would play Pangloss and Martin again in the touring stage production, which Madeline hoped and expected to join. In a profile in *Newsday* the next year, she spoke of Cunegonde: "'You know how you always dream of doing something and you cherish the dream . . . ' she trailed off with a wistful look in her eye. 'I was scared. But it was everything I thought it would be.'"[35]

• • •

While the number of credits on her résumé during this period may seem slight, Madeline didn't keep a thorough accounting of the work she did early in her career. She consistently landed one-shot jobs throughout the 1960s on television—both in advertising and on talk shows— as well as in "industrials," promotional shows staged at trade fairs and conventions. Because of the gaps in Madeline's surviving records, there's no way for a biographer to know precisely how many TV ads she did—though in interviews she referred to at least three, for products that included chicken soup and pharmaceuticals. Other references and relics do crop up, however. A national commercial for Ban deodorant dating from about 1968, for example, survives on YouTube, and television listings in old newspapers confirm that Madeline was a frequent guest on shows hosted by Merv Griffin, Mike Douglas, Dick Cavett, and Johnny Carson. Such appearances meant greater exposure than she could expect from her stage work, and they sometimes led to more substantial jobs, much as Madeline hoped.

Industrials entailed far more than simply acting as a spokesmodel. Replete with sketches and music, they were often more like nightclub revues, and some were lavish song-and-dance spectacles. Sometimes industrials involved travel within the United States and to Europe, Mexico, and Canada, Madeline's *New Faces* co-star Dorothy Danner remembers. The shows gave dancers like Danner a chance to try comedy and comedians like Madeline a chance to try dance in front of an appreciative, non-judgmental audience.

Talk shows gave Madeline her biggest audiences during the early phase of her career. But these showcases—and the paychecks that talk-show guests receive—came at a price that Madeline found steep. Almost immediately, all of the hosts effectively typecast her as an attractive, naïve, or spacy woman who was funny without meaning to be. For most of her life, Madeline didn't understand why people found her funny, and on talk shows, where she tried to give thoughtful, intelligent answers, the hosts' and other guests' attitudes baffled her. The result of Madeline's talk show experience was heightened anxiety or stage fright. And as she told Rex Reed in 1974, "[O]ne night I watched myself on Merv Griffin, and there I was, sandwiched between [standup comics] George Jessel and Marty Allen, and just being treated like a dumb kook for them to bounce their jokes on, and I said that's it. Where did it ever say I have to do that? What's happening to me? So I just stopped doing talk shows."[36]

Later in her career, she had to make appearances, like it or not, to promote her latest projects. Although the hosts treated her more respectfully once she attained stardom, her anxiety didn't subside. Promoting *Clue* on *The Tonight Show* in 1986, she told Carson toward the end of the interview segment, "I've been anticipating being on for a couple of weeks now. I have known I was going to be on. And you know, I mean, it's scary. It does feel like surgery to me, coming on this program. Although I have never had surgery. But . . . ."

Carson, who had been low-key and even gentle throughout the interview, and who appeared quite fond of Madeline, interrupted: "I enjoyed this, talking like this." "Yes," Madeline said, "it isn't bad when you actually do it. But the anticipation is so scary. And then it's over! And you leave, and you just feel . . . ." "And then the depression," Carson said, alluding to their earlier conversation about how actors feel after completing a movie. "That's life, I guess," Madeline said.[37]

Two of Madeline's final talk show appearances, promoting the show *Cosby*, provide an illuminating contrast. Talking to David Letterman on CBS (January 13, 1997) would set off her anxieties. Typically, producers for the show contacted guests about a day in advance, discussed at length any stories that might appeal to Letterman, and wrote out notes and questions for him on little blue cards—which he ignored. He might even pursue questions despite her repeated requests to change the subject, as he did on his NBC show in 1989.[38]

But Charlie Rose (December 16, 1996), with his quieter, more thoughtful program and long segments devoted to each guest, filmed in a studio without an audience, afforded Madeline something like the serious treatment she'd wanted for so long. Talking about typecasting, Rose asked, "How would you define the perception of you, do you think, by audiences?" The question prompted a revealing response from Madeline: "I'm always asking that question. I'm always curious to know. I don't know what people—I'm happy to find that many people do see that I'm an actress and that I'm not a kook. It's not just, 'Oh, that's her. You know, that character, that kooky person, is her.'"

Even so, Rose moved on without acknowledging Madeline's question, "I wish you would answer that. How am I perceived?" We'll never know how she might have reacted had he responded.[39]

10

Only Make-Believe

Promenade and *Show Boat* (1969)

MADELINE EXPECTED TO ROUND OUT THE 1960S WITH A ROLE IN *PROMENADE*, a music-theater piece with book and lyrics by the avant-garde playwright María Irene Fornés and a score by the Rev. Al Carmines. Though Madeline and the production won favorable reviews, "None of us knew what the hell was going on, and I remember I was actually booed in that show," she told the *New York Times* in 1974. "Now that's a feeling to remember!"[40]

Much of the trouble lay with Fornés's script, which the critics lambasted even while praising the music and staging so highly that the show became a hit. George S. Irving, who played the Mayor in *Promenade*, gives an idea what they were up against. He remembers turning to the playwright and asking, "'Irene, what does this line mean?' She replied, 'Whatever you want it to be!' That's great direction for a poor fucking actor!" A curious mixture of expressionism and absurdism, *Promenade* is set in motion by two Prisoners, who escape from under the nose of the Jailer, then crash a society party. There, they meet the Servant (Madeline), with whom they rob the socialites before taking off in pursuit of more misadventures, with the Jailer in pursuit. Fornés and Carmines first staged the play in 1965, at the Judson Memorial Church on Washington Square. The same year, *Promenade*, along with another play, *The Successful Life of Three*, earned Fornés the first of her nine Obie Awards. Revised and expanded from one act to two, *Promenade* reopened on June 4, 1969, re-inaugurating an Upper West Side theater that, until it closed in 2008, continued to bear the play's name.

In the *New York Daily News*, James Davis denounced "a book that is simply dreadful" and complained of "an aimlessness that made for lack of interest in the incredible dialogue."[41] Even while describing the play as "a joy from start to finish," the *New York Times*'s Clive Barnes allowed that there was "no book in any conventional sense . . . close to no book in any unconventional sense."[42] But Walter Kerr devoted one of his long Sunday essays in the *Times* to praise for Carmines's score. Under the headline "Hooray! He Gives Us Back Our Past," Kerr compared the composer to Sigmund Romberg. He also singled out Madeline's performance:

> Madeline Kahn announces, with jazz bravura, that she has discovered what life is all about. It's all about the glory of walking down the street with a mean look on your face, a cigarette in your right hand, a toothpick in your left. Miss Kahn is contented, gay, nearly ecstatic, as she alternates cigarette and toothpick, right foot and left, syncopated bass notes and riffed treble. . . . And the longer we watch Madeline Kahn's waitress, skirt starchily flared, hair ready to dance in the breeze, the more we are convinced that she is really Marilyn Miller gone tough-minded.[43]

Madeline received favorable mention in most of the reviews, as did George S. Irving and Alice Playten. Madeline also landed her first personality profile, in *Newsday*, on July 10, 1969. But *Promenade* was an ensemble piece, not a star-making vehicle. Even when referring to Madeline as one of "the bewitching trio of honest delinquents," Barnes professed himself reluctant to identify any standouts in the cast. There was little reason for Madeline to stay.

And then came the booing. The incident—or one of the incidents—provoked an extraordinary, long letter to the *Times*, the sort of amateur criticism that nowadays would circulate on the Internet. The writer, Don Dunn of Queens Village, NY, reports that "Madeline Kahn's eyes—mischievous, sparkling as a rule—glazed over for just an instant when the single shout, 'Booooo!,' rumbled foghorn-like from a male member of the audience." Insisting that "a musical should say *something*," Dunn complains that Carmines's forgettable melodies and Fornés's "incomprehensible" lyrics were at fault. He also blames the critics, whose reviews led audiences to expect a different kind of show. The fellow who booed, he says, stormed out with several friends. And Dunn isn't done:

> Is it possible to boo or jeer something onstage without meaning any disrespect toward the hardworking performers? Miss Kahn is a lovely, talented actress with a magnificent voice, but she was standing onstage singing gibberish. She was singing it well, full-throated

and proudly—but she was singing gibberish . . . . Now, if a patron realizes he has paid $10 to listen to well-trained voices sing gibberish, may he express his displeasure toward the writers—not the performers, who are only trying to earn a paycheck—or must he wait until they answer the call of "Author!" and appear onstage?

Dunn even suggests "that someone was seriously thinking of attacking Miss Kahn in blind fury—or of storming the box office. I know that it would not have taken much to set me in hot support, and I wonder how many other theatergoers would have joined in."[44]

Getting booed is tough for any performer, but for a sensitive artist like Madeline, it was unbearable. Around this time, she came to feel that those in charge didn't appreciate her, either. Producer Joseph Beruh came to the cast with contracts to record the cast album. He offered only a session fee, with no residuals, and the actors unanimously refused to sign, Irving says. They later relented, but by then both Madeline and Irving were gone, and their replacements recorded the parts.

Virtually all that Madeline took away from *Promenade* was a copy of that cast album and a number written for another character, Miss O. "The Moment Has Passed" entered Madeline's standing repertoire. A world-weary, Weill-tinted comic number that may be seen as a kind of stepping-stone between "Das Chicago Song" and "I'm Tired," "The Moment Has Passed" was included in most of her sketches for her unrealized nightclub act, "Kahn-Cepts." She also sang it on *The Tonight Show* in 1986.

Madeline fled first to Philadelphia, for one more *Candide* concert (almost certainly her last), and then, for the first time in her life, made her way to California. In Sacramento, she played Magnolia in Jerome Kern's *Show Boat*, produced by the Sacramento Light Opera Association at the Music Circus, an enormous tent venue. Magnolia's sweetly lyrical lines have proven congenial to other classically trained sopranos, notably Irene Dunne and Kathryn Grayson in two film adaptations of the show. Opposite Madeline, baritone Richard Fredericks sang Gaylord Ravenal. Immediately before coming to Sacramento, he'd sung Lescaut in Massenet's *Manon*, opposite Beverly Sills. Magnolia's first number is a duet with Ravenal, "Make-Believe"—Madeline would have to work to keep up with her co-star.

She didn't, quite. "The first couple of days, she was so insecure," Fredericks remembers. Magnolia was unlike other roles Madeline had played, and he suspects that she'd never kissed a man onstage except for laughs. When it came time to rehearse the kiss, he had to ask her to remove her chewing gum first. (She stuck it behind her ear, but at the end of the scene, she stuck the gum back in her mouth.) In rehearsals, the rest of the cast worked "at performance level," but Madeline didn't. In dialogue scenes, he could barely hear her. He confronted Russell Lewis, one of the Music Circus's founding producers, who admitted he'd gotten the idea to hire Madeline when he heard her sing on a talk show.

Yet Madeline's apparent diffidence wasn't, as Fredericks believed, the fault of bad habits brought on by television cameras and microphones, which do encourage smaller-scale work. Instead, she was finding the character according to her own internalized method, which most opera singers in those days would have found alien. However, Fredericks says, after a couple of performances, "she started coming on like a herd of turtles. *Then* we started to have a show." He found Madeline "too sophisticated and too old" for Magnolia, and she lacked period style. But "[t]o her credit, there was a performer in there. She did her job." Fredericks disputes reports ("horse pucky") that Madeline played Magnolia for laughs. She played the character as written, he says, and when she got laughs, it was "because the lines are funny. She did nothing to distract from that."[45] As a singer, Madeline felt—and to an extent, Fredericks agreed—"she had no business being there" in an operetta among professionals. In 1969, he knew she'd done sketch comedy, but he didn't believe she'd ever done a book show—much less that she'd sung Cunegonde for Bernstein.

Conducted and directed by Milton Lyon, *Show Boat* ran the week of August 4–10, 1969. The heat was over one hundred degrees during the daytime, and it was still sweltering in the tent by evening—"And then they'd turn the lights on," Fredericks says. Reflecting on the production, Madeline later told the *New York Times* that it was "so hot, my makeup fell off."[46] She got terrific press for *Show Boat*, not only reviews, but also a personality profile in the *Sacramento Union*, in which she revealed the kind of ambivalence that Fredericks sensed in her, not only about opera but also about old-fashioned musical comedies like *Oklahoma!* or the one in which she was about to star.[47] Her best review came from Richard Simon in the *Union*, who called her "a rising star on the musical horizon" and "a real find." He added, "She possesses both a winsome charm and an absolute sincerity that makes irresistible her portrayal of the riverboat captain's daughter. Allied to a very nice lyric soprano voice, it is evident that Miss Kahn will be up, up and away in her beautiful career."[48]

In the *Show Boat* program, Madeline mentions one upcoming engagement. Having dabbled in operetta, at last she was ready to try the real thing: opera. *Candide*'s conductor, Maurice Peress, had hired her to sing one of the leading roles in Puccini's *La Bohème* in Washington, DC.[49] If not committing entirely to the fulfillment of her mother's dreams, at least Madeline would give it a try. But as far as Fredericks could see, "She was so self-conscious, God love her. She knew, for all intents and purposes, she really shouldn't be there—her own self-evaluation."

Ahead on the horizon was an even bigger challenge, the biggest thus far in her career. She would have to survive *Two by Two*.

PART II

The 1970s

IN THE 1960S, MADELINE DEMONSTRATED REMARKABLE PRECOCITY, refining her talents and revealing an already-recognizable performing persona. In the 1970s, she truly matured as an artist. At the beginning of the decade, she was still seeking direction, yet in the space of three years, she secured stardom, a Tony nomination and a Drama Desk award (1974), back-to-back Oscar nominations (1973, 1974), and the movie roles for which she's best remembered. Then, her biggest failures followed with comparable swiftness: the movies *At Long Last Love* (1975) and *Won Ton Ton* (1976), and the Broadway musical *On the Twentieth Century* (1978). After those stumbles, she didn't truly regain her footing until 1992.

Only twenty-seven as the decade began, she could boast of a clutch of great reviews and a couple of recordings. She'd made good contacts with talented peers, and she'd caught the notice of Leonard Bernstein and Richard Rodgers, two of the most influential men in America. "She was a known quantity," says lyricist Martin Charnin. "But I don't think she had really reached full throttle, if you will. Nobody really knew all of the gifts that she had as a comedian"—least of all Madeline herself. She was still challenged by the kinds of typecasting she'd rebelled against at Hofstra, and in her two most prominent acting jobs in the 1960s she played the wanton (in *Candide*) and the servant (in *Promenade*) yet again. At the time, New York didn't seem to know what to make of her, any more than the music and theater departments at Hofstra had. She didn't have the luxury of choice.

It seems strange to those who came later, but as the 1970s began, Madeline was best known as a talk-show guest, certified as such in a

January 14, 1970 *New York Times* feature on women and comedy. Identifying "a new breed of funny girl," who "can be both funny and feminine at the same time," the article presents brief interviews with five performers.[1] It's a distinguished group that includes Joan Rivers, Lily Tomlin, Fannie Flagg, and Jo Anne Worley, Tomlin's co-star on *Laugh-In* at the time. When the article ran, Madeline was the least famous of the lot.

"Madeline Kahn is curvaceous and red-haired, and looks as though she should be entering beauty contests instead of making people laugh," reporter Judy Klemesrud writes. She goes on to focus not on Madeline's work, but on her marriage prospects: "I think that the fact that I'm funny scares a lot of men," Madeline said. Noting that she still lived with her mother in Queens, Klemesrud concludes, "She said she might consider marriage if she met a man with a sense of humor. 'It would be like being in jail otherwise,' she added." Madeline says nothing about recently having dated two comedians, Jim Catusi and Robert Klein, without any thought of marrying either. And there's scarcely a word to suggest that, for the preceding five years, music had been more important to Madeline's livelihood. The only professional engagement mentioned is an appearance on *The Merv Griffin Show*. Television exposure seems to have been the criterion for inclusion in the article, and Madeline couldn't compete with *Laugh-In*—not yet.

11

"Educated Shrieks"

La Bohème (1970)

BECAUSE OF *CANDIDE*, MADELINE HAD WON A LIFELONG ADMIRER IN conductor Maurice Peress, who engaged her to sing Musetta in Puccini's *La Bohème* at the Washington Opera Society, the forerunner of today's Washington National Opera. Three performances (March 6, 8, and 11, 1970), marked the beginning and end of her professional career in opera.

Baritone Alan Titus sang the role of her lover, Marcello. He would later win acclaim at New York City Opera and, in Europe, as Wagner's Wotan. In talking with him, Madeline framed *Bohème* as an experiment. She would see whether her mother's ambitions for her had any merit, whether critics and audiences would approve, whether her voice was sufficiently "operatic." Yet what he remembers most is her approach to the comedy in the role of Musetta: "It seemed to me that she puzzled over her ability to make people laugh and was trying to become more conscious about how she said things, i.e., her 'delivery.'"

Because Puccini worked out most of the delivery in advance (in 1896, in fact), Musetta would have been an ideal vehicle for Madeline as an actor, and any enterprising soprano can learn to work an audience simply by performing the role. A wily flirt, Musetta has already broken Marcello's heart when we first see her in act 2, but she wins him back with a song. It's foolproof comedy. In act 3, the lovers quarrel and break up (again comically). In the final act, they're reunited at the deathbed of their friend, Mimì. Madeline and Titus made a charming, thoroughly credible pair, and at the time, Titus's wife believed they were having an affair. (Later, this sort of suspicion would become a leitmotiv for partners of Madeline's co-stars.) "I don't think there's ever been a Musetta like this," Peress says. "Every opera singer should study the way she used the stage. You couldn't take your eyes off her." While praising her comedy in act 2, he singles out "the pathos of the final scene": "That was a great event."

Musically, however, Puccini's score seems heavier than Madeline's light, lyric instrument could handle with ease. She had the range, certainly, but did she have the sheer muscle to project Musetta's lines in an opera house, or to hold her own alongside professionals? Titus and Peress approved, but according to Paul Hume, critic of the *Washington Post*, Madeline "turned out more than her share of educated shrieks in a role that is supposed to be sung quite as much as Mimì."[2] Although Musetta's aria "Quando m'en vo" had been Madeline's audition piece at Green Mansions, she never sang it in public after the curtain fell on *Bohème*. For her, the musical high point of the opera was the opening-night party, when she got to sing jazz with Peress's friend Duke Ellington on piano.

Later, during a broadcast of *Live from the Met*, Madeline recalled her performances as Musetta as "utterly terrifying," and she explained that, as far as an opera career went, "The muse was definitely *not* in attendance."[3] At other times, she was more philosophical: "I think I had the raw material for an operatic career, but I really don't regret it," she told a reporter. "Being an opera singer is like being an athlete; you have to stay in training all the time."[4]

Over the years, she did have other prospects for operatic engagement. She auditioned several times for Bernstein for a 1973 television production of his *Trouble in Tahiti*. A few years later, she entered into serious talks with Julius Rudel about a premiere at New York City Opera, though in 2009 he didn't remember the work in question. In the 1980s, Madeline looked seriously at Offenbach's *The Grand Duchess of Gerolstein*, and the composer Thomas Pasatieri pitched the idea of Madeline in a new production of Offenbach's *La Périchole* to Beverly Sills (by then Rudel's successor at NYCO). There was even the possibility of reprising the role of Musetta in 1981 in Santa Fe.

With the exception of *Trouble in Tahiti*, Madeline didn't pursue these opportunities with much enthusiasm or confidence, and impresarios seldom pursued her. Sills told Pasatieri she considered Madeline's voice "too small" for the New York State Theater, the company's home at Lincoln Center, though Peress scoffs, "If she could be heard in that awful place called Avery Fisher, she could be heard in the State Theater." Several years after *Bohème*, Peress worked with Madeline in Kansas City in a hall he describes as "a barn, a football field, it's horrible. And she could be heard there."

At the Metropolitan Opera, conductor James Levine was a fan of Madeline. Soprano Teresa Stratas recalls him "flying through the air" to greet Madeline when she came backstage. Madeline might have made a terrific Adele in *Die Fledermaus* at the Met in the 1980s, in a production featuring Dom DeLuise as Frosch and Robert Klein's wife at the time, mezzo Brenda Boozer, as Orlofsky. Klein believes Madeline could have excelled; her singing "was not living-room bullshit," he says. Peress speculates that Madeline, "a total theater person," could have had "a Callas-like, go-for-broke career, where she'd be the great actress–singer, in that order." But, he adds, Madeline would have needed the right roles. To exercise control over her repertory, "You'd need money like Onassis."

Several associates say Madeline determined that in opera she would fall inevitably short of her own high standards. Her last voice teacher, Marlena Malas, says that, "in her kooky, wonderful way, I could see her experimenting" with leading roles such as Gilda in *Rigoletto* and Lakmé, but both Malas and Madeline preferred to focus on lighter fare. While Matthew Epstein, an unrivaled guide for singers, believes Madeline might have found a berth in Mozart and operetta, Pasatieri disagrees— to a point. The composer used to play and sing through the score of Strauss's *Salome* with her, for example, in addition to attending her public performances. "Her voice was a coloratura," Pasatieri says, "but it was not what one would consider a first-class instrument, and she would not have made a first-class career as an opera singer. Her dramatic [and] comedic talent was so great that her path as a Broadway and film star was evident."

Yet Madeline's turn away from the opera house was largely the result of circumstance, dictated more by other people's casting choices and by her need for income than by her own predilections. This state of affairs naturally led to uncertainty, especially in the early years of her career, and Pasatieri remembers that she returned from shooting *Paper Moon* with souvenirs of the film, "as if she thought she'd never be asked to do another movie."

The City Slickers' Goodtime Hour

Comedy Tonight (1970)

FOR MADELINE, *COMEDY TONIGHT*, A SKETCH-VARIETY SHOW ALONG the lines of NBC's *Laugh-In*, marked a number of auspicious reunions and first encounters. Robert Klein, the show's star, invited her to join a cast that included Judy Graubart, as well as a recent graduate of Second City, Peter Boyle, with whom Madeline had never worked. Staff writer Thomas Meehan had just wrapped *Annie: The Women in the Life of a Man*, the first of many projects with Mel Brooks and Anne Bancroft, and producer Joe Cates worked closely with lyricist Martin Charnin. Referring to the old Sid Caesar show, Klein calls Madeline "my Imogene Coca—except she's much prettier."

An early salvo in CBS programming executives' "rural purge," a shift away from countrified programs toward more urbane fare, *Comedy Tonight* was a summer replacement for *The Glen Campbell Goodtime Hour*. It resembled *Laugh-In* in many ways: the grouping of sketches by theme, blackouts, topical humor, songs, monologues, and unusual guest stars (baritone Robert Merrill, novelist Jacqueline Susann). Although satirical targets included Washington politicians, Madison Avenue, the military, and hippies, the writers steered clear of the kinds of material that had gotten the Smothers Brothers into trouble with CBS the previous year. The show was videotaped and employed a laugh track rather than a live studio audience, a challenge for a stand-up comic and a cast of nightclub and stage performers.

Madeline generally took part in sketches featuring the entire cast, but she did sometimes get the spotlight. In one "Man Against . . ." segment about parents and children (August 23), she played the domineering mother of a comic-book superhero, played by Boyle.[5] For Klein, Madeline's most memorable sketch was "Oh, When Times Were Bad in

Vienna" (August 2), another Weill-flavored song. Madeline threw her leg up on a table and shrieked, "Garbage! We ate garbage!" "I died, even in rehearsal," Klein says. "You can't buy that, and you can't write that. She was the kind of performer—there are a few out there, all virtuosos— they can give you invaluable laughs that were never written, that they can find by instinct."

Unfortunately, Klein says, "All the tapes to the '70s shows drowned in Joe Cates' basement." The connections Madeline made and remade on the show would prove far more enduring, with almost immediate rewards.

13

The Man Who Came to Dinner

Two by Two (1970–71)

BAD LUCK IN A BROADWAY MUSICAL MAY COME IN MANY FORMS. YOU may get fired on the road, as Madeline did in *How Now*. Your show may fold after just a few weeks, as *New Faces* did. Or you may get cast in a show written by America's most popular theater composer, starring one of the country's most beloved entertainers, and wind up running for a long, long year.

No question, getting cast in *Two by Two* was an honor, giving Madeline the opportunity to work with a score by Richard Rodgers and with a superstar, Danny Kaye, in the lead. Advance ticket sales were impressive, and the show, a retelling of the story of Noah's Ark, promised fun for audiences. Peter Stone's book, based on Clifford Odets's play, *The Flowering Peach*, found new relevance in the Bible story, with its generation gap and fears of global annihilation. A resemblance to *Fiddler on the Roof*, which was still running on Broadway, boded well. Like *Fiddler*, *Two by Two* is a heartwarming family story based on Jewish traditions, concerned with the pairing off of three children (one of whom marries a Gentile), and featuring a father who frequently stops to address God—though in *Two by Two*, God answers. There might be fun, too, for the cast of eight, which performed a pantomime during the title number to illustrate how the animals boarded the ark—constructed by the actors themselves during the earlier scenes of the play. Images projected on screens upstage showed the animals, as well as visual clues to messages from God that only Noah hears.

After Noah himself, Goldie is the funniest character, and Madeline got big laughs at every performance. Even her first costume, a clingy golden gown with an elaborate hairdo, was an attention-grabber.[6] Goldie is an outsider, a celebrant from the pagan Temple of the Golden Ram. She wanders in to see whether the crazy rumors about an ark are true, and Noah and his wife, Esther (Joan Copeland), immediately size her up as a prospect for their youngest son, Japheth (Walter Willison). Marriage isn't what Goldie has in mind, but during the flood, she and middle son Ham (Michael Karm), who's already married, fall in love. When he touches her at last, Goldie exults in song, using the only frame of reference she knows: an invitation to the pleasures of "The Golden Ram."

That number was Madeline's ticket to the show. According to Charnin, he and Rodgers had already sketched the song when auditions began, but they weren't sure they could find an actress who could handle the challenging vocal line they had in mind. Willison, already cast by then, remembers that they saw Bernadette Peters and "all the cute girls of the time." Having seen *Comedy Tonight*, Charnin knew Madeline was funny; having heard *Candide*, Rodgers knew what her voice was capable of. They hired her and finished the song. The result may not be quite the tour-de-force that "Glitter and Be Gay" is, but it's a coloratura extravaganza—a classic Rodgers waltz, lopsided. Rodgers was handing Madeline a valuable prize, and she was ready to run with it—a little too far, she discovered, when she eagerly played for him the cadenzas and ornaments she'd written for the song. Rodgers was deeply offended; she in turn was mortified. Thereafter, she sang the aria precisely as he'd written it, which was, after all, what he'd hired her to do.

Two by Two brought changes to Madeline's personal life, as well. She started an affair with Karm and developed a close friendship with Willison, and she used an argument with Paula as an excuse to move out of the house on Romeo Court once and for all. Working on the show should have been a dream for Madeline, but it turned into a nightmare for everyone in the company. The troublemaker was Danny Kaye.

Decades of public adulation hadn't brought Kaye emotional security. He hadn't performed in a book musical on Broadway since 1943, and Noah was unlike any part he'd ever played. Nervous, he fell back on what he knew best: scene-stealing. From the first day of rehearsals, Kaye began to demand more and more attention. At first, he might insist on re-blocking a scene, or complain that the audience wouldn't recognize him when he made his entrance in old-age makeup as the six hundred-year-old Noah. (The resulting changes to his makeup diminished the impact of his song in act 1, when God makes Noah "Ninety Again.") He also rejected several actresses for the role of Esther, Noah's wife, and the show had been in rehearsal for a week before Copeland joined the cast.

Harold Prince, a protégé of Rodgers, told the composer during Boston tryouts that *Two by Two* needed Helen Hayes, or an actress of comparable age and stature, to play Esther and to counterbalance Kaye onstage and off. Copeland couldn't, though eventually Peter Stone dubbed her "Mother Courage" for her efforts to hold the *Two by Two* company together. Copeland, the sister of playwright Arthur Miller, was already far along in her distinguished career, but she says, "I'd never been in a play where there was a war like that backstage." Company members still talk about the show like combat veterans and treat each other like army buddies.

Ultimately, nobody could defeat Kaye's power grabs. The company was "held hostage to the fact that Kaye had sold so many tickets on the announcement of his return to Broadway," Charnin says. "You couldn't thumb your nose at a $3 million advance in those days." During rehearsals and tryouts, Kaye managed to take away "all the jokes" from the other men, but he "couldn't really touch what Madeline did," Charnin says, "because she's the outsider . . . with a funny story that has to be honored in order to make it work."

But Kaye found other ways to make sure Madeline didn't upstage him. During rehearsals, her act 1 solo, "Getting Married to a Person," caught his notice. He demanded that she share the song with him as a duet. Then, as the show ran long, the song was cut altogether. During Boston tryouts, Kaye decided that a number Karm sang to Madeline, "Forty Nights," was getting too many laughs. Kaye threatened to leave the show if the number wasn't cut. As the creative team tucked and trimmed, the spotlight on Madeline dimmed. Though critics in Boston singled her out, in New York her co-star, Tricia O'Neil (as Ham's wife and Japheth's love interest), got more attention once the show opened on November 10, 1970.[7]

Madeline persevered, no matter what changes the creative team threw at her. In performance, "There was always something funny and hidden in what she did. She was, I thought, a very secretive kind of girl." Able to "be sexual and innocent simultaneously," Madeline "was screamingly funny and truthful onstage," Charnin says.

Critics generally cited Kaye's performance and, to a lesser degree, Rodgers's score as reasons to see the show, while Stone's book found less favor. In the *New York Times*, Clive Barnes lavished affection on Kaye— "so warm and lovable an entertainer, such a totally ingratiating actor, that for me at least he can do no wrong"—while summing up the rest of the "very good indeed" cast in a single paragraph.[8] Madeline's most substantial review came from John Simon. Writing in *New York* magazine, he described her as having "at least two 40-inch busts" and delivering "an outrageously vulgar caricature of a Mrs. Ham."[9]

Nevertheless, *Two by Two* was still the play much as it had been conceived and written, and Kaye was still an actor playing a character. For a time after the opening, he didn't take many liberties with the show, Willison says—except when he interacted with Madeline. Kaye was always looking for ways to break her up onstage. Nervous laughter came naturally to her, and it made the audience laugh, too. Such behavior wasn't necessarily out of character for Goldie or for Noah, but Kaye went further, playing variations on a burlesque act by ogling her breasts. "To Danny, Madi was just a big tit joke," Willison says.

For a while, both Madeline and Willison remained on friendly enough terms with Kaye. When he was honored as *Cue* magazine's entertainer of the year, they performed a tribute number, "Oh, Kaye!" written by Sylvia Fine, Kaye's wife. And in February, 1971, when Kaye injured himself during a dance, Madeline and Willison accompanied him to the hospital, waiting anxiously with him into the night. Kaye had torn a ligament in his leg, an injury requiring him to wear a cast on his foot and limiting his movement. For two weeks, Harry Goz (who ordinarily played oldest son Shem) took over, and box office figures dropped precipitously.

Alternating now between a crutch and a wheelchair, Kaye was more insecure than ever. When director Joe Layton tried to restage the show to accommodate him, the actor declared "I can't do that" so often that Layton conceded defeat. The next sign of trouble came just before Kaye rejoined the show. During "The Golden Ram," Kaye stood in the orchestra pit, making faces and mock conducting—a specialty of his—as the aria began. Madeline began laughing, and the performance degenerated into such chaos that, at last, Kaye worried he'd gone too far. "He slithered out of the pit," Karm recalls, and conductor Jay Blackton started over.

The night he returned to the stage, Kaye made his entrance and greeted the audience applause with an unscripted line: "Well, I finally showed up." From that point forward, he milked his injury, whether for laughs or sympathy from the audience. Offstage, a real-life version of Sheridan Whiteside in *The Man Who Came to Dinner*, he tyrannized the company.[10] In performance, Kaye would break character, insult and humiliate other actors, and chase them offstage with his wheelchair. He improvised while they tried in vain to keep up with him as he performed bits of his nightclub act and, on occasion, changed the ending of the play.

Polite, pretty Madeline was "butch insurance" for the sexually re-pressed Kaye, Willison says, and she was particularly vulnerable. To a ham, any kind of laughter becomes a license, though Copeland specu-lates that Madeline laughed as a conscious defense. "She was giggling to get what she wanted and giggling *not* to get what she didn't want," she says. If Madeline humored Kaye, then he might spare her worse indignities. But there was no chance that he'd ignore her, and he didn't limit himself to leering. Years later, after Kaye's death and with palpable reluctance, she told David Letterman that when she was singing, Kaye would come up behind her and stick his finger under her arm. This was only part of the story, Karm confirms. Using her little-girl voice to make light of the incident, Madeline told him that Kaye "tried to touch my til-lies." "Danny Kaye was very proprietary about her," Robert Klein says. "When I took her to [the] opening-night party, I had the feeling about it, and she actually suggested, that he was a little jealous." What's more, Jef Kahn says, "Danny Kaye hit on our mother."

When Kaye was unhappy, he'd "pout," giving an intentionally bad performance. The general fear was that he'd leave the show if anyone tried to rein him in. The company had little recourse. Actors Equity (where Paula Kahn worked at the time) was less powerful then than it is today, and when Kaye heard that Layton was planning to intervene, he banned the director from the theater. Only Willison stood up to the abuse. One by one, the cast stopped speaking to Kaye. Copeland was the last to do so, after Kaye blew up at her for walking offstage when he launched into an impromptu monologue. Backstage, he raged at her: "You're so temperamental! Nobody could work with you!"

Milton Berle had signed to play Noah in the upcoming national tour and might have stepped in, but the producer (Rodgers himself) was un-willing to take that risk. Meanwhile, Rodgers's office was inundated with complaints from theatergoers, Willison remembers. Two such letters, published in the *New York Times*, prompted Kaye to defend himself in *Va-riety*. Though many audiences were perfectly happy to see Kaye do as he pleased, the backlash built. When Tony nominations were announced, Willison received a nomination as best supporting actor in a musical, widely construed as a reward for his grace under fire, while Kaye re-ceived a public reprimand from a member of the awards committee. If Willison won, Kaye told Copeland, he had a plane waiting and would fly home to California.

Madeline tried to sail above the conflict backstage. This tactic led to the impression that she was "slightly disconnected," Copeland remembers, "as if she were a little in between reality and what she was thinking. She had a different kind of relationship with the world. That was enchanting but also sometimes confusing to the onlooker." Even as the cast divided ("Danny on one side, everybody else on the other," as Charnin puts it), everybody adored Madeline, and Willison still speaks of her as if she were his kid sister. But the stress took its toll in the form of severe back pain. "I think emotionally things would just attack her back," Karm says.[11]

During the rehearsal period she began to travel by taxi, lying flat on her back. The first time Karm saw her arrive, he asked, "How are you feeling?" Ever wary, she answered, "Why do you want to know?"

"Because I care about you," he said. He meant it. He'd met her at the Upstairs, and now, working closely and spending every day with her, he began to feel for her what Ham felt for Goldie. She was falling in love with him, too. A few years later, as their affair wound down, Madeline wrote in her personal notebook, "One needs to believe in the existence somewhere of that uniquely different face, the mind mysteriously in tune with one's own. . . . But with a 'first love' there's no need of questioning, no room for doubt, just the simple loving certainty that here is my person and that I am only at home in the world when we are together."[12]

They didn't move in together, but Karm spent most of his time at her apartment on East 73rd Street. They hosted dinners and took long walks together. He remembers her infectious laughter, and offstage as well as on, once she started, he couldn't help but join in. She took a childlike delight in "secrets," refusing to tell him where she'd found a new dress or the special "no-calorie" candies that she and Brenda Vaccaro craved. Marriage didn't come up. Matrimony didn't match the tenor of the times, and as Bernie Wolfson prepared to leave Shirley and take a new bride, Madeline grew even more certain that divorce was in her DNA. But until she met John Hansbury in 1989, her affair with Karm would be her longest-lasting romantic involvement. It had a direct impact on her professional life, too.

Karm found the experience of *Two by Two* so miserable that after the show closed, he gave up his career and started teaching acting. He welcomed Madeline and Paula to his classes, and he coached Madeline for some of her most important early film roles, including her Oscar-nominated turn in *Paper Moon*. Her work with him recalls the way she prepared "Glitter and Be Gay" with Michael Cohen, in meticulous coaching sessions long before she won the part. She was learning that sometimes actors must rely on resources outside the rehearsal room, and that a trusted friend can be as good a coach as—or better than—a movie director.

Seeking to escape *Two by Two*, Madeline began to look for other work. Before the end of the run, she'd lined up her first feature film, *What's Up, Doc?* After a Sunday matinée she flew to Los Angeles for the first read-through, flying back in time to be at the Imperial for the Tuesday night performance.

14

The Eunice Burns

What's Up, Doc? (1972)

WHEN MADELINE FIRST MET PETER BOGDANOVICH, "[H]E SAID HE WAS going to make a movie called *What's Up, Doc?* Well, I thought that was a pretty tasteless title, and I wasn't ready to do a bad movie," she told Shaun Considine, a reporter for *After Dark* magazine. "I had just landed on Broadway, finally, and I didn't want to cancel myself out by doing a tasteless film. A lousy movie, especially if it's your first, can kill you. But then I read the script, and I knew it would be good, and working with Ryan and Barbra couldn't hurt."[13]

With an Oscar nomination for his previous movie, *The Last Picture Show* (1971), Bogdanovich was riding high. A film critic, he brought to bear on his directing the lessons he'd learned from studying and interviewing veteran filmmakers such as John Ford, Orson Welles, and Howard Hawks. His upcoming project would pay homage to the screwball-comedy tradition, particularly Hawks's classic *Bringing Up Baby* (1938). He needed comic actors, and casting director Nessa Hyams brought Madeline to meet him in New York. Bogdanovich dislikes readings, so they simply talked. "She had this wonderful, funny voice," he remembers, "and this very straight delivery, and I just thought she was hilarious." But this was effectively a job interview, not an audition, and Madeline wasn't trying to be funny. "Why are you laughing?" she asked Bogdanovich repeatedly. "Because you're funny," he answered. She looked "surprised," he says now. It was a conversation that they would have often, but that first time, her surprised look came with laughter of her own—as if she found his reaction strange.

Madeline went into the meeting believing she'd read for the role of Judy Maxwell, but Barbra Streisand had already accepted that job. Instead, Bogdanovich wanted Madeline to play Eunice Burns, the shrill fiancée of an absent-minded musicologist, Howard Bannister (Ryan O'Neal), who dumps her for the free-spirited Judy. Co-starring Kenneth Mars as a rival musicologist and Austin Pendleton as a philanthropist, *What's Up, Doc?* would be Madeline's feature film debut and her first collaboration with Bogdanovich. That she didn't audition for the role, but won it instead *as herself*, proved an exceptionally ill omen.

Eunice was "my great good fortune, and sort of a blow to my spirit," Madeline said in 1989. "I knew that Eunice was as far removed from my essence as she could be—as opposed to what Streisand got to do, which was to play herself. And her first role [Fanny Brice in *Funny Girl* (1968)] encompassed many wonderful features—comedy, singing, adorableness. So she was always perceived that way. And here I am the ugly stepsister, which was absolutely not true! So then, what do I do? Continue to be the ugly stepsister to everyone—Cybill Shepherd, Tatum O'Neal, and everyone else in the entire world?"[14]

"Ugly" is a key word. Eunice isn't supposed to be pretty. In the screwball paradigm, it's the woman who chases the man, and in *What's Up, Doc?* O'Neal is the object of desire. Bogdanovich and his production team heighten the contrast by making Eunice as unattractive as her fiancé is tanned and tempting. Her wig was bad enough, but her costumes gave her still zaftig figure barely any shape at all. And while the world hadn't yet learned to apply the word "beautiful" to Streisand's distinctive features, in the film as in life, she gets the man (O'Neal had dated Streisand just before shooting began). Now Madeline grew concerned that she really was unattractive and that people were laughing *at her*. Every night, she called her brother "Is this really how people see me?" she would ask, in tears. She wound up in therapy.

Funny women are often insecure about personal appearance, Martin Charnin says. "They never think they're pretty, until they learn that part of what makes them attractive is that they're funny." Madeline hadn't reached that point of understanding. What made her attractive, so far as she could see, was her best behavior, her carefully polished exterior. In her personal life, propriety (one of Eunice's pet words) had been her first defense. Comedy was a way to make a living, and always before, she'd looked pretty when she did it. Now she looked awful, and the cast and crew—and, later, audiences—reacted uproariously.

Charlie Rose once asked Madeline whether she thought she was "naturally funny." "I'm very smart," she replied. "I'm very understanding. I'm *serious*. . . . I always see sort of the tragedy beneath what's funny. And that's only important to me. Then that tells me how to make something work, or I think it's what makes something work, beneath it all. The gravity. And I also *am* funny. I also can see the humor."[15] Yet until the end of her career—on the set of *Judy Berlin* in 1997—Madeline still expressed surprise when she got a laugh. As her friend David Marshall Grant observes, her quest for the "gravity" of a character enhanced her comedy, because she took ridiculous situations so seriously. But that same empathy sometimes blinded her to the reality that the character herself might be ridiculous, as Eunice is. In private, Madeline had a great sense of humor and loved to laugh, but as an actor she remained "someone who said things funny, not someone who said funny things," as Lily Tomlin describes her.

"Why are they laughing?" Where Eunice Burns is concerned, Madeline also wondered: Are they laughing because that's what they really think of me? Bogdanovich, who found Madeline perfectly attractive and who knew little if anything about the fathers who left when she was ugly, didn't detect the anxiety underlying her question. He did become increasingly aware that "She didn't like the way she looked in our pictures." Her unhappiness would become a bigger problem for him with each successive film.

At the first table read, Bogdanovich says, Madeline's every line—even "Howard! Howard Bannister!"—provoked laughter from the entire cast, "except Barbra and Ryan, who were not amused, because she got a laugh on everything she said, and they didn't get one laugh." Though O'Neal says both he and Streisand did laugh, Bogdanovich later found Streisand crying in her dressing room and saying, "I'm an extra in this picture, I'm an extra." She generally disliked the script, he says, and O'Neal remembers her complaining, "It's not funny, it's not funny. I know funny."

Sensitive as always and scrutinizing Streisand closely, Madeline picked up on the star's lack of confidence in the material. From the first read-through, however, O'Neal believed that *What's Up, Doc?* would be a hit. "I thought Madeline was sensational," he says. "She was naturally funny. It was her instinct. She could make you belly laugh." He'd never have guessed this was her first feature; already she held her own with pros like Streisand and Mars. "We had to keep up with *her.*"

Despite her misgivings, Madeline threw herself into her role. Her performance is supremely vocal, a delirious display of inflections and intonations that instantly proclaim Eunice's character. As Bogdanovich says, audiences laugh whenever she says "Howard Bannister"—not in itself a funny name. But she didn't limit herself to language. For the scene in which gangsters on the waterfront confront Eunice, Bogdanovich wanted her to back away in fear. "Make funny noises," he told her. We hear the result, a tightly suppressed whimper, three times in the picture, with slight variations: first, when Eunice is reading *The Sensuous Woman* (much dismayed); next, when she meets the gangsters; and later, during the chase scene, when she's taken hostage. She needed little direction, Bogdanovich says, citing her shrieked "I'm coming in!" during the extended scene in Howard's hotel room. She got big laughs, though on the page it's a simple declaration. Later in that scene, when the room catches fire, Eunice's shrieks are different: Madeline was standing too close to the burning curtains. "We had fire marshals on the set, and it was terribly controlled," O'Neal says, "but she got scared. You can tell, that's not acting. We had to hold her; she was trembling."

Madeline's physical characterization is almost equally accomplished. Most notable is the scene in which she forces her way into the musicologists' dinner party, swinging her arms and fighting off one and all, whether or not they try to stop her. In subsequent films, she was seldom called on to perform this kind of broad, physical comedy, since most directors preferred to use her as a (physically) calm center of the high jinks. Yet in *What's Up, Doc?* even Madeline's basic posture, a sort of fallback manner of carrying herself, is expressive. As Eunice, Madeline clenches everything. She keeps her arms close to her torso, and she seems to swell upward from her toes. It's as if she's always inhaling, puffing herself up to seem more intimidating.

Madeline would work again with several *What's Up, Doc?* cast members, including Liam Dunn, Kenneth Mars, and Austin Pendleton. Pendleton says that Madeline was "incredibly easy to act with, the kind of actor where you think, 'That actor is so open that if I can't act with her—or him—I should seek guidance for another vocation.'" Over the years, he says, she didn't change much, except that she grew less shy. Owing to her shyness at the time, neither Pendleton nor O'Neal had any idea Madeline was unhappy playing Eunice.

The set was a heady environment for any young actor. Bogdanovich consulted with Howard Hawks by phone, and O'Neal remembers that John Ford, King Vidor, and Samuel Fuller visited the set. However, the greatest star—by far—was Streisand. Before shooting started, Madeline had been "petrified" of Streisand, whose personality clashes on the set and whose ruthlessness in the editing room regularly made gossip headlines. However, Bogdanovich assured Madeline she wouldn't be cut from the movie. As she recalled, "It was a movie about three people, and there's only so much you could cut out of it and still have the movie make sense."[16] On the set, Madeline and Streisand got along reasonably well, though Bogdanovich stresses that they're seldom in the same shot. Pendleton found that they "had a lovely rapport." Streisand sometimes offered advice on screen acting, which Madeline took well. "There was no sense of competitiveness on Barbra's part at all," Pendleton says.

O'Neal believes Madeline and Streisand were, to a degree, kindred spirits. The death of Streisand's father and her relationship with her step-father left her with a need for paternal approval similar to Madeline's. "That's what makes these women so good," he says. Streisand respected Madeline as a performer, as well, he recalls. Once, between takes, Madeline started singing and dancing, little realizing that Streisand was watching behind her. When Madeline turned around, Streisand smiled. "That was good," she said. "I must have listened to a different radio station." A few years later, Madeline told O'Neal she'd seen Streisand in concert doing the same routine she'd performed on the set of *What's Up, Doc?* "Barbra always looked to see what people were doing, and then would steal it," he says. "She could do that because she could do anything."

"I really liked her and we had some good talks," Madeline told Rex Reed, "and I thought we could really be friends, but she has so many pressures, and she's unavailable a lot on the set, and we never became close or anything. I got a glimpse of what it's like to be a really big superstar. I don't think I'd like that."[17] "I understand now what being in her position must be like," Madeline told another reporter. "Everything Barbra does is so noticed and so important: every look, every word, every gesture. That's got to be terrific pressure. And I don't think you can control it."[18]

What's Up, Doc? opened at Radio City Music Hall on March 9, 1972. Bogdanovich called O'Neal from the lobby and held out the phone. "Can you hear it? Can you hear the laughter? There's a thousand people here and they love the movie!" A hit was born.

Madeline received third billing in the closing credits and mostly favorable reviews. One eminent exception came in *Time* magazine from Jay Cocks, a fierce detractor of Bogdanovich's work. Describing "a comedy made by a man who has seen a lot of movies, knows all the mechanics, and has absolutely no sense of humor," Cocks rounded up the "singularly strident" supporting players in a paragraph. Madeline, he wrote, "rolls over her part like one of Patton's tanks."[19] Writing in the *New York Times*, Vincent Canby was more appreciative and more representative of the consensus. "The people who give the film its particular style are the superb (and largely unknown to me) new character actors . . . most especially, Madeline Kahn. Miss Kahn, who has a voice that sounds as if it had been filtered through a ceramic nose, just about walks off with the movie."[20]

When he saw the movie, Jef Kahn was so anxious that he could barely enjoy it. He wanted the audience to like his sister, but her late-night calls made an impression on him. "I couldn't allow her to be the character she was playing," he says. Even later, seeing Madeline in other movies, "I got used to her being a celebrity, but I was always thinking of her as a person, as well as the character. I was robbed of the experience other people had of her movies."

For Madeline, the most meaningful response may have come from the audiences at Radio City Music Hall. "I used to go there every day just to see the people's reactions," she remembered. "I loved it. I could have sold programs in the lobby—no one knew me from Eunice." She thought she'd never make another movie, she said, and she showed the interviewer all the memorabilia she'd collected in California, from the back of her canvas chair with her name on it, to the plaque for her parking space on the Warner lot.[21] But Hollywood loves a hit, and in its first release, *What's Up, Doc?* earned sixty-six million dollars at the box office, making it the third-highest grossing film of the year. "Only *The Godfather* and *The Poseidon Adventure* did better," Bogdanovich proudly recalls. It was inevitable that Madeline would be asked to make another movie, and Bogdanovich asked.

15

Bon Voyage

Missing *Candide* (1971)

ACCEPTING *WHAT'S UP, DOC?* FORESTALLED MADELINE'S CONTINUED association with *Candide*, the major stage revival that had grown out of Bernstein's birthday gala. Through her agent, the *Candide* producers had "put a hold" on Madeline: They'd given a verbal commitment to hire her. "Holds" were standard practice, to secure performers whom producers really wanted, while steering around Equity rules for auditioning. After other actors had been seen for a role, the "held" actors would be given contracts. If another engagement came up before the show went into production, agents were expected to contact producers to obtain either permission or a contract.[22]

Because of the scheduling conflict with *What's Up, Doc?* Madeline's "hold" stipulated that she would join the *Candide* cast only on the final leg of the tour, which began in San Francisco, then continued on to Los Angeles and to Washington, DC. Thereafter, she and the production would head to Broadway. For the tour, producer Edwin Lester wanted Mary Costa for Cunegonde. The voice of Disney's Sleeping Beauty, Costa had already sung Cunegonde in an American concert tour and in the first British stage production, in 1959. She was qualified and exceptionally attractive. But she'd recently turned forty, and Sheldon Patinkin's concept accentuated the youth of the characters. Bernstein had an extra reason to prefer Madeline over Costa, as Theodore S. Chapin, a production assistant during the San Francisco leg of the tour, explains: Costa had difficulty with the coloratura in "Glitter and Be Gay." "When she sang it, by her admission, she used to get gook on her cords," Chapin says. "What that would mean was simply that the notes would not come out." He imitates the "gooky" singing, then adds, "But she was a great trouper and she was a great spirit."

What's Up, Doc? had begun location shooting in San Francisco when *Candide* started rehearsals, and Madeline came in to apologize for not being able to do the show. Visiting the rehearsal was excellent strategy, because it gave her a chance to check out the production without having to tell anyone that she expected to replace Costa. Since she was already in town, it was entirely like her to observe the propriety of saying hello to Patinkin, with whom she hoped to work again, whether in *Candide* or another project. But as the shoot went on and her anxieties increased, Madeline yearned to reunite with her friends and to play the pretty leading lady once more.

She phoned William Lewis repeatedly, begging him to help find a way to get her back into the show. He made inquiries with the producers, even though he believed that Madeline's primary interest was an expense-paid trip to Hollywood, where she could audition in her spare time. His suspicions rose when she learned that through his work with Sid Caesar he knew Mel Brooks. Right away, Madeline asked whether Lewis could land her an audition. He replied, "A word from me isn't going to help you, my dear." Patinkin loved working with Madeline, and bringing her back to *Candide* "certainly would have improved the show," he says. However, he approved of Costa, too. Moreover, "Everybody was on contract. . . . I don't know how it would have been accomplished." Madeline didn't know, either, but that didn't stop her from making inquiries in the midst of an increasingly confused production.

As Patinkin was shoved aside and replaced by director Michael Kidd, even Bernstein's morale drooped. It became obvious to everyone that *Candide* was in trouble. According to Patinkin, things got to the point that once, when the chorus came in a bar late in Lewis's big number, "Bon Voyage," Bernstein fell to his knees and bit Ted Chapin on the leg.[23] Moreover, as Lewis points out, "We sang 177 performances in a row of those things! That was a real singing show." As Madeline was soon to discover, eight performances a week in a tough sing was not the key to her happiness. With no hope of a New York engagement, *Candide* limped its way to the Kennedy Center and closed there without her. She went back to looking for work.

Because she'd been "put on hold," Madeline hadn't lined up other jobs. She later told columnist Arthur Bell that after the completion of *What's Up, Doc?* she worked only once in the next year, in an industrial show.[24] (Either her old friend Michael Cohen or a new friend, Steve Novick, both in advertising at the time, might have gotten the gig for her.) Apart from this, Madeline took singing lessons and acting and dance classes.

She studied dance not for professional reasons alone. (At least a few lessons were for belly dancing, something she never needed in any role.) Before, she had been "zaftig, sexy, voluptuous," Robert Klein says, but even during *Two by Two*, she was sensitive about her weight. When a Boston theatergoer gushed, "You're so much thinner in person!" Walter Willison had to spend two hours reassuring Madeline. Now, having seen herself on a big screen at last, and determined not to be perceived as Eunice, Madeline wanted to lose weight. Michael Karm remembers that after inviting friends over for dinner, she'd throw away any leftovers. But that wasn't good enough. After all, what was to stop her from fishing the dessert out of the trash for a late-night snack? Her solution was to sprinkle the garbage with kitchen cleanser. "Nothing could be better than to lose weight and be thin," Madeline wrote in her personal notebook. "Yet, when you succeed (and *esp.* as in my case, finally, without trying, because of *real* change) people look worried, as though you were dying."[25]

For the rest of her life, she continued to police her weight, and she showed considerable discipline. Reporter Claudia Dreifus remembers a lunch meeting, around 1973, when Madeline's meal consisted of a single boiled egg. In an interview with me, her close friend Gail Jacobs suddenly realized that, though they'd dined together often, she'd never seen Madeline eat an entire portion of anything. By the mid-1970s, the girl who looked like an opera singer was gone for good, and in her place stood a movie actress.

• • •

Despite her protestations of joblessness, Madeline did field other work during this period. In 1972, when Jimmy Stewart returned to his signature role as Elwood P. Dowd, in a *Hallmark Hall of Fame* adaptation of Mary Chase's *Harvey*, Madeline played Ruth Kelly, a nurse in the sanitarium. The role isn't large—and in this adaptation, it's smaller than usual—but it provided important early exposure on a prestigious, nationally televised program certain to draw large audiences. She shared several scenes with Stewart and Helen Hayes, and for the rest of her life, Madeline could say that Jimmy Stewart told her she was pretty—it's in the script, after all.

Madeline also took the part of Antonia, Quixote's niece, in a curious studio recording of *Man of La Mancha*, released by Columbia Masterworks in 1972. The cast featured the television star Jim Nabors as Quixote/Cervantes and the opera star Marilyn Horne as Aldonza/Dulcinea. Madeline received fifth billing, after actor Jack Gilford (Sancho) and tenor Richard Tucker. Antonia has one number, an ironic lament in which she and Quixote's housekeeper (Irene Clark) claim "I'm Only Thinking of Him," all the while betraying transparent self-interest. Spanish-flavored, like the entire *Man of La Mancha* score, this number is a trio, as the Padre (Tucker) consoles the two women. Madeline sails through her high-lying cries of "Woe!" and gets the thrill of harmonizing with Tucker, one of the Metropolitan Opera's most acclaimed artists. Madeline was in the recording studio only for that one number, Horne says. She wouldn't meet Madeline until their mutual friend, Matthew Epstein, introduced them a few years later.

Meanwhile, Bernie and Shirley Wolfson divorced, and Bernie married his third wife, Marti, who was close to Madeline's age. The couple moved to Manhattan, which would remain Bernie's home for the rest of his life. Madeline made an effort to see them at least a few times each year, and this period marked the most frequent contact she'd had with her father since he divorced her mother. Robyn Wolfson stayed with Shirley, and so she and Madeline saw less of each other. They never bridged the gap between them, Robyn says wistfully, and they didn't have an advocate to bring them together, as Jef tried to do with Madeline and his father. When a friend once remarked that Madeline had a half-brother and a half-sister, Madeline snapped, "No, Jef is my *brother*."

● ● ●

The world met Eunice Burns on March 10, 1972. With mostly terrific reviews and great box office, Madeline's debut commanded attention—including at home. "We were all very proud," Jef Kahn recalls. "*What's Up, Doc?* was the first clear sign that the door was open. Whether she would be able to capitalize on it, we didn't know, but it was a great thing."

Already the income Madeline had earned from a long run on Broadway and in Hollywood meant greater financial security than she'd ever known. She did continue to help pay for her mother's expenses, and soon, Paula Kahn quit her job with Actors Equity. Once Jef started college, Paula, determined to break into movies herself, rented out the house in Queens, and moved to Westwood, in western Los Angeles. Seeing Madeline's success, Paula "may have had jealousies or resentments, but she's very clever," Jef says. "If I were Paula, I would be thinking, 'This may work out very well for me. So you *go*, girl.'"

16

Honky-Tonk Parade

Paper Moon (1973)

IN PETER BOGDANOVICH'S NEXT FILM, *PAPER MOON*, MADELINE DELIV-
ered what would long stand as her most nuanced screen performance.
Her characterization of Miss Trixie Delight includes a standout scene,
a long speech on a hillside that had the cast and crew talking about an
Oscar nomination as soon as the director cried "Cut."

Adapted from Joe David Brown's novel *Addie Pray* (1971), *Paper Moon*
is a picaresque tale about a small-time confidence man, Moses Pray
(Ryan O'Neal), and his precocious sidekick, Addie (Tatum O'Neal, just
nine years old when shooting started). While the script leaves room for
doubt that Moses (also called Moze) is really the orphaned Addie's father, the casting of a real-life father and daughter pretty much settles the
question—and also provides much of the fun of watching the picture.
Drawn to the project because he's the father of two girls, Bogdanovich
used black-and-white photography and deep-focus compositions to locate his characters in a time, the Depression, and a place, Kansas, where
individuals stand out against flat landscapes, vast skies, and never-end-
ing roads. Alvin Sargent's script takes a three-act approach: In the first,
Moze and Addie meet and strike up an uneasy but gradually warming
alliance; in the second, their relationship is threatened by Miss Trixie, a
cooch dancer who must be dispatched by Addie; in the third, Moze runs
afoul of a bootlegger and a corrupt sheriff (brothers, both played by John
Hillerman), bringing the tale to its conclusion.

"Lots of people thought I was wrong for that role after *What's Up, Doc?*"
Madeline told the *New York Times*, "but Peter knew I could be different.
I don't know how much more different two parts could be, although I
guess they both concern desperate ladies, don't they?"[26] In many ways,
Bogdanovich's treatment of Miss Trixie marked a step up from *What's Up,*

Doc? for Madeline. Not only a burlesque performer, but also a burlesque of femininity and the opposite of the no-nonsense, tomboyish child, Addie, Miss Trixie isn't glamorous, exactly, but she's sexy. And this time, Ryan O'Neal can barely keep his hands off of her, a marked improvement over Eunice's sorry lot. Physically, Miss Trixie is all burgeoning curves and curlicues, from her wavy hair to the frilly dresses that cling just a *little* too tightly to her body. The first time we see her, walking toward the camera as she leaves a carnival tent, she's jiggling in a way that Madeline never did on camera before or after—thanks to a brassiere, with support but without restraint, that production designer Polly Platt, Bogdanovich's ex-wife, created especially for her. That entrance still elicits laughter, and it identifies Miss Trixie's character. Instantly, Addie (like the audience) sees through her, and the ensuing scenes confirm our first impression. Miss Trixie is on the make, flattering Moze in exchange for gifts, though she withholds sex because she's hoping for something more substantial than a free ride and a new wardrobe. To appear respectable, she tries to pass as a refined Southern lady, even traveling with a lady's maid, Imogene (P. J. Johnson).

At first, Addie dislikes Trixie simply because she's an interloper: She usurps Addie's place in the front seat of the car and as the only female in Moze's life. Addie rebels, refusing to return to the car after a picnic, and Trixie climbs up a hillside to cajole her, bribe her, appeal to her vanity, and cuss at her, in succession. Addie is unmoved. Finally, Trixie drops all artifice and asks, "So how 'bout it honey? Just for a little while? Let ol' Trixie sit up front with her big tits."

In the screenplay, the line was merely "Let ol' Trixie sit up front," and when Bogdanovich proposed the change, Madeline balked. "She had a certain moral code," O'Neal observes. After *Paper Moon* premiered Madeline—pulling out the script to prove that "big tits" didn't appear on the page—told a reporter, "I don't find things like that easy to say."[27] In rehearsal, she told Bogdanovich she would prefer to say "big ones" instead. "All right, well, say that," Bogdanovich replied. Yet whenever they got to the speech, Madeline said something different. At one point, seeing her struggle with the line, young Tatum piped up, "Why don't you just say 'knockers'?"

The scene is composed of two long shots of Madeline, crosscut with close-ups of Tatum. In the first shot, Trixie comes up the hill and tries to win over Addie. In the second, the camera has moved in closer, and Trixie speaks from her heart. "As we got ready to make the second set-up," Bogdanovich remembers, "just before we did the first take, I went over to her and I whispered in her ear, 'Just say "tits," just once. Just try it.' Then walked away. Didn't even wait for her to react, I just walked away. I didn't know if she'd do it."

She did. "And that was the first and only time she said it in her life, because we only did one take," Bogdanovich says. "What I love is the little smile, a kind of embarrassed smile she gives after she says it, which is just Madeline reacting to the moment." At the end of the scene, Madeline "slipped and fell but caught herself and played it into her character," O'Neal remembers. "That was an accident; she could have rolled down the hill, actually," and she'd only just recovered from a broken leg. O'Neal admires the way Madeline "could turn a moment that wasn't rehearsed into something nicely spontaneous."

The last we see of Trixie, she's in her peignoir, inviting a hotel clerk (Burton Gilliam) into her room, and thus falling into the trap that Addie and Imogene set for her. We hear her briefly though a closed door, but what Moze finds when he walks in on Trixie and the clerk we understand from the expression on Moze's face. He's been betrayed, and he and Addie leave Trixie behind. The last image, however, is of Imogene, tiny and alone in the hallway as the camera recedes.

While Trixie is over-the-top, Madeline's performance isn't. Ever on the hunt for what she called "classics" on which to base her interpretations, she pegged Trixie as "a Tennessee Williams character, if Williams had written a comedy." "Trixie was such a good part. She had a shine all her own," Madeline said. "Personally, I've never known anyone like her, but I had similar feelings to situations, and if you use them you can bring the part home. She reminded me a lot of Blanche in *Streetcar*—trying to be genteel and clinging to airs when she was down on her luck. I don't know if Trixie was from the South . . . but some of those lines I couldn't say *without* using a Southern accent."[28]

Indeed, Trixie is the last vestige of the Deep South, the original setting of Brown's novel (Bogdanovich transported the story to Kansas). Madeline had hardly set foot in the South, though she'd worked with Fannie Flagg, whose Alabama accent was strong to begin with and became stronger in some of her Upstairs sketches. "The fact that I'm good at mimicry and imitating voices surprises me every time I do it," Madeline told Rex Reed. "The Southern accent in *Paper Moon* just came out of me like a ghost. I don't know where it came from. I just do these voices."[29]

Refusing to mock the character, Madeline invests Trixie with a tender vulnerability, a clear sense that she's never been quite tough or pretty enough to rise above life's hardships. She chatters to stave off more serious, unpleasant kinds of conversation, and her every flutter seems to be calculated (by Trixie, not by Madeline) for maximum effect. Ultimately, though Trixie sees her downfall coming, she can't prevent it. An undercurrent of seriousness resonates throughout her characterization, most especially in the hillside speech. "I always have in mind a complete picture when I do a role," Madeline told syndicated writer Dick Kleiner in 1975, "and it's not my fault the picture comes out with only one facet showing. The character I played in *Paper Moon* was a very serious lady, although the picture only showed her comedy aspect."[30]

"Madeline got things very quickly with Trixie," Bogdanovich says. "She was a real natural. That was the main thing about Madeline. She wasn't like a Method actor, or any of that kind of stuff. I don't know how she worked; we didn't get into that." In reality, Madeline did much of the work without him. Before shooting started, she found Trixie's "complete person" by coaching privately with Michael Karm and also, separately, with Larry Moss, her co-star from *Mixed Doubles*. These sessions were so private that Ryan O'Neal had no idea that anybody coached Madeline, and he refers to Karm as Madeline's "secret boyfriend," who never came to the set. "You're gonna win an award for that," Karm remembers telling her. "[J]ust keep doing what you're doing, and you're gonna eat up the screen." In the finished film, he says, "I saw everything, everything that we'd worked on."

With *Paper Moon*, Madeline joined the unofficial troupe of actors that Bogdanovich had been developing in several pictures, in conscious imitation of directors like John Ford and Preston Sturges. John Hillerman, for example, appeared in *The Last Picture Show*. Though he shares no scenes with Madeline in *What's Up, Doc?* or *Paper Moon*, he would co-star with her in *At Long Last Love*. Offering insight into the advantages of Bogdanovich's rep-company approach, he told a columnist, "The time that is wasted on getting to know each other is automatically out of the way. There's no time wasted on ego play. Actors, you know, have delicate egos. It takes time to prove themselves to each other." Because Bogdanovich used the same crew, too, "It's a marvelous atmosphere and I think it's conducive to good work."[31]

But shooting the movie entailed hardships large and small. During the rehearsal period, Madeline was still wearing a cast on her leg, and O'Neal had to carry her to her hotel room each night. The weather in and around Hays, Kansas, made exterior shoots, including the hillside scene, uncomfortable. "My part was shot in November, and the locals were saying, 'Aw, it never gets this cold out here usually at this time of year.' But it snowed," Madeline remembered. "It was supposed to be spring in the movie and it was just freezing. I mean we were in pain!"[32] Under her frilly dresses, Madeline wore thermal underwear and, whenever she wasn't on camera, a heavy jacket, while she huddled by a stove. "I was afraid the picture was about this girl who was cold," she told the *Village Voice*. "I'd whip my coat off, they'd take a shot of me in my flimsies, then throw the coat back on to defrost me."[33]

Inexperienced as Madeline was in film work, Ryan O'Neal was the only other professional actor in the Trixie sequence. He doesn't recall that the differing levels of experience of the cast members posed particular problems, and Bogdanovich elicited marvelous performances from Tatum, Johnson, and Gilliam. But the long takes required extensive rehearsals and multiple shoots whenever any actor flubbed his lines. "I never heard her complain about Tatum, who took forty takes to get anything right," O'Neal remembers, adding that he sometimes lost patience with his daughter. At one point, he snapped at her, and Tatum replied, "I've only been acting for three weeks." "She thought if you could *see* a movie in two hours, you could *make* a movie in two hours," O'Neal says.

"Working with a child can be delightful and interesting," Madeline told the *New York Times*. "It can also be very trying."[34] But experience as a student teacher had taught her how to get along with children, and she genuinely liked her little co-star. On the set, O'Neal says, Madeline and Tatum "worked quietly together and never had a problem with each other. They were kin. Their characters had a problem, but they loved each other. We all did." Madeline sang between takes, usually Dietrich or Piaf numbers, O'Neal says, adding with a laugh, "I wish I had some dark stories. She was sunshine, always a pleasure to see, warm and engaging and down to earth when it came to the work."

Bogdanovich shot *Paper Moon* in black-and-white not because he conceived of it as a companion piece to *The Last Picture Show* or an homage to John Ford, but because both O'Neals had suntans that were wrong for Moze and Addie. After some 16-millimeter tests in color, Ryan O'Neal remembers, Bogdanovich exclaimed, "You look so healthy! We're gonna have to do this in black-and-white. You both look so sun-kissed!" Madeline worried that Laszlo Kovacs's photography was unflattering to her. Her post-*What's Up, Doc?* weight loss was a work in progress, and in profile shots, she has a slight double chin. Her first costume is not only jiggly on top but also tight across the hips, and she had to suffer the indignity of it more than once—first with an ordinary brassiere and again with Platt's special creation. Madeline found the costume so awful that she shut herself in her dressing room. O'Neal found her crying. Pointing to his own costume, which had been pulled from the Paramount wardrobe, he told her, "I'm wearing George Raft's pants and Bing Crosby's jacket. They look right. It's okay, it doesn't have an effect on who you are."

As a precaution, Bogdanovich didn't let his actors watch the dailies—a wise choice in Madeline's case. "When she saw the picture, she hated the way she looked," he says. Conceding that black-and-white "isn't flattering, particularly," he says he wasn't trying to make her look good or bad. "She was supposed to be a kind of cheap stripper; she wasn't supposed to be glamorous. And then she liked Mel Brooks, because Mel made her look good. In *Blazing Saddles* and *Young Frankenstein*, she looked much better than she did in my pictures." Off-camera, Madeline looked so attractive that Ursula Andress, the first Bond Girl, whom O'Neal was dating at the time, grew jealous—not least when she saw O'Neal carrying Madeline to her hotel room. "She was convinced that we were having something," O'Neal says. "Beauties are so insecure!"

Michael Karm's prediction proved correct: Madeline received Academy Award and Golden Globe nominations in 1974. Also up for the best supporting actress Oscar that year were Sylvia Sidney (*Summer Wishes, Winter Dreams*), Candy Clark (*American Graffiti*), Linda Blair (*The Exorcist*), and Tatum O'Neal. "I think just being nominated is very important," Madeline told the *New York Times*. "It's lovely and very moving to be chosen by other actors. But I don't see how you can compare what a child does, however remarkable, to what an experienced actress like Sylvia Sidney does. She's also a nominee . . . and I'd probably vote for her. Anyway, I don't expect to win."[35] Oscar buffs still grumble that because Addie appears in almost every frame of *Paper Moon*, Tatum should have been nominated in the best actress category. But on April 2, 1974, at age ten, she won the award; she still holds the record as the youngest person ever to win an Oscar in a competitive category.

Among film critics, *Paper Moon* found a champion in Judith Crist at *New York Magazine*, who praised Madeline as a "sheer delight as the whorish and pathetic Trixie." Jay Cocks, writing in *Time*, found that Madeline "makes a smashingly dippy Trixie," even as he lambasted the rest of the picture. Madeline's star was in the ascendant. "At least when I go out there [to Hollywood] they know who I am now, so I feel like I've got a right to be there," she told a reporter. In her personal notebook, however, she wrote, "[M]y fantasies, and the opportunity to make them alive [and] real is what turns me on—the stardom is something else and

I must deal with it as I don't really feel at home with fame altho' I like starring in a project."[36]

Paper Moon was the tenth-highest grossing picture in a year that also saw release of *The Sting, The Exorcist, American Graffiti,* and *The Way We Were.* For Bogdanovich, the movie marked the end of an era: It was his final collaboration with Polly Platt. Their marriage had ended in 1971, after the director began an affair with Cybill Shepherd, the star of *The Last Picture Show.* His next film, *Daisy Miller* (1974), would provide another vehicle for Shepherd, and she would also star in his *At Long Last Love* (1975), alongside Madeline. By coincidence, in the scene in which Addie plots Trixie's downfall, she's listening to a Cole Porter song, "A Picture of Me Without You," on the radio. The song returns in *At Long Last Love*—but in that movie, Madeline sings it.

17

Gooch's Lament

Mame and Other Curiosities (1972–73)

PAPER MOON WAS SHOT IN NOVEMBER 1972. STILL IN THE PLANNING stages at the time, *Mame*, a big-screen adaptation of Jerry Herman's Broadway musical, was slated to star Lucille Ball, a beloved entertainer under considerable pressure. She was—and still is—a controversial choice for a part created by Angela Lansbury, and both Herman and Patrick Dennis, author of the source novel, *Auntie Mame*, expressed reservations about Lucy's casting.[37] At age sixty-one, she was old for the part, and her dubious singing ability was an oft-mined vein of comedy in her sitcoms. Her movies had never achieved the kind of widespread success she'd found in television, and even on the small screen, her career was winding down. To top off her problems, she'd injured her leg in a skiing accident. Now she was on a collision course with the young actress hired to play Mame's assistant, Agnes Gooch. How Madeline won and lost the part is a mini-*Rashomon*. Which version you believe seems to depend on whether—or how much—you love Lucy.

One pro-Lucy account is predicated on a tale of artistic differences and Madeline's lack of diplomacy. The star disapproved of Madeline's interpretation, as screenwriter Paul Zindel confirmed. Madeline was cast "without clearing it with Lucy, or not listening to her grumbling," Zindel said, and before the first rehearsal, they'd never met. When Madeline began to read, Ball interrupted: "Listen, what kind of voice are you going to use in this? . . . [Y]ou've got to use a trick voice here, why don't you start using it right now? Let me hear the voice." Zindel remembers, "There was silence in the rehearsal room as Madeline coldly stated, 'I will arrive at the voice *after* some rehearsal and building of the character.' Lucille Ball affirmed, 'Oh, no. You use the voice *now*!'"[38]

In an interview in 1973, Madeline suggested that the clash was not only artistic but also generational, an analysis that squares with Zindel's account. Madeline's approach to a role was typical of younger artists with a theater background, but it might have been foreign to Lucy, who honed her craft in a different era and who tended to work from the outside in—on those occasions when she delved at all. Madeline told *After Dark* that the producers "wanted to go with something different for Agnes . . . a more contemporary approach, and then Lucy got wind of what they were doing. She didn't want some young, fresh interpretation. She wanted what Jane Connell did [as Gooch on Broadway]. Well, I don't look like Jane and I don't act like Jane, so they got Jane."[39]

A variant account, repeated by Madeline in an interview with Rex Reed, holds that Lucy had seen *What's Up, Doc?* and expected Madeline to resemble Eunice Burns. Eunice might indeed have been a good fit for the frumpy Agnes Gooch, whom Auntie Mame transforms into a sadder-but-wiser party girl. But Eunice "was just a part," Madeline said. "I mean, you can see I don't look like that in real life. But I thought that was what the movies were about. Hey, nobody walks around Hollywood looking the way they really look." Even without fancy makeup or a costume change, she said, "I can look like forty different people . . . ."[40]

Of course, Madeline had no desire to look anything like Eunice ever again. When she showed up on the Warner lot to begin shooting *Mame*, she was sleek, beautiful, thirty years younger than Ball, and a redhead, too. Lucy "took one look at me, went straight to her trailer, closed the door, and a few minutes later, I was told that I had been fired," Madeline said. Years later, co-star Robert Preston told Michael Karm that he could tell from the moment Lucy set eyes on Madeline, she'd be gone before the end of the day. "We went to my office," director Gene Saks remembered, "and Lucy started to weep, saying, 'I swore I wasn't going to cry.' She was so manipulative, so controlling, that she absolutely wouldn't have Madeline, who was too young and too pretty."[41]

These stories portray Lucy either neutrally or negatively, but there's an anti-Madeline story, too, ostensibly originating with Ball herself and circulated by her partisans. According to this story, Madeline was already angling for the role of Lili von Shtupp and actually tried to be released from her contract for *Mame* in order to make *Blazing Saddles*. In Lili, she had a better role with a sure-fire scene in the spotlight that ultimately won her a second Oscar nomination. Madeline came looking for trouble, this story goes, and when the opportunity arose, she seized it—and circumstances obliged the producers to pay her nonetheless.

But that story falls apart under scrutiny. Throwing away work wasn't Madeline's practice, and Gooch was a surefire role that, in the original play and film *Auntie Mame*, made Peggy Cass a star. Nobody could know whether *Blazing Saddles* would succeed, and Brooks's previous movies, *The Producers* and *The Twelve Chairs*, had flopped. Michael Karm refutes the "pro-Lucy" story altogether, and Brooks says he'd never heard it before. Possibly Lucy was trying to save face when she realized that the young actress she'd fired wound up with an Oscar nomination for her next movie. "It was right under her nose and she didn't see it!" Brooks says, suggesting that the story was something Lucy "concocted to make herself feel better." In reality, Madeline lost one job and lined up another as soon as she could, auditioning for Brooks while she was still in Hollywood.

Madeline wasn't the only one who clashed with Lucy. On December 22, 1972—well before cameras started rolling—the *Hollywood Reporter* announced that Beatrice Arthur, recreating her role as Vera Charles, had quit *Mame* over "conceptual differences" with Ball. To replace her, the paper said, the studio had called on Bette Davis. Ruth Buzzi had been tested to play Gooch.[42] Arthur did complete the movie, and it surely helped her cause that she was married at the time to Saks, who also directed the Broadway production. An unapologetic perfectionist overseeing every aspect of production, Lucy wanted *Mame* to reflect the Broadway show as much as possible. She insisted on the original choreographer, Onna White, and she got Connell, too. Dismayed by the growing permissiveness in American entertainment, Ball also wanted to make a family picture. But *Mame* exposed her to wounding criticism, and she never returned to the big screen.[43]

"Losing a role, no matter how secure you are in your craft, still hurts," Madeline said in 1973. "I felt bad about *Mame*, but I didn't take it personally."[44]

• • •

While Madeline was still in Hollywood, she guest-starred in a two-part episode of *Adam's Rib*, a sitcom based on the 1949 film directed by George Cukor and written by the husband-and-wife team of Ruth Gordon and Garson Kanin. On TV, as in the movie, the principal characters are Adam Bonner, an assistant district attorney in Manhattan, and his wife, Amanda, a private attorney active in women's rights. In the series premiere, a two-episode recapitulation of the plot of the movie, Adam and Amanda clash when she defends Doris Attinger (Madeline), a woman accused of shooting her husband.

Playing roles indelibly associated with Spencer Tracy and Katharine Hepburn were Ken Howard and Blythe Danner (sister-in-law of Madeline's *New Faces* co-star Dorothy Danner). Most actors feel uneasy about following in the footsteps of icons, and as Doris, Madeline took on a role created by Judy Holliday. Years later, she would wrestle with conflicting emotions when Kanin asked her to take another Holliday role in his play *Born Yesterday*. But in 1973, as she told interviewers at the time, she could hardly afford to pass up paying work, no matter how much she wanted to be her own performer.

Holliday was one of a few great stars with whom Madeline was sometimes compared. Both grew up in Queens and had a gift for playing ditsy characters in comedy, though both were highly intelligent. Like Madeline, Holliday got her start in New York cabaret. Her troupe, the Revuers, also launched Betty Comden and Adolph Green and established the prototype for the kinds of shows Madeline performed at the Upstairs. Holliday's distinctive speech—a strangely husky sort of baby talk—coupled with her good looks, led to success in Hollywood and on Broadway. Madeline might have done well to embrace the Holliday comparisons more often, and *Adam's Rib* is a case in point. Cukor and Kanin effectively used the movie as Holliday's screen test for the movie adaptation of *Born Yesterday*, in which she'd starred onstage. The trick worked, and for *Born Yesterday* she won a best actress Oscar, instantly graduating from character actress to leading lady in Hollywood, a feat that Madeline never entirely managed to achieve.

The television version of *Adam's Rib* didn't have the impact that the movie had, either on the career of the actress playing Doris or on audiences. The series lasted only thirteen episodes. Though Blythe Danner thought Madeline was "great," even she has few memories of the series, since it began during what she calls "a chaotic time" immediately after the birth of her daughter, Gwyneth Paltrow. However, it's certain that if Garson Kanin didn't know already who Madeline was, she couldn't have escaped his attention in the premiere episode of *Adam's Rib*.

Returning to New York, Madeline proved her aptitude as a character actress in her third feature, *From the Mixed-up Files of Mrs. Basil E. Frankweiler*, also released in 1973.[45] An adaptation of E. L. Konigsburg's ingenious, Newbery Award-winning novel (published in 1967), the movie concerns a sister and brother who run away from home to live in the

Metropolitan Museum of Art. In one quick scene, they tag along with a school group and a teacher who's so harried she doesn't notice that two of these students aren't hers. She's played by Madeline, drawing on her own teaching experience, and she's the best thing in the movie. The scene is funny, and it conveys the fun kids could have if they lived in a museum; it's also the rare occasion when Madeline got to play a character so much like herself. Despite the star power of Ingrid Bergman as Mrs. Frankweiler, *Mixed-up Files* flopped. But the other movie Madeline shot in 1973 proved to be the biggest hit of her career.

18

It's Twue

Blazing Saddles (1973–74)

WHEN MADELINE FIRST HEARD ABOUT MEL BROOKS'S NEW PROJECT, A spoof Western to be entitled *Black Bart*, she was intrigued. Brooks had written a character based on Frenchie, Marlene Dietrich's part in *Destry Rides Again* (1939), and Madeline thought she'd be right for it. But she'd met Brooks only briefly in the Warner Bros. commissary, and as she later recalled, "No one knew that I had spent time working in Hofbrauhauses and sung German Lieder and stuff like that. How would [Brooks] ever know that? I must try and see if I can inquire about this, even though I'm not a Marlene Dietrich type at all, but I understand that sort of thing, mentally."[46] For her meeting with him on the Warner lot in 1973, Madeline prepared "Das Chicago Song" and a couple of German numbers. What she hadn't prepared for was Brooks himself. She later told an interviewer, "My audition for Mel for *Blazing Saddles* was . . . intense. It lasted two hours. I felt like I was at the Mayo Clinic. For a funny man, he's *very* serious."[47]

Brooks remembers the scene vividly. As soon as Madeline saw that her character would be called Lili von Shtupp, she said, "Are you really gonna go with that name?" After all, *shtupp* is the Yiddish equivalent of the English slang "screw" (from the same root as the English "stuff"). Then Brooks said, "Can I see your legs?"

· "Don't you want to hear me read?" she asked, but Brooks insisted. She blushed, he remembers, and she asked, "What, are you crazy? What is this? I thought I was auditioning for a part in your movie. I didn't think you wanted to screw me on your desk." Brooks assured her he was happily married and not the kind of man who chases starlets around his office. He simply wanted Lili to straddle a chair and to wear net stockings, à la Dietrich. "So she showed me her legs," Brooks remembers.

"She straddled the chair, and that was it. 'You've got Dietrich legs.' The first two or three minutes we met, she was insulted. I had a lot of explaining to do." At first, he thought she was "incredibly prudish, and incredibly societally closed-off and bound," but as she relaxed, he began to revise his impression.

Moreover, she had a terrific German accent, and he responded immediately to her musicality. He decided to hire her, and he and Anne Bancroft began to socialize with her. They went to dinner often, Brooks says, "so she could see how much I loved Annie, and there was no straying from that love." The result was a long friendship among all three. Brooks had good reports of Madeline from Liam Dunn, who would play Rev. Johnson in *Black Bart*. But in retrospect, Brooks believes Bancroft also steered him toward Madeline. Because Thomas Meehan and Martin Charnin had worked with Bancroft on her television specials in the 1960s, she'd have been familiar with Madeline's work in both *Comedy Tonight* and *Two by Two*. "Don't miss this one! She's the best," Bancroft told her husband. Madeline's collaboration with Brooks would be the most significant of her career—for better and for worse.

Like Frenchie in *Destry Rides Again*, Lili von Shtupp falls for an unlikely sheriff and sings a suggestive song. But Brooks carries those essential ingredients farther. His sheriff isn't merely a pacifist, as Jimmy Stewart was in *Destry*; played by Cleavon Little, he's also black and policing a deeply racist community. Lili's "I'm Tired" isn't merely suggestive, like Frenchie's "Laziest Girl in Town"; it's "probably the dirtiest song I ever wrote," Brooks observes. And Lili isn't merely a saloon singer; she's a Wild West Mata Hari, paid to use sex for political ends. Enlisted by corrupt Gov. William J. Lepetomane (Brooks) and his nefarious henchman Hedley Lamarr (Harvey Korman) to undermine the renegade sheriff and make way for a new railroad, Lili accedes readily. She arrives in the town of Rock Ridge with all her weapons: well-stocked corset, tapering legs, and mouth-watering *moue*. The only trouble is, she's tired. "Tired of being admired. Tired of love uninspired. . . . Let's face it, fellas, everything below the neck is *kaputt*."

Madeline gives her best-known performance as Lili, doing an uncanny imitation of Dietrich. Her peroxide rinse and bustier garnered her pin-up status with a couple of generations of fanboys, and with *Blazing Saddles* as with *Paper Moon*, a single scene sealed the deal on an Oscar nomination. In this case, it's the song, and much of the number is pure Madeline. Brooks told her to "harmonize the way Dietrich would," so she came up with the meandering "Ah" in the middle of the song, "in a key that was just a little wrong. Ordinarily, she was always in the center of the note," he says. The moment when Lili reaches out to lean on the set and misses was also Madeline's. Her most important contribution, however, was to point out that the song had only verses and a chorus. Brooks went home and, in one night, wrote the words and music to the introduction that begins "Here I stand, the goddess of desire." Madeline was thrilled, and so was Brooks, though it meant restaging the number. Summing up her performance, he recalls a moment that "always makes me laugh and cry" at the end of the number. As the cowboys shoot up the saloon and the chorus of Prussian soldiers carries her off, she looks around as if to say, "Oh, the hell with it all." "You gotta watch her all the time," Brooks says, "because she's always doing something unique and Madeline-esque."

During the filming of *The Producers*, Brooks despaired when takes were ruined because the crew cracked up at Zero Mostel's performance. The solution was to buy handkerchiefs and distribute them: "If you feel like laughing, stick this in your mouth." Brooks resorted to the same tactic for "I'm Tired." "I knew I had a great scene when I looked around and the whole crew was standing there with white handkerchiefs in their mouths," he says. "I must have gone through a whole case of white handkerchiefs on that picture." Between takes, he says, Madeline sang Weill songs and coloratura arias, sometimes bringing work to a halt as the crew listened to her. "Trills for her, thrills for us. . . .. We just marveled at her."

Though Gene Wilder shares the screen only fleetingly with Madeline in *Blazing Saddles*, he made sure to be on the set during the filming of "I'm Tired." "I told Mel that if the movie were just her one number, it would be worth the price of admission," he says. With *Young Frankenstein* already in the planning stages, Wilder—that movie's co-writer, as well as its star—began to consider casting Madeline in a key role.

Ultimately *Blazing Saddles* was the first of three pictures with Wilder and four with Brooks. Madeline found herself working again with Liam Dunn and met Dom DeLuise and Harvey Korman for the first time. She'd co-star with each of them again. She was now a valued player not only in Bogdanovich's de facto repertory company, but also in Brooks's, and in *Blazing Saddles* she's not just the leading lady, she's virtually the *only* female.

Though she never worked with him again, Madeline established a remarkable rapport with Cleavon Little. In few other pictures does one sense a comparable ease between Madeline and her leading man. Much of this comes from Little. Handsome, silky-smooth, and affable, he makes the movie's message of racial awareness not merely palatable (as the studio executives hoped he would when they rejected Brooks's first choice, Richard Pryor, who co-wrote the screenplay) but delicious. During Bart's tryst with Lili, Madeline participates in one of many penis jokes Brooks would throw her way: "Tell me, Schatzi, is it twue what they say about the way your people are *gifted*?" At the studio's request, the next line ("I hate to disappoint you, ma'am, but you're sucking on my arm") was cut, a concession Brooks regrets. Madeline's exclamation, "It's twue! It's twue!" becomes the punch line to the scene.

Off-camera, she wasn't comfortable with Brooks's bawdy humor. "The language is absolutely filthy," she told a reporter several months before *Blazing Saddles* opened. "They say things like, 'Up—.' Oh, my God! Why am I telling *you* this? Everyone will think *I* am dirty. Please, can we talk about something else —something my mother can show her friends?"[48]

Premiering on February 7, 1974, *Blazing Saddles* was the top-grossing picture of the year, besting the disaster epics *The Towering Inferno* and *Earthquake*, *The Godfather II*, and a little picture called *Young Frankenstein*. Madeline earned excellent reviews for her "marvelously unkind takeoff on Marlene Dietrich"[49] and her second Oscar nomination in two years. She lost the Academy Award for best actress in a supporting role to Ingrid Bergman for *Murder on the Orient Express*, but nevertheless, she was on a winning streak. She'd made three hits, and all of Hollywood knew who she was.

Her performance in *Blazing Saddles* is still so powerful that one forgets she has only a few scenes and all but disappears at the end of the movie. (She turns up briefly in drag, another Dietrich homage, though she says nothing). A great deal of her training came together at once: her mimicry, her facility in sketches and in comic songs, her portrayals of saucy wenches—and yes, her extensive knowledge of Weimar culture. This background explains why she's funny even to people who have no idea who Dietrich was, just as "Das Chicago Song" is funny to people who never heard Lenya. She knew exactly how to put across this material. And true to form, she even managed to supply Lili with a bit of depth. After a night of love, she closes the door on Bart and exclaims, with rapturous purity, "Vot a nice guy!"—signaling that other guys in Lili's life haven't been nice, and letting us know how she wound up where she is. "She was so bright," Brooks says. "Not only did she get jokes, she got *nuance*."

19

The Half-Vision of What I Might Be

Boom Boom Room (1973)

BOTH *ADAM'S RIB* AND *FROM THE MIXED-UP FILES* PREMIERED IN THE fall of 1973, a few weeks before Joseph Papp launched his first season as producer of the New York Shakespeare Theater at Lincoln Center with a new play by David Rabe, whose work he had championed at the Public Theater downtown. Unlike Rabe's other plays to that point (notably *The Basic Training of Pavlo Hummel* and *Sticks and Bones*), *Boom Boom Room* centered on a woman. A go-go dancer in the eponymous Philadelphia club, Chrissy is barely intelligent enough to realize that everyone she knows exploits her. When at last she achieves her dream of a career in New York, it's as a stripper—a step down.

The part was such a stretch for Madeline that some, seeing her name listed in the published script, wonder whether another actress named Madeline Kahn was working in New York in the early 1970s. Theater critic Michael Feingold, who saw her performance, says, "She didn't come across as a go-go girl, but remember that the character is a person who has long, emotional scenes and speeches, and who is to a certain extent a reactive element to all the other people." Madeline didn't play Chrissy as stupid, he says, but as confused or uncomprehending; she didn't condescend to the character. "Chrissy is a person who makes mistakes in her life, and it's easy to believe Madeline as that," he says. "She was very moving in it." Her rehearsal script contains two additions that give one a sense of Madeline's approach to *Boom Boom Room*. One is a photograph of a Playboy bunny, alongside a note in her handwriting on the first page: "[S]o trapped in the half-vision of what I might be . . . while having to wallow around in what I actually am . . . that anyone who can make my half-visions alive [and] breathing has a power over me." It's as good a description of Chrissy as anyone (arguably including Rabe) ever managed.

As the production started, Rabe felt that his script wasn't ready, but as he told Papp's biographer, "You'd have to be an idiot to turn down a chance at Lincoln Center, and I was not prepared to deal with Joe's kind of argument and force."[50] The rehearsal period was even more difficult than might have been predicted. Believing that a woman should direct, Papp hired Julie Bovasso, a distinguished actress, teacher, and director of experimental theater. He didn't know her and wasn't familiar with her work. She lacked experience in commercial theater, and the material she usually directed was comparatively outré. However, Rabe's sensibility appealed to her, and she envisioned a surreal production that would take advantage of the Vivian Beaumont Theater's expansive stage, with simultaneous action on multiple playing areas, and Papp and Rabe approved.

Bovasso disagreed with Papp on casting the lead role. "I really did not ever like Madeline Kahn," Bovasso said. "She was imposed on me. She is charming and she can be funny, but she doesn't have that kind of power. When it comes to wailing, she cannot wail. It ain't there." But as a newcomer to Papp's fiefdom, Bovasso didn't feel she could veto his choice, and she sensed that Papp wanted stars—like Madeline and her co-star, Julie Newmar—to lend glamour to his inaugural production, regardless of their abilities. Madeline "played everything straight out front, wouldn't relate, she was concerned with her own self-survival," Bovasso remembered. "This has nothing to do with acting."[51]

Yet during rehearsal, Bovasso began to believe she could coax the performance she wanted from Madeline, and Madeline later recalled Bovasso as "very helpful to me. She was a woman and she seemed to have a real ability to portray rage, while my fear would have been that I couldn't be really believable portraying rage. I hadn't come from a family background where everyone was really yelling at everyone else, and maybe she did, so I had courage with her leading me along a bit."[52] But the actress who couldn't say "tits" in *Paper Moon* was scarcely able to dance topless, as the script required in the final scene when Chrissy's degradation is complete. At a dress rehearsal, Madeline kept her breasts veiled, a choice that lacked the impact Rabe sought. In frustration, Bovasso suggested another rewrite. Instead, Papp fired her. But she didn't give up without a fight, returning a few days later to confront him in front of Rabe and the cast. Papp ordered her out of the theater. Characteristically,

Madeline disengaged herself from the unpleasantness. Bovasso's firing, she later said, "just kind of happened."[53]

With only days before opening and no time to hire anyone else, Papp directed *Boom Boom Room* himself. He must have been a whirlwind. When Madeline balked, he called her understudy onstage. According to Mary Woronov—the Warhol superstar who replaced Newmar during rehearsals—it took about fifteen minutes of watching another actor do her job to persuade Madeline to cooperate. She even found the nerve to flash her breasts at the end of the play as the stage went dark. "I was so full of what I had to do yet," Madeline said. "I can't explain the feeling, except to say it's like you're out there in the ocean swimming, and you've got to get to shore. You can see the shore, and you simply have to keep going. God, it's great when you're working that hard, I have to say."[54]

Though Rabe later conceded that Papp was responsible for much of what went right with *Boom Boom Room*, their relationship crumbled. The coup de grâce came on opening night, when Papp humiliated Rabe by phoning critic Clive Barnes and haranguing him for his negative review—all under the watchful eye of a *Times* reporter invited by Papp to cover the play's preparation. Unaware that many people on both ends of the conversation could hear them, the two men heaped invectives on each other. A sanitized account of the conversation appeared in the *Times* reporter's article shortly thereafter, helping to deflect attention from Rabe's work and toward Papp's outsized personality.[55] Indeed, the producer got more press than the play, Rabe felt,[56] and *Boom Boom Room*'s sordid subject matter and (at the time) graphic sexuality and language found little favor with some audiences.

Despite all the turbulence in the background, Madeline gave what she would long consider her finest performance, earning a Drama Desk Award and a Tony nomination for best actress in a play. *Time* critic T. E. Kalem praised her "performance in depth of an intrinsically shallow soul."[57] In the *New Yorker*, Brendan Gill wrote, "Madeline Kahn is superb as Chrissy; with the wary stance of a boxer accustomed to being clipped from behind and with a child's voice of mingled hope and doubt, she is a true heroine, indomitable in her pursuit of who she was, and is, and can be."[58]

But Barnes was no more persuaded by Madeline's performance than by Rabe's play. "Madeline Kahn, a gifted performer, has been allowed to mug the play as if she were doing a series of blackout sketches for a revue," he wrote in the *Times*. "It is the kind of acting more suitable for Johnny Carson's *Tonight Show* than Lincoln Center." Given Madeline's desire to move beyond revues and her longstanding ambivalence about talk shows, Barnes could hardly have found a more wounding description of her work.[59] The next year, in a profile in the *Times*, she alluded to Barnes's review, then suggested that people who didn't understand the play were people with whom she simply couldn't communicate.[60]

Whenever Madeline spoke of her frustration with parts that were "just sketches" or "bits," and of her desire to play something with greater range, she had Chrissy in mind. Chrissy was the most complex character Madeline ever portrayed, and the last role she would play that wasn't primarily comedic. (Years later, she was approached to play Chrissy's mother in a film adaptation, never realized, to have been directed by Barbara Kopple.) "At heart, no one thinks of himself as a comic," Madeline told the *Washington Post* in 1997.

Speaking of Chrissy, she said, "I was never the same after that role. I felt validated as an actress. For the first time in my career, I felt known. So much of the time I don't. That's not to say unappreciated, but rather not properly perceived. Most of the roles I get are not close to me in essence, and I have to retrieve those elements in my experience that are useable. [With] *In the Boom Boom Room*, I had an unexpected connection. And Joe Papp had the courage of his conviction to cast me in something no one else would have."[61]

20

Sweet Mystery

Young Frankenstein (1974)

COMING OFF A WINNING STREAK OF FOUR HIT MOVIES RELEASED BE-
tween 1972 and 1974, "I was spoiled," Madeline told her friend George
Bettinger in a radio interview. "I thought they were all going to be like
that."[62] In 1975, syndicated columnist Dick Kleiner called her "the biggest thing in pictures since talking popcorn," and compared her with
Marilyn Monroe and Carol Burnett. Even so, she told Kleiner, she felt
pigeonholed, much as she had at Hofstra. But, he wrote, "[S]he says
now she'd like to try some serious roles."[63] They weren't forthcoming.
As ever, Madeline's work was determined by other people. Writers, directors, and casting agents more than ever now saw her as a comic. The
means to control her career—holding out for serious parts, writing or
producing her own material—were unavailable to Madeline and to almost any other woman in Hollywood and New York at the time.

Men had more options, and Gene Wilder's desire to shape his career
inspired him to write a screenplay. Wanting to create not only a juicy
role for himself, but also to guarantee himself a good time making the
picture, he'd already begun writing the script for *Young Frankenstein* (and
Mel Brooks had agreed to direct it) before *Blazing Saddles* started shooting. Wilder wrote the first draft; Brooks advised him, then helped to polish the final script; they shared co-author credit onscreen.[64] Once they
heard Madeline sing "I'm Tired," they determined to find a role for her in
their new movie. But which role? Wilder thought Madeline would prefer to play the sexy lab assistant, Inga, while Brooks wanted her to play
Elizabeth, Frederick Frankenstein's fiancée. "She was Park Avenue," he
says. But he left the choice to her. Madeline knew what *she* wanted: Taffeta beats a lab coat any day, and as photographed by Gerald Hirschfeld,

she glitters like starlight. Ultimately, Wilder succeeded in both his goals for the picture: Frederick is one of the best parts he ever got, and as he wrote in his memoir, "Making *Young Frankenstein* was the happiest I'd ever been on a film. . . . It was like taking a small breath of Heaven each day."[65] With a cast that included Peter Boyle, Marty Feldman, and Teri Garr, Madeline found herself among friends old and new, and whenever she was on the set, Brooks made a point of eating lunch with the actors—something he wouldn't ordinarily do, he says.

The camaraderie on the set can be seen in outtakes saved by editor John Howard. In the scene in which Elizabeth arrives at Frankenstein's castle, Madeline and Feldman worked out their business before the cameras rolled. But when Feldman did something unexpected—punctuating a line with a growl and a nip at the fox-fur stole around Madeline's neck—the actors burst out laughing. Each time Feldman bit the stole, a tuft of fur (and eventually an entire leg) came away in his mouth. Madeline, Feldman, Garr, and Wilder kept more or less straight faces for the first take, but thereafter Wilder himself was usually the first to laugh, and even in the final take he's on the brink of another burst of laughter. "It was the toughest moment in [Madeline's] life," Brooks says. "How could I not laugh?" she asked him afterward. "I had to play angry."

Madeline delivered a few surprises, too. For the crucial scene in which the Monster (Boyle) rapes Elizabeth, the script called for her to burst into song: "Cheek to Cheek," an Irving Berlin number (as is "Puttin' on the Ritz"). The night before shooting, Madeline wondered whether another lyric might sound more like lovemaking than "Heaven! I'm in heaven!" If only there were a song that started out with "Oh!" or "Ah!" Suddenly, she had her answer, and the next morning, she approached Brooks on the set. He thought for a moment, then said, "Sure, let's try it."

"Ah! Sweet Mystery of Life" is so apt that it's hard to believe it wasn't on Wilder's mind from the moment he started writing the story of a scientist who discovers the mystery of life both in the lab and in love. Composed by Victor Herbert, with lyrics by Rida Johnson Young, for the operetta *Naughty Marietta* (1910), the song is as faithful to the period as other details in the movie, and in Madeline's trained soprano voice, it's over-the-top ecstatic. The result is a classic moment in cinema, forever associated with Madeline—though in the film Garr sings more of the song than she does. The first "Ah!" was all it took, though, and it was all Madeline's. Arguably no other soprano has made as great an impact with a single note.

The last full day of shooting was devoted to the honeymoon scene between Dr. Frankenstein and Inga. Brooks found Wilder sitting thoughtfully on the edge of the bed. "You know, I've never had a better experience in my life," the actor said. "Would it be crazy to write a new scene or two, just to keep going?" "No, we can't," Brooks replied. "But I'll keep the set, if you want to just sit around for a while longer."[66] Instead, Wilder began writing a new movie, with leading roles for Madeline, himself, and Marty Feldman.

It's become customary to describe *Young Frankenstein* as the most "disciplined" of Mel Brooks's films, and certainly it eschews the chaos of *Blazing Saddles*, making it easier to appreciate the beauty of the physical details (from the quasi-expressionistic cinematography to the zippers on the Monster's neck) and the thoughtful, coherent exposition of psychology. Even the *New Yorker*'s Pauline Kael was won over, though she reserved the bulk of her praise for Wilder and for Madeline:

> When she parodied Marlene Dietrich in *Blazing Saddles*, it wasn't the usual Dietrich imitation, because she was also parodying herself. Madeline Kahn has an extra dimension of sexiness; it's almost like what Mae West had—she's flirtatious in a self-knowing way. And everything that's wrong about her is sexy. You look at her and think, What a beautiful translucent skin on such a big jaw; what a statuesque hourglass figure, especially where the sand has slipped. She's so self-knowingly lascivious that she convinces you she really digs the monster. Madeline Kahn is funny and enticing because she's soaked in passion; when you look at her, you see a water bed at just the right temperature.[67]

Given Madeline's anxieties about her weight and appearance, she surely considered this one of the nastiest good reviews she ever got.

It's easy for kids to focus on the broadest comic elements (and the ultra-sexy performances of Madeline and Teri Garr), yet when we return to *Young Frankenstein* as adults, we may appreciate a minute concern with questions of Jewish identity, as Frederick emigrates from America to Eastern Europe in search of his roots, and struggles until he can pronounce his name correctly: "Franken-STINE." In this context, Madeline's character is daring, a joke that Gentiles would be smacked for repeating: She's a stereotypical Jewish princess. A daddy's girl more interested in preserving her coiffure, her nails, and her taffeta gown (to say nothing of her virginity) than in kissing Frederick, she succumbs to the Monster's advances as soon as he unzips his trousers. What starts as rape turns into something else altogether, and we see that Elizabeth needs "an enormous Schwanzstücker" to tame her.

Today, in an era when "No means no," the comedy is more daring than Wilder and Brooks intended, since Elizabeth does say no at first. But even in 1974, this scene was outré, and Madeline herself once asked, "What's funny about that? It's grotesque. I know when I'm in a Mel Brooks movie, we're going to be doing some low, grotesque stuff. A lot of what makes sufficient numbers of us laugh, me included, is sometimes very broad, very low, grotesque, horrible stuff."[68] Some of her friends still balk at Brooks's humor, and Betty Aberlin winces at the memory of Madeline's "Let me see your legs" audition. Aberlin also objects to the characterization of the first encounter between Elizabeth and the Monster as "a rape scene." To her, it's "a love scene," and she resists even the politically incorrect possibility that the script depicts a rape that turns to love. Lily Tomlin finds much of the movie objectionable on political grounds. Surprisingly, Tomlin recalls that she was offered the role of Frau Blücher but turned it down. "I was much too feminist in those days—my own politics," she says. "I don't even remember what happens to that character. Whatever it was, I didn't like it. I would never be able to throw myself into a part like that, at that time especially. The fact that Madeline would throw herself into a style of comedy that didn't necessarily speak to what she would like to represent, and still pull it off, was remarkable. She was extremely sensitive, and her own sensibility was very developed. I would have been a disaster. Whatever I thought was wrong politically, I wouldn't have been able to do it and make it work."

Again and again, working in Brooks's films obliged Madeline to compromise her natural reserve. In a 1975 profile of Brooks for *Newsweek*, she—perhaps unwittingly—summed up her dilemma: She worked with a man she adored, who made her do things she didn't necessarily like. "Mel is sensual with me," she said. "He treats me like an uncle—a dirty uncle. He's an earthy man and very moral underneath. He has traditional values."[69] Off-screen, Brooks wasn't going to take advantage of her, and he made her feel appreciated and protected. Yet his movies threw her into Transylvanian rapes and Roman orgies.

While Madeline admitted to laughing at Brooks's movies, on only one occasion—a syndicated late-night talk show in 1979—did she suggest that his humor was in any way a reflection of her own. Brooks, she said, "understands me somehow and loves me somehow, and allows me to be myself, to a greater degree than a lot of people do. And that's wonderful, that's a great feeling. I feel very liberated around him. He accepts my raunchier humor."[70] To no other interviewer, to no friend or family member did Madeline say anything similar. On the contrary, she worried that fans expected her to be like Brooks's characters, and from the start, she insisted in the press that she wasn't. She described herself as "the antithesis" of Brooks's "gross, flat-out humor. . . . I think I am rather delicate and subtle."[71] Yes, Brooks created an atmosphere on the set that made her more comfortable with rough language and outrageous behavior, and there's no question she loved working with him. But as Tomlin says, Brooks's sensibility was not Madeline's.

Brooks believes otherwise. "She was a natural, entertaining commentator on the human condition," he says, "and she always felt a little hidebound about not letting some of what we call 'dirty stuff' out. She felt with me, with *Blazing Saddles* and our adventures together, that there were no holds barred. I would be glad to express anything, you know, anything that was real, that expressed the human condition. I was a good conduit for her, for letting it all out." The reason she trusted him, Brooks says—"very egotistically, you have to take it with a grain of salt"—was his intelligence. "Intellectually and mentally, she was probably superior to anyone and everyone she worked with, and actually probably had to hide her brilliance a little, not to in any way make them feel that they weren't the kingpin. . . . And she admitted to me, 'In the end, I never met anybody like you. You're actually brighter than I am. You're smarter than I am, and I feel such a great relief in working with you.' It's hard to meet somebody who was as smart as I am, and she was."

Smart enough to persuade him that she enjoyed raunchy comedy, even though she didn't.

• • •

Off-camera during the filming of *Young Frankenstein*, everyone from Peter Bogdanovich and Mel Brooks to Wilder's teenage stepdaughter believed that Madeline and Gene Wilder were having an affair. As Wilder explains, "Now and years ago, my stepdaughter and Madeline Kahn both had the same idea. My daughter thought it was true and my favorite acting partner and greatest actress wondered why it wasn't true. But I was always attached to someone else." In fact, he began seeing Teri Garr, but Wilder and Madeline got along so well that even he thought they'd make a good couple. If her feelings for him went deeper than the speculative stage, they didn't interfere with her friendships with him and with Garr—or with Gilda Radner, whom Wilder later married. But the rapport between Wilder and Madeline was important artistically, and it's one reason they're so closely associated, despite having made only three films together (in one of which they don't interact). With Wilder, as with Brooks and with Boyle, the personal relationship made it easier for Madeline to take risks as an actor, and Wilder would capitalize on that trust in his directorial debut.

For Brooks, *Young Frankenstein* confirmed that he was now a powerhouse in Hollywood. The picture opened on December 15, 1974, and took third place at the box office for the year, just two spots behind *Blazing Saddles*. The disappointments of *The Producers* and *The Twelve Chairs* were forgotten, and to sweeten the moment, Brooks and Wilder received an Academy Award nomination in 1975 for best screenplay adapted from other material. At the Golden Globes, Madeline received a nomination for best supporting actress in a motion picture, but lost to Karen Black for *The Great Gatsby*.

To promote the movie's premiere, Madeline appeared on *The Tonight Show* on November 11, along with the idol of her college years, Jeanne Moreau. The perks of stardom were beginning to add up. "I'm enjoying this," she told a reporter. "It's nice to be able to sleep at night and not have to worry about unpaid bills. It's a very good feeling. And now I'm indulging myself—why not? I'm redoing my apartment. I'm buying lots of nice clothes, I'm spending lots of money. Listen, I worked for ten years to get here, so why not?"[72]

21

Down in the Dumps in the Hollywood Hills

At Long Last Love (1975)

MADELINE'S APPOINTMENT BOOK NOTES CONTRAST THE SHOOTING of *Young Frankenstein* (five days, plus one day of pick-up work that doubled as a wrap party) with that of *At Long Last Love*, her final collaboration with Peter Bogdanovich (five and a half months). The latter picture, released in 1975, is representative of the majority of her subsequent movies: It must have looked good on paper, and it involved people she (for the most part) liked, but the result is an artistic misfire and a box office failure. Co-star Cybill Shepherd and Bogdanovich refer to it simply as "the debacle."

Nothing if not a serious student of old movies, Bogdanovich is also a musician who revealed in *The Last Picture Show* and *Paper Moon* a visual lyricism, a sustained melody of images. *What's Up, Doc?*, in contrast, plays its characters and confusion in jazzy counterpoint. In his earlier movies, he applied what he'd learned not only through study but also through his personal relationships with directors from the golden age of film. Now he wanted to apply lessons learned from another friend, Fred Astaire.

Who better than Bogdanovich to pay homage to Cole Porter and the classic Hollywood musicals of the 1930s? When Shepherd gave him a book of Porter lyrics, Bogdanovich latched onto the melancholy "I Loved Him (But He Didn't Love Me)" and began to conceive of a lavish movie. Consulting musical-theater historian Miles Kreuger, he settled on sixteen Porter songs in their original versions—that is, with the original, racier lyrics written for sophisticated Broadway audiences and not the watered-down lyrics heard on recordings and movie soundtracks purveyed to the wider, more conservative public of the 1930s. In "Down in the Dumps (On the Ninetieth Floor)," for example, Madeline sings that "Even the minister's wife / Has a perfectly good sex life." In "Most Gentlemen Don't Like Love," Eileen Brennan sings,

> *A slap and a tickle*
> *Is all that the fickle*
> *Male ever has in his head*

and in the same song, Shepherd sings,

> *. . . A rock and a quickie*
> *Is all little Dickie*
> *Means when he mentions romance.*

This sort of suggestive language might not have played in Peoria during the Depression, but times had changed—or so the filmmakers hoped. Accordingly, Bogdanovich wrote a screenplay in which the plot was simultaneously simple and sophisticated, depicting the romantic foibles of the wealthy and glamorous, just as Hollywood musicals of the 1930s did. But he tweaks the formula with the sensibilities of the 1970s. It's not quite a '70s-style key party or swingers' club, transplanted into the context of a '30s-style musical—but it's close. And in the authority-questioning style of the times, some cast members sang and danced more like ordinary people than like old-fashioned musical stars.

And so millionaire playboy (Burt Reynolds), madcap but penniless heiress (Shepherd), Broadway star (Madeline), and worldly gambler (Duilio del Prete) meet, pair off, break up, then pair off again with one another's partners, all while drinking vast quantities of alcohol. Commenting from the sidelines—and eventually pairing off, too—are the heiress's lusty maid (Brennan) and the playboy's standoffish valet (John Hillerman). As an extra treat, one of John Ford's favorite actors, Mildred Natwick, plays Reynolds's mother. However, instead of the usual happily-ever-after Hollywood musical finale, Bogdanovich opted for what he calls a "bittersweet," "sort of up-in-the-air ending, where nothing is really resolved." As the couples look wistfully at the lovers they've left behind, they sing and dance to the final song, "A Picture of Me Without You." Bogdanovich wasn't displeased when a reporter pointed out that no other musical comedy had had an unhappy ending since Lubitsch's *The Smiling Lieutenant*, in 1931.

In hindsight, that ending may have sealed the doom of *At Long Last Love*. The movie is deeply flawed, and yet it does boast incidental pleasures. Audiences and critics alike might have found it easier to rally around the picture had it sent them out of the theater feeling good, as old-fashioned musicals generally did. Perhaps, in the cynical '70s, a happy ending would've risked appearing corny, but even in the extensively restored version that's seen today, the picture doesn't leave a viewer with much to cheer about.

As Kitty O'Kelly, the Broadway star, Madeline joins other cast members in eight numbers. She took tap lessons to prepare for the role, though choreographer Rita Abrams remembers that the dancing was "basic tap" and "elegant movement." In the original cut of the movie, Madeline sang two solos: "Find Me a Primitive Man" (Kitty's stage act, with a chorus of galumphing cavemen), as well as, "Down in the Dumps," the movie's most audacious stunt and its opening number, filmed in a single, unbroken tracking shot as she sings and staggers drunkenly through her apartment. The scene was cut from the picture shortly before its theatrical release.

Much of the movie's reputation stems from Bogdanovich's hasty re-editing under pressure from Fox executives. "The studio said they loved the film," Shepherd remembers, "but they kept saying, 'We love it. Make it better. Make it shorter.'" By this they meant less Madeline, less del Prete, and more Shepherd, more Reynolds. Meanwhile, the grand opening at Radio City Music Hall on New Year's Day was fast approaching. "That's a lot of pressure for a filmmaker to be under," Shepherd says. Bogdanovich concedes he "made some mistakes in the original cut." After a disastrous first preview, he re-cut the movie for a fresh preview. The second cut "was pretty good," he says, but then he tinkered with it further and released the new version without a preview, "a huge mistake, because the worst version of all was the one that was released." Moreover, rumors of the last-minute editing excited critics who'd been waiting to bring down the ambitious young director. We'll never know whether his original vision would have met with success in 1975, but Fox pulled the released version from theaters early, earning no more than $1,600,000 (and costing an estimated six million dollars). According to Bogdanovich, the movie had started to see an uptick at the box office, but the studio preferred to write off the picture as a loss.

• • •

At every step of the production, Bogdanovich posed immense challenges to himself and to the entire cast and crew. Gene Allen's production design relies exclusively on shades of black and white, to give the feeling of an old Paramount musical, but this scheme complicated the work of cinematographer Laszlo Kovacs, who had to find ways to keep the images interesting. Long takes proliferate, including the three women's complaint, "Most Gentlemen Don't Like Love" (another unbroken take, this one set in the ladies' lounge at Lord & Taylor); and the sextet, "Friendship" (set in a moving car, with two establishing shots followed by a long, unbroken take). As if those challenges weren't enough, the ladies' lounge is decorated with mirrors, though the camera must remain out of the shot. And in the confined space of the car, the camera has to dart to keep the actors from blocking whoever's singing. In dance numbers, just as Astaire insisted that his whole body be photographed so that audiences could appreciate his every move, Bogdanovich keeps his cast on full view. The grand vision meant that cutaways couldn't be inserted to cover missteps, and these limitations in turn required extra rehearsals and extra takes, and choreographers Albert Lantieri and Rita Abrams found themselves with a narrower range of options. Above all, every one of the sixteen numbers required new solutions to "the whole issue of how they were going to hear and sing without accompaniment," Abrams remembers.

In most Hollywood musicals, audio tracks were recorded weeks before filming began. Bogdanovich objected to the practice. If he did the same, he believed, the actors wouldn't have found their characters when they sang, and their interpretations might have changed by the time cameras rolled. Most of all, he wanted spontaneity. In only one number, Shepherd and Brennan's duet, "It Ain't Etiquette," did he go back and loop in pre-recorded audio. "But the rest of the picture," Bogdanovich says, "what's shot is what was used. It had a certain energy that I liked." As he explained to Miles Kreuger, the goal was not "to make a musical that was about singing and dancing: I wanted to make a musical about some people who sing and dance instead of walk and talk."[73]

Each dance number required four to six weeks of rehearsal, Shepherd remembers. "That's how they did it in the musicals with Fred Astaire. Not that we were Fred Astaire and Ginger Rogers! By no means!" Indeed, apart from Madeline and Eileen Brennan, nobody in the cast had much experience with American musical comedy, and Reynolds had virtually never before sung in public. Despite two months of daily singing lessons before shooting began, Reynolds remained uncomfortable, and living with Dinah Shore, one of America's great song stylists, only point-ed up his own awkwardness. Madeline boosted his confidence, though, with a bit of actorly advice: The trick wasn't to *be* a singer, but to play a character who sings.[74]

Throughout the filming, the cast wore transistor radio earpieces in order to hear an electric piano off the set. For the several outdoor track-ing shots, Bogdanovich put the piano in a flatbed truck that followed at a discreet distance. Just as a misstep in a dance meant another retake, so did a sour note in a song. But evidently some things, such as del Prete's thick accent, were too much trouble to correct. A singer and songwriter, del Prete had perhaps more professional experience than anyone else in the cast, but the complexities of filming effectively sabotage his perfor-mance, and *At Long Last Love* put an end to his American career. His lack of ease seeps through the screen, and it posed problems for Madeline, since she played opposite him in so many scenes.[75]

Looking back, Abrams cites language in del Prete's case, and sing-ing and dancing in Reynolds's, to illustrate the liabilities the cast had to overcome. Ultimately, she believes these struggles made it too difficult for the actors to communicate the "tongue-in-cheek" irony that Bogda-novich sought to convey, the opposite of what she calls "the straight-out Nelson Eddy–Jeanette MacDonald kind of musical" that many audiences expected. She points to Madeline's "Primitive Man"—"a very spoofy, fun number"—as an example. Madeline wore a transistor earpiece, but the chorus didn't. Unable to hear the music, they followed Bogdanovich's off-camera cues, "not really dancing" but stomping around and paw-ing Madeline. "That was a strange one," Abrams says. "She wasn't real happy that day, I remember."

The handwriting in Madeline's appointment book reveals her mount-ing frustration as the shoot wore on. She resorted to block capitals and drew rigid boxes around her engagements. Almost as therapy, she turned to Brennan to commiserate, talking late into the night. The bond they established didn't narrow the gap in their relationships with Bogdanov-ich, however, and without recalling many specifics, the director says that Madeline was "difficult" during the shoot. Though he'd written the role with her in mind, she seemed unappreciative, and "I was just a little bothered that she was so insecure about Cybill. She thought that both Cybill and I were trying to plot against her. She was a bit paranoid."

If so, it was a paranoia that Reynolds and Brennan shared. "Because Peter was so in love with Cybill, if she was right on in a scene I could fall down and have a nosebleed and it was a print," Reynolds wrote.[76]

As Brennan saw it, Bogdanovich "gave Burt and Cybill all the attention, all the work." She'd worked with Bogdanovich and Shepherd in *The Last Picture Show* (and its sequel, *Texasville*, many years later) and *Daisy Miller*. "I tried and tried to like her. I tried," Brennan said. But during *At Long Last Love*, those efforts were hampered by misgivings about Shepherd's talent, mingled with reservations about her relationship with Bogdanovich, since Brennan liked Polly Platt very much. Abrams believes that Bogdanovich and Shepherd did themselves no favors by going off together during lunch breaks, while the rest of the cast ate and chatted together. "The line was drawn there," she says. One visitor to the set, Ryan O'Neal, remembers, "Nobody got along on that movie! That was a mess! . . . I was nervous for everybody."

Madeline had looked forward to working with Reynolds and harbored a passionate, years-long crush on him. In his memoir, he confesses to an unrequited crush on her, too: "Bambi's father is still (especially lately) standing alone on a high cliff and thinking of white skin, brown freckles, and ships that pass in the night."[77] Privately, she told friends—and even her future husband—that mutual attraction went farther. Yet on the set, she felt cut off from him, too. After all, he was the source of many of the production delays. Bogdanovich remembers that the studio talked him into casting Reynolds. His first choice, Elliott Gould, had sung and studied tap, but couldn't match Reynolds's marquee value.[78] "We spent a lot of time trying to get Burt through it," Bogdanovich says. "He was sick most of the time, hyperventilating because he was so nervous." Madeline, by contrast, was a pro, and today Bogdanovich says her scenes are his favorite moments.

If Madeline had any sense of the director's approval at the time, however, it wasn't enough to calm her insecurities. "She'd been burned twice in two pictures of mine, one that made her a star and the other one that got her an Oscar nomination. But she didn't like the way she looked," Bogdanovich recalls with audible sarcasm. Now, working on *At Long Last Love*, she suspected that "because I was with Cybill I was gonna make her look bad." Against his specific instructions, she went sunbathing, though tanning was wrong for the period style and brought out her freckles. "She looked like a lobster," he says, "and next to Cybill, it was even worse." The freckles are especially noticeable in Madeline's section of the title song, in which she wears a short-sleeved blouse. Madeline didn't like her costumes, either, and she made her unhappiness apparent to everyone. Several of her gowns are tight across her waist and lower abdomen, correct 1930s fashion but not reassuring to a woman who's concerned about her appearance in 1975. And in "Primitive Man," one of those gowns is torn away, leaving her in a short slip, which prompted Pauline Kael to mention her "lavish, teasing thighs" in her review of *At Long Last Love*.[79] While she'd lost weight since her debut, Madeline may have focused on one or two areas and worried that she looked fat. And as Bogdanovich says, standing next to Shepherd didn't help.

Abrams, unlike Bogdanovich, remembers the best of Madeline's time on the set, particularly her sense of humor and professionalism. "There was a certain amount of conflict between the three women," she concedes, "but I think that's natural when you put three ladies together in beautiful costumes, and all vying for Peter's attention."

Madeline and Brennan had never met before the start of rehearsals, but Brennan broke the ice at a read-through at Bogdanovich's home, and they quickly found common ground. Both had worked with Bogdanovich before and had a background in musical theater in New York. Brennan starred in *Little Mary Sunshine* in 1959, and she co-starred with Carol Channing in the original cast of *Hello, Dolly!* in 1964. Both loved music, which made *At Long Last Love* more trying for them. "Music means more to me than anything," Brennan exclaimed. "Even more than dogs! Even more than *cats!*"

She recalled that neither Shepherd nor Reynolds made much effort to improve their (as she perceived them) limited musical abilities. "When you love music and it means so much to you, you want to have it right," she said. During rehearsals and around the piano at Bogdanovich's home, "Nobody wanted to work! Cybill didn't want to work. You gotta work, you gotta practice!" Memory didn't soften her impressions of Reynolds ("Why did Peter pick him? Box office? He [already] had that with Cybill!") or of Hillerman, her partner in many scenes. "There was no class to our parts," she said, "*and* you have to be with John Hillerman all the time. It really is not a pleasant thing to do." Del Prete, she said, made "no impression. He was sweet . . . . At least he was a professional singer." And yet, despite the hardships, "I'd love to work with Peter again," she said, four years before her death. "I'd do it in a minute."

To some on the set, the camaraderie between Brennan and Madeline seemed like an alliance every bit as intimidating as the one between Bogdanovich and Shepherd. During a dance rehearsal for the female leads, Lantieri misunderstood their "clever banter," believing they'd insulted his wife, Abrams recalls. A scene ensued, upsetting everyone, and Madeline turned to Mel Brooks—not to her agent or to the producer, Frank Marshall—to intercede on her behalf. Thereafter, Lantieri worked only with Reynolds, and he hardly appeared on the set for the rest of the shoot. Abrams was promoted from "drilling" the dances to sharing dance coordinator billing with Lantieri.

Admiring Brennan and Madeline, Shepherd was unaware of their unhappiness, and she considers the original cut of the movie one of Madeline's masterpieces, if not *the* masterpiece. Indeed, Madeline has few advocates as passionately outspoken as Shepherd. This admiration would have astonished her, just as Shepherd was astonished to hear that Madeline was intimidated by her, by the attention Bogdanovich paid her, and especially by her looks. "She looks so beautiful in the movie," Shepherd says. "Astoundingly beautiful! And she was intimidated? I was a cover girl, that's intimidating, maybe," she muses. If anything, Shepherd remembers being intimidated by Madeline, especially by her singing. Like Madeline, she'd had classical vocal training as a girl, but watching *At Long Last Love* now, she says, "I can't believe what she's doing with her voice." Much of Kitty's music lies in Madeline's alto register—to the degree that a lyric soprano has one—and Shepherd says Bogdanovich wanted her, too, to sing in a lower register during filming.

Though Shepherd sings pleasantly in *At Long Last Love*, in 1975 critics simply didn't want to hear her, and some still don't. Whether because of laziness (lumping all the cast together) or lack of musical background, a number of critics to this day dismiss the entire cast, including Madeline. The all-damning summary, "They can't sing," hangs around the picture's neck. The trend began with Vincent Canby in the *Times*, who praised Madeline's comedic talent ("indestructibly funny"), but wrote off the cast as "performers who don't dance and whose singing abilities might be best hidden in a very large choir."[80] In *Time*, Jay Cocks observed, "Even the few with musical training . . . flounder badly."[81]

The director has wondered whether his relationship with Shepherd didn't antagonize people (he recalls being told it did by no less than Cary Grant). Having left his wife and the mother of his children for a cover girl whose talents would remain hotly debated for years, Bogdanovich was showcasing Shepherd in yet another big-budget feature—this time insisting that audiences accept her as a singer and dancer, as well as an actress. The movie is something of a celebration of infidelity, too. By the time the picture opened, a backlash against Bogdanovich had built up, with Cocks at its forefront. After attending a press preview, critic Judith Crist phoned Bogdanovich to warn him, "They've got the knives out for you." Though Cocks opined, "This may be just the moment, then, if only out of simple charity, to attempt an uneasy truce with Peter Bogdanovich," he gave no quarter: "*At Long Last Love* cost $6 million, but might almost be worth it if the movie represented the low point of Bogdanovich's talent—the point from which he can only ascend."[82] Pauline Kael found almost nothing to her liking in "a stillborn picture . . . this relentless vapidity."[83] *At Long Last Love* would be a notorious flop, "a career-killer," as Ryan O'Neal puts it. Bogdanovich took out a newspaper ad to apologize for the disaster. A few years later, he re-cut the movie, restoring "Down in the Dumps." But ultimately, he says, "It was a favorite project of mine, and it didn't turn out the way I wanted it to. So I sort of turned my back on it."

Bogdanovich, Shepherd, and Reynolds received the worst reviews. Madeline walked away from the wreckage with a few words of praise ("the real pastry here," Kael called her). Yet watching the movie today, it's hard to understand why most critics were so harsh. Bogdanovich makes a number of miscalculations, and yet they hardly add up to a debacle. Perhaps the single greatest flaw is that listening to the same few people sing over and over becomes tedious, no matter how much one loves Cole Porter. At least in old-time musicals, singing chores were distributed more widely. The characters in *At Long Last Love* are less compelling than those in the movies that inspired them. Brennan's wisecracks, no matter how expertly delivered, don't rise to the level of those Helen Broderick put across in *Top Hat* and *Swingtime,* and audiences root for Fred Astaire's characters because, no matter what, he dances well. No one in *At Long Last Love* shines in any comparable way. But each actor does bring a distinctive personality and at least a little charisma. Reynolds is visibly uncomfortable whenever he sings, yet he's a natural athlete and fun to watch when he dances, light-footed and less self-conscious, as if his body can take liberties that his voice can't. But neither the cast nor the script does much to involve the audience emotionally.

For modern viewers, the great surprise of the movie may be how much the characters drink. Madeline's Kitty is soused when she sings "Down in the Dumps," which informs her interpretation of the song. She slides from her lowest register to her plummiest operatic timbre; she staggers and reels and breaks into tap steps. The number ends when she collapses on her bed with a bottle of gin. It's as impressive a performance as Bogdanovich hoped—in one unbroken take. At least audiences now have the chance to judge for themselves. "Down in the Dumps" wasn't included on the soundtrack album; the number wasn't even included in the commemorative songbook. But it's the prize of the restored version that's now available for home viewing on Blu-Ray, painstakingly reassembled by James Blakely, the head of Fox's editorial department.

Well before the Blu-Ray release, Shepherd argued in favor of a reevaluation of *At Long Last Love*, primarily as a means of granting Madeline, del Prete, and cinematographer Kovacs overdue recognition. "When I watch the movie, I'm constantly going, 'How did we do that?'" she said. "How did we shoot Madeline Kahn and 'Down in the Dumps' without a cut? When Peter and I see it, we're still holding our breaths!"

Madeline later referred to *At Long Last Love* as the most unpleasant shoot of her career, and in its aftermath, Bogdanovich says, "We sort of lost touch." That's a shame, because he had exciting plans for her: a solo record album much like the Porter album he'd produced for Shepherd, and a second musical based on the songs of Rodgers and Hart. It was not to be, he says: "There was a joke going on at the time that said if Peter Bogdanovich was seen near an orchestra, he should be arrested for loitering."

If You Loved as I Do

The Adventure of Sherlock Holmes' Smarter Brother (1975)

MADELINE'S DAYS OF BEING "SPOILED" BY HIT MOVIES WERE OVER, but her next picture seemed like an embrace from old friends—three of whom were Gene Wilder. For *The Adventure of Sherlock Holmes' Smarter Brother*, his debut as a film director, Wilder played the lead, enlisted a screenwriter he trusted (himself), and tailored roles to co-stars he loved: Madeline, Marty Feldman, and Dom DeLuise. Even before writing the script, he made sure they were willing and available; he's often said that he wouldn't have made the movie without them. As an added gift, Wilder shot in England, and Madeline had never been to Europe. Once again practically the only woman in the picture, she plays Jenny Hill, a London music hall artiste *and* opera singer who turns to Sigerson Holmes for help in a baffling case.

A hitherto unmentioned sibling to Sherlock and Mycroft, Sigerson is eager to prove his mettle as a detective—though doing so means pursuing a school of red herrings and seducing Jenny, who's incapable of telling the truth except when sexually aroused. It's precisely because of Jenny that Sherlock (or, as Sigi calls him, "Sheer Luck") doesn't want the case for himself. He means for his younger brother to fall in love, get married, and settle down. Sigi is far too resentful of Sherlock ever to tolerate any direct matchmaking, and so Sherlock orchestrates the entire case to its happily-ever-after coda, intervening at key moments to ensure that Sigi doesn't screw up. Sigi is smart but not *smarter*, and it isn't only because he's in his famous brother's shadow that he has to take what cases he can get. While he immediately sees through Jenny's imposture at their first meeting, he stumbles badly in other, more routine areas of detective work. Every misstep provokes Sigi's barely controlled hysteria, which in turn leads to high comedy. As a screenwriter, Wilder knew how to make himself look good.

And just as he approached monster movies, Wilder makes *Smarter Brother* less an outright parody than a loving application of Baker Street conventions to alternative circumstances. His Holmes and Watson remain true to their original personae, and Wilder builds his plot from three Conan Doyle stories. Sigerson's name is one of Holmes's aliases. To transport the audience to 1895, Wilder engaged cinematographer Gerry Fisher (Joseph Losey's collaborator on *The Go-Between*), as well as Oscar-winning scenic designer Terence March (*Dr. Zhivago, Oliver!*), who lavished meticulous period details on the film. Though the ingredients don't always gel, Wilder had accumulated a wealth of ideas and influences that poured onto the screen: not only Conan Doyle, but also Ealing Studios, the Marx Brothers, and even Ingmar Bergman, as he admitted in his director's commentary on the DVD of the film.

Above all, Wilder designed *Smarter Brother* as a showcase for the actors. A leading man and an action hero, Wilder's Sigi explores a range of emotions as he falls for Jenny, and he fences in three scenes, drawing on Wilder's theater training. Since both Madeline and DeLuise were opera fans, naturally they play opera singers, and the film's climax takes place during a performance of Verdi's *Un Ballo in Maschera*. Madeline and Feldman enjoyed working with each other on *Young Frankenstein*, so Wilder gave them scenes together now. Playing Sacker, Sigi's sidekick, Feldman gets some lunatic business, but he also shows an almost romantic sensitivity in his scenes with Jenny. Later to win fame as Rumpole of the Bailey, Leo McKern is a hilariously deranged Moriarty. Even Mel Brooks gets in on the act, with a brief voiceover. "Apart from *Young Frankenstein*, it was the best experience I've ever had in a movie," Wilder says.

However, he remembers, things got off to a rocky start, and again, Madeline's concern for her looks created trouble. "Madeline, who was trying on wigs the day before filming, suddenly went crazy, yelling and acting like a spoiled brat," Wilder says. "Fortunately for me, Dom DeLuise was there and calmed her down. The next morning, as we were all getting into costume and makeup, I was handed a note. It contained a drawing of a witch, with the message underneath that read: 'You will never see that lady again. Love, Mad.' And I didn't."[84]

Among Madeline's lesser-known movies, only *Judy Berlin* offers fans greater rewards than *Smarter Brother*. Seen today, the movie looks like a lacy valentine to Madeline, who's decked out in graceful costumes (and who's at her thinnest for the occasion) and elevated to leading-lady status. As she charts her course from "Miss Liar" to Mrs. Holmes, she is by turns artificial, vulnerable, sexy, and brave. (Look for her violent attacks on DeLuise in the *Ballo* sequence.) It's no accident that Brooks beefed up her role in their next picture together, *High Anxiety*, in which, once again, she plays a neurotic damsel in distress who develops into a love interest with heroic qualities.

Madeline summoned all her resources in *Smarter Brother*, including her more "serious" acting ability. When Jenny can't bring herself to tell Sigi the truth and turns to leave, Madeline was really crying. But seconds later, she joins Sigi in "Kangaroo Hop," an out-of-nowhere song-and-dance number that Wilder says is among his favorite scenes in the film. And because Wilder "could listen to Madeline sing all day,"[85] *Smarter Brother* is also a musical comedy. The names Jenny Hill and Bessie Bellwood (Jenny's alias) are those of real-life Victorian music-hall stars, and Jenny has hardly arrived at Sigi's door, answering to the name Bessie Bellwood, when he demands that she sing Bellwood's signature numbers. In the course of the film, Madeline also sings "Kangaroo Hop" (and its reprise), "Simply Crazy," and "You Don't Love As I Do" (joined by Sigi). (Some of these numbers, uncovered by assistant director Gail Mutrux, are associated with Gertie Millar, an Edwardian operetta star.) Madeline also sings portions of the *Ballo* pastiche. This is Madeline's most prominent singing role onscreen, and it makes abundant use of her classical training.

• • •

Shortly before leaving for London, Madeline began keeping the personal notebook in which she recorded her observations and experiences as part of her psychotherapy. She continued to write sporadically in the same spiral notebook for the next twenty years. Near the start, she wrote two pages of character analysis, a fascinating documentation of her approach to a role. Jenny was

> trying to control situation—manipulate him into helping—You're playing "the game of life" very unwillingly because you're not suited for it—but gamely and with spirit as long as it must be done I'll do it well—so it's thrust + parry I go—When he seems to be getting the upper hand—gamely + gently try to get the ball back as best you can which is with *charm*—let them try to break you but treat them as school boys-will-be-boys and change the subject (saying excuse me, of course): All this put over great *fear* [and] *insecurity in self-abilities* and *deservance* [sic] of winning so when they start

breaking thru this rather fragile, unsteady defense system, oh the panic that it's going to break down, all systems will start running amuck in just a few moments and not only will you revulse everyone around you, but you'll ruin any chance of getting help as well.

And of the song "Simply Crazy," she wrote:

A little girl—precocious—"*singing a song*"—testing and then reveling in her voice; + getting off on the sexy parts—her chance to pretend she's a "woman"; One *would* sneak out at night to sing this (even as the character who is playing that she's an adult) and, Jenny who can be 5 again when everyone loved her[.]

"To me," Wilder says, "the beauty of Madeline's performance was that she could sing English music hall and opera, plus do comedy and drama . . . all equally well. She could, occasionally, do comedy and drama at the same time." Essentially, he wrote a part for her that would give him, many times over, the same kind of pleasure that he found on the set of *Blazing Saddles* when she sang "I'm Tired."

Madeline's onscreen chemistry with Wilder is stronger—and given more chance to develop—here than in *Young Frankenstein*, and we see the true measure of her trust in him. In a dressing-room scene, Jenny makes it as easy as possible for Sigi to seduce her, so that she can tell him how to help her. He finds her dressed in pantalettes and a corset, reclining on a chaise longue. When, despite herself, she can't confide in him, he places a hand on her breast and massages it; as the scene continues, his hands roam, they kiss, and he undresses. It's one of the most intimate scenes Madeline ever filmed. Wilder has said that as originally written, the physical seduction didn't appear in the script, but that the scene fell flat without it. All the rest grew out of improvisation, and would serve only to enhance the widespread belief that Madeline and Wilder were lovers. Even now, Brooks insists that Wilder and Madeline must have been having an affair. "Gene, maybe he was just being brilliant," he says when reminded that Wilder consistently denies any romantic involvement. "She was working for him, so why not be in love with her, for the time they were working together?" (Told of this, Wilder replied in an e-mail, "I never thought or was aware that anyone thought Madeline and I were lovers. It certainly wasn't true.")

Madeline never found a better onscreen vehicle for all of her talents at once. In the *New York Times*, Vincent Canby hailed her as "possibly the funniest woman in films today."[86] Released at Christmas, just a year after *Young Frankenstein*, *Smarter Brother* received similarly appreciative reviews, and ranked twentieth on the list of top-grossing movies of 1975. That status was more than enough to win approval for Wilder's next picture. His new career was officially launched.

This situation put him in the enviable position of weighing options: whether to spend two years directing a single movie, or to make several pictures in the same amount of time by working under other directors. When other people didn't offer him good material, he'd write his own.[87] Madeline, like most actors, didn't have these options. She had to wait for the good scripts, and in-between times make a living with not-so-good scripts.

Neither good nor bad would come to her from Wilder. He didn't write another part for her, and they never worked together again. In his next movie, *The World's Greatest Lover*, he cast her friend Carol Kane as a naïve baker's wife who fixates on Rudolph Valentino. The part, as he wrote it, would have been wrong for Madeline, whose sophistication we'd seen too often. She and Wilder both would have had to work too hard to persuade us that, for once, she was unworldly and innocent. An additional female lead would have unbalanced the picture, and Wilder didn't write one. The leading roles for women in his subsequent writing and directing efforts went (understandably) to his wife, Gilda Radner. From an objective perspective, one can justify these choices easily, yet one wonders whether both Madeline's *and* Wilder's stars might have burned brighter if they'd explored further the creative partnership they'd barely begun. Madeline would learn this lesson again as the years went by: A colleague may love you as a person and admire you as a talent, but when it comes time to make a movie, if he's an artist and a pro, chances are he'll put the script ahead of friendship.

"Gene left me to *make* movies," Brooks says, "and Madeline left me to *star* in movies. In my pictures, she was always one of many, never the star. Then she realized that you can't star in something unless it's really good. You need a good script." It was a problem that would plague her for the rest of her movie career—beginning immediately.

What a Dog

Won Ton Ton, the Dog Who Saved Hollywood (1976)

HER INCOME GREATLY IMPROVED, MADELINE UPGRADED, MOVING from the apartment on East 73rd Street to a larger place at 975 Park Avenue. It was still, however, a rental, and when the building went co-op, she hesitated. New York City was in the midst of a fiscal crisis, making real estate investment riskier than usual. But Madeline was always "insecure, because of Paula," Jef Kahn says. "She always felt like she was going to lose everything. She was conservative in her investments, always concerned whether she would make it, when her next job would happen." Ultimately, Madeline decided to buy in, and the apartment would become "her sanctuary," as Jef calls it. She furnished it with books and a piano, and not long afterward, her friend Gail Jacobs, a decorator, would help her create an ideally tranquil, gracious environment. At Jef's home today, it's easy to spot which pieces were once his sister's. Madeline's tastes were her own, and Gail understood them perfectly. Nobody but Madeline Kahn could have owned these things.

By the mid-1970s, Jef was living at Twin Oaks, an intentional community in Virginia. He was always welcome to visit Madeline's home, and Paula visited her often, but on Park Avenue "There was *no* sense that there was a place for Paula!" Jef says. There was a guest room, but it was never designated as "Paula's room," or, for that matter, "Jef's room." "Paula could come and visit," he says, "but that was about it. No, there was no sense of inclusiveness." The purpose of the apartment was to shelter Madeline. By this time, she and Michael Karm had broken up, but the pattern she established with him would continue for the rest of her life: Boyfriends didn't move in with her, and she didn't move in with them. Jef approved of very few. "The one way you could bullshit her was to be in an intimate relationship with her. Then she was blinded," he says. "I saw a lot of men wanting the title of 'I was Madeline Kahn's boy-friend.' It's kind of a big mark on your bedpost. It's a bragging right. And I think she would allow herself to be mistreated—to a point." Madeline deserved better, but "[n]obody could" convince her of that, Gail Jacobs agrees.

Jef speculates about his sister's psychology. Doubtful of Paula's love, Madeline sought approval from the public, but that didn't satisfy her. She sought approval in intimate relationships, yet even then "you don't think you're really worthy of it, because from the start, you never got it from your mom," Jef says. These are tough words from a man who shared that mother, but in Madeline's case, there also were doubts about the love of two fathers and her sense that their emotional distance was her fault. The adults in Madeline's early life didn't just provide her with bad examples (conflict, divorce), and they didn't merely abandon her physically. In trying to construct a satisfying emotional life, she had no models and many deep wounds. Madeline spent the next few years de-veloping crushes on her co-stars. Sometimes her feelings were recip-rocated, sometimes not. She entered into relationships with "civilians" that, for various reasons, didn't last. With one exception, her love affairs didn't affect her work in any significant way—but that exception con-tributed to her early departure from the musical *On the Twentieth Century* (1978), the most painful episode of her career.

• • •

While Mel Brooks's analysis isn't entirely accurate—Madeline didn't ex-actly "leave him to become a star"—she did sign up for other directors' movies, in which the spotlight might be focused more narrowly on her. Star status meant more money, of course, but for her as an actor, it could also mean better roles and perhaps the chance to venture beyond come-dy. Her next movie met only one of her goals. She was the star, certainly, yet she was also "one among many"—more than ever before. *Won Ton Ton, the Dog Who Saved Hollywood* was yet another broad comedy, but one with virtually no laughs. She'd have been better off working with Brooks in his next picture, *Silent Movie* (also 1976), but he thought the woman's role was too insignificant for her, and he hired Bernadette Peters instead.

A satire of moviemaking in the 1920s, *Won Ton Ton* concerns a canine star that resembles Rin Tin Tin. Madeline plays Estie Del Ruth, an as-piring actress whose career is stymied because the dog in question will perform only at her command. Her co-star Bruce Dern has written that the script seemed like "the funniest thing I ever read,"[88] and the talent assembled for the production included two reliably funny second banan-as, Teri Garr and Art Carney; a reputable director, Michael Winner (*Death Wish*); and dozens of cameos by intriguing old-time stars, from Joan Blondell and Ann Miller to William Demarest and Johnny Weissmuller. *Won Ton Ton* may have promised to be an all-talking, no-dancing update on *Singin' in the Rain* (1952, still the best comedy about Hollywood), but the picture bombed. It deserved to. From Madeline's shrill Estie to Ron Leibman's shriller, cross-dressing burlesque of Rudolph Valentino, the lead characters are shallow, unsympathetic, and often offensive. In *Singin' in the Rain* terms, it's as if all of them are Lina Lamont—without the redeeming characteristics. The Hollywood legends, including several in their final film appearances, are poorly used, and most cameo turns are so brief the viewer has little time even to identify the actor. This insensitive treatment is particularly painful because Blondell gave the acting performance of her career just one year later, in Cassavetes's *Opening Night*. Who knows what the veteran stars might have done, given a chance?

Won Ton Ton depends in some measure on the audience's knowledge or appreciation of old movies. Dubious though the pleasures are in rec-ognizing the stars, the exercise is even less fun if one doesn't know them at all. The script, by Arnold Schulman and Cy Howard, grows out of (relatively) little-known history. As the novelty of movies wore off, Hol-lywood floundered until Rin Tin Tin sailed into town in 1922, on a tide that raised all boats. Leibman's character finds its origins in speculation about Valentino's sexuality (largely confirmed by later research), which movie buffs engaged in while the actor was alive. But there's a difference between gossiping about Valentino's "pink powder-puff" proclivities and watching the hysterical, effeminate character in *Won Ton Ton*. Leibman's performance is painful.[89]

While watching, one wonders for whom this picture was intended. Between the sometimes racy content and scenes depicting the dog's sui-cide attempts (noose, oven, etc.), *Won Ton Ton* is inappropriate for the younger audiences that typically enjoy dog movies, even as the hasty cameos and unfunny dialogue alienate grownups who care about clas-sic films. Perhaps most astonishing is Winner's inept handling of slap-stick gags. Short takes, jumpy cuts, bad lighting, bungled set-ups, and obscured payoffs make it difficult to tell what's going on, and thus make it impossible to laugh. Winner puts Madeline at the center of a particu-larly audacious rip-off of a gag from Buster Keaton's *Steamboat Bill, Jr.* (1928), in which a building's façade collapses on her without touching her, thanks to a fortuitously placed open doorway. Though the original could have been studied, or copied frame for frame, Winner doesn't appear to have taken the trouble to do so. His timing is off, and while it's not so far off as to risk Madeline's safety, the gag, like the façade, falls flat.

Through it all, Madeline "was just funny," Dern writes in his memoir. "And sexy and nasty but without ever advertising it or broadcasting it. She had a fabulous figure. She was as pretty as she wanted to be. She could be a mess if she wanted to be. She was a wonderful, wonderful actress." But, he adds, she "had no confidence in [her] ability at all."[90] In her notebook, Madeline wryly compared her acting with that of Gus, the dog in the title role. For example, while she had "to conjure up feelings," Gus could stare at a piece of liver off-camera. "He has his technique, I have mine," she wrote. "But there are certain things he wouldn't do (he's not a complete robot)—he wouldn't pee on Art [Carney]'s leg (neither would I do anything in poor taste)."[91]

She was spared the worst reviews, and in the *New York Times*, under the headline "Miss Kahn Lifts 'Won Ton Ton,'" Richard Eder lavished extraordinary praise on her, setting her alongside Keaton, Chaplin, and W. C. Fields by dint of her "unwavering purpose at right angles to reality, a concentration that she bears, Magoolike, through all kinds of unreasonable events. . . . The dog is all right. But Miss Kahn upstages him."[92]

Won Ton Ton was Paula Kahn's big break in Hollywood: she worked as an extra during a sequence at a movie screening and can be seen prominently seated behind Teri Garr and Billy Barty. But the box office verdict seemed clear. Madeline's name on the marquee couldn't save the picture, and even the superior returns for *Smarter Brother* indicated that, with or without her buddies from the Brooks movies, she was the kind of star audiences enjoyed but didn't go out of their way to see.

24

Live from New York

Saturday Night Live (1976)

AFTER *ADAM'S RIB*, MADELINE TURNED DOWN OFFERS TO APPEAR ON sitcoms. She never again guest-starred on one. She reasoned that if she became too regular a presence on television, she'd diminish her value in movies. Talk shows, on the other hand, could enhance that value by permitting her to promote her latest film projects, and she did gravitate to TV specials. In 1976, for example, she guest-starred on *The George Burns Special*, successfully taking the Gracie part in an old Burns-and-Allen routine. Treating the script as a score, she finds Allen's peculiar music and timing— to Burns's evident delight. The next year, she reunited with her *Comedy Tonight* friends Robert Klein and Peter Boyle for *Klein Time* for CBS. One sketch, "How Rembrandt Got Started," suggested that the artist debuted by painting cigar boxes. Madeline and Boyle played adulterous lovers, whom Rembrandt (Klein) painted *in flagrante*. By now, Madeline and Boyle were established stars who got star salaries, Klein says, but working together was still as "beautifully copacetic and fun" as ever. Madeline remained extremely judicious about other programs, but in 1976, she accepted invitations that resulted in two of the most important appearances of her career: *Saturday Night Live* and *The Carol Burnett Show*.

On May 8, two weeks before the premiere of *Won Ton Ton*, Madeline guest-hosted *Saturday Night Live*. This was near the end of the show's fabled first season, and several sketches are among Madeline's best-remembered work. In "Not for Ladies Only," Baba Wawa (Gilda Radner, doing Barbara Walters) finds herself flummoxed by interviewee Marlene Deutschland (Madeline, doing Dietrich again): Both "wadies" are unable to pronounce their *R*'s. This is, as the sketch's writer, Rosie Shuster, describes it, "a beautiful meeting of nonsense and wordplay and incredibly gifted actresses." Another sketch, by Marilyn Suzanne Miller, "Slumber

Party," concerns a know-it-all little girl named Madeline and her attempt to instruct her friends (Radner, Jane Curtin, and Laraine Newman) in the truth about sex. They refuse to believe her. Madeline also plays a drunken, embittered Pat Nixon in a Watergate satire written by Al Franken and Tom Davis.

Given the course that *SNL* would later take, the amount of musical material given to Madeline is remarkable. Today, the writers and producers seldom shape the show in a host's image to such a degree, especially when someone else (in this case, singer–songwriter Carly Simon) is officially the musical guest. But Madeline sings several numbers, and one sketch, a *Chinatown* parody with John Belushi, is entirely constructed around songs. Most strikingly, Madeline sings Weill's "Lost in the Stars" as a solo, with discreet accompaniment, in a tight spotlight, and "I Feel Pretty" from Bernstein's *West Side Story*, in costume as the Bride of Frankenstein—all the while mimicking Elsa Lanchester's lurching and hissing in the eponymous monster movie.[93]

Hosts would arrive at 30 Rockefeller Center on a Monday to meet with the show's staff and to discuss ideas for material. The writers would work—often through the night—until Friday, when sketches would be culled, reshaped, and rewritten. "On that show, you're rehearsing all the time," frequent host Buck Henry told an interviewer. "Even when you're just sitting around, you're rehearsing."[94] Though he seldom contributed much to the sketches, Henry is himself a writer; Madeline was not. For her first meeting with the *SNL* team, Madeline "came to the set with these incredibly big clown shoes," Shuster remembers. "She thought they were funny. It took delicacy to get her to give them up." That awkward moment aside, Shuster says, "She played it straight, beautifully. She was great. But that one moment, it was like—*oh, dear.*" Madeline "was able to do feminine stuff and yet project funny without coming across like Martha Raye and Jo Anne Worley on *Laugh-In*," Shuster says. "She had a dynamic tension of opposites, a female thing and a lot of power at the same time. It was a beautiful weave, and it came out funny."

Airing the night before Mother's Day, Madeline's first hosting gig marked the first time she worked with Gilda Radner. Their rapport shines in another highlight of the show, when the two women perform their impressions of a baby eating ice cream (Madeline) and a parrot (Gilda). Two of America's best-loved comics became, for those few minutes, a team, though they would have few subsequent opportunities to work together.[95] Close friends behind the scenes, they'd met sometime earlier—though not later than January 11, 1976, when Paula Kahn beat

Madeline to Studio 8H. Elliott Gould was the host of *SNL* that night, and in a recurring sketch, Radner's infatuation with him escalates to the point where they marry at the end of the show. But first Radner introduces Gould to her mother, played by Paula with few lines but warmly maternal grace. The sketch would remain the most significant credit on Paula's résumé, and the combination of her brief appearances in *Won Ton Ton* and *SNL* triggered her ambitions. For the next few years, she pursued her acting career more aggressively, with no qualms about trading on her daughter's fame.

25

So Glad We Had This Time Together

The Carol Burnett Show (1976)

IN AUGUST, MADELINE FLEW TO LOS ANGELES FOR HER OTHER SIGNIFI-
cant television appearance of the decade, an episode of the most popular
prime-time comedy-variety program of the day and the capper on CBS's
classic Saturday night lineup. Through *The Carol Burnett Show*, Madeline
could reach a bigger audience in a single night (as many as twenty million, Burnett says) than she could during the entire run of most of her
movies. The process was launched in the most flattering way possible,
with a fan letter from Burnett herself, handwritten on January 10, 1975,
shortly after Madeline appeared on *The Tonight Show* to promote *Young
Frankenstein*.

"Well, I meant every word!" Burnett says now. Madeline kept the letter in her desk until the time of her death, and she and Burnett refer to it
during her episode on *The Carol Burnett Show*, explaining how they know
each other before joining in a duet, "Friend." The two did in fact hit it off,
though theirs was the sort of show-business friendship that lasts as long
as the run of a show—in this case, a single week. Afterward, their mutual fondness endured without much follow-up. Still, the episode stands
out in Burnett's memory. Though it was merely one of dozens she taped
over the course of eleven years four decades ago, she can still quote the
dialogue verbatim. "It's one of my favorites," she explains. She'd wanted
to book Madeline at least since seeing *Paper Moon*, and she admired the
Brooks films, too. "My God, the talent is just enormous, and she's beautiful. And she sang up a storm."

Madeline's episode is almost a time capsule, containing elements that
represent the essence of *The Carol Burnett Show*: a question-and-answer
session with Burnett and the audience; a "Family" sketch about Eunice
(Burnett) and her soul-crushing mama (Vicki Lawrence); a song for the

guest (in this case, the duet with Burnett); a Mr. Tudball sketch featuring Tim Conway's relentless attempts to crack up Harvey Korman; and a spoof of old movies. By the show's tenth season, the production team, led by Burnett's then-husband, Joe Hamilton, had perfected the formula for presenting guest stars advantageously, astutely combining their well-known talents with others that had been otherwise untapped. And so, in addition to her celebrated comedic skill, Madeline's episode exploited her operetta background, of which few in the audience would have been aware (though Korman had heard her trilling between takes of *Blazing Saddles*).

Ordinarily, Burnett says, guests were booked three or four weeks in advance, giving the writers time to develop material. (In this case, Burnett and Hamilton probably knew *months* ahead of time, since Madeline attended a rehearsal and the taping of *Sills & Burnett at the Met* in March 1976.) Burnett doesn't remember whether she or the writers Dick Clair and Jenna McMahon came up with the idea, but somebody said, "Let's put her in with Eunice." The result was among the most substantial, significant roles Madeline ever played.

In the "Family" sketch, Madeline plays Mavis Danton, a hugely pretentious actress who has fled inhospitable Hollywood to direct and star in a community-theater production of *Mary, Queen of Scotland*. Eunice plays her lady-in-waiting. Dissatisfied with Eunice's work, Mavis comes to her home for a private rehearsal and coaching session. Eunice proves an eager but unpromising pupil, and of course her husband, Ed (Korman), and Mama distract and criticize her. Mavis loses her patience—and her hoity-toity accent—before storming out of the house. Burnett can't confirm that Madeline based Mavis Danton on Miriam Tulin, the Hofstra theater professor, but she says the character's look and voice came from Madeline. She encouraged Madeline to work with the show's designer, Bob Mackie, to create her costume, a fluttering dress in burgundy chiffon, always in movement—and thus always upstaging any other actors. Throughout the scene, Madeline explores the musicality of her voice, from queenly soprano to Queens-ly braying, and she sweeps and glides around the room in a parody of grace. Mavis's exalted goals for Eunice's scene work ("numb despair combined with a kind of doomed frivolity," "an urgent weakness") betray a profound familiarity with acting teachers, and her repeated exhortations to concentrate ("In our circles, in our circles!") became, at least for a while, a catchphrase among real-life actors.

Madeline sings with Burnett, as well as in one of four brief sketches that contrast the great stars of yore with their present-day decrepitude. According to a title card, this is the eighty-sixth installment of the popular *That's Entertainment!* movies, and by now MGM is scraping the barrel. Alongside Lawrence's ebullient Ann Miller, Conway's inept Fred Astaire, and Burnett's unsinkable Esther Williams, Madeline appears as Jeanette MacDonald in a spoof of *Rose-Marie*. As Nelson Eddy, Korman joins her at the climax of a parody of Friml's "Indian Love Call," here rendered as "We always used to oooh." Madeline clearly enjoys mocking the music on which she'd overdosed at the Hofbräuhaus, and vocally, she holds nothing back. Finally, the entire cast assembles in their "modern-day incarnations" for the finale. Madeline's Jeanette is frail and barely upright.[96]

The episode grants Madeline more screen time than many of her movies did, and in accordance with the show's traditions, it concludes with Burnett's theme song, "I'm So Glad We Had This Time Together," and her ear-tugging tribute to her late grandmother. Madeline signed Burnett's autograph book, and received a copy of that week's script. (Bound in velveteen, it remained one of her personal treasures.) There was one final tradition: "Every Friday night, my husband and I would take the guest out to dinner after the show, at Chasen's," Burnett says.

• • •

While not on par with the conflict between Eunice and Mama, perhaps, Madeline's relationship with her own mother had hit another rough patch. On Tuesday, September 7, 1976, Madeline drew a box around the words "BAD DAY" in her appointment book, jotting next to that, "Ma over." Jef Kahn believes that this was the occasion when Paula informed Madeline about a real-estate scheme gone awry in California. It began when Paula's tenants on Romeo Court trashed the house just as she wanted to sell it. Jef was summoned from Virginia to clean up the place, and Paula made the sale. Immediately thereafter and against all advice, she used the proceeds as a non-refundable deposit on a house in Santa Barbara. Jef, who saw the house, hesitates to call it a mansion, but he recalls a more lavish environment than Paula required. When he told her so on the way home, she began to drive faster, hitting one hundred miles per hour before he could calm her.

Only after paying the deposit did Paula explain that she expected Madeline to put up the rest of the money for her. Ever cautious, Madeline balked, and Paula lost both the house and the deposit. Now she came to break the news—and to ask Madeline to pay rent on her latest home. This was three weeks before Madeline's thirty-fourth birthday, and the timing of the visit was typical of Paula's method. Birthday cards sometimes arrived with bills enclosed for Madeline to pay.

Paula knew perfectly well how to make Madeline feel guilty if she didn't provide for her, but Madeline's concern wasn't entirely the result of manipulation. Paula was Madeline's confidante, adviser, coach, and also of course, her mother. Moreover, Madeline hadn't had the benefit of Hiller Kahn's perspective, which helped Jef to understand that "Paula's many desires [were] pretty much endless and insatiable," as Jef puts it. Soon, Madeline decided that her duty was "to take care of our mother" and pay all her expenses. She shared this decision with Jef one September afternoon when they were staying on Fire Island. Jef thought Madeline was taking on too much responsibility, too much pressure, but her mind was made up. (A friend, Denny McElyea, was taking photos that day, and captured Madeline and Jef in the midst of that conversation.) From that point forward, she gave Paula an allowance and paid many of her bills directly. Though she explained to Jef that Paula "couldn't take care of herself," it was another twenty years before Madeline fully grasped what the words meant.

26

Prelude to a Train Wreck

Marco Polo Sings a Solo and *She Loves Me* (1977)

FOR THE NEXT SEVERAL MONTHS—WELL INTO 1978—MADELINE worked nonstop, returning to the New York theater three times and, after the disappointment of *Won Ton Ton*, reuniting with Mel Brooks for a third film. As career strategy, this busy schedule made sense. She wasn't merely returning to her roots, but reminding people why she was a star. Things didn't turn out as she'd planned.

Ever an uptown girl, Madeline began with a rare excursion downtown to Joe Papp's Public Theater. For a limited engagement, she took the female lead, Diane, in the premiere of John Guare's absurdist comedy *Marco Polo Sings a Solo*, opposite Joel Grey as her husband and with a cast that also included Anne Jackson, Chris Sarandon, and a then-unknown Sigourney Weaver. Set in the distant future (1999) on an iceberg off the coast of Norway, *Marco Polo* mixes elements of drawing-room comedy and political satire with dense, lengthy speeches and an incomprehensible plot. Despite the challenges, Madeline was eager to work again with Papp, who'd provided her with her most gratifying stage role, Chrissy in *Boom Boom Room*. And to actors at the time, Grey says, the Public was "a magical box that was doing the most edgy and unusual plays. You felt privileged to be a part of something new."

Guare's script was perhaps a little *too* new, however. Though the playwright had already written *The House of Blue Leaves* and co-written (with Mel Shapiro) the Tony-winning book to the musical *Two Gentlemen of Verona*, both those plays are more conventional than *Marco Polo*, and in 1977, little of Guare's work was familiar territory. Guideposts, if there were any, would have to be found during the rehearsal process, itself complicated by Guare's "fluid" approach to writing, Sarandon says. Each morning, the cast would receive new script pages—sometimes as many as twenty. To facilitate collating, Papp's staff copied new pages on paper of different colors: "The joke was that they were running out of colors at the Public Theater office," Sarandon remembers. "Literally, we'd say, 'On Vermillion 13, Puce 84.' It was a rainbow of a script."

Shapiro directed, as he'd done for *Two Gentlemen* (also produced originally by Papp). After about six weeks, Shapiro, Guare, and Papp decided to freeze act 1 and run it, though it was extremely long, about sixty pages. After the run-through, the cast assembled onstage. They could hear Papp and Guare muttering, and after a long wait, Shapiro leaned on his desk and announced, "We talked it over, and we think what we need to do is cut the first 20 pages." Madeline immediately burst into tears. Her "visceral response" shocked the other actors, Sarandon says. Madeline apologized: "I know, I know, this is just about my ego, *but that's why I'm doing this*!" By which she meant working in theater in the first place. "It was such pure Madeline," Sarandon says, "because she was at times painfully honest about her feelings, but at the same time extremely incisive in her estimation of the temperature in the room and also where we all needed to be in the moment."

Calling Madeline "tender," "guarded," and "fragile," Grey says, "There was something that frightened her more than we're all frightened, before we open in a play." He was struck by the difference between her screen persona ("It was like she had no fear of really going wild") and the woman he met in *Marco Polo*. "In person, she was very—*withdrawn* is probably another word." Sarandon spent time with Madeline outside the theater. From what he observed, "When something affected her, she reacted. She didn't hold onto it and wait and wait and let it fester." He found her combination of honesty, intelligence, and vulnerability "devastating . . . in the sense that it's very appealing."

Climbing all over the iceberg set designed by John Wulp, Madeline "came within inches of breaking her leg . . . before stretching herself out like a dead haddock on a vast cake of ice, where I feared she'd be quick-frozen," Walter Kerr wrote in a late-season essay for the *Times*. Parenthetically, he added, "I like Miss Kahn, and I don't want any harm to come to her." His real purpose, however, was to reflect on memorable scenery in recent shows, and he suggested that some designers "seem to have turned against actors, even to the point of doing them bodily harm, and some have lost touch with what used to be called reality."[97] But then, in an earlier essay, Kerr declared that *Marco Polo* "took place on a planet with which I am unfamiliar."[98]

"I think we in large part confused the critics," Grey says now. "They didn't like it. They didn't get it. When you feel left out, you get cranky." Indeed, Clive Barnes began his review in the *Times* by admitting he didn't understand the play. Ordinarily in such circumstances, he wrote, "you try to bluff it." In this case, "I had no idea what Mr. Guare was trying to do to my mind, which was possibly my loss rather than Mr. Guare's fault. But I rather doubt it." Barnes was more generous to the "distinguished," "marvelous," "lovely cast." Reserving the highest praise for Grey and Jackson, he wrote, "Madeline Kahn as the wife, a blasé ex-concert pianist of a genius and Chris Sarandon as a mystery man are also, when the playwright permits, fitfully delightful."[99]

In conversation thirty-five years later, critic Michael Feingold recalled a long speech in which Madeline's character imagines that composers are flashing her. "You have to hear that monologue in her voice," he says, "and I always see this troubled little face, and this funny body language, which is saying, 'I want to assert this to you, but I don't want to be assertive.'" Referring to Zerlina in Mozart's *Don Giovanni*, who "wants and doesn't want," he added, "That may be why she made such a strong impression on me in the Guare play, because his plays are full of that: He wants to be funny and yet he doesn't want to be funny. 'This is what I believe. *This* is what I believe?'"

Marco Polo closed on schedule, on March 6. Madeline followed up with another limited engagement, a semi-staged concert revival of Bock and Harnick's *She Loves Me*, at New York's Town Hall. The cast—including top-notch musical comedy stars Barry Bostwick, Rita Moreno, and George Rose—dressed formally and used scripts and music stands, which director John Bowab ingeniously configured to represent props and set pieces. Today, this kind of performance is almost routine, thanks to the successful *Encores!* series, but in 1977, it was uncharted territory, and the company had only one week to rehearse before opening to the critics and the public. For Madeline, the process was especially stressful, since Paula was on hand at all times, "not underfoot but sort of omnipresent," remembers Michael Hayward-Jones, a cast member as well as the assistant stage manager. "My feeling of it was that [Paula] was trying to be helpful, and her helpfulness often got in both of their ways." What's more, this was one of Madeline's first visits with Paula since the failed real-estate deal the summer before.

Madeline "had a lot to prove, going from Broadway to film, and now she was back in New York," Hayward-Jones says. She was once again playing a role created by Barbara Cook, whose longtime accompanist, Wally Harper, conducted the concerts, thus inviting comparisons not only to Cook but also to Madeline's own early triumph as Cunegonde. The show's choreographer, Joseph Patton, believes her agent may have advised against *She Loves Me*, spelling out the risks in a low-paying theater gig with limited rehearsal, so she'd have been insecure from the start.

Generally, Hayward-Jones found Madeline "aloof but pleasant," but during the brief run she displayed several flashes of prima donna temperament of a kind she'd rarely if ever indulged before. The worst came just before the opening-night performance, when Moreno generously called her over to speak with a reporter who was interviewing her. Madeline high-hatted them both, and Moreno took her aside, explaining that her behavior was inappropriate. Madeline broke down. "I can't go on," she said, retreating to her dressing room. Only Patton dared to go in. He found her in tears. "I know how vulnerable you are. I get it," he said, and he talked about fear and control. Gently, he added, "I think we're pretty close to half-hour." "Then I need to get ready," Madeline replied.

Writing for the *Times*, Richard Eder devoted one-third of his review to Madeline's performance, praising her above all as an actress.[100] In *Time*, T. E. Kalem gave her a mixed review: praise for her singing, but for her acting, an accusation of self-caricature. Thus, only five years after Madeline's feature-film debut, her work was already sufficiently well known that the critic from the leading news magazine could make such a charge. When an actress isn't recognizable, nobody can tell whether she's caricaturing herself. More ominously for Madeline, Kalem's review appears to be the first suggestion that she might be too old for a part: "She lacks the vernal innocence intrinsic to the role."[101]

A pirate recording, despite rather dim sound, reveals Madeline in radiant voice and a fully realized character. Surely benefitting from Harper's experience with Cook, Madeline's account of "Vanilla Ice Cream," alternating song with speech and concluding with an elaborately ornamented cadenza, has the audience in stitches. Patton says, "What she did with that role was astounding, with no rehearsal. There was not a moment that was not absolutely truthful and honest in her performance. Every choice she made was based on what the other actors were giving her." Her rendition of "Help Me Find My Shoe" was also brilliant and very funny, Hayward-Jones recalls, but her performances varied wildly, as she altered her lines, blocking, and characterization. "It was always what we called 'the show *du jour*' once we began performing. We even had 'the key *du jour,'"* and Harper prepared three arrangements for each of her songs.

Both director Bowab and Bostwick adapted to Madeline's methods, but George Rose lost patience with her entirely. Actor–playwright Ed Dixon says that, for the rest of his days, the otherwise genial Rose ("everybody's best friend," as Hayward-Jones puts it) refused to hear Madeline's name spoken in his presence. "George was old-school: 'This is the way you do it, you do it consistently,'" Hayward-Jones says, whereas Madeline "never gave the same performance twice. There's nothing wrong with that, but in other people who expect consistency, show to show, it can be disconcerting." Harold Prince would react similarly, blaming Madeline's time in Hollywood for a lack of discipline in her stage work. According to Dixon, Rose ascribed Madeline's behavior to another cause: cocaine abuse.

27

The Drug Rumor

GEORGE ROSE WAS MURDERED IN 1988; I NEVER MET HIM. IT'S IMPOS-
sible to know whether he originated the drug rumor, or whether he
merely repeated it because it seemed to explain Madeline's behavior,
which fell short of his standards of professionalism. But the rumor
spread, and long before I began researching this book, I'd heard it often.
For many years after Madeline's next theatrical venture, the Broadway
musical *On the Twentieth Century*, if you walked into a piano bar in New
York and asked why Madeline Kahn left that show prematurely, you'd
be told, with absolute authority, that she was a cocaine addict. Even
Walter Willison heard this story and believed it to be true, though when
pressed, he admitted he'd never seen Madeline doing drugs or known
anyone who claimed direct knowledge of her alleged addiction. He and
a few other veteran Broadway actors tried to find witnesses for me, and
they failed. Ed Dixon came up with just one person, who refused to
speak with me or to let Dixon give me his name.

Everyone I spoke with who knew Rose used the same words to describe him: "old school" and "by the book." Madeline was neither. Certainly cocaine might explain her stage performances in 1977–78, which
some (but not all) eyewitnesses considered "erratic." And certainly some
people with whom Madeline associated at the time, both in Hollywood
and in New York, did abuse cocaine, particularly around the set of *Saturday Night Live*. But to imagine Mel Brooks on cocaine is impossible (or
terrifying). And as Rosie Shuster points out, Madeline was Gilda Radner's
friend, not John Belushi's, and Gilda "called cocaine 'God's dandruff,'"
Shuster remembers. Chris Sarandon and Robert Allan Ackerman, friends
both to Madeline and to Gilda, agree: Gilda didn't do drugs. "She did a
lot of other ridiculous, crazy things to herself," Ackerman says. "She was
bulimic, she was anorexic, and she drank a lot, but she never did drugs.

I never saw Madeline do anything. I don't even remember her smoking a joint." Sarandon worked with Madeline immediately before *She Loves Me* and *Twentieth Century*, and says he never saw her affected by anything other than her own nature. "She was a very highly tuned bird, Madeline," he says. "Birdlike in the sense that she had a very delicate emotional constitution. She was mercurial in some ways. . . . I never had the sense that she was under the influence of anything but her own demons."

While Madeline's performances in *Twentieth Century* reportedly varied, it's telling that neither that show's director, Harold Prince, nor its music director, Paul Gemignani, ever suspected drug abuse. Gemignani reminds me that, from the orchestra pit, he was staring right at Madeline at every performance. If she behaved oddly, he'd have noticed. Prince never heard the rumor before I asked him about it, and Madeline's co-star, Kevin Kline, told me that he hadn't heard the rumor, either, until Prince repeated it, asking Kline whether he knew anything about what "Madeline's biographer" had said a few days earlier.

Kline also worked with George Rose, in *The Pirates of Penzance*. Because of his work with Madeline but also his experience of other singers, he doesn't believe the rumor. Before switching to a theater major at Indiana University, Kline studied music as a pianist, and worked on crews for the school's acclaimed opera program. "I knew a lot of singers at that point," he says. "I just think, if she was on a drug, cocaine would be the *last*! Notwithstanding the fact that it was the drug of choice for many rock'n'roll singers, but they're not worried about what an opera singer is worried about." In an e-mail he explained, "For a trained singer like Madeline, the vocal cords, voice box, sinuses, etc., are the center of your universe and you protect them, coddle them, and avoid anything that would compromise them in any way." One opera singer just a few months older than Madeline, baritone Richard Stilwell, was active professionally during the 1970s. He agrees that cocaine was far from prevalent among singers at the time, although some did smoke marijuana. "Even then, there was that addictive stigma attached to cocaine among my opera friends," Stilwell says. "Those serious about mounting a career did not go there."

A few years after *Twentieth Century*, while preparing the role of Nathan in *Sophie's Choice*, Kline studied the symptoms of cocaine abuse. "I went to Phoenix House and studied all the symptoms, and in retrospect, I just never saw [in Madeline] the sweaty upper lip or the [hyperactivity] that cocaine can do to people. She seemed consummately professional. . . . I can't imagine her doing anything that would be that potentially harmful to her vocal cords or any part of her vocal apparatus."

Maris Clement, another colleague from *Twentieth Century*, says, "She never pulled cocaine and went into the bathroom. Her mother was a voice teacher; she wasn't going to wreck her voice." Clement often spent time with Madeline and never saw her or her close associates doing cocaine. Although she was not yet the licensed therapist that she is today, Clement came up with a diagnosis other than drug abuse in Madeline's case. "Those notes were very difficult to sing," she says. "It took an unusual voice, and also I think what happened was that Madeline got scared of it, and then she became more nervous, and she started getting panicky." This made the score all the more challenging for Madeline, and offstage, relationship troubles—among myriad other pressures—may also have played a role. Clement herself had experienced panic attacks, and after she saw Madeline onstage "look[ing] like a deer in the headlights," she urged Madeline to see a therapist, who confirmed her (at the time) lay diagnosis. Though Clement and the therapist both tried to help Madeline, she left *Twentieth Century* two weeks later.

If Madeline's drug habit was bad enough to threaten her career, then it's probable that at some point she'd have sought help. She never discussed a drug problem with her closest associates, such as her brother and her best friend, Gail Jacobs. Neither did they see her doing drugs or coping with recovery. On the contrary, Jacobs remembers Madeline's being so disciplined that she never drank red wine, for fear that it would stain her teeth, and when she did drink white wine, she limited herself to a single glass. Madeline's appointment books don't show her going into a rehabilitation facility, and during the period 1974–97, there are no blocks of unaccounted time sufficient to accommodate a stay at a clinic. Yet the rumors persist, and it hasn't helped Madeline's reputation that between *She Loves Me* and *Twentieth Century* she flew back to that well-known den of vice, Hollywood.

28

Dames in Distress, Pigs in Space

High Anxiety, The Cheap Detective, and the Muppets (1977–78)

BOTH OF MADELINE'S NEXT MOVIES WERE ELABORATE PARODIES. MEL Brooks's *High Anxiety* sends up Hitchcock classics such as *Spellbound, Vertigo,* and *The Birds,* while Neil Simon's *The Cheap Detective* offers a more affectionate takeoff of Humphrey Bogart's greatest hits.

High Anxiety was Brooks's first picture since *Silent Movie,* and now Madeline returned to the fold, playing the troubled Victoria Brisbane. A Hitchcock blonde, Victoria is the most glamorous and subtle of Madeline's collaborations with Brooks. Victoria serves, more or less, as a straight man to the rest of the characters (played by a cast that includes Harvey Korman, Cloris Leachman, Ron Carey, and Brooks himself). They get most of the comic business and the best-remembered lines, and Brooks sings the film's only musical number. Nevertheless, Madeline grabs a few good scenes, including a phone call she mistakenly believes to be obscene (and thoroughly enjoys), and a romp through airport security while disguised as an elderly Jewish woman. *High Anxiety* is the only one of Madeline's films with Brooks in which she's not the object of a penis joke, and apart from her drivers license, it's the only recorded proof of her ability to drive a car. She does so in a scene in which Victoria goes to Golden Gate Park to meet Dr. Richard H. Thorndyke (Brooks), who's running from the law. From her first entrance, Victoria carries a Louis Vuitton purse, and by the time she arrives at the park, her brand loyalty has expanded. Now she's carrying the Vuitton purse, wearing a Vuitton pantsuit, and driving a Vuitton car. It's a terrific sight gag, and its humor wasn't lost on fashion-conscious Madeline. Every time she got out of the car, Brooks remembers, she'd break up laughing.

She won the approval of no less than Hitchcock himself, whom Brooks consulted while making the picture. Madeline looked so much like Grace Kelly, Kim Novak, and Tippi Hedren that when Hitchcock saw *High Anxiety*, he asked where Brooks found Madeline. "You know she's not really blonde," Brooks replied, teasing him. "You never saw a woman that wasn't blonde!" Hitchcock paused, then said, "That's true, that's true."

The hair color Madeline used in *High Anxiety* was actually called "Hitchcock Blonde," Brooks says, and during filming, she remarked to him that he took greater care to make her look good than other directors did (presumably she was referring to Bogdanovich). "I knew she had all the features," Brooks says now. "You just had to paint it and light it properly. . . . Even in *Blazing Saddles*, I said, 'She's still got to be really handsome, she's got to be German-beautiful.' And she was." Brooks took particular care with backlighting, shooting Madeline from the forehead down, giving her flattering hairstyles, making up her eyes to bring them out. "Because I knew she was a great comedian, but you don't necessarily gotta make her funny looking," he says.

High Anxiety gave Madeline the pleasure of looking both gorgeous and funny, since she also got to wear Victoria's little-old-lady disguise. The airport scene requires Madeline to create another character, entirely different from Victoria and from the majority of Madeline's other roles. She played age rarely, and the Yiddish accent she uses makes this the most overtly Jewish character she would play until she appeared in Wendy Wasserstein's play *The Sisters Rosensweig* in 1992. Here, Madeline develops a character that is basically the wife of Brooks's famous 2,000 Year Old Man, and Madeline has a terrific time with the scene.

Victoria was Madeline's largest role in Brooks's films, allowing her to develop a more rounded character. In her first scene, Victoria is not merely worried about her father, she's downright frantic. Terrified that she's being followed or observed, she orders Thorndyke to draw the curtains—but to crawl on the floor to do so. (Brooks says this scene also required multiple takes because Madeline kept laughing.) Victoria is paranoid at the outset and neurotic to the end, but once she kisses Thorndyke, her confidence and courage begin to grow. When she's faced with real threats—getting through airport security, thwarting an attempt to murder her father—she keeps her cool, more or less. We see a woman who is no longer sheltered, but instead excited by new experiences. Not least of these is the "obscene" phone call, when a psychopathic thug (co-screenwriter Rudy De Luca) tries to kill Thorndyke at a pay phone, and she can hear only his gurgles and gasps. Victoria is less inwardly vulnerable than Lili von Shtupp and less outwardly frigid than Elizabeth in

Young Frankenstein (a kindred character in some ways). Playing Victoria wasn't exactly the "dimensional" acting Madeline yearned to do, but it was a step in the right direction.

Brooks studied psychology briefly in college and has undergone therapy. Much of *High Anxiety*, set in the Institute for the Very, Very Nervous, is a spoof of psychiatry that feels like a patient's payback. However, he says that, when writing, "I don't examine the chemistry. I just enjoy the result. . . . I'm not gonna take it upon myself to break down Madeline's unconscious. Much too complicated." Brooks's study of Hitchcock, on the other hand, is on full display. His obvious inspiration is *Spellbound*, in which the new director of a mental asylum grapples with a dark secret, just as Thorndyke does. Thorndyke's "high anxiety" is vertigo, but the telltale word is never mentioned. Other memorable scenes refer to *Psycho* and *The Birds*. Thorndyke's name echoes that of Cary Grant's character, Roger O. Thornhill, in *North by Northwest*. Another Hitchcock trope, the director's cameo, is inflated here, since the director is the star of the entire picture. And, on Hitchcock's recommendation, Brooks hired Albert Whitlock to create matte paintings of the institute. Upon hearing Whitlock's English accent, Brooks asked him to play Victoria's father.[102]

At the box office, *High Anxiety* performed respectably, the seventeenth-highest grossing picture of 1977, though it didn't reach the level of *Blazing Saddles* or *Young Frankenstein*—or even that of *Silent Movie* (twelfth-highest grossing in 1976). Not all the reviews were rapturous. Describing Madeline's Victoria as "the kind of girl who has everything— and it all matches," *People* magazine dismissed *High Anxiety* as "a takeoff that, despite a few funny traumas, never quite leaves the runway."[103] In the *Times*, Vincent Canby praised the movie, calling it "as witty and as disciplined as *Young Frankenstein*," and calling Madeline "a woman who can be gloriously funny simply by attempting to control an upper lip. She's a cocktail waitress' loving concept of 'the real Kim Novak.'"[104]

• • •

Taking only a three-day pause after *High Anxiety*, Madeline shot her scenes for *The Cheap Detective* in little more than a week. The picture (released in 1978) found her working with Neil Simon, who was, like Brooks, an alumnus of Sid Caesar's writing staff. (Caesar himself plays a brief role in the film.) Like Simon's first mystery spoof, *Murder by Death* (1976), *Cheap Detective* featured an all-star cast and exploited Peter Falk's loving imitation of Bogart. As Simon later observed, studio heads ordinarily reject parodies, because they depend on the audience's familiarity with the original.[105] However, after *Murder by Death*'s success, producer Ray Stark persuaded Columbia Pictures to green-light the second film, also directed by Robert Moore. With faithful recreations of the sets of *The Maltese Falcon* and *Casablanca* (including some of the original light fixtures from Rick's Place), *The Cheap Detective* mashes together some of Bogart's best-known films.

The incorporation of plot lines from different movies required ingenuity on Simon's part. Since another *Maltese Falcon* spoof, *The Black Bird*, failed just three years earlier, it made sense to set *The Cheap Detective* apart as much as possible. Thus Falk's Sam Spade character, called Lou Peckinpaugh, solves the murder of his partner and juggles a search for a legendary treasure (here, eggs with jewels in them) with an attempt to secure the necessary paperwork for his ex-lover's husband to open a French restaurant. He does this in much the same way that Rick Blaine secures Victor Laszlo's escape from Casablanca— which is to say despite the interference of a Nazi officer and his henchmen. (These Nazis, however, are stationed in Cincinnati.) Simon also gives a nod to *The Big Sleep* and *To Have and Have Not* as Falk shuttles among story lines and glamorous women.

Madeline plays a variation on *Maltese Falcon*'s Brigid O'Shaughnessy (Mary Astor), a duplicitous dame in distress. Whereas Brigid changes her name only once, Madeline's character is so deceitful that she can't keep her aliases straight. In her first scene, she runs through eight names before arriving at "Carmen Montenegro. That's my last one, I promise!" She's lying, of course. Before the picture is through, she'll have changed her name—and hair color—several more times. She also claims she's her identical twin and her father's wife, one of the few references that have more to do with contemporary movies (*Chinatown*, 1974) than with classics.

Madeline's material in *Cheap Detective* is less bawdy than that given to her in Brooks's films. While some of the other women come onto Peckinpaugh or torment him with tales of their intimate relations with other men (another running joke), Mrs. Montenegro is comparatively demure. And in a succession of gorgeous period costumes, Madeline is even more glamorously photographed than in *High Anxiety*. Simon's snappy rhythms posed no challenge to her, and having been denied the chance to work with him when he was brought in to revise *How Now, Dow Jones*, she hoped to do so more often. In the shorter term, taking a role in *The Cheap Detective* after *Won Ton Ton* was a smart career move. The movie was an easy way to reassert herself in Hollywood. If this film and *High Anxiety* were hits, so much the better, but if either picture flopped, no one would blame her. As further incentive, her friends Eileen Brennan and Dom DeLuise co-starred.

Another movie that rewards rediscovery by Madeline's fans, *The Cheap Detective* garnered generally good reviews and came in twenty-first at the box office for 1978, though it hasn't enjoyed the kind of lasting popularity of Madeline's spoofs with Brooks, or even *Murder by Death*. Vincent Canby's review in the *Times* identifies one possible reason for the movie's limited success: "[M]ostly, watching it is like being with a group of friends as they recall their favorite movie-going experiences. It's not as a movie that it's so much fun, but as a multimillion-dollar, all-star parlor game."[106] In so far as the movie *is* a parlor game, Madeline's work falls somewhere below Falk's and Louise Fletcher's spot-on impressions of Bogart and Ingrid Bergman. Madeline doesn't mimic Mary Astor so much as she creates a character who is all artifice. At the end of the picture, she explains that she just wants the money so that she can get her hair done; after all those dye-jobs, Mrs. Montenegro is a multi-colored fright. Yet what sets Madeline's performance apart is her eyes. She tries her best, but Mrs. Montenegro can't *quite* control her nervous glances.

• • •

In midsummer, Madeline flew to London for the first of her appearances with Jim Henson's Muppets, who proved boon companions for the remainder of her career. First came a guest-starring role on *The Muppet Show*, then shooting its second season. Produced in Britain by ITV and syndicated internationally, the program had become a worldwide hit in its first season, and exposure to audiences beyond America appealed to Madeline. Then, in September, she taped the first of her *Sesame Street* appearances. Among her most charming performances, these built a lasting fan base among viewers too young to see her films.

Most episodes of *The Muppet Show* entail a good deal of "backstage" material, as the Muppets prepare their weekly vaudeville routines and interact with their guest star. For Madeline's episode, the backstage plot takes a dramatic turn when Gonzo the Great (Dave Goelz) misunderstands a kind word from her and falls hopelessly in love. Although Miss Piggy (Frank Oz) has no particular use for Gonzo, she's indignant to learn that he's given his affection to another woman. In fact, he intends to marry Madeline. Before Piggy can wreak vengeance (which might have been fun to watch), Madeline sets Gonzo straight: She likes him, but only as a friend. He sings a maudlin "Wishing Song" but soldiers on, and thus ends his brief crush on Miss Piggy.

Meanwhile, Madeline stars in two "onstage" turns. A musical number finds her in a harem, surrounded by gigantic Muppets (actually dancers in costume) with outsize feet. The choreography features the constant threat of Madeline being stepped on. In a subsequent sketch, another gigantic Muppet sets out systematically to ruin Madeline's stroll in the park. He causes a rainstorm, knocks over trees, and shoots a songbird, but she's unflappable and gets the better of him. The episode first aired on October 1, 1977.[107]

Madeline's first assignments on *Sesame Street* proved even more congenial to her gifts, most especially the "echo song," "Sing After Me," that she performs with Grover (Frank Oz). Cuddling the Muppet on her lap much as she would a small child, she explains what an echo song is (as Tony Geiss's lyrics helpfully remind us, "You sing what I sing / Follow the leader and sing after me") and promises him "a really, really swell time." Once the song is underway, however, Madeline gets carried away, tossing off roulades and a trill that Grover can't match. "Show-off," he grumbles—yet there's nothing mean-spirited about the way she outsings him, and the number ends in a hug.

On October 8, Madeline also returned to *Saturday Night Live* for a second guest-hosting gig, which turned out to be less artistically rewarding than her first turn. Throughout the episode, the writing feels tired, especially in a long, almost laugh-free sketch in which Madeline plays Bianca Jagger dispensing "wisdom" at a dinner party with other jet-set icons. Far more satisfying is Marilyn Suzanne Miller's character-driven sketch, in which Madeline and Gilda Radner complain about men over a bottle of wine. The show's highlight is "Bad Opera," in which Leonard Pinth-Garnell (Dan Aykroyd) introduces *The Golden Note*, "as difficult to sing as it is to listen to." With a little help from the sound effects team, Madeline, dressed as a Valkyrie, caps a quick mish-mash of Wagner themes with a high note "of such pitch, tone, and character, and it must be sustained for so long, that it causes 'larynx lock': The singer's larynx simply locks onto the note *forever*" (actually more than two minutes, until the commercial break). The sketch ends as EMS technicians administer oxygen to Madeline and lead her away, while Pinth-Garnell gloats, "That was bad, wasn't it? Delightfully bad!"

• • •

Madeline's busy professional schedule during this period may have been motivated in part by something having nothing to do with her career. She had ended her relationship with Ted Bentell, an executive with a garment company and her first long-term boyfriend since Michael Karm. At one point, Bentell confronted her with a choice: either marry him or break up with him. As she explained to *People* magazine in an interview the next year, Madeline was too mindful of her parents' divorces to commit. She and Bentell separated, and by the time the *People* article appeared, he'd already married another woman. Only in 1979 did Madeline begin another long-term relationship, with Dr. Myles Gombert.

But there was a practical strategy behind Madeline's activity, as well. The Monday after Thanksgiving, 1977, Madeline started rehearsals for *On the Twentieth Century*. By making two movies and appearing on television, she sought to bring in money and to keep her profile high among audiences outside New York. Working on *Marco Polo* and *She Loves Me* allowed her to stretch her stage muscles before returning to Broadway, not as a featured actress but as the marquee star of a musical comedy written with her in mind. Yet the show proved the biggest setback of her career, and to this day, controversy surrounding *On the Twentieth Century* continues to damage her reputation.

29

Train Wreck

On the Twentieth Century (1978)

ON THE TWENTIETH CENTURY IS AN ADAPTATION OF BEN HECHT AND
Charles MacArthur's play *Twentieth Century* (1932), itself an adaptation
of Charles Bruce Milholland's unpublished play, *Napoleon of Broadway*.[108]
Oscar Jaffee, a theatrical producer down on his luck, hopes to resuscitate
his fortunes with a new play, but to attract backers and guarantee his
success, he needs the right leading lady: Lily Garland, his ex-mistress, an
actress whom he discovered, dominated, and drove away years earlier.
Now she's a Hollywood star. Finagling his way into the train compart-
ment adjacent to hers on the Twentieth Century Limited from Chicago
to New York, he uses wiles, blandishment, and physical force to persuade
Lily to work with him again. A munificent check from a fellow passenger
gives Oscar the backing he needs, and Lily is ready to sign—but the bene-
factor turns out to be a religious fanatic recently escaped from an asylum.
Only by faking his own death does Oscar win over Lily.

Originally directed by George Abbott, Hecht and MacArthur's farce
has been revived twice on Broadway (1950 and 2004) and adapted for
television three times between 1949 and 1956, yet it's Howard Hawks's
film adaptation (1934) that endures as a landmark among screwball
comedies. In adapting the piece as a musical, Betty Comden and Adolph
Green had to keep their hands off the movie, because the rights still belonged to Columbia Pictures. The film made a star of Carole Lombard,
and in Comden and Green's hands, the role is still a tour-de-force offering a wide comedic range, as one Mildred Plotka is transformed into
a glamorous screen goddess who has absolutely no intention of having
anything more to do with Oscar. Playing Lily would give Madeline the
opportunity to stammer like a schoolgirl and swan like a diva, while
engaging in knockabout antics—and, unlike every Lily who came before
her, she'd have to sing her guts out.

Comden and Green had struck gold before with show-biz tales of yore; after all, they devised the screenplay for *Singin' in the Rain*. For *On the Twentieth Century*, they contributed book and lyrics to an ambitious score by Cy Coleman, the composer of such shows as *Wildcat* (starring Lucille Ball, 1960) and *Sweet Charity* (1966). Coleman believed *On the Twentieth Century* required something unlike the usual musical-theater vocabulary, or even pastiche of '20s and '30s jazz music, of which there had been plenty on Broadway lately. Kander and Ebb's *Chicago*, for example, is set in 1925, and it ended its two-year run in August 1977. As Comden and Green explained in an essay published in the *Times* on the morning of *On the Twentieth Century*'s New York premiere, the show's musical language grew out of Oscar and Lily, "two larger-than-life, extravagant, egomaniacal giants of the theater."[109]

Looking with Coleman for "an overblown, bravura musical style," they arrived at European opera traditions, hastening to say they hadn't written an opera, merely "a demanding score." There's even a sextet, not unlike the one in *Lucia di Lammermoor* (though this one is about money, not love, both numbers do involve contracts), and Comden and Green described Oscar and Lily's finale as "a kind of Love-Death duet," a reference to the *Liebestod* aria from Wagner's *Tristan und Isolde*. Oscar, by turns domineering and romantic, becomes Méphistophélès and Roméo in a single baritone; Lily is exalted beyond the status of movie star to that of prima donna, with the temperament and high notes to match. But the stakes in their drama are pettier than those in an opera, and the music mocks them at every step.

Keeping jazz to a minimum, Coleman cut loose his gift for invention, with the result that the vocal lines for Lily are especially strenuous, from *Sprechgesang* to chest voice to coloratura, through a very wide range. Tempos are frequently rapid—after all, on a speeding train, what could be more natural than *accelerandi*? Few actresses could meet all those demands and be funny, too. Invited to Comden's apartment to hear a few numbers from the show, Madeline was assured not only that the creative team and producers wanted her for the role, but also that they had created it expressly for her. As things turned out, Comden and Green made prophecy when they wrote, "[T]he stress is on the impact of the music."[110]

Comden and Green's association with Harold Prince dated back to *Wonderful Town*, which he stage-managed in 1953–54 under director George Abbott. Prince went on to produce such hits as *The Pajama Game*, *Damn Yankees*, and *Fiddler on the Roof*, and his directing credits include the original productions of *Cabaret, Company, Follies, A Little Night Music, Sweeney Todd, Evita,* and *Phantom of the Opera,* to cite only a few. He's a Tony Award record-holder, with eight wins for best musical, two for best producer of a musical, eight for best director of a musical, plus three special awards and an additional sixteen nominations.

But *On the Twentieth Century* was an exceptional experience for Prince. "It's the only show I've ever come into late," he says. Indicating his office, he adds, "Shows always start here." For *On the Twentieth Century,* however, the conceptual work was largely complete before he arrived. "I did some editorial work, and I certainly am responsible for overseeing the design, and all of that, which was smashing." Comden, Green, and the producers approached Madeline a year before rehearsals began, and Prince had no say in hiring her. When he walked into rehearsals, he expected to find another actress: Bernadette Peters. "I have that kind of a mind," he says with a shrug. "You could say I'm nuts. Why wouldn't I know? But it was probably not much more than a matter of yin and yang. I thought Bernadette Peters would be very funny." (He concedes that she would have needed to work hard to get through the score as Coleman wrote it.) Madeline was hired for her marquee value as much as for her abilities, Prince suggests, describing Comden and Green as "star people. They loved stars." They may have been the ones who suggested that Danny Kaye play Oscar, prompting Madeline's reply, "Sign him, lose me." For Prince's part, "In a million years, I would never work with Danny."

To play Oscar, Prince chose John Cullum, who made his Broadway debut as Sir Dinadan in the original cast of *Camelot* and created the lead roles in *On a Clear Day You Can See Forever* and *Shenandoah.* To play the supporting role of Bruce Granit, Lily's dashing but dumb actor boyfriend, Prince hired Kevin Kline. He also cast Madeline's understudy, Judy Kaye, an exceptionally talented, relatively unknown soprano he'd first spotted in California. Other casting choices Prince either made himself or agreed with, including George Coe and Dean Dittman as Oscar's sidekicks, and Imogene Coca, for whom Comden and Green reconfigured the role of the religious fanatic. A man in the original play, she's now Letitia Primrose, though the essence of the character remained unchanged. But Cullum says Prince "considered the set the star of the show, and in many ways he was right—it was incredible, with railway stations, hotels, spacious connecting Pullman suites, rolling locomotives from every angle." Technical problems and the complexity of Robin Wagner's set design frequently drew Prince's attention away from the actors.

As Prince perceived her, Madeline was merely a movie star, unable or unwilling to come up with consistent performances onstage. He doesn't want "cookie-cutter performances," he says, but Madeline's energy and involvement varied wildly. Prince was unaware of her difficulties with Coleman's score, to say nothing of her being terrified—which she was. To the contrary, he says, "I thought she was—*emboldened*. By a huge career in hit movies, and that voice, that speaking voice, which was always funny." This impression led to what he calls "an odd relationship with Madeline. I knew she was wildly creative. . . . I don't think she had a lot of staying power."

From the start, Madeline knew she'd have to fight to win Prince's approval. He might not remember—but she did—that in 1970 she had auditioned eight times for him before he rejected her for the cast of Sondheim's *Company*. In rehearsals for *Twentieth Century*, Prince's attitude clearly hadn't changed. He expected Bernadette Peters, and he believed Judy Kaye could do a better job. This made it harder for Madeline to approach him. "My problem is, I'm not who I appear to be," Prince says. "I am not stern, I am not someone to be frightened of. But I'm a little removed. I'm not a cozy actor. I'm also not a bully. Not remotely. I'm just not cozy, and I wish sometimes I were."

Insecure as always—and becoming ever more so as she faced the demands of the show—Madeline had agreed to play Lily long before learning she'd be working with Prince. The first day of rehearsal, she was already talking about the "Hal Prince machine," referring not to Wagner's set design, but to the director's briskly efficient, "results-oriented" methods, Judy Kaye told an interviewer. "Already she was scared."[111] But in Madeline's relationship with Prince—as in her relationships with Bernie Wolfson and Hiller Kahn—remoteness, whether physical or emotional, she believed must be something *she* had caused by being less than perfect. She would respond by looking for any way she could find to impress him. When at last she saw she would never win Prince over, she panicked—while he began lobbying the show's producers to fire her.

The conflict between Madeline's working method and Prince's resembled in some ways those that she'd encountered with Lucille Ball and George Rose. She worked from the inside out, beginning by locating the character's motivations and exploring her emotional life, something like but not identical to the Method of the Actors Studio. "She was all about process," Judy Kaye said, and Maris Clement describes Madeline as "an organic actor." But in 1977, three decades after Marlon Brando appeared in *A Streetcar Named Desire*, the Method was still likely to inspire mockery in the musical theater. (Comden and Green themselves had lampooned a Method actor, the character Blake Barton, in *Bells Are Ringing* in 1956.) At the time of *On the Twentieth Century*, the specific needs of musical comedy—in which an actor's line may cue not only a scene partner, but also an entire orchestra, chorus, and (in this case) a complex change of scenery—still dictated a by-the-book approach.

That wasn't Madeline's way of doing things. Because of her background in revues and also in film, she liked to improvise with a script. In film, this technique is often welcome; sudden inspiration can make one take superior to another. But some of Madeline's collaborators in musical theater—certainly including Prince—interpreted the improvisational approach as inconsistent or undisciplined, even somehow disqualifying: "She's not a theater actress." *Twentieth Century*, like every premiere production Madeline had worked on so far, underwent substantial revision during rehearsals and tryouts, and Comden and Green had a legitimate interest in hearing and judging lines as they'd written them.

With Prince and Coleman, Comden and Green undertook the "editorial work" that Prince recalls, and as the first read-through began, the director worked through scenes, making cuts that "were permanent, with no questions allowed," Cullum remembers. "[B]y the third scene, the actors were fighting desperately to hold on to as many of their lines as possible. Auditions are scary, but this was hair-raising, terror-time." Prince cut some of Kline's dialogue, and Kline thought, "Oh, great, it isn't as if it's an overwritten part as it is." But Madeline, sitting next to him, whispered, "Don't you worry about a thing, darling, it'll be fine." During rehearsals, she helped him look for ways to improve his part, working with him on comic business, which was mostly physical comedy. "People don't write that in scripts. [W]e just invented it," he says. Somewhat to his surprise, the creative team approved, and thanks to Madeline and Prince, Kline says, "I ended up with a showier part."

Kline's interpretation found him falling flat on his face and climbing up walls, a trial run of sorts for his Oscar-winning turn in *A Fish Called Wanda* (1989). Already in his still-nascent career, he'd "discovered that, instead of trying to do it *right*, just try to do it *well*. And that can mean playing in rehearsals and exploring, sometimes, not only in rehearsal but in performance, too," as Madeline did. He contests the widespread use of the word "erratic" to describe her work in *Twentieth Century*. "I would say fun, spontaneous, in the moment, all the things I love about actors." The show's conductor, Paul Gemignani, suggests that the "erratic" label stuck "due to [Madeline's] ability to ad lib within a scene. . . . With

comedy, she was like a jazz musician. Improv was her comfort zone."
And ensemble member Maris Clement approvingly describes Madeline's
performances as "different every night. She listened to a line from another actor and interpreted it differently all the time. That's why she was
so brilliant, so incredibly funny."

By the second week of rehearsals, Kline became aware of Madeline's
anxieties about the score, though he didn't grasp their extent until many
years later. He remembers her saying to him, "Cy Coleman's scores are so
rangy. It's like Cole Porter . . . really a challenge." Today Kline describes
On the Twentieth Century as a "fucking impossible score! It's an opera!"
Even so, he says that Madeline wasn't complaining. "She seemed consummately professional. When she started taking the alternate notes,
instead of hitting the high B-flat, she would take the G." "I did my best to
convince her that she was doing fine," Cullum remembers, "but I noticed
that she was transposing some of her lines in the sextet. I didn't think
this was a big deal, but I later learned that Cy was furious."

Whether or not she behaved like a diva, she was the leading lady of
a brand-new operetta, one of the most stressful jobs a singer can take.
Anxiety distorted her critical perception of Coleman's work ("I do *not*
like the music," she wrote in her notebook), diminishing her confidence
further. Singing was never a simple process for Madeline; she couldn't
get past associations with Paula. As a girl, Madeline sang to please her
mother, or to please people her mother wanted to please. As an adult,
Madeline sang in order to pursue the kind of career her mother dreamed
about. Singing required intense preparation; it had to be *perfect*. And like
many another soprano before and since, Madeline felt insecure. Could
she hit today the high note she hit yesterday?

Compounding her anxieties, Madeline became romantically involved
with a married man, and when the affair ended, shortly before *Twentieth
Century* returned to New York, Madeline didn't break it off by choice.
From the start, she understood that he would return to his wife, but she
was hardly the first woman to think, "This time will be different. I can
change him." While the circumstances certainly differed, they brought
back memories of Bernie and Hiller, the anxieties abandonment naturally produced in her, and the sense that a man had left because something
was wrong with *her*. Rather than being able to lose herself in her work,
she was obliged to spend her time onstage reenacting the ups and downs
of Lily's affairs and yearning for a lost love. There was no way to escape
constant reminders of her own situation, and because he was involved in
the production, he was never far away when Madeline, as Lily, sang, "I

want him back." These anxieties and the physical strain of singing Lily's numbers led to behavior that Maris Clement recognized as panic attacks.

• • •

To understand the vocal demands of the role of Lily Garland and to appreciate the ways Madeline tackled them, one begins by listening to the original-cast album, recorded on February 28, 1978. Lily is assigned significant portions of seven numbers, and from the album, one easily gets a sense both why Madeline could be so good in the part, and why she found it daunting.

In "Veronique," Oscar insists that the drab Mildred Plotka read a synopsis of his latest show, the inspirational tale of a French girl whose refusal to sleep with Otto von Bismarck starts the Franco-Prussian War. Mildred is the least likely candidate to play a patriotic martyr, as she's the first to realize. She begins to read in character voice, with a Bronx accent and a limited, even amateurish tonal quality below the middle of Madeline's range. But as she continues, her accent fades and her voice swells. By the end, she's even pronouncing French correctly (Veronique dies "dans la rue") and her voice is soaring over the orchestra as, in a helmet and skimpy tunic, she's hoisted aloft by the ensemble. The audition becomes reality, transforming Mildred the rehearsal pianist to Lily Garland, star.

"Never," Lily's next number, similarly ranges from lower-middle chest range to the upper extension of Madeline's lyric soprano. At points, she's almost shrill—and she means to be. It's an interpretive choice, not a flaw. As Lily informs Oscar's lackeys of precisely when she would be available to work again with Oscar, Madeline gives a phenomenal display of character singing. She teases out the lines as she goes through her calendar, employing her most elegant diction. But the music accelerates, and the orchestra shifts from lilting grace to rumbling menace— until Lily explodes: "Never? Never. Never!" In chest voice, she tells off Oscar's sidekicks, rising gradually to lyric voice, then dropping back into chest and rising again. As the song reaches its climax, she groans and shrieks, at two points ascending from the very bottom of her range to the very top, most notably in the finish:

> *Go back with him? Here's my reply!*
> *Ah-ha, ah-ha, ah-ha!*
> *Aaaahhh, let me see.*
> *I'd rather die! Die! Die!*

She floats in her upper register for the first lines. The "ah-ha"s are upward spirals. The long "Aaaahhh" begins as a guttural low note, then rises to her upper register for "Let me see." The final "Die! Die!" is delivered at the top of her range.

Two duets with Oscar are fascinating compositional variations on standard operetta themes, largely because Lily and Oscar sing together only on the final notes in each. "Our Private World," a tender waltz sung in remembrance of their love affair, begins with Oscar. As Lily is caught up in the memory, she joins in, but *after* Oscar, in a round. Madeline's singing here is lyrical throughout, nicely complementing Cullum's warm baritone. Even when they agree, they're in competition—in fact, they're in separate rooms. Face-to-face for their next duet, "I've Got It All," they're *not* in agreement. Oscar begins by trying to cajole and flatter Lily, who sees through him immediately. She answers him, gloating in her success and his failure. Losing patience, Oscar belittles her: Hollywood has cheapened her, and her fame is hollow. "You've lost it!" he sings, to which Lily replies, "I've got it all!"

The sextet finds Oscar and his sidekicks exulting in Mrs. Primrose's munificence, a check for $200,000. (Having heard that Oscar's new play will be the story of Mary Magdalene, Primrose believes her gesture will further the cause of salvation so dear to her.) Now Oscar can offer Lily a contract, but when Lily and Bruce enter, Bruce tries to stop her even from reading it, while Oscar and his friends implore her to sign it, and Primrose stands back and marvels at the scene. Against this backdrop, Lily wonders why she's even considering working with Oscar—then realizes she wants him back. Madeline begins with an extended passage of soft singing in her soprano register to piano accompaniment that recalls a Rachmaninov concerto. As she comes out of her reverie, the rhythm accelerates ("You can't go back!"), and all six characters come together as Oscar, Owen, Oliver, and Primrose sing in surging repetition, "You must come back! Sign it, Lily!"; Bruce sings in plaintive isolation, "Don't sign, Lily!"; and Lily wonders, "Should I sign it?" She concludes the sextet on a high "Sign?," sailing over the other voices.

As the passengers realize the truth about Primrose, declaring that "She's a Nut," Lily enters after Owen, Oliver, and Oscar have made the discovery. At first, like the others, she sputters in disbelief, at a frenetically galloping tempo (much like a runaway train.) Her next line, naturally, is self-centered and full-flying soprano: "What will become of my movie? Wait 'til I get my hands on Oscar!"

Lily resolves to sign with a rival producer (who is Oscar's former office boy). In "Babbette," she reads the eponymous new play, a drawing-room melodrama. As an exercise in vocal characterization, it's a marathon. Lily begins reading with the lilting Lily leitmotif underscoring, which breaks into a brassy Charleston when she comes to a party scene. She skims past other characters' parts to get to her own. But she can't banish thoughts of Oscar and of Mary Magdalene. She lapses into a stately hymn ("We shall be saved!" on a Gounod-flavored melody), then pulls herself back to the "Babbette" play. In one passage, she flips back and forth word-by-word between the two plays, before summoning her strength and announcing, "Max, I'll do this play!" to the freewheeling Charleston theme, which Madeline sings in a squealing character voice (something like her little-girl voice) in her upper register. She scats on the phrase "do it" and, for the big finish, on the name Babbette.

At the end of *Twentieth Century*, after Oscar's "fatal" accident and his brilliant *scena*, "The Legacy," Lily rushes to his side to bid him farewell in one last duet, "Lily, Oscar." The most fully operatic number in the show, it abides by the rule: Lily and Oscar take turns, rather than singing together, until they reach the final notes of the song. On the cast album, Madeline's soprano is at its most secure in this number, and a listener hears both Lily's tears as she calls out to Oscar, and her smile as she grants his dying wish by signing the contract for the Mary Magdalene play. She soars in her upper register, just as so many sopranos in grand opera do when cradling their dying lovers, and the recording ends with her barely suppressed sob. As far as the plot of *Twentieth Century* goes, it's all a trick: Oscar isn't really dying. But then, Lily didn't really sign the contract.

Performing this part in a studio, with retakes, producers, and sound engineers is one matter. Doing it live in the theater eight times a week is another.

• • •

Unlike Madeline, Judy Kaye was completely unfazed by Coleman's score. As Kline says, she "has pipes that are just inhumanly extraordinary. . . . She could belt out fifteen performances a week. She had steel pipes, a great, amazing voice." Whenever she went on for Madeline, first in rehearsals and later in the theater, "We were like, 'Great, Judy Kaye just kicked ass! Listen to those notes!'" he remembers. "We always cheer the understudy when she goes on." But Kaye found understudying rough on her ego; *Twentieth Century* was the only time she tried it. With her, as with

Madeline, Prince offered little feedback, saying something only when he didn't like what she did. At last he suggested that she "find another template," Kaye remembered. "If Madeline was Carole Lombard, I was a Jean Harlow. Something a little tougher." Kaye went on for Madeline in several rehearsals, displaying her growing mastery of the material each time, Cullum remembers. After the gypsy run-through, "Madeline asked me, 'How did Judy do?' 'She knows all the blocking,' I said." By the time *On the Twentieth Century* got to Boston, Cullum told Madeline, "She now knows the show." And by the end of the Boston run, Cullum said, "in no uncertain terms, 'Madeline, don't miss any more performances.'"

In blizzard-bound Boston, Madeline's offstage love affair blossomed. Even more discreet than usual, she mentioned neither her married lover nor personal engagements in her appointment book during this time. But her misgivings about the show persisted, and the critical response didn't reassure her. Kevin Kelly, writing in the *Boston Globe*, found the show "about as much fun as taking the Amtrak to Providence." While he admired the score and Cullum's performance, Kelly found structural flaws throughout *Twentieth Century* and merely "lie-in-wait dazzle briefly glinting" in Madeline's work. Kelly proposed a few ways to remedy the show's weaknesses, including a big, old-fashioned production number for Lily—as if "Veronique" weren't enough. A new number only would have added to Madeline's burdens.[112]

At the end of the Boston run, Madeline learned that Prince asked the show's producers to fire her. They refused, pointing to two million dollars in advance ticket sales. But as *Twentieth Century* returned to New York, Madeline contended with Prince's hostility and the breakup of her affair. Even showing up for rehearsals now risked an emotional ordeal. Before, when she'd mixed her love life with her work, the experience sustained her (Michael Karm being the principal example) or made no difference. But now she couldn't escape reminders of her unhappiness. Very little was going right for Madeline. The creative team did make changes to the show, though nothing as significant as a new production number for Lily. Madeline's anxieties got worse, not better, and Prince seemed firm in his opposition to her.

"In New York, the show was in trouble, and Hal knew it," Cullum remembers. "[H]e came to me complaining of the trouble Madeline was giving him and the rift between her and Cy Coleman," Cullum remembers. "I told him, 'Madeline is my leading lady, and you're not going to get me to say anything negative about her. I think she's terrific and I love what she's doing with the part.' That ended that"—at least as far as complaining to Cullum went. But on opening night, February 19, 1978, Prince still didn't believe he could get a consistent performance out of his star. "I sat there very nervous," Prince remembers. "'Will she or won't she?' . . . The two guys, I could count on. But she delivered. Every nuance, everything." A pirate recording of the opening-night performance in its entirety confirms that Madeline was "on," and the audience loved her. "Babbette," in particular, found her at the height of her powers; ultimately, it's a miniature mad scene. Cullum calls opening night "an unforgettable evening."

After the curtain fell, Prince ran to Madeline's dressing room, where she sat in front of her mirror. "That's what I've been talking about for weeks!" Prince told her. "You can do it! You can do better than do it, you can knock the ball out of the park! It's wonderful!" Without taking her eyes off the mirror, Madeline replied, "I hope you don't think I can do that every night."

Prince went cold. "That's when I decided she hasn't the energy for eight performances a week," he says now. "Not necessarily just the energy, maybe the discipline. But I thought she's too used to cuts. 'Cut! Let's take it again! Or let's not.'" Madeline was "very funny. Smart. Eccentric. Loony, and very—it was good casting. The problem was that she can't sustain. And I thought, 'She's killing the show.' And you know, I really did think this, because it never happened to me before."

At the opening-night party, Madeline put on a brave face. With her ex-lover and his wife expected to attend, she asked Paula to escort her. Soon, however, the writer Shaun Considine arrived. He'd become a friend since he profiled Madeline for *After Dark*, and now she posed with him for photographers and teasingly suggested he was really her date. A few minutes later, she asked what Considine "really" thought of the show. "You were first class," he said, "but the play wasn't." "See?" Paula cried.

Madeline received excellent reviews for *Twentieth Century*. Though *Time*'s T. E. Kalem found the show itself "about as much fun as getting stranded on a station platform," he praised Madeline's "arsenal of talents. She is kooky, vulnerable, and seductive in succession, and her voice has a near-operatic authority."[113] In the *New York Times*, Richard Eder, too, found that the show had "rough spots," but he especially enjoyed Madeline in the Mildred Plotka scene.[114] Also in the *Times*, Walter Kerr observed that Madeline was "spending much of her romantic time bent double and backward, unraveling herself long enough to snarl at the very memory of Mr. Cullum in a song [presumably "Never"] that requires her to use a cellar coloratura (what else are we to call trills that seem to scrape ground regularly, possibly digging a convenient grave?)." But he also praised her "gentle handling" of "Our Private World," and compared her with Judy Holliday.[115] In *New York* magazine, however, John Simon found Madeline "downright offensive" in the Mildred scene and accused her of "campy gurgling and shrilling during the songs." "[I]t would be nice," he concluded, "if Broadway leading ladies could occasionally represent the heterosexual image of a woman."[116]

Eder's remark that "the performances seem to lose their drive" toward the end of act 1 now seems ominous. As the run continued, some audience members recollect, Madeline's performances varied, not only night to night but scene to scene. Her energy level was sometimes frenetic, other times low. Some suspected drug abuse. In reality, she was either protecting her voice or panicking—or both. Prince remembers that Madeline "proceeded to play it some nights, or not play it other nights." Striking his hand for emphasis, he continues, "Audiences could tell the difference, totally."

By now, Madeline had lost all confidence in the material she'd been given, from script to score to costumes—especially the skimpy tunic in "Veronique," which required a quick change in the wings. Madeline had to undress in full view of the stage crew. "Even Marlene [Dietrich] *chose to* cover up for uniqueness, rather than showing (lovely) flesh," she wrote in her notebook. As a feminist, she disliked the Pygmalion–Galatea relationship between Oscar and Lily: "This is not a show, music, point of view, that I am proud of. I do *not* look forward to my friends seeing me in it."[117] After opening, she declared that Coleman had told her she no longer had to take all the high notes in her numbers, something that didn't square with the "stickler" Kaye knew or the "very demanding" composer Cullum describes. The show's choreographer, Larry Fuller, told Coleman's biographer, Andy Propst, that Madeline began taking alternate notes as soon as the first rehearsal.[118] However, Madeline later told composer Fred Barton that she interpolated many of Lily's high notes during rehearsals, improvising within the music as she'd improvised within the script. Therefore, she said, she considered it her prerogative to take lower notes, despite Coleman's insistence that any changes he approved were now part of his score. She took the lower notes anyway.

As Kaye remembered it, Madeline "gave away the show . . . neither sharing it nor taking it. And I would listen and think, 'Why is she doing that? Why is she squandering this opportunity?' . . . I started to get extremely angry about it." She determined to have a good time whenever she stepped in for Madeline, to share the fun she found in the material. But many in the audience would walk out when they heard that an understudy would play the lead. Madeline picked up both on Kaye's resentment and on the producers': "An understudy is a person who only performs—fills in for you in a star role when you are *shamefully* incapacitated!" she wrote in her notebook. "You *wretch* you. How dare you commit such a crime[?] (We swallow this.)" If she so much as asked for a cup of coffee, she wrote, she was made to feel like the Ugandan dictator Idi Amin.[119] When Madeline began to miss performances, Prince thought, "She wants out."

In fact, she did not. By now it should be clear that Madeline didn't throw away work. She needed money to support Paula, and for that reason she would accept all kinds of jobs that possessed little more appeal than a paycheck. Because she'd signed on to *Twentieth Century*, she'd lined up no other work for a period of several months (a year and a half, by some accounts). If she had any inclination to quit, then she might have done so as soon as she learned Prince wanted to fire her, if not sooner. Determined to stay in the show, even as she worried that Coleman's score would permanently damage her voice—her single greatest asset as a performer—she began to seek out people who might help her.

Nine times in the month and a half before she left *Twentieth Century*, Madeline consulted with Dr. Wilbur Gould, a throat specialist whose patients included Frank Sinatra, Luciano Pavarotti, Beverly Sills, Elizabeth Taylor, and Angela Lansbury. He performed surgery on Lyndon Johnson, removing a nodule from the president's vocal cords, and he encouraged Dan Rather to wear sweater vests on *The CBS Evening News* to combat the chill of the television studio.[120] Also, beginning on March 31, 1978, Madeline began taking lessons with Beverley Peck Johnson, perhaps the most celebrated voice teacher in New York at the time. Johnson also had a reputation for helping voices in distress. After Gould operated on LBJ, she coached the president (who was no relation). She helped soprano Anna Moffo with a condition that's still known as "Moffo throat." Her other students included such sopranos as Renata Tebaldi and Renée Fleming. Among actors, she coached Blythe Danner and Kevin Kline. Kline went to Johnson when he began to work on the movie adaptation of *The Pirates of Penzance* (1983). "She was very, very strict about protecting the voice and not damaging in it any way," he says. At his first lesson, she told him that if he smoked, he had to choose between cigarettes and her, and this is another reason he believes Madeline didn't have a cocaine habit: Johnson wouldn't have continued to work with her if Madeline took drugs.[121]

Both Gould and Johnson had reputations for being the best people around to solve problems like Madeline's. That she saw them demonstrates that she responded in the most professional, responsible way she could to what she perceived as a crisis. In this regard, at least, she refused to let her thwarted love life affect her. However, she didn't tell Prince or Gemignani about her difficulties with the score or her efforts to protect her voice and carry on. Both men say they were unaware of her anxieties about Coleman's music. Joel Grey finds her reticence typical of "actors who need the job, and who want the job, and want it to work, but don't feel they can voice their opinion." Grey, who has enjoyed a long, collaborative friendship with Prince, adds, "Actors are sort of the last people that are considered. [Directors and producers] say, 'Get up and do it! Stop complaining!'" And indeed, Prince is still using words like "tired easily," "lazy," and "bored" to describe Madeline.

Today, Prince says he'd have tried to steer Madeline away from Gould, "the most suspect doctor in the throat business" who "was much more interested in being Svengali and keeping [performers] out of the show than in delivering them." Gemignani takes a different view. "Firstly, Gould did not suggest performers taking off unless he felt that they would be doing permanent damage to themselves," he says. Like any actor singing eight shows a week, Madeline worried about remaining healthy vocally, and "she was a soprano being asked to use her chest voice more often than she had in the past." Going to Gould and Johnson was, in Gemignani's view, the smart thing to do. "In this business, singer–actors have to protect themselves," he says, and it's up to them "to know your limits and to protect your instrument. Perhaps a good musical director will suggest things to help you, but ultimately it's your call. Not an easy one to make. Management never makes it easy. Ask any opera singer who has to cancel. It's one hundred times worse in the musical theater."

In New York, Madeline missed the first three or four days of rehearsal at the St. James Theater (probably due, at least in part, to her emotional upset after breaking up with her lover). Once the show opened, she complained of laryngitis and appeared at the recording session against her will. Her voice gave out at the Sunday matinée on March 5, and she fell ill again on March 21 and 22, missing both the matinée and evening performances. Immediately, she began consultations with Gould. She missed two more performances on April 12, and stayed out late on April 14 to give a press interview. She found the two shows the next day especially difficult, writing "Oy" in her appointment book on April 15. She missed one more performance, the matinée on April 19—but this time, her health had nothing to do with it.

Madeline had thought of one possible solution: to cut back the number of performances she gave per week. Across the street, Liza Minnelli was starring in Kander and Ebb's *The Act*, and though Minnelli sang virtually every number, she lip-synched some to pre-recorded tracks, to facilitate her dancing. Minnelli played only seven performances a week; an advertised substitute went on for Wednesday matinées. Upon inquiring, Madeline was told that no such arrangement would be possible for her in *Twentieth Century*. The producers were right to refuse her, Prince says. Minnelli's dubbing and her afternoon off didn't help her, he says, and cutting back on the number of shows wouldn't have helped Madeline, either. She could have given eight performances a week "just fine. She just did not have that frame of mind." He didn't know she was terrified of losing her voice, but her cancellations and stated desire to work less forced the producers to reconsider their position. She was no longer a box office asset, but a potential liability.

The simplest solution, at least from the producers' perspective, was to let Judy Kaye take over the show. She had Prince's enthusiastic support, and everyone in the cast (including Madeline) loved her. She consistently played the part as it was written, and she had no difficulty with the music. This last asset in itself made hiring her especially attractive to Coleman, and the favor he showed Kaye led to further friction between him and Madeline. While it might be somewhat late to publicize the launch of a talented unknown, the prospect of Kaye's stardom generated excitement, both inside and outside the St. James. "[T]his was a dream story for Broadway, and they embraced it with open arms," Cullum says now. Buoyed by good reviews and audience response to the reliable Cullum, Coca, and Kline, even the loss of Madeline's marquee value no longer seemed an insurmountable obstacle. There would be liabilities. Madeline was on the cast album, and it was too late to re-record and release the album with Kaye. Madeline featured prominently in the television advertising campaign (which would continue to air, with Kaye's name and Madeline's image). Madeline would have to be paid off. And Madeline, not Kaye, would be eligible for the Tony Award. Yet all of these realities were preferable to the risks of retaining a star who, by her own reluctant admission, wasn't up to the demands of the show.[122]

In an interview years later, Cullum expressed his disappointment. Madeline was "very sensitive, and a shy kind of person. I don't think that they handled it with her right. . . . They didn't treat her like the star she deserved to be treated like."[123] Today, Kline still seems somewhat stunned by Madeline's departure. At the time, he thought, "This is a serious business." If he missed shows, he'd better be *really* sick, because otherwise Prince wouldn't put up with it. "That was my take-away. Not that Madeline was an impossible diva, and you thought, 'Oh, it's a wonder they put up with her this long.'"

On April 19, Madeline received a letter from the producers, informing her that they would prefer to let her go. Overwhelmed, she missed the matinée that day but returned to the theater that night. She gave her final performance on April 23. As she told *People* magazine a few days later, "Finally, I had my agent ask just what [the producers] wanted me to do. 'To leave,' I was told. So I left."[124] In her notebook, she wrote, "May an angel take my place—it will serve you right."

• • •

As *Twentieth Century*'s opening night approached, the editors at *People* magazine began lobbying Madeline for a feature, possibly a cover story, on her Broadway comeback. Meeting with resistance, they asked Shaun Considine to interview her, and one of the show's producers, Marty Richards, did his best to cooperate, despite Hal Prince's objections. Madeline trusted Considine, yet she continued to balk, telling him she needed to save her voice. He attended the recording session, where he found her strangely distant, but after Richards intervened again, the interview took place after the April 14 performance. Madeline wouldn't pose for pictures, and without illustrations, the editors at *People* couldn't run the story before she quit the show. After she quit, the editors scrapped the idea of a cover story. Now the article would be a news feature, and Considine returned for a follow-up interview, in which Madeline went public for the first time about her vocal problems. Still refusing to pose, she told Considine to use one of the pictures he'd taken of her in Central Park a few years earlier. The article appeared in the May 15 issue.

Madeline knew that by speaking up, she might deprive herself of future singing jobs; producers might not hire her because they would believe that she couldn't handle the challenges. By then, however, she faced a larger threat to her reputation: She'd left a starring role in a major Broadway musical after only two and a half months. The gossips on Broadway had been humming ever since her voice gave out on March 5.

She couldn't merely sit back and hope that the producers might provide explanations that would cast her in a flattering light. She had to tell the story herself, and her interview with Considine amounted to the first salvo of a damage-control campaign.

"The schedule was ludicrous," Madeline said. "Three weeks of singing a semi-operatic score nonstop? I needed a rest." She cast herself as the victim, telling Considine, "[I]t became very unpleasant with the management. I was harassed constantly." Even so, she couldn't help but speculate that her vocal trouble might be "psychosomatic." Neither statement was likely to dispel rumors that she was difficult to work with. When the article appeared, it wasn't the personality profile Madeline expected. She felt that Considine had betrayed her. He explained that the editors waited a long time for their cover story, and her departure from *Twentieth Century* required a change of focus. Appeased, Madeline told Considine that, contrary to what he'd been told and what *People* published, the producers had bought out her contract for less than one hundred thousand dollars. He offered to request a correction, but she replied, "Let it stand. It will allow people to think I'm a rich woman."

Already the Broadway equivalent of public opinion found fault with Madeline, and one member of the theater community, Walter Willison, feels that Madeline unwittingly had become the kind of problematic star that Danny Kaye was in *Two by Two*. Certainly Prince found her so disagreeable to work with that initially he was reluctant even to speak about her three decades later. Alienating the most powerful man on Broadway is never a good career move. Madeline's closest associates were unaware of the drug rumor (which Willison says was rampant in Hollywood at the time of *Twentieth Century*), but they did worry that she'd been blackballed from Broadway. If she was, Prince says, then "I can't regret that. She absolutely did it herself."

While she did manage to improve her relations with Comden and Green, Madeline believed that other influential people on Broadway were reluctant to work with her. The chief example was Stephen Sondheim, who collaborated often with Prince. Madeline wanted desperately to be taken seriously by the composer, but opportunities to perform his work came only at gala concerts. Sondheim's next premieres, *Sweeney Todd* and *Merrily We Roll Along*, didn't have roles suited to Madeline, and both were directed by Prince, so there was little point in her making any attempt to find a part in those shows. Gemignani, another frequent collaborator with Sondheim, says that Madeline wasn't blackballed so much as undone by her own anxieties about returning to Broadway.

"[B]ecause she didn't really understand the rigors of theater performing[,] she herself got nervous about trying it again," he says, and for the
next few years she avoided theater. However, Gemignani adds, "I know
that her fellow performers loved and respected her." As Judy Kaye remembered, Madeline "actually came to the show after I went in for her
and brought a bottle of Champagne. Very nice. Really, really dear. I think
she wanted more of a dialogue than I was capable of, because I was embarrassed at what had happened, and I couldn't change it. And I didn't
want to make her feel bad."

On May 15, the day her *People* interview hit newsstands, Madeline's
nomination for the Tony Award for leading actress in a musical was announced, and she stepped up her campaign of damage control. Certain
economic considerations typically factor into the decisions of Tony vot-
ers, and awards seldom go to shows that are no longer running. Though
Twentieth Century continued to run, Madeline had virtually no chance of
winning, even had her rivals in the category not included stars like Minnelli and Eartha Kitt. Nevertheless, Madeline made a point of attending
the luncheon for nominees at Sardi's two days later, and posing for news
photos with the other nominees (Frances Sternhagen was the fourth).

She also attended the awards ceremony on June 4. Naturally her attendance meant being caught on camera, and she risked running into
her ex-lover, Prince, and the rest of the *Twentieth Century* company. While
Madeline sat in the audience, the cast performed a medley of songs from
the show, which garnered eight other nominations. Ultimately, Comden
and Green won for best book and, with Coleman, for Best Score, while
Cullum, Kline, and Robin Wagner won their respective categories. Despite that tally, Prince is still resentful: If Madeline had bowed out of
the show during Boston tryouts or New York previews, he says, then
Judy Kaye would have been eligible for and won the Tony. "We could
have promoted that," he says, and Kaye's victory could have boosted the
show's box office and extended the run beyond March 18, 1979, when
Twentieth Century closed.[125]

Attending the Tony events required considerable courage, and Madeline wrote a note in her appointment book as a sort of pep talk to herself: "[A]tmosphere of clean, young, country beauty—the feeling of a
contented baby. [S]weetness. [P]ristine. I am a teacher, too. One of them.
Queen." (Such notes are rare in Madeline's appointment books, which
she maintained almost exclusively for their intended purpose. This note
surrounds a reminder of a massage appointment on the Friday before the
ceremony.) And indeed she tried to be kind to herself after leaving the

show. In the coming months, she took a week's vacation in Bermuda, and spent two weeks sightseeing in Rome, Zurich, and London. But first she booked a series of stays at the New Age Health Farm, a spa in Neversink, New York: a week in early May, a long weekend later that month, and another week at the beginning of June. Defenders of the drug rumor might point to this as evidence of Madeline going into rehabilitation, though Deborah Birch, who works at New Age today, says the spa was famous at that time for weight-loss programs. Elsa and Graham Graydon opened New Age in 1976, and they promoted juice fasting, massage, yoga, meditation, hiking, and swimming. They didn't permit drugs or alcohol on the farm, and it's located in a dry county. In any case, it appears that—beyond a desire to relax in a resort that was more spiritually oriented than most, and thus more attuned to her own personality—Madeline's primary interest was weight loss. In her appointment book, she recorded her weight each day of each stay.[126]

For solace, she turned to friends, including Mel Brooks and Anne Bancroft, Dom and Carol DeLuise, Steve Novick, Gail Jacobs, and Michael Cohen. For the remainder of 1978, her appointment book is relatively empty of professional engagements. That's understandable; she'd planned to be in *On the Twentieth Century* during these months. After her busy calendar for 1977, the contrast must have been poignant.

Madeline saw Bernie Wolfson a few times in New York, and she also turned to her brother, Jef, making an extended visit to the Twin Oaks Community in Virginia. Jef's girlfriend at the time, Heidi Berthoud, was also a member of the community, and she'd met Madeline before on trips to New York. She recalls Madeline as "full of energy, sprightly, very outgoing—which I think would be a requirement for any superstar. It goes with the territory." "I was well entrenched into feminism," Berthoud says, "so I was at once impressed with this woman who was a little powerhouse of her own, and [I was] at the same time feeling a little guarded . . . kind of wondering what it would be like" to travel in Madeline's circles. "And I soon found out." She describes a town mouse/city mouse split in her sensibilities and Madeline's when each entered the other's territory.

At Twin Oaks, Jef recalls, Madeline "was fascinated. It was like going on safari. She felt safe with me, but—." "The kind of amateur sociologist that she was," Berthoud interjects before agreeing with Jef, "[s]he needed her guide." "She was just impressed with how open people were," Jef continues. Berthoud adds, "And you can't do that in her world." During her stay at Twin Oaks, Madeline attended a party and got to know Julio, or "Hoots," a little boy from Honduras with whom Jef had grown close, before "she had her fill of it and went back" to New York, he remembers.

During this time, Madeline's longest sustained professional activities were a media tour of Los Angeles in June to promote *High Anxiety*, and a three-day shoot for *The Muppet Movie* in August. The Muppets' first big-screen adventure is a road picture that owes more than a little to *The Wizard of Oz*, including a wistful opening song about rainbows. Throughout the film, directed by Jim Frawley, the Muppets interact with human stars, much the way the characters interacted with guests on *The Muppet Show*. The villain and his reluctant henchman are played by two of Madeline's favorite colleagues, Charles Durning (who played her father in *Boom Boom Room*), and Austin Pendleton. Mel Brooks, Dom DeLuise, and Cloris Leachman also appear. But Carol Kane was the only one of Madeline's friends who shared screen time with her, and Pendleton confirms that during his time on the set he never saw Madeline at all.

Madeline appears in the El Sleezo Café, a low dive into which Kermit (Jim Henson) stumbles. Dressed like an Apache dancer and using her Dietrich voice, Madeline tries to vamp the frog, then sics her burly boyfriend (Telly Savalas, after whom one of the hairiest Muppets was named) on him, while Kane looks on—and that's all we see of Madeline. Here, as on *Sesame Street* and *The Muppet Show*, her work with the Muppets is exceptional. The writers had a strong grasp of her persona, and she worked well with them. It's apparent that she enjoyed herself, as did so many other stars. (Lily Tomlin once remarked that the only trouble with working with Muppets was you couldn't go to dinner with them after the show.) However, there's a technical flaw in Madeline's acting: She tends to look over the Muppet's head, instead of at its face.[127]

Released in July 1979, when many of the Muppets' biggest fans were on vacation, *The Muppet Movie* grossed $76,657,000, the seventh-highest grossing picture of the year. That figure becomes more impressive when one remembers how many children saw the movie at reduced ticket prices. In any event, the take was sufficient to propel Henson and his Muppets into more movies, and it also served as a template for *The Muppets* (2011), which targeted the children who'd grown up with the original movie—and the children of those children.

Despite its success, at first the picture didn't seem to do much to raise Madeline's profile. She was billed prominently on the poster advertising the movie, but most reviewers simply listed Madeline among the cast or omitted her altogether while raving about the ways in which Kermit played banjo and drove a car. However, when the home video revolution flowered, just a few years later, *The Muppet Movie* became a staple of the VCR, played endlessly for young children. Over the years, Madeline's performance has won her a tremendous audience—though many of those watching had no idea who she was.

• • •

Madeline spent the rest of 1978 taking singing lessons—including at least one session with her mother in Los Angeles—and studying French at the Alliance Française in New York. Madeline reconnected with her friends, ran errands, dined out, and went to a *lot* of movies. On October 14, she saw Terrence Malick's poetic *Days of Heaven*, which concludes with the teenaged narrator (pint-size New Yorker Linda Manz) escaping from an orphanage at night, then wandering the deserted streets of a small town. Madeline noted in her appointment book, "Just like when I was little. Alone in N.Y.C."

Already, she was starting to rally. She spent January 1979 reading film scripts, and in February, she met with Woody Allen. Nothing seems to have come of their conversation, but she was lining up projects, and over the ensuing months she made four movies in quick succession. Not one would be a hit. Engineering a comeback would take more than hard work.

Her most remarkable engagement during these months is the least known. On Thursday, May 3, 1979, she flew to Kansas City, where Maurice Peress had invited her to participate in another Bernstein gala. By this time leading the Kansas City Philharmonic Orchestra, Peress had watched in dismay as Bernstein's sixtieth birthday came and went without the kinds of tributes he'd been accorded in 1968. Peress resolved to remedy the situation, programming a weekend-long festival of Bernstein's music, with the composer in attendance. The performances were divided into chamber music (Friday evening), theater music (Saturday evening), and symphonic works (Sunday afternoon, after Bernstein and Madeline had left town). Guest artists included pianist Lukas Foss, members of the American Ballet Theater, and dancer-choreographer Judith Jamison from the Alvin Ailey American Dance Theater. On Friday, following *Songfest*, Bernstein himself conducted the finale.

Madeline joined the performance on Saturday night, when the dancers performed the ballets from *On the Town*, and Larry Kert, the original Tony, sang "Tonight" from *West Side Story*. Madeline didn't sing "Glitter and Be Gay," but Bernstein's amanuensis, Jack Gottlieb, devised a terrific set-up for her. On a screen behind the orchestra, a clip of the rape scene from *Young Frankenstein* played—up to the point where Madeline sings "Ah! Sweet Mystery of Life." Just then, the lights went up, revealing Madeline onstage. "Ah, the movies!" she said, and then performed an aria from *Trouble in Tahiti*, "What a Movie!"

The reunion with Peress and Bernstein—and what amounted to one last *Trouble in Tahiti* audition—was by no means the only big event that night. Also on the bill, singing numbers they'd written for *On the Town* and *Wonderful Town*, were Betty Comden and Adolph Green. In addition to the concert on Friday, Comden, Green, and Madeline would have rehearsed together on Friday afternoon, and presumably they all stayed at the same hotel, the Alameda Plaza, in Kansas City. This was the longest-sustained encounter they'd had, at least since the Tony Awards ceremony the year before. While Green's daughter, the Broadway lyricist and composer Amanda Green, says her father bore Madeline no ill will, Madeline herself may not have been so confident. But once again, she was determined to show the world that *On the Twentieth Century* hadn't broken her.

PART III

The 1980s

LOOKING BACK IN 1988, MADELINE TOLD THE *WASHINGTON POST*, "Most of the stuff I've done, the good stuff, was done a long time ago. The stuff that I've done in TV and the movies has not been of high caliber, but who knew at the time?"[1] The 1980s had been difficult for her.

Most actresses worry as they enter their forties, and some panic. Sexism and ageism have always been problems in the entertainment industry, and good parts are rare for any actor. Again and again, Madeline signed up for movies that fell short of their promise, while in hits like *Ruthless People* (1986), *Outrageous Fortune* (1987), and *Big Business* (1988) Bette Midler fielded plum roles that—as Madeline saw it—might otherwise have gone to her. For her, the decade began with back-to-back failures on the big screen. In 1980, Madeline co-starred in the forty-eighth and fifty-third top-grossing films of the year, respectively *First Family* and *Wholly Moses!* With an estimated gross of $6 million, Marshall Brickman's *Simon*, Madeline's first picture that year, would have ranked eighty-first, but mediocre or poor box office figures don't convey the artistic disappointments of these movies. Her forays into television would earn her a People's Choice Award in 1984 and a Daytime Emmy in 1987, but every one of her sitcoms failed. She remained a much-loved star, albeit one not so widely seen as she'd been in the mid-1970s.

30

Annus Horribilis

Simon; Happy Birthday, Gemini; Wholly Moses!;
and *First Family* (1980)

PLAYING CYNTHIA, A DISTINCTLY INTELLECTUAL FEMME FATALE, IN MAR-
shall Brickman's *Simon*, Madeline is elegant, restrained, and fully dressed,
the polar opposite of Lili von Shtupp—though both characters are hired
by a bad guy to seduce the hero. Her hair looks soft and lovely in the light
of the Hudson Valley (standing in for the state of Maine), and she wears
chic outfits like those she preferred to wear offscreen. Cynthia doesn't
need fancy lingerie to ensnare a man, and when she sings, it's not "I'm
Tired," but the aria from Villa-Lobos's *Bachianas Brasileiras*, number 5.
Madeline's participation in *Simon* suggests that somebody had noticed
her popularity among college boys: In the movie, as in life, she's precisely
the sort of woman about whom a bookworm might fantasize.

Working from his own screenplay, Brickman made his directorial debut with the film, having co-written three movies with Woody Allen:
Sleeper, Annie Hall (sharing the screenplay Oscar in 1977), and *Manhattan*.
Simon is the rambling tale of a Columbia professor who's brainwashed by
scientists into believing he's an extraterrestrial. In quick succession, he
becomes a media sensation, a threat to national security, and a fugitive.
Brickman's script is crammed with arcane cultural and scientific references, demanding a fair degree of sophistication from the audience and
from the actors. As Austin Pendleton observes, great portions of the dialogue are "deliberately full of shit. . . . That's actually the brilliance of the
script."

The title role went to Alan Arkin, with whom Brickman performed
in a folk trio, the Tarriers, in the late 1950s. Pendleton plays the master-
mind of the brainwashing, and Judy Graubart plays Simon's girlfriend.
Both of these are far more substantial roles than Madeline's, though she

receives second billing. She's onscreen for only about five minutes, sharing her scenes either with Arkin or with Pendleton and the cheerfully amoral scientists. Her reunion with Pendleton was especially happy, he remembers, but *Simon* had terrible word of mouth. Many moviegoers found the plot too weird to be entertaining, and Simon's messianic rants are neither as funny as a standup comic's nor as lunatic and true as Howard Beale's in *Network* (1976). In the *New York Times*, Vincent Canby laid much of the blame on Arkin's performance ("much too dour for these kinds of shenanigans") and on Brickman's screenplay, which "is never as funny as almost any two of its dozens of one-liners."[2] Even hardcore fans of Madeline and Arkin stayed away.

Madeline got top billing in Richard Benner's *Happy Birthday, Gemini* for her performance as Bunny Weinstein, a trampy single mother in South Philadelphia, though the plot barely involves her. Posters (incorporating caricatures by Jack Davis of *Mad* magazine) promoted the movie as a wacky Madeline Kahn comedy, a test of her box office drawing power— a test she failed. A hit at Playwrights Horizons in 1976, Albert Innaurato's play *Gemini* had transferred to Broadway, where it ran for more than four years (1977–81), closing after the film adaptation had come and gone. Written without input from the playwright, the film script fuses familiar tropes from urban comedy—a close-knit community of noisy ethnic neighbors—with what was at the time daring sexual frankness and social observation. The "Gemini" of the title, Francis Geminiani (Alan Rosenberg), is a Harvard student home for the summer. His birthday celebration is upended by the arrival of Judith Hastings (Sarah Holcomb), the girl he's been sleeping with, and her brother, Randy (David Marshall Grant), to whom he feels more profoundly attracted.[3] Translated to the big screen without input from the playwright, *Gemini* gained a longer title (presumably because movie audiences otherwise might have expected to see astronauts) and lost its balance. The zanier supporting characters overpower the Harvard students.

With her "hepatitis-colored hair" and tight dresses, Bunny is a juicy part, and Madeline pulls out all the stops. Just about everybody in the ensemble cast does, and that's a problem: What's broadly funny onstage can be overwhelming onscreen.

In her most substantial film role dating from this period, Madeline overcompensates for the differences between her own personality and Bunny's. When Bunny is loud, Madeline gets *louder*. As usual in her acting, however, she does try to portray a richer emotional life for her character than the outlines of the script suggest. Bunny is shrill, outlandish, attention hogging—but she's also the mother of an emotionally needy, probably autistic son, Herschel (Timothy Jenkins), and she's terrified of growing older. Among her stronger scenes is a tender moment when, after a blowup with Herschel, she sits at an upright piano, playing and singing "Moon River." Beginning in a lower register, with dubious pitch, Bunny gains in force and confidence. Better still is a drunken monologue before a mirror in which Madeline reveals Bunny's unwillingness to grow up. She's become the neighborhood tramp because she fears no one will find her beautiful anymore, and she'll wind up alone.

But there's no firm directorial hand to bind together the character's disparate traits or the movie's seemingly contradictory motives. Even Bunny's suicide attempt becomes just another screeching, extroverted distraction from what is, at heart, a simple coming-out story. Benner had broken ground with his 1977 film *Outrageous!* (about the friendship between a drag queen and his schizophrenic roommate), but gay-themed movies of any kind were still a novelty in 1980, and there were few guideposts. To his credit, Benner did emphasize that Francis sees his homosexuality as neither fearful nor shameful, and he wrote a new scene in which Francis and his macho father (Robert Viharo) come to terms.

Though the movie's gay themes went unremarked in posters and other promotional material, Madeline took a risk by starring in *Happy Birthday, Gemini*. The subject matter was daring, and the comedy might not appeal to mainstream audiences—and it didn't. Playing to primarily gay audiences also carried the personal risk of feeling less "feminine," as had been the case when she worked at the Upstairs. But gay audiences were among her most loyal, Madeline knew, and she worked with and enjoyed close friendships with plenty of gay men. For her, making the movie—which, for all she knew at the outset, could have turned out to be as successful as Innaurato's play—was a show of solidarity.

The movie had another, more immediate impact on her personal life: She began dating David Marshall Grant. When as Bunny Weinberger Madeline flirts with Randy Hastings (Grant), he flirts back. They're color-coded, too, as Randy's tight-fitting yellow T-shirt corresponds to Bunny's tight yellow dress. And the attraction between the actors wasn't play-acting. Thirteen years younger than Madeline, good-looking, funny, and with a talent for writing, Grant charmed her completely, and she charmed him. The two saw each other almost constantly during location shooting in Toronto. Night after night, her appointment book is marked simply "David." "He was the love of her life" up to that point and for at least several years to come, Madeline's closest associates say. "[S]he really thought he was the one." Though she resumed seeing Myles Gombert when she returned to New York, Madeline and Grant continued to spend time together, and she continued to wonder whether things might work between them. However, Grant says, "I don't think I turned out to be who she thought I was, and she didn't turn out to be who I thought she was: the heterosexual and the formidable star. We were neither of those things."

In Los Angeles in 1984, he came out to her. As he remembers, she spent hours talking with him, actually holding his hand as he tried to navigate the course he was setting. She called on the qualities that other friends remember in her: the ability to listen, to ask the right questions, to apply her intuition and her compassion. As an established actor, she also provided professional advice. Grant was at the start of a promising career. The year before filming *Happy Birthday, Gemini*, he'd made his Broadway debut in the premiere of Martin Sherman's *Bent*, and he'd played a lead in the film comedy *French Postcards*. By 1984, Grant remembers, "I was tormented; I had aspirations as an actor, and I was very concerned for my career. I think she was concerned for my career, as well. She asked whether maybe I didn't have to be gay. I think she wondered whether it was worth the risk: Why do it if it's going to destroy your career?" But, he says, she was more concerned with his happiness.[4]

What she didn't tell him was that her heart was broken. Before, she'd consciously avoided certain kinds of closeness so as not to repeat her parents' failures. The relationship with Grant suggested new possibilities, and she'd established a connection unlike any she'd found with other men. She continued to spend time with Grant and made a point of introducing him to people who might help with his career both as an actor and as a writer. Though the hope of romance vanished, she didn't deprive herself of the pleasure of his company.

The difference in their ages made her disappointment more painful. *Happy Birthday, Gemini* was the first movie in which Madeline played anybody's mother, and while she would do so again in *First Family*, the same year, nobody really believed Gilda Radner was her daughter. Thus far, Madeline had earned her living primarily by playing sexy, glamorous creatures. When Grant came out, she was turning forty-two. She still looked terrific, but nobody needed to remind her that Hollywood holds fewer opportunities for mature actresses.

Madeline's next movie, Gary Weis's *Wholly Moses!*, was yet another that seemed like a sure-fire hit, with another all-star cast of reliably funny actors. Weis had directed a short film with Madeline (*Autumn in*

New York) when she hosted *Saturday Night Live* in 1977. A box office disappointment, grossing $14,155,617 in its original release, *Wholly Moses!* suffered by comparison with *Monty Python's Life of Brian*, another tale of mixed-up biblical destinies, released the year before. *Moses* is short on laughs and long on pointless raunch. Historical and biblical references surface tentatively, as if the filmmakers couldn't decide how sophisticated the target audience might be. In one brief scene, Madeline (as the Witch) drives a cart full of love potions and stops to pick up the hitchhiking Herschel (Dudley Moore), the biblical Moses's brother-in-law. Wearing an immense silver wig, Madeline impersonates a yenta as she offers a couple of minutes' worth of exposition, then tosses Herschel out of the cart. The movie offered her no opportunity to work with anyone other than Moore in a cast that also included Laraine Newman, Dom DeLuise, Richard Pryor, Jack Gilford, and Andrea Martin. As far as Madeline was concerned, the best that could be said about *Wholly Moses!* was that her role was so small few people remember it.

Madeline's professional path had almost crossed writer Buck Henry's several times. He skillfully overhauled the screenplay for *What's Up, Doc?*, worked with Mel Brooks on the sitcom *Get Smart*, and hosted *Saturday Night Live* several times in the 1970s. Now, in 1980, he was ready to try his hand at directing his own work. He cast first-rate talent: *First Family* stars Bob Newhart as the President, Madeline as the First Lady, and Gilda Radner as their daughter, with Harvey Korman, Austin Pendleton, and Richard Benjamin in prominent roles. Oddly enough, Henry's writing, not his direction, undoes the movie, as the political satire grows bitter and unfunny over the course of the movie. Pendleton says Henry was so dismayed by audience response to a preview screening he reshot the movie's ending: The accidental death of the family becomes a miraculous resuscitation. But the changes didn't help much, and the movie earned just $15,198,912 at the box office, far less than the studio hoped. Henry never directed another film.[5]

Madeline doesn't have many lines in *First Family*, though she's in plenty of scenes. The movie sets forth the premise that the pressures of the presidency create stress for the president's loved ones, too. Obliged to adhere to a strict code of conduct, his daughter is a deeply frustrated twenty-six-year-old virgin. His wife drinks in secret, not unlike the Pat Nixon Madeline played on *SNL* in 1976. In most scenes, the first lady remains somewhat in the background, trying to hold herself steady, and Madeline subtly varies her portrayal of the character's levels of intoxication. In her most substantial dialogue scene, she tries to console her daughter in one more example of Madeline and Gilda's extraordinary chemistry.

Despite the dismal results of the films Madeline made in 1980, that quick succession of roles confirmed that she was still in demand as a motion picture star, and the steady work helped her continuing recovery from the disaster of *On the Twentieth Century*. One person in particular hoped to capitalize on Madeline's heightened visibility: her mother.

31

It's Good to Be Somebody's Mother

A Little Off-Broadway and *History of the World, Part I* (1980–81)

PAULA KAHN, STILL CERTAIN THAT STARDOM WAS HER RIGHTFUL DES-tiny, decided that now was the time to reveal her talents to the world. But a mere showcase, such as those that aspiring actors stage all the time, would not do. A one-woman show was required, she felt, and she asked Madeline to bankroll it. Understandably nervous, Madeline asked Walter Willison to direct the show. "Walter, you gotta protect me here," she told him, and he took the job, also writing lyrics for two songs, including the opening number, "I'm Somebody's Mother," with Jeffrey Silverman, the show's music director. The script consisted of a loose collection of anecdotes—"Paula's take on womanhood," as Jef Kahn calls it—as well as reenactments of scenes from her life. Just in case anyone was unaware that she was Madeline Kahn's mother, she insisted that her one-woman show be expanded to include an actress representing the Daughter, though the character had no lines. This daughter, unlike the real-life one, would merely look on, almost like a stage prop, while Paula went about her business. Willison cast his friend Joanna Rush in the role.

Paula had wanted all along to extract Jef from the Twin Oaks community, so she summoned him to work on the show. Jef was ready to leave, so he drove out to Los Angeles with his cousin, Dan Kahn. Frustrated by his inability to get Paula to stick to the schedule and learn her songs, Jef next asked his girlfriend, Heidi Berthoud, to make the trip out, for emotional support. But Willison and Rush found Paula as undisciplined as she was temperamental, and they soon went into a huddle with Jef and Heidi, then quit the show. Undaunted, Paula cast another actress as the Daughter, hired another director and, ultimately, another musical director, and forged ahead.

A Little Off-Broadway & Slightly North of Wilshire played first at UCLA. Paula invited Madeline's friends, and a few did attend, more as a display of solidarity than out of any expectation that a star would be born that night at age fifty-seven. "Who wants to see Madeline Kahn's mother when Madeline Kahn is in the audience?" Mel Brooks asks. Nevertheless, he and Anne Bancroft watched as Paula sang and revealed "funny" details of her relationship with Madeline. Always striving to be a polished professional herself and resolutely guarded about her private life, Madeline was humiliated in front of some of her most important Hollywood connections. Today, Brooks politely declines to remember any details of Paula's show. "It was okay," he says. "[I]t was a blur. I was just so unhappy for Madeline."

Seemingly unaware that her show was anything but a hit, Paula arranged to sign on for a longer run—Monday nights for six months, with the possibility of an extension—at the Westwood Playhouse, beginning June 16. This time, Madeline refused to pay the upfront money. Undaunted, Paula "borrowed" it from Jef. For the second show, however, Paula neglected to rehearse or even to learn her lines. On opening night, she tried to wing it, humming when she forgot song lyrics, laughing as she repeatedly asked for cues. Now Madeline put her foot down. The show closed, and Paula resumed her primary occupation, "being taken care of," as Jef says. She continued to stir up activity without following through, blaming others for her failures, and then asking Madeline to pick up the pieces.

At the time of Paula's show, Madeline was shooting *History of the World, Part I,* her fourth and final picture with Brooks, in which she plays the Roman Empress Nympho. Spanning centuries, from the cavemen to the Spanish Inquisition to the French Revolution, *History* may be the most lavish of Brooks's directorial efforts. With an estimated budget of $11 million, and gross earnings of $31,672,907 (ranked nineteenth at the box office for 1981), it nonetheless didn't rival *Blazing Saddles* and *Young Frankenstein* in impact. Only years later did the line "It's good to be the king" (uttered by Brooks as Louis XVI) become a catchphrase, thanks to viewings on cable and video. The highlight of Madeline's performance is a musical moment in which she selects the best-hung imperial soldiers to escort her to an orgy. "Yes, yes, no, yes, no, no," she sings to an accelerando rhythm, but it's not really a song. And she gets nothing more to sing, though Broadway hoofer Gregory Hines plays her favorite, a runaway slave. "After seeing the movie about 30 times, I realized that was a mistake," Brooks says. "I had Madeline Kahn and Gregory Hines! And

Madeline Gail Wolfson, circa 1943. Photo courtesy of Jeffrey Kahn.

Daddy's girl, for now: Madeline and Bernie Wolfson on Revere Beach, circa 1943. Photo courtesy of Jeffrey Kahn.

"Madalin Wolfson," age eight, a student at the Manumit School. Photo courtesy of Jeffrey Kahn.

Madeline's relationship with her brother, Jeffrey, was among the closest and most gratifying of her life. Photo, circa 1953, courtesy of Jeffrey Kahn.

Hiller Kahn, with Jeffrey (circa 1957). No comparable picture of Madeline and Hiller survives. Photo courtesy of Jeffrey Kahn.

Singing for her supper: "Madi Gail" at the Bavarian Manor, circa 1963–64. Photo courtesy of Jeffrey Kahn.

Like a college student impersonating the movie star Madeline Kahn: a scene from *L'Amfiparnaso*, Hofstra, 1964. Photo courtesy of Jeffrey Kahn.

Like a young Jeanne Moreau:
the Hofstra graduate, 1964.
Photo courtesy of Jeffrey Kahn.

New York debutantes (left to right)
Madeline, Fannie Flagg, and Betty
Aberlin at the Upstairs, 1965.
Photo courtesy of Jeffrey Kahn.

New Faces of 1968: Madeline and Robert Klein (both seated) with George Ormiston and Marilyn Childs (both standing). Photofest.

Making the garden grow: Curtain call for *Candide* with (left to right) Leonard Bernstein, Alan Arkin, Madeline, and Irra Petina, 1968. Photo courtesy of Jeffrey Kahn.

Musetta's Waltz: Madeline in *La Bohème*, her only professional operatic engagement, Washington Opera Society, 1970. Photo courtesy of Jeffrey Kahn.

Golden Girl: Madeline, in her act 1 costume, with (left to right) Michael Karm, Danny Kaye, and Harry Goz in *Two by Two*, 1970. Photofest.

Built like an opera singer: Seeing herself onscreen convinced Madeline that she needed to lose weight. Between takes during the filming of *What's Up, Doc?* Photo, taken in 1971, courtesy of Jeffrey Kahn.

Why are they laughing? The role of Eunice Burns in *What's Up, Doc?* (1972) made Madeline miserable and sent her into therapy. Photofest.

Miss Trixie makes her entrance: rehearsing the shot while trying out a new brassiere in *Paper Moon*, with P. J. Johnson trailing behind. Photo, taken in 1972, courtesy of Jeffrey Kahn.

Portrait of a serious actress: Madeline and the dancers in *Boom Boom Room* (1973). Mary Woronov stands in the center background. Photofest.

"Let me see your legs": Madeline as Lili von Shtupp (*Blazing Saddles*, 1974). Photofest.

The most important collaboration of her professional life: Madeline with Mel Brooks during the filming of *Young Frankenstein* (1974). Photo courtesy of Jeffrey Kahn.

Hello, stranger: Madeline with Peter Boyle in *Young Frankenstein* (1974). Photofest.

No entourage. No stylists. No artificial lighting. No mirror checks or "fabulous" chitchat. *Portrait of Madeline* (circa 1974). Photo © Shaun Considine. Used with permission.

An extraordinary level of trust: Madeline with Gene Wilder in a scene from *Sherlock Holmes' Smarter Brother* (1975). Photofest.

"Down in the Dumps": Madeline during the original opening scene of *At Long Last Love* (1975). Photofest.

The would-be star of the family: Paula Kahn's headshot from the 1960s, and posing with Madeline on the set of *Won Ton Ton* (1975). Photos courtesy of Jeffrey Kahn.

Live from New York: Madeline's appearances on *Saturday Night Live* in the 1970s were among her most important professional engagements. Photo from 1977, taken during her second hosting gig. Photofest.

"Numb despair and doomed frivolity": Mavis Danton rehearses with Eunice Higgins (*The Carol Burnett Show*, 1976). Photo courtesy of Jeffrey Kahn.

"Paula is my responsibility. I have to take care of her": A fateful conversation between Madeline and Jef (1976). Photo by Denny R. McElyea. Used with permission.

If the 2,000-Year-Old Man had a wife: Mel Brooks and Madeline in *High Anxiety* (1977). Photo courtesy of Jeffrey Kahn.

"I hope you don't think I can do that every night": Madeline in the "Veronique" finale (*On the Twentieth Century*, 1978). Photofest.

Madeline's appearances with the Muppets exposed her to several generations of younger audiences that had no idea who she was. With Kermit and Telly Savalas in *The Muppet Movie* (1979). Photofest.

Clowning with Jerry Lewis on the set of *Slapstick* (1982). Photo courtesy of Jeffrey Kahn.

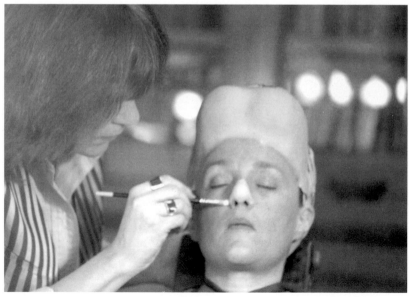

Not quite ready for her close-up: in the makeup chair for *Slapstick* (1982). Photo courtesy of Jeffrey Kahn.

A Lucy Ricardo for the 1980s: a promotional still for *Oh Madeline*, with James Sloyan (1983). Photofest.

Peter Hujar's eloquent portrait of Madeline is a document of her friendship with Charles Ludlam. Photo © 1987 The Peter Hujar Archive LLC; Courtesy Pace/MacGill Gallery, New York, and Fraenkel Gallery, San Francisco.

A black widow, web and all: as Mrs. White in *Clue* (1985). Photofest.

Speaking truth to power: Madeline and George C. Scott in *Mr. President* (1987). Photofest.

The gin game, act 1, *Born Yesterday*, with Edward Asner as Harry Brock (1989). Photofest.

A rare sighting of the Bear Lady and her "pizza hat": Madeline in costume during the shooting of Woody Allen's *Shadows and Fog* (1991). Photo courtesy of Jeffrey Kahn.

Madeline with her long-term boyfriend and eventual husband, John Hansbury. Photo courtesy of John W. Hansbury, Esq.

Harmonia Gardens, here I come: Madeline in costume as Dolly, backstage in Atlanta (1992). Photo courtesy of Jeffrey Kahn.

"Like Dolly on the ramp": Madeline as Gorgeous Teitelbaum in *The Sisters Rosensweig* (1992). Photo courtesy of John W. Hansbury, Esq.

In costume as Billie, the homeless sage, with John Hansbury on the set of *For Richer, for Poorer* (1992). Photo by Carol J. Bawer, courtesy of John W. Hansbury, Esq.

Singing for Sondheim: Madeline performs "Getting Married Today" at Carnegie Hall (1993). Photofest.

Like playing jazz: Madeline as Pauline, with Bill Cosby as Hilton, in a scene from *Cosby* (circa 1996). Photofest.

Relaxing on Fire Island in the 1990s. Photo courtesy of John W. Hansbury, Esq.

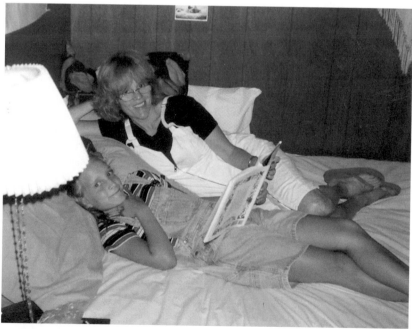

Madeline in one of her favorite roles: Eliza Kahn's aunt (circa 1997). Photo courtesy of John W. Hansbury, Esq.

"I'm so glad I made that movie before I died": Madeline with Novella Nelson in her final film, Eric Mendelsohn's *Judy Berlin* (shot in 1997). Photofest.

The last summer: Madeline with Jef and Eliza Kahn, 1999. Photo courtesy of Jeffrey Kahn.

I didn't give them a musical number!" He did, however, give Madeline jokes and shtick that were vulgar even by the standards of his comedy. She goes along gamely, as far as one can tell from watching the screen. But to friends and family she again revealed her discomfort with this kind of material. In private, she wasn't entirely uptight, and to her dying day she kept old love letters that include rapturous paeans to her breasts. But what she wanted to present to the public wasn't necessarily what Brooks asked for.

At least the material Brooks gave her was *funny*, unlike so many of the roles that other moviemakers offered her. "Mel gave sexy ladies a chance to be funny, and he allowed Madeline Kahn to be sexy *and* funny. There's a big difference," Joan Rivers told a film interviewer. In the same documentary, Tracey Ullman describes Brooks as one of the rare "men in the business that like women and get women and are comfortable with women being funny."[6] Madeline almost certainly would have agreed with this assessment. But there was a catch: Brooks's films brought Madeline prominence and acclaim, but also a widespread belief that she really *was* bawdy, and that broad comedy was her preferred field—her specialty, if not her one-trick pony.

Nympho is hardly a substantial role. She may be empress, but she's not the leading lady, as she had been in *High Anxiety*. In the Roman episode she is overshadowed by Brooks, who plays a standup comic helping Hines to escape to freedom. But she enjoyed working again with Brooks and with Dom DeLuise, who plays the emperor Nero, and she established a good onscreen rapport with Dena Dietrich (playing her lady-in-waiting), with whom she'd appeared on *Adam's Rib*.

Over the next several years Brooks directed three films without making any substantial offers to Madeline. She took this as a personal slight. Admittedly, it's hard to imagine an appropriate part for her in Brooks's next movie, *Spaceballs* (1987), since she was by then too old for the role of the Princess (played by twenty-five-year-old Daphne Zuniga) and the wrong type to play the android Dot Matrix (Joan Rivers). To Brooks's credit, he'd already doubled the number of female leads in the film he was parodying, *Star Wars*. It's far easier to picture Madeline as Brooks's love interest in the class comedy *Life Stinks* (1991), and yet that character's best scene is a dance number. With Lesley Ann Warren, who studied ballet as avidly as Madeline studied voice, the scene achieves an arresting beauty that Madeline could never have brought off, no matter how hard she tried.

Madeline's family and friends report that Brooks's representatives offered her the part of Latrine, the cook in *Robin Hood: Men in Tights* (1993), at a fee too low for her to consider. Brooks tells a different story. There was no question of money, he says, but the part itself "was simply not enough." Tracey Ullman played Latrine, and Brooks never worked with Madeline again. When asked whether he considered her for other roles, Brooks said that he wanted to expand the role of Elizabeth in the Broadway musical adaptation of *Young Frankenstein*, and with Madeline in mind, he'd wanted to do so long before his adaptation of *The Producers* opened on Broadway in 2001. But the musical version of *Young Frankenstein* wouldn't see its New York premiere until eight years after Madeline's death.

32

Slipshod

Slapstick (Of Another Kind) (1982–84)

SLAPSTICK (OF ANOTHER KIND), AN ADAPTATION OF KURT VONNEGUT'S novel *Slapstick: Or Lonesome No More*, teamed Madeline with Jerry Lewis and Marty Feldman, but the results were so bad that the picture was held back from American release for two years, seeing its US premiere only in March 1984 (European audiences saw it beginning in late 1982). According to the film's director, co-screenwriter, and producer, Steven Paul, critical and audience responses were so negative that distributors around the world tried to break their agreements with him. Although Vonnegut joined in writing the screenplay—and, according to Paul, enjoyed himself at a preview screening in New York—the author ultimately dismissed the movie, and the Golden Raspberry Award Foundation nominated Lewis for a "Razzie" for worst actor in 1985. Even today, Internet critics continue to throw insults at the picture. "Horrifying," runs a typical comment on the IMDb website. "[T]he movie takes the book, shreds it, puts a Hollywood sheen on it, dripped slime on it, then pooted it out into the world."[7]

Vonnegut's novels are reputedly unfilmable, and *Slapstick* is a hodge-podge of science fiction and social and political satire that the author described as "the closest I will ever come to writing an autobiography."[8] The problem with this movie doesn't lie so much with the material as with the approach. Paul, a wunderkind actor and producer (whose relationship with Vonnegut dated back to childhood), was less experienced as a filmmaker, having only one prior credit, *Falling in Love Again* (1980). Today Paul cheerfully accepts responsibility for *Slapstick*'s failure, but he points out that as a producer, he managed to make a complex film on a tiny budget with popular stars. His biggest mistake was hiring himself to direct, and he wistfully recalls meeting with Terry Gilliam to discuss the project. Gilliam found *Slapstick* intriguing, and he outlined his vision, which embraced suggestions of incest between the principal characters, a brother and sister who are also twins. However, Gilliam was committed to the final Monty Python movie, *The Meaning of Life*, and with money lining up, Paul couldn't afford to wait.

By producing and directing, Paul effectively held down two full-time jobs simultaneously. He was responsible for the film's completion bond and financing, for securing distribution, and for paying every bill—to the point that he had to interrupt takes to sign checks. As an inexperienced director, he opted for what he now believes was the wrong tone—"comedic and softer," less bizarre than that of the novel or, for that matter, Gilliam's scheme. Also, he should have "pulled more" from the cast. He sought out Lewis because he admired the "young, innocent, idiot kid" the comedian played in his early films, but he came to understand that in middle age Lewis could no longer tap into that persona. "I kept pushing to get that character from him," Paul remembers, "and he couldn't find it. I think we finally got close to it, that childish quality."

Finding an actress to play the dual role of the sister and the twins' mother proved a challenge, but after considering a number of candidates, Paul remembered Madeline, with whom he had worked on *Comedy Tonight*. Joining forces with her agent, Johnnie Planco, he persuaded Madeline to commit to *Slapstick*, and prepared a press release. Only then did Paul share the news with Lewis, who replied, "I won't work with her." The two had never met, but Lewis believed that Madeline's work was "not my kind of comedy," suggesting that he, like so many others, expected Madeline to be Lili von Shtupp. After repeated assurances from Paul, Lewis relented, and Paul was spared the ordeal of retracting his press release and tearing up Madeline's contract. Lewis may not have been completely convinced, and when he met Madeline at last, it was on neutral ground, at the Polo Lounge. Later, he hosted several rehearsals at his home in Beverly Hills, and by the end of shooting, he told Paul that working with Madeline "was the closest he had come to working with Dean Martin."

Because *Slapstick* was a non-union project, Madeline was able to secure jobs on the set for her brother and for Heidi Berthoud. But coming to work meant crossing a picket line every day, which heightened tensions on the set—particularly for Lewis, since the Teamsters were longtime supporters of his Labor Day telethons. At one point, Lewis lost patience with his director ("You're appalling. A-*Paul*-ing"), but apart from this outburst, Jef and Heidi say, he remained quiet, professional, and somewhat aloof on the set. Shoots tended to run long, and Madeline often worked ten- and twelve-hour days.

As the continuity person, Heidi had a front-row seat for the ad-libs and teasing that followed flubbed lines. Feldman "would go off on these riffs and make everything funny and fine. And of course Madi would play off of him. They had fun together," Heidi remembers. Madeline tried to "stay above the fray," Jef remembers, and she kept her opinions to herself. On one occasion, however, the fray came to her. A popular television actress came to the set and confronted Madeline, believing that she was having an affair with her husband, a member of the production team for *Slapstick*. Madeline "handled it very diplomatically and didn't raise her voice and kept her integrity about it," Jef says. Her capacity for arousing suspicion among other women (Alan Titus's wife, Gene Wilder's daughter, Ursula Andress) may have contributed to her aplomb. She'd endured such situations before, but she would've preferred to avoid them altogether.

Other film sets have seen more tensions and more outright conflict than this one, and they've turned out just fine. *Slapstick* turned out to be an unfunny, cheap-looking mess that wasted the talents of its stars and the goodwill of Vonnegut's fans. As freakish twins—brilliant so long as they're together, but infantile idiots when they're apart—Madeline and Lewis are saddled with grotesque makeup, one-piece pajamas for costumes, and no way to salvage creditable performances. For Lewis, who had only just completed Martin Scorsese's *The King of Comedy*, *Slapstick* must have been especially painful. He and Madeline also play the twins' parents, "the most beautiful of the Beautiful People," and he seems to channel his discomfort into his portrayal of the father. Though the character is supposed to be ill at ease, the audience can sense the actor's desire to escape from the movie.

For Madeline, *Slapstick* did come with a few perquisites, including the opportunity to work with Michel Legrand, who composed the score to the soundtrack, as he had done for Paul's *Falling in Love Again* (as well as *The Umbrellas of Cherbourg* and *The Summer of '42*, among many others). Madeline recorded one song for the film, "Lonesome No More," to a lyric by Vonnegut; Legrand himself provided piano accompaniment. But the US release featured a new score by Morton Stevens, the composer of the theme to *Hawaii Five-O* and Jerry Lewis's preferred bandleader. Madeline's song went unheard in America, and it is omitted from a soundtrack album that featured orchestral excerpts from both Legrand's and Stevens's scores.

Vonnegut visited the set on February 23, giving Madeline the chance to meet him. Paula Kahn also visited the set for her birthday, and after hours, Madeline spent time with Jef and Heidi. Once a week, the three of them went to eat together, in restaurants much fancier, and featuring more fattening food than anything the young couple had been accustomed to at Twin Oaks. The excitement didn't stop there. "When she drove us around L.A.," Heidi remembers, "she wouldn't stop for stop signs. No way. It was like a thrill, a racecar-driver thing for her."

Although Heidi and Jef had spent time with Madeline at Twin Oaks and in New York, Heidi's perspective deepened during the shooting of *Slapstick*. For her, Madeline and Jef were simultaneously the adoring big sister and baby brother—and the famous actress and her fan. Jef was "deeply enamored of Madeline," Heidi says. "Whenever we were with Madeline, he was focused on Madeline and, like, with *blinders*." Neither Heidi nor Jef needed much attention, she says ("If you want name and fame, you don't go join a commune"), but Madeline thrived on it. When they were with her, "it became really uncomfortable for me, to be like this appendage that wasn't really needed. The fall-out of superstars! Living in the wake—in the ruins! That continued through the years to be difficult." Heidi and Jef broke up some time later, but they remain close friends.

33

The Safe Place

Santa Fe (1982–83)

"THERE'S SOMETHING ABOUT THIS PLACE, A LOT OF MYSTERIOUS AND primitive stuff going on—faith healing, sorcery, herbal therapy," Madeline told a reporter from *People* magazine who had come to see her as Madame Arcati in Noël Coward's *Blithe Spirit* at the Santa Fe Festival Theater in 1983. "Santa Fe is beautiful, and I'm moved by what I see and how I feel here."[9] As she prepared the role of the addled medium, the spirituality of Santa Fe had already begun to work on her.

For most actors, New Mexico is "fly-over country" between Hollywood and New York, but for Madeline in the 1980s it became a haven. Visiting Hiller Kahn's ex-sister-in-law, Ginny Kahn, Madeline could recharge her emotional batteries, and performing with a local theater troupe, she could take creative risks. Even when she wasn't working, she sometimes flew out to enjoy the scenery and the opera festival, as well as the mystical atmosphere. Ginny had longstanding ties to the area around Santa Fe dating at least as early as 1948, when, as an anthropology student at Vassar College, she did field work among the Navajo. Many years later, having divorced Ernie, Ginny summered in Santa Fe, and around 1979, Madeline and Jef Kahn first visited her there. Madeline's contacts with Ginny and her children were "intermittent," Ginny says. "We didn't write to each other, because she wasn't a writer. We'd talk on the phone sometimes, but not a lot. But there was a bond between us."

Because of their time together in New Mexico, Madeline's relationship with Ginny and her children found its mark. It helped that Ginny's son, Dan, is close in age to Jef Kahn, and the two were fast friends. To an outside observer, it's as if the various divorces never splintered the family ties. Ginny's younger daughter, Sarah, knew Madeline better than Robyn Wolfson did. Robyn believes geographical distance contributed to the limited roles she and Madeline played in each other's lives, but the neutral ground of Santa Fe gave Madeline space to enjoy the company of Ginny's family. Madeline never discussed her mother with Ginny, but the two did sometimes share details of their private lives. On a visit in 1992, for example, they talked about marriage. Madeline had been seeing John Hansbury for three years, and Ginny had recently been through what she calls "a disappointing but exciting relationship." Madeline treated her as an older sister, Ginny says. "She was safe with me, and we had a good time together." Often, Madeline was in Santa Fe to work. Though she'd seen her niece's movies, and her performances at the Upstairs and in plays, it was only in Santa Fe that Ginny realized, "My God, Madeline's become famous!"

By the early 1980s, the Santa Fe Opera Festival, founded in 1957, had become a national and international destination for music lovers. Among the singers who performed with the company were William Lewis, Madeline's co-star from *Candide*, and mezzo-soprano Frederica von Stade, one of Matthew Epstein's closest associates. Madeline herself nearly performed with the company in 1981, when a virus ran rampant through the cast of Strauss's *Daphne*, necessitating a switch to Puccini's *Bohème*. The Musetta fell ill, too, and Madeline considered stepping in, extending her stay by a few days to accommodate the opera schedule. The Musetta recovered, and Madeline never rehearsed the role; she flew home the next day. That she even considered a return to the opera stage is one more indication of the emotional security she found in Santa Fe.

For years, both locals and visitors wondered whether the town could support a theater festival, too. Artistic advisory board member Angela Lansbury echoed this thought at a press conference on June 16, 1981, announcing the opening of the Santa Fe Festival Theater,[10] and the project seemed promising to Madeline, who was involved from the start. Seasoned professionals from "back East," as a local news account described them (producing director Thomas Gardner, executive director Christopher Beach, stage director Robert Allan Ackerman, and designer Robert Wojewodski), had their location already, the National Guard Armory on Old Pecos Trail. Somewhat removed from the downtown area frequented by tourists, the armory is one of the last constructions of the WPA. The building opened in 1940, just in time to be put to use as a processing facility. By the late 1970s, the armory saw less use. Gardner and Beach renovated it, with private money and a grant from the state legislature, taking over the entire structure for their theater.

Their first production, Hecht and MacArthur's *The Front Page*, opened on July 29, 1981, with Madeline in attendance. The founders aspired to create an environment where both seasoned professionals and emerging actors could stretch their wings, where they were often cast against type in less-familiar repertory, and sheltered from the scrutiny of larger venues. Ultimately, though, their vision worked against them. As one of the Festival Theater's original company members, Nicholas Sabato Jr., observes, audiences tended to skip plays without celebrity actors, such as Ted Tally's *Terra Nova*. Instead, they held out to see Michael York in *Cyrano de Bergerac*, another of the company's first season productions. *Terra Nova* "was brilliant, but no one came to see it," Sabato remembers.

At a benefit in New York, Madeline had helped to raise funds for the Festival Theater, singing "I'm Tired" and appearing with Gilda Radner in a short play directed by Ackerman. Susan Sarandon and Stephen Collins also participated in the event. That lineup is a good indicator of the star power the company hoped to deploy in Santa Fe. Ackerman would direct Madeline in two productions at the Festival Theater: in 1982, a world premiere music-theater adaptation of Franz Kafka's *Amerika*, with a book by Israeli playwright Yoram Porat and music by Shlomo Gronich, and in 1983, *Blithe Spirit*.

The second production is in some ways more representative of the Theater's aims. While Madeline might have excelled in the role of the beautiful, disruptive ghost, Elvira, she played against type as Arcati. Both Ackerman and Madeline's co-star, Victor Garber, agree that Madeline would be a wonderful Arcati *today*, but in 1983, she was too young for the part. Another star actor, Amy Irving, took the role of Elvira. But as Ackerman says, the *New York Times* didn't dispatch critics to review a play in Santa Fe, and producers and casting agents were unlikely to turn up in the audience. The Santa Fe journalists who reported on theater and interviewed actors were also the critics who reviewed the plays, engaging in a kind of dualism that, in the era before industry-wide cutbacks in arts coverage, larger papers in bigger cities tried to avoid. Even today, Sabato says, "It's not a theater town."

But as Madeline told *People* magazine, "There's a different feeling in the theater here. You aren't as self-conscious as you would be on Broadway or a big city. You take more risks." Working with the Festival Theater was important to Madeline, Ackerman says, because "It was so free, and I'm sure people have told you, she was kind of a frightened person. I think being there made her feel calm and secure, and she . . . enjoyed being surrounded by friends who really cared for each other." That atmosphere was important to her. She hadn't worked in theater since *On the Twentieth Century*.

Amerika tells the story of a young German, Karl (played by Scott Burkholder), whose parents ship him off to the United States after catching him with the housemaid. Madeline played three roles: the maid, the proprietress of a hotel where Karl works as a bellboy, and—most memorably, according to all accounts—an opera singer who spent most of her stage time in the bathtub. Yoram Porat didn't write these roles for a single actress, he told the *Santa Fe New Mexican*, but, he said, "There is a thread of similarity in the three women, and with Madeline Kahn playing all three roles, that continuity is enhanced."[11] Madeline lost herself in her characters, Burkholder says. As the maid, a non-comic role, Madeline was "very, very girlish, not very well educated, very low-class," he remembers, a strong contrast to her "imperious and very controlling opera singer." And much of the "hilarious" business she came up with, especially for the bath scene, was unscripted. "She was constantly inventing things." To get the accents right, she turned to Ginny Kahn, who put her in touch with a Viennese émigré.

Porat had premiered *Amerika* without music in 1976. Yet Shlomo Gronich's score was the strongest element of the play, Ackerman and Burkholder agree, and Madeline approached it seriously (though sometimes she used her voice "to sing in a funny way, [as if] making fun of her own talent," Burkholder remembers). Music "was like a religion" to Madeline, Ackerman says. He also worked with her in a number of benefits and special events when she sang. "If she was going to sing a song, she really *became* the song," he says. "She analyzed the song. She built a character."

Meanwhile, the demands of the show—a large cast in multiple roles, a two-level set (designed like a giant machine by Wojewodski), an eleven-piece orchestra—were compounded by extensive revisions to the script. Officially, though, it was a technical challenge, upgrading the sound system, that caused Gardner and Beach abruptly to postpone opening night. The reporter–critic for the *New Mexican* disapproved, and, returning to the theater on August 6, she found the show overlong, "a case of Kafka overkill"—then lumped her review in with that for another production. She praised Madeline, while warning that "if theater-goers expected her to out-act and out-sing everyone else, they were disappointed. . . . [The] play is written in a way that equalizes roles, forbids a 'lead' to emerge."[12]

Burkholder, however, remembers an "overwhelming" audience response to Madeline at curtain calls.

Especially because of the unhappy outcome in *Twentieth Century*, "I don't think Madeline would have done *Amerika* anywhere but Santa Fe," Ackerman says. "We all felt this was a safe place to try this out." Burkholder agrees. Because theater affords actors the chance to repeat their work, to correct their errors, to relive a portion of their experience each night, "You can edge towards perfection," he says. "It's a very safe place to be."

Madeline returned the next summer for what seemed a less risky choice of repertory, in what she believed to be the funniest role in *Blithe Spirit*. It's an unusual instance of her getting to choose a role and choosing wrong. She had the eccentricity for Arcati, but not the maturity, Ackerman says now, and her "different kind of energy" ran up against the audience's expectations of a Margaret Rutherford-type. Madeline had turned forty the previous September, and remarkably, she opted to depict Arcati as an older woman, following the standard interpretation of the play and adding this to the short list of roles for which she "greyed up."

Here again, the protected atmosphere of Santa Fe encouraged her. Had she expected Hollywood casting directors to see the show—and to see her opposite the stunning Amy Irving—she might have played Arcati as younger and more attractive than usual, while still bringing her lunacy to bear. Instead, Ackerman remembers that Madeline stooped her shoulders and changed her voice, and photographs show her with age makeup and a wig. Embracing Arcati's age may be one reason everyone remembers her as too young for the part, since her portrayal was artificial from the start. "She analyzed things to beyond the nth degree," Victor Garber says. "She was so smart, and such an intellect, but I think it kind of worked against her in some ways." Nevertheless, Ackerman says, Madeline dove into the role, with an attitude of "Let's do this for the theater." He found her inventive and collaborative, though Garber remembers, "Madeline's process was sometimes frustrating, because she just didn't nail stuff down. She was kind of all over the place—in a wonderful way. I mean, I adored it. But there were times I would think, 'Are you actually going to move over *there* now?'"

At least by the Festival Theater's standards, *Blithe Spirit* was a success. Sabato retains vivid memories of Madeline's grand entrance on a bicycle, spinning across the back of the house. "Audiences and the local critics appreciate her comic inventiveness in the role," *People* noted. Yet the safety of Santa Fe wasn't inviolable. In the article, a mention of Madeline's exercise routine was used to remind readers of *Twentieth Century*, "when fatigue and a faltering voice forced her out of the Broadway hit . . . . This time no replacement is likely to be necessary."[13]

Offstage, Madeline found a welcoming community of colleagues and friends. Younger company members expected to find a movie star—or at least the kind of personality Madeline played onscreen. Instead, Burkholder was surprised by how tiny, shy, and soft-spoken she was. Sabato noted that she treated everyone, from novices to Lily Tomlin, with the same "wonderful spirit and energy." *Amerika* was only Burkholder's second professional acting job, and he was under great pressure in a huge role with constant revisions. He remembers that Madeline sometimes "translated" Ackerman's directions in order to help him during rehearsals. When his parents drove in from Tucson to see the show, she joined them for dinner but made sure he remained the center of attention. Both Ackerman and Garber had known Madeline since the 1970s, each having been introduced to her by Gilda Radner. Working together in Santa Fe brought them closer, Garber says. The three had dinner together almost every night, and tea on Sunday afternoons. After hours, they might socialize with other members of the troupe and the opera company, too.

During *Amerika*, producers Gardner and Beach found a rental for Madeline, the Pit House, outside town. Inspired by traditional Anasazi structures, it was almost completely underground and blended in with the desert scenery. Ultra-urbane Madeline found the Pit House claustrophobic and remote. Fearful of bugs, she walked around "on semi-tiptoes," Ackerman says. "Madeline was not the sort of person you would think would go camping." But she didn't want her friends to think she didn't appreciate the effort they'd made for her. She phoned Ackerman often: "Tell them I love it!" Then she would squeal, "Come over, don't leave me here alone!" (For *Blithe Spirit,* she rented a one-bedroom adobe house more to her taste.)

Because of film and television commitments, Madeline couldn't return for another season with the Festival Theater, and the company closed in 1985. She'd wait until 1992 for her only other professional engagement in the area.

34

Madness and Mourning

Yellowbeard (1983)

THE EARLY 1980S SAW A NUMBER OF PIRATE MOVIES. MOST WERE COMedies; all were failures. None was starrier than *Yellowbeard*, featuring *Monty Python* veterans (Graham Chapman, Eric Idle, John Cleese); British comedians old (Spike Milligan, Peter Cook) and young (Nigel Planer); *Young Frankenstein* favorites (Peter Boyle, Marty Feldman, Kenneth Mars); acclaimed "legit" actors (Michael Hordern, James Mason, Susanna York, Beryl Reid, Peter Bull); one rock star (David Bowie); two American counter-culturists (Cheech and Chong); and one female comedian, Madeline. But as Bob Thomas of the Associated Press asked in his review, "How could so many comedic talents produce such a mirthless movie?"[14] Warning signs were evident even during shooting. "They're saying it's very funny, which is usually the kiss of death," Milligan told two documentary-makers on the set.[15] Curiously, *Yellowbeard* works better as a straightforward swashbuckler, interrupted by scattershot bursts of humor.

For her part, Madeline fares rather well, with a creditable Cockney accent and a fetching costume. A paragon among the many saucy wenches Madeline played, Mrs. Yellowbeard is the common-law wife of an especially ruthless pirate (Chapman). When he's imprisoned, she ensures the security of his treasure map (and of her own desire for wealth sufficient "to own Denmark") by tattooing it onto the scalp of their infant son. Years later, Yellowbeard escapes from prison and finds the boy (Martin Hewitt), now grown and a tremendous disappointment who's more devoted to books than to plunder. Yellowbeard kidnaps him and sets off in search of the treasure, with the British government, the boy's foster father, rival pirates (Boyle and Feldman), and Mrs. Yellowbeard in pursuit.

Many of the problems with the film originate with Chapman, who conceived of the movie as a vehicle for himself and the drummer Keith

Moon, who loved pirate movies. Even after Moon died in 1978, the pirate theme persisted, and he's memorialized in Boyle's character's name. The script, written by a mini-committee that included Chapman, Cook, and Chapman's lover, was the worst Cleese had ever seen, and it required harum-scarum antics of Chapman that were sadly unlike the authoritarian stuffiness at which he excelled. But he wanted the lead, and he wanted a hit to rival the post-*Python* successes of Cleese, Idle, and Terry Gilliam.

Chapman's efforts to control the movie extended to the selection of Mel Damski as director. A seasoned television director making his feature-film debut, Damski's experience in comedy was limited to one episode of *M*A*S*H*. Chapman expected to dominate him, though Damski pushed back as well as he could. The cast proved unruly, however, leading to production delays when shooting moved from London's Pinewood Studios to the resort town of Ixtapa, Mexico. And Damski never managed to integrate the different comedy styles of his actors. Cheech and Chong, for example, strike discordant notes whenever they interact with other cast members.[16]

While *Yellowbeard* is an ensemble picture, it can't have escaped anyone's notice—and it didn't escape Madeline's—that she was the only female lead among all the funny men, confirming her status as the reigning queen of film comedy. The other women in the film have far less screen time and few lines, and the juvenile lead, Stacey Nelkin, doesn't make her first appearance until the movie is half over. No matter that Madeline had to play the mother of a grown man even as she celebrated her fortieth birthday. She found it "flattering to be one of the few women who work with these guys who are so clever."[17] But as Lawrence Van Gelder observed in his review in the *New York Times*, "What *Yellowbeard* establishes is that even for the funniest of performers, a good script may be as essential as pitching is to baseball."[18]

Yellowbeard holds the dubious distinction of being the 107th-highest grossing film of 1983. For Madeline, it signaled the end of the Brooks era in another important way. After she'd returned to New York, production moved to Mexico City, where Marty Feldman died of a heart attack in his hotel room on December 2, 1982. Receiving a phone call, she noted in her appointment book "M. Feldman," drawing a black box around the name. Never again in movies would she find the mix of fun and good fortune she'd derived from her collaborations with him, Brooks, Wilder, and Boyle.

35

Breaking into Television

Scrambled Feet (1983)

YELLOWBEARD WAS THE LAST IN A SERIES OF GLOOMY PORTENTS.
While she remained a popular—and evidently bankable—star, Madeline
wouldn't appear onscreen in another hit movie for the rest of her career.
(Only a few animated films succeeded.) Paradoxically, perhaps, it was in
the early 1980s that the phrase "a Madeline Kahn movie"—distinct from
yet related to "a Mel Brooks movie"—gained currency with audiences,
especially college students. The phrase was shorthand: Madeline's participation in a movie instantly connoted an irreverent comic sensibility,
an ensemble cast of familiar and well-liked faces, and, in all likelihood,
genre parody. Madeline's pictures promised—and usually delivered,
however fitfully—a generational cry of rebellion, refusing to take seriously the icons of earlier filmmakers.

Success in character parts had helped her to postpone many of the
anxieties that typically come to Hollywood actresses over thirty. After all,
Madeline made her feature debut just as she *turned* thirty, and nobody
suggested she was too old for her roles in the Bogdanovich, Brooks, and
Wilder movies. She wasn't a conventional starlet, and the appearance of
youth didn't determine her casting. But as she turned forty, and as film
after film flopped, she began to worry. Paula continued to run up bills
and to concoct schemes that proved more expensive than get-rich-quick.
Meanwhile, despite the reassurance that her role in *Yellowbeard* offered,
Madeline believed her tenure as the top comic actress in Hollywood was
in jeopardy.

The biggest warning sign may have been *To Be or Not to Be*, Alan Johnson's remake of Ernst Lubitsch's comedy from 1942, in which two actors, husband and wife, thwart the Nazis in occupied Warsaw. While Mel
Brooks didn't direct the film, he did produce it, and he took the lead role

(played originally by Jack Benny) for himself. Since the role of the wife had been played by Carole Lombard in the Lubitsch movie, one might have supposed that the part in the remake would go to an actress who was often compared with Lombard and who had worked so well with Brooks in the past: Madeline herself. Instead, Anne Bancroft got the part.

While Brooks emphasizes that his wife admired Madeline and considered her a friend, Madeline worried privately that Bancroft had grown jealous or resentful of her. Surely Bancroft must have wanted in on the fun of making a Mel Brooks movie. Watching Bancroft's cameo in *Silent Movie*, you see her becoming almost giddy as she ventures into broad comedy, a field far distant from the serious dramatic roles she usually played. You can see her pleasure in her smile, and she's smiling much the same way in the opening scene of *To Be or Not to Be*, in which she and her husband sing "Sweet Georgia Brown"—in Polish. Brooks recalls that the scene required a full month of intensive private instruction at home.[19]

In 1997, when Madeline met with Eric Mendelsohn, the director of her final film and a lifelong Brooks fan, the subject of her movies with Brooks came up. She "spoke of them very dismissively," he says. How much of her response was an attempt to boost the morale of a fledgling director who was trying to create a comedy at once airier and darker than *Young Frankenstein*? It's impossible to say. But in the 1980s, the primary question was blunter: If Madeline couldn't be sure of playing the lead in a Mel Brooks movie, what could she be sure of?

Television appeared to hold the answer. She tried to make the move sound like "a practical matter of opening new vistas and expanding my career," as she told the UPI. "I wanted some continuity in my life for a change, a chance to work with a company of people week after week in a consistent structure. I'd just finished doing *Yellowbeard*, and the constant starting and stopping of movies was getting to me a little bit. I wanted to lead a more normal life personally. On a professional level, I hope to be able to develop a character in greater depth and detail than the kind of roles I've played in movies."[20] In effect, she was following the example of Lucille Ball and Eve Arden, who turned to television and situation comedies when they hit middle age and movie studios had less use for them. With *I Love Lucy* and *Our Miss Brooks*, Ball and Arden suddenly were bigger stars—and more regularly employed—than actresses to whom they used to play second banana.

So when ABC offered Madeline a sitcom, she did what she'd done before in high-stakes ventures: She tried something smaller-scale first. The songs or sketches she'd performed on other television shows required at most a week of rehearsal time, but *Scrambled Feet* would be more demanding. A theatrical revue videotaped as a one-off for the Showtime cable network, it positioned Madeline as first among equals, the only marquee name in a cast of four, and she appears in most of the scenes, singing, dancing, clowning, and even playing piano.

A lighthearted look at theatrical life, *Scrambled Feet* originated in Chicago, where a group of friends—John Driver, Jeffrey Haddow, and Evalyn Baron—assembled in Baron's living room. Like all good Chicago actors, they began to improvise scenes, based on their experiences and on stories they'd heard from other friends. Enlisting Jimmy Wisner and John Vaccaro to produce, Driver and Haddow shaped the material into sketches and wrote several songs. Wisner and Roger Neil contributed musical arrangements, as well. With Driver, Haddow, Baron, and Neil performing, Chicago audiences responded enthusiastically, and the team headed to New York, where the show was a smash hit at the Village Gate, running for two years. By the time the show was taped, the team had also traveled to Boston and Los Angeles and returned in triumph to Chicago. Cast members cycled in and out of the show as it ran, so it wasn't unprecedented to replace Baron, though neither she nor Haddow remembers who decided to replace her with Madeline, a better-known performer. Not even Baron objected. "It makes total sense, if you want to sell a program and put it on Showtime," she says.

Songs for the female role in *Scrambled Feet* include three high C's, Baron says, and like Madeline, she had classical vocal training. Both women knew what life was like for a struggling actor in the big city, and both had performed in revues. (Today, Baron describes *Scrambled Feet* as "the new Upstairs at the Downstairs.") Beyond this, however, the two women weren't much alike. While Baron was statuesque, Madeline was petite and a decade older. And Madeline had never even met the men in the company, who were Baron's lifelong friends. Indeed, Haddow doesn't remember interacting with Madeline at all outside their scenes together. Madeline didn't share anecdotes from her early years or any of the background that might have suggested why *Scrambled Feet* could be particularly meaningful for her. "She was cordial, as I recall, but not terribly communicative or social," he says.

He had expected to perform *Scrambled Feet* much as they had done in theaters. The studio was decorated like a cabaret, and a live audience sat at tables. But, Haddow says, the stage show had a forward momentum, facilitated by rapid costume changes—casual street clothes in the original Chicago run, and more formal dress as the show moved on to greater success in other theaters, but nothing that required more than a few seconds. For the video production, costumes became more elaborate—especially Madeline's. While shooting proceeded in the same running order as the stage show, Haddow remembers long, frustrating breaks between scenes, when Madeline went back to hair and wardrobe. Madeline wears everything from formal dresses to a Valkyrie costume and old lady drag. Her hair, curled modishly, goes through a few changes, too. Haddow understood the need for an actress to look good; he also suggests that the producers demanded the fancier costumes, perhaps from a desire to make *Scrambled Feet* more appealing by presenting not just a famous movie star but a glamorous one. He didn't know Madeline well enough to recognize her anxieties about her appearance or to understand that television might exacerbate them. As the taping continued, he felt the audience response grow less spontaneous.

Viewed today, *Scrambled Feet* holds up remarkably well. The life of an actor hasn't changed much in the intervening years, and despite a few references to then-current plays, the material eschews the kind of topicality that requires similar revues—notably *Forbidden Broadway*—to update regularly. If audience response is less than enthusiastic, there's no way to tell, and Madeline's work is remarkably self-effacing. Apart from the fact that she's the only woman onstage, she blends in with her colleagues, seizing the spotlight only when it's handed to her, exactly as the men do in their turn. Showtime may have intended for Madeline to be the big-name star, but she doesn't act like one.

"She was letter-perfect," Haddow remembers. Madeline excelled in the special number that he and Driver wrote for her, "Child Star" ("My career is finished if I start to grow!"), a surprisingly hard rock song that owes something to Gilda Radner's punk character, Candy Slice. Elsewhere in *Scrambled Feet* however, Madeline is very much in her own realm. The Valkyrie speaks with a German accent redolent of Lili von Shtupp. The little old lady in the "Theater Party" song is clearly related to Victoria Brisbane's charade in *High Anxiety*. Since the comedy of "Sham Dancing" depends on tricks deployed by actors who can't dance, it still lies comfortably within the scope of Madeline's abilities. She plays piano in three songs, and sings in more, including a wistful duet with Driver, "Send Me Two Tickets." But the *pièce de résistance* is the final sketch, which purports to focus on opera and finds Madeline singing "Un bel dì," the only extant record of her hit number from the Bavarian Manor. Then, a previously unseen performer interrupts her. This is the show's mascot, a white duck named Hermione, whose well-timed bodily function leads to the number "Never Go Onstage with an Animal." Seeing the duck's interest in one of the audience members, Madeline quips, "I think she wants you. She *does* want you. And she will *have* you! Don't you understand?" She times each phrase to get a laugh before moving on to the next.

The Showtime network had been distributed nationally for only five years and didn't penetrate as deeply into American households as its rival, HBO, did at the time. The home audience can't have been as large as it was, for example, for *SNL* (though cable networks' penchant for repeats would have boosted the numbers). But Madeline wanted the television equivalent of an out-of-town tryout, and she got it. As she proceeded to tape the pilot for her new sitcom, she crossed paths at last with Baron, cast as her neighbor. "I recall her being catatonic with fear, she was so nervous about going in front of a live studio audience," Baron says. "She wanted a TV career so badly." After the taping, they sat in Madeline's dressing room, shared a drink to calm down, and swapped stories about their mothers. Both were in therapy, "and.that's what you do," Baron says. "She was so relieved that it was over." The sitcom went forward, Baron lost her role—and Madeline's anxieties kept on roiling.

36

A Banana Boat to Nicaragua

Oh Madeline (1983–84)

TOGETHER AND SEPARATELY, MARCY CARSEY AND TOM WERNER, FOR-
mer executives at ABC, had a hand in developing comedies that included
Happy Days, Mork & Mindy, the serialized satire *Soap*, and the brilliant *Taxi*.
Carsey left first, in 1981, to form an independent production company,
and Werner joined her a year later. Over the next several years, they
would meet with acclaim for their work. Often, they built shows around
stars such as Bill Cosby (*The Cosby Show, Cosby*), Roseanne Barr (*Roseanne*), and Cybill Shepherd (*Cybill*). In that regard, their venture with
Madeline was a template for their future shows—but in many ways,
it was more like the sitcom equivalent of that first pancake that never
turns out right.

Just two years younger than Madeline and a native of Massachusetts,
too, Carsey was also a former actress. Bright and possessed of discerning
taste (perhaps more so than some of the shows on her résumé might
suggest), Carsey was arguably more high-minded than other people in
authority in television. The opposite of a stereotypical network syco-
phant, she charted her course at ABC by speaking her mind. Eventually,
she rose to the position of senior vice-president of prime-time series.
Werner's similarly straightforward style led Carsey to believe they could
work well together—as they did, both at the network and in the Carsey-
Werner Company. As they prepared their first production, they enlisted
such behind-the-scenes talents as the veteran writer–producer Irma Kalish and the young, albeit experienced, producer Caryn Sneider Mandabach, as well as the director J. D. Lobue, who had directed twenty-eight
episodes of *Soap* and who would direct every episode of Madeline's show.
Madeline was in good hands, though that was hardly a guarantee of
success.[21]

Yes, But I'm Married, as the series was originally titled, pushed against the confines of what was ultimately a highly conventional husband-and-wife comedy. In the pilot, a married couple, Catherine (Madeline) and Charlie (James Sloyan), argue and separate. Charlie decides to start an affair with Annie (Francine Tacker), an attractive blonde kindergarten teacher, little realizing that Catherine and Annie are friends. Charlie invites Annie to dinner with the intention of sleeping with her, while Catherine goes to a party. Drunk, she demands to sleep with Bobby, Charlie's best friend (Louis Giambalvo). Bobby's half-inclined to agree. The farce is brought to a close with a bed trick, when Charlie discovers that the woman beside him isn't Annie; it's Catherine, passed out. The sanctity of marriage is upheld—for now.

This was racy stuff for an American sitcom at the time, and viewed today, it can be unpleasant. American television depends on likability, the quality that makes viewers invite performers into their living rooms week after week. Madeline had that quality, tinged with a vulnerability that makes it difficult to watch her being treated unkindly by her husband. But the source material for *Yes, But I'm Married*, a British sitcom called *Pig in the Middle*, had no need to consider the sensibilities of American viewers. Produced by London Weekend Television between 1980 and 1983 and taking its title from the name of a children's game (known as "keep-away" in the United States), *Pig in the Middle* depicts the sex lives of middle-class suburbanites—particularly one married man's unrequited infatuation with another woman. Adaptations of Britcoms had been Werner's portfolio early in his career at ABC, and he triumphed with *Three's Company*, an adaptation of the British *Man About the House*, in the 1970s. That show, like *Soap* and some other productions on which he and Carsey had worked, relied on sexier humor and themes than did sitcoms of earlier decades, and it made sense to set out in that direction for their first independent production.

Unlike some of their subsequent series, *Yes, But I'm Married* wasn't created with a specific star in mind. Madeline joined a project already in progress with a premise that didn't focus primarily on her character. In the British series, the "pig in the middle" is the husband. Still, she found the prospects encouraging, and ABC snapped up the show—only to have second thoughts about the material as the start of regular production neared. Abruptly, the network asked for changes, and with new executives in charge there, Carsey and Werner didn't wield the kind of influence that would allow them to debate, much less refuse the demands. Interviewed in 2003, Carsey recalled, "We unfortunately took some network notes that were not very good, because we were desperate to make this last, now that it was on the air. And we softened the concept and kind of watered it down to their liking, to such a degree that it kind of lost its center." She and Werner learned "to really put those blinders on and follow the vision that you start with, because otherwise, things can go haywire." There was no chance to apply that lesson to their first show.

The title was first to go. *Yes, But I'm Married* could have starred anybody, but *Oh Madeline* put the focus directly on the leading lady. Beyond that, Carsey and Werner's team retooled the series with evident haste, throwing out the *Pig in the Middle* blueprint while continuing to credit the British show, retaining most of the cast and the sets, and recycling certain elements from the pilot in subsequent episodes. This process revealed a number of flaws—not only with the new approach, but also with the original premise—that rippled through the series as a whole. For example, Mandabach suggests that if they were following *Pig in the Middle*, they should have cast the male lead first. Today, they might have made Madeline the pig in the middle, choosing between her husband and a teacher, but in 1984, that premise wasn't feasible.

Above all, ABC insisted that Madeline herself be made into "a Lucille Ball for the '80s." Carsey gamely played along, describing *Oh Madeline* as "in tone more like a *Honeymooners* or a *Lucy* than anything on television now," in an interview during the television critics' summer press tour.[22] Lobue still believes it was a mistake not to capitalize on Madeline's gifts, rather than someone else's. The new premise portrayed a zany, redheaded housewife in a variety of comical misadventures. As network publicity put it, her goal was "to keep her marriage fresh," rather than following Lucy's lead by attempting to break into show business—but the debt is nonetheless weighty. The revamped show also required a far greater emphasis on physical comedy, which, as Lobue agrees, was Lucy's trademark, but never Madeline's.

Madeline's character was now called Madeline, not Catherine, setting her up as "the new Lucy," who used her own name, and also trading on her name recognition—by far the show's greatest selling point. Charlie was a romance novelist, and Francine Tacker now played his editor, but she would be eased out of the show after just two more episodes. Filling that gap, *Soap* veteran Jesse Welles stepped in as Doris Leone, the estranged wife of Bobby, still played by Louis Giambalvo. Their interplay is meant to bring an edge to their otherwise generic second couple. It's as if Fred and Ethel Mertz have gone beyond bickering to divorce.

The resemblance to *I Love Lucy* continued to dominate the series, as the producers and writers cherry-picked sitcom plots from three decades before. Madeline takes a magazine quiz and decides her marriage is in trouble. Madeline gets jealous of Charlie's ex-girlfriend, a glamorous Hollywood actress. Madeline and Charlie go camping and land in jail. Madeline is supposed to sing in a local troupe's operetta evening but loses her voice. After criticizing Charlie for playing poker, Madeline loses money at the roulette table and schemes to hide the truth. And so on. There's even an ultra-*Lucy* setup, a guest appearance by a celebrity playing himself (Johnny Mathis).

Granted, the show is more concerned with sex than *Lucy* was. For example, during a vacation with her parents (guest stars Geraldine Fitzgerald and Ray Walston), Madeline learns that her mother once had an affair with an employee (Bill Macy) at the family's favorite resort hotel. This episode and one featuring Madeline's younger sister contain the show's most serious, character-oriented scenes, signaling another direction that might have been explored further. But when *Oh Madeline* approaches the territory covered in *Yes, But I'm Married*, it backs off. The plot of "The Lady with the Lamp" closely resembles that of the pilot, but this time, when Madeline passes out, she sleeps alone, and there's no pretty younger woman to tempt Charlie. The show's other sexual references are generally more leering than knowing, and they seldom harmonize with the conventional premise and plots.

That's a point that Tom Shales, the influential critic of the *Washington Post*, drove home in his review of *Oh Madeline*'s premiere when he observed that "the burnt-roast sitcoms of the '50s" didn't include "talk of 'alabaster breasts' and 'deflowering.'" The show "essentially squanders Kahn's singular broad-comic gifts on frazzled and tattered material. . . . [N]o intriguing concept is ever developed. It's just Madeline thrown into a sitcom like a child dropped into a sandbox and told to play."[23] In the *Miami Herald*, critic Sandra Earley went so far as to suggest that even Madeline's hairstyle, upswept in some scenes in the premiere, was copied from Lucy Ricardo's—though she declared that Madeline "has the kind of TV presence that requires ours." *Variety* approved of the show: "Kahn brings her odd voice and her capacity of using her body in odd ways to the series and generates a strong amount of big laughs. . . . The cast and concept, as revealed in the opener, looked like 'Madeline' might have the stuff to be around for a long while." But Fred Rothenberg, writing for the Associated Press, dismissed the entire series as "forgetfully funny,

with characters you wouldn't find in real life, or want to know anyway."
And, in an extremely brief "Picks and Pans" review, *People* magazine said,
"This sitcom about a woman trapped in a mid-life crisis likewise traps
comedienne Madeline Kahn."[24]

For one early episode of the series in which Madeline attends a costume party, a network executive suggested that she wear a sleek, sexy
tiger outfit, replete with an immense, S-curved tail. (Naturally, the tail
gets caught in a door.) Just before dress rehearsal, with the studio audience waiting, Lobue received a call: Madeline wouldn't come out of her
dressing room. He went to her, and found her wearing the costume and
in tears. "I thought I was on a cruise to the Caribbean," she said, "and
now I find out I'm on a banana boat to Nicaragua."

It's difficult to overstate the degree to which *Oh Madeline* ignored
breakthroughs in the sitcom genre made by contemporary shows such
as *Taxi* and *Cheers*, to say nothing of *All in the Family*, *The Mary Tyler Moore
Show*, and *M*A*S*H*. Sitcoms had come a long way, but Madeline Wayne
lived closer to Debbie Thompson in *The Debbie Reynolds Show* (1969), another Lucy-esque, redheaded housewife married to a writer. That show
lasted one season.

Ostensibly, the new premise of the series was that, instead of adultery,
Madeline tried every new fad and activity to stave off boredom after
ten years of marriage. Madeline Wayne might wink at the possibility of
an affair (notably, in an episode where she flirts with a younger man),
but at heart she had no interest in such a thing. Actually going out and
pursuing a fulfilling career didn't seem to occur to her (she tried aero-
bics instead) until halfway through the season, when "Monday Night
Madeline" showed her briefly landing a job as a sportscaster and winding up in the ring during a wrestling match. Nevertheless, the show did
include situations in which the star could show off her versatility, and
in various episodes she sang everything from "Poor Wand'ring One" to
the theme from *Shaft*, from Rossini's aria "Bel raggio lusinghier" to "Ah!
Sweet Mystery," and, in a scene in which she does her patented little-
girl act, the Norwegian national anthem. Even in physical comedy, she's
surprisingly effective. Not a natural like Lucy, Dick Van Dyke, or John
Ritter, Madeline nonetheless found ways to merge physical comedy with
her vocal gifts. For example, in "To Ski or Not to Ski," Madeline sprains
her ankle on the slopes and tries to keep Charlie from finding out. To
her hobbling and wincing she adds a variety of wails that begin as cries
of pain and become a spontaneous rendition of "Oh, Susannah"—or,

in a very funny square dance scene, whoops and hollers that are *almost* appropriate.

For the most part, whenever an opportunity arose to stand out or surprise, the team behind *Oh Madeline* rejected it. There was no question of, and perhaps no time for innovation. Even Madeline's character's name—Wayne, née Vernon—is relatively bland and signifies a neutral, largely unexplored background. This leaves the only hints of ethnicity to Bobby and Doris, whose last name is Leone—never mind that the Waynes are played by actors named Kahn and Sloyan. The Waynes live in a spacious home that could be situated anywhere in the upper-middle-class American suburbs, in a town sometimes referred to as Eastfield, with occasional suggestions that they're near Chicago. By contrast, *Cheers*, which premiered the previous season, couldn't have taken place anywhere but Boston.

Moreover, none of Madeline's co-stars was a household name—to say nothing of "the world's funniest lady," as a season preview article described her.[25] Other such articles mentioned her in the same breath as another actress who would be launching her first weekly TV series: Bette Davis, slated to star in the prime-time soap opera *Hotel*, also on ABC.[26] As Madeline understood perfectly well, she was the first and perhaps only reason viewers would tune in. Her status in television and in Hollywood generally was at risk.

"The show premiered with a number which would be a megahit by today's standards," Lobue says, and it ranked twenty-first for the week, promising to shore up the Tuesday-night lineup, which depended heavily on *Oh Madeline*'s lead-in, *Three's Company*, then starting its final season. Soon, however, Madeline felt misgivings about the show and expressed them openly in the press. She tried to make a run-of-the-mill sitcom sound like something that would satisfy her as an actor—or else she was making a direct appeal to the network to let the producers add more depth to her show. After just one month on the air, she chafed at comparisons to *I Love Lucy* and told the Associated Press, "Yes, I'm a housewife, but that's just a start. The show has to do with the complexities of human behavior. The way people can be grown-up and children at the same time. She has a certain restlessness, not having to do per se with her marriage. Maybe she feels she's missing something."[27]

Madeline wasn't the only one dissatisfied with her show, and she may have felt something like peer pressure. "I got very unhappy when she was settling for minor parts on TV," Mel Brooks remembers. "But she said things like, 'It's a job, it pays more a week than you paid me for the whole movie.' I said, 'Well, salaries are different.'" If she felt the temptation to tell Brooks he could solve her problem by writing more parts for her in his movies, she resisted it.

• • •

It's a measure of Madeline's insecurity that she rented, rather than buying a house in Los Angeles, where *Oh Madeline* was produced. Much of her life was still in New York, and she shuttled back and forth every few weeks to enjoy her well-established routines, such as a play or an opera with Gail Jacobs. And on November 1, 1983, at the behest of Matthew Epstein, she narrated a concert performance of Offenbach's *La Périchole* at Carnegie Hall, where Epstein was an artistic consultant. The performance starred Frederica Von Stade and Neil Rosenshein, under Bliss Hebert's direction.

Hebert wrote Madeline's narration, with the premise that she was Périchole's great-great-great-great-granddaughter. "She walked out after the entr'acte with this giant book," remembers Darren Keith Woods, who sang the role of the Notary, "and in her Madeline Kahn way, she blew the dust off of it, and a cloud of dust went flying into the first two rows at Carnegie Hall—and the laughter never stopped." Conductor Mario Bernardi evidently agreed with some of the concert's critics that *Périchole* didn't require narration.[28] At rehearsals, Woods remembers, every time Madeline was supposed to say her lines, Bernardi would insist, "No, no, we go on with music!" Things got to the point that, each time they came to one of her lines, "she'd open her mouth and look at him and say, 'I won't say anything,'" Woods says. "Only at dress rehearsal did we get through the narration."

Before the performance, Madeline spoke to the *New York Times* for a preview article that constitutes one of the more accurate public accounts of her musical background. It duly notes both *Candide* and *Bohème*, as well as describing Madeline as a coloratura soprano. "I never thought about singing in Carnegie Hall when I was studying," she said. "If anything, it was the Met. At the beginning, I was surprised to discover I could sing at all, and before my life began to take the direction it has, I kept on studying music. When I wasn't working, an opera role was something I could learn and store up for the future. Then one day people discovered I was funny, and things went in a different direction . . . . Comedy is hard, but it comes naturally for me. Singing never did. If I had to sing opera again,

I'd have to spend all my time offstage preparing for it. I'd have to stop speaking to people. I couldn't even laugh."[29]

• • •

Returning to Hollywood, Madeline didn't socialize much. Throughout the run of *Oh Madeline*, her appointment book shows almost nothing but rehearsals and tapings, plus a few professional commitments, such as the Emmy Awards ceremony, guest appearances on talk shows, and parties hosted by the network. She also saw Paula from time to time, and they spoke often by telephone, though Madeline tried to keep at least some distance between them while they lived in the same city. Early in the run, she made an effort to get to know her colleagues, attending a party at Giambalvo's home and going to lunch with Tacker, for example. With Caryn Mandabach, she formed a friendship that prefigures those she established with other young women in later years, notably her co-starring "nieces" from *Mr. President* and *The Sisters Rosensweig*, Maddie Corman and Julie Dretzin. Mandabach says Madeline "just wanted people to understand her, like most people who are talented. . . . I understood her. I felt she had this really rare gift, and it was impossible to put it in a kind of simple place."

Week to week, Madeline bore the brunt of responsibility for getting laughs. Charlie displays flashes of wit, and Bobby's vulgarity is meant to be funny, as are Doris's waspish tongue and her lingering attraction to her ex-husband, but virtually all the sight gags and most of the dialogue depend on Madeline. Again and again, a viewer is reminded of the appraisals of collaborators like Lobue, Tomlin, and Bogdanovich: Madeline could be funny no matter the material given to her. From the live studio audience, she consistently gets big laughs on fundamentally flat lines, simply with an inflection, a pause, a modulation of tone, a gesture. "Her line readings were sort of classically wrong," Tom Shales says today, "but because it was her and part of her persona and her shtick, it was just perfect. It was quixotic and appropriate and right. Her timing was so wonderful."

One can't help wondering what she might have done with sharper material and stronger artistic support from her co-stars. *Oh Madeline* is a show in which, as Mandabach puts it, "She's doing one movie and they're doing another." In their subsequent sitcoms, Carsey and Werner demonstrated a phenomenal ability to surround a star with a top-notch supporting cast—notably in *Roseanne*, where theater actors John

Goodman and Laurie Metcalf compensated for the star's limited acting experience. In *A Different World*, the supporting cast was so strong that it carried the show for five more seasons after the lead, Lisa Bonet, left. In *Oh Madeline*, however, the supporting cast doesn't register as strongly, and they're seldom given the opportunity to do so.

Acting is like tennis, and any actor performs better opposite a skilled scene partner. Madeline and Sloyan never appear fully at ease with each other. "It was hard to get them to do any love scene at all," producer Irma Kalish told an interviewer. Kalish's husband, writer–producer Albert "Rocky" Kalish, chipped in with the recollection that, whenever Charlie is supposed to kiss Madeline, she'd usually "bend her head down, so he would kiss her on the forehead."[30] Naturally, this reticence posed challenges for a series ostensibly depicting a loving married couple. In any case, with less than a single season to work together, the cast of *Oh Madeline* never got much of a chance to establish a rhythm or to work past any differences. As Mandabach observes, Sloyan was an unusual casting choice to play the "pig in the middle" in *Yes, But I'm Married*, and the change in format did little to improve matters. "We should have cast a stronger person to play opposite Madeline," she says. Sloyan "didn't approach the project with the same sort of directorial intensity. He wasn't a lead. And that's just the truth. He was a much better character actor, and we forced him to be a lead." With a stronger actor, such as Peter Boyle, opposite Madeline, the show would have been better overall.[31]

At the same time, Mandabach feels Madeline was a character actor at heart. "One time I remember thinking how hard it must have been: 'This is a brave woman, because it doesn't come naturally,'" she says. She contrasts Madeline with John Lithgow, another actor she classifies as "a character person," with whom she worked on the sitcom *3rd Rock from the Sun*. Lithgow "is a leader. He can teach others while he's [acting], but Madeline was so fastidious in her own work that it was hard to be generous." And indeed, there's a striking lack of chemistry between Madeline and all three of her co-stars, nothing like the rapport one feels when watching her with Boyle, Wilder, Feldman, or Cleavon Little in the movies, or later in sitcoms with George C. Scott and Bill Cosby. The sense of mutual enjoyment simply isn't there.

Lobue confirms that Madeline disliked Sloyan, and he echoes Mandabach's criticism. "I found Jimmy overly broad," he says. "He was a good actor, it's just that he had never done this kind of comedy. It was difficult for Madeline." He remembers the camping episode, and a scene in which Madeline sat on Sloyan's lap and smiled at him. "We're going to be okay,"

Lobue thought at the time, "because there's been no chemistry here, and at least there's a moment." He recalls that Madeline was "difficult" whenever she and Sloyan shared an important scene—as happened in nearly every episode. But she was conscientiously professional on the set, Mandabach and Lobue agree. "I saw her come to work unwilling, but never unprepared," Lobue says with a chuckle. Despite her singing background, he says, she never displayed any "diva" behavior. "Once she committed, she committed in every way," Mandabach says. "She was amazing in rehearsals. There was nothing more joyous than watching her musical approach to comedy, which was particular and high-minded, as if she were conducting herself in an opera or an aria. She had no peer, I thought, in that kind of approach to comedy, which was astonishing for television."

Lobue, who has played keyboards professionally, also praises Madeline's musicality. However, he says, "We got into a little bit of trouble on the series, because Madeline, for a woman who was innately, hysterically funny, she didn't understand why she was funny." During the run of *Oh, Madeline*, her long-standing doubts led to anxiety that Lobue and the rest of the team had to address. "We were constantly trying to reinforce the things that she did so well, and try to lead her through the physical things, which she wasn't good at but *became* good at, because of the work she did." Madeline "could read the phone book and make it funny, but she wasn't totally comfortable with physical comedy," says Lobue. Nevertheless, each week she found herself in "mega-scenes" such as a recreation of *Lucy*'s chocolate-making scene (but with newspapers), or an ice-skating scene, though she'd never skated before. Much of Lobue's work with her, especially in physical comedy, entailed improvisation. "I'd give [the actors] full rein . . . at least the first time through. I found over time that as soon as they exhausted their imagination, they were far more ready to receive direction." As always, Madeline wanted to find the "truth" in a scene, and Lobue would offer suggestions. "For any actor–director relationship," he says, "the real key is to have the actor believe it was their idea."

He tried not to pry into Madeline's concerns about her appearance, but he told the cinematographer, "I don't care if it's dark on the set, as long as Madeline looks good. Care for her as if she's your girlfriend," he recalls. "And she looked beautiful. Even when she had her hair messed up, we made sure the makeup was perfect, the lighting was perfect, so that the hair was like a funny hat."

Madeline's keen critical perceptions developed as early as her time at the Upstairs, where she judged material and co-stars shrewdly. By now she was a seasoned veteran, and thus a tougher critic. Ordinarily she remained circumspect about the shows she did and the people she worked with. But by Christmastime 1983, Madeline was on the brink of open rebellion. In a feature story for the UPI that ran on New Year's Day, 1984, she said, "I have the distinct sense that there were many concerns voiced by people which have, shall we say, clipped my wings? Someone is making a lot of decisions—people who have nothing to do with the show [i.e., network executives]. The thing has to go through a carwash practically before it gets on [the air]." She continued: "They start to fix it up, neaten it up, clean it up and they strip it of everything they originally loved." She'd proved herself, she said, and if the show failed—or if it "continue[s] in its present form, let's say"—then she was not to blame. She pointedly told the reporter that she had no intention of giving up her New York apartment.[32]

At the time the article appeared, *Oh Madeline* was "generally in the top 20" in the ratings, Lobue says, and as the season progressed, the writing grew sharper. Changes kept coming. During its run, the show went through three different opening credit sequences, with different theme songs, the last of which featured Madeline's vocalise. And in the final two episodes, Madeline's sidekick Doris got her own sidekick, played by Randee Heller. Given the way Francine Tacker was eased off the show, Heller's arrival looks like a cast change in progress, but by this point the ratings had declined, and everyone knew the series was ending.

With a few episodes yet to be shot, ABC told Carsey and Werner that it was canceling *Oh Madeline* before the end of the season. Alerted to this news, Madeline remained committed to the show, Lobue says. But she was also more adventurous, asking the producers to find a role for her classmate from Hofstra, Charles Ludlam. His theater work—campy, gender-bending, and crammed with references to drugs, sex, old movies, and high culture—resembles nothing seen on television, even today, but Madeline was determined to use to good purpose what was left of her show. She began conferring with Ludlam frequently by telephone, and he signed for the penultimate episode in the series. His television debut, "Play Crystal for Me," aired February 28, 1984.[33]

Lobue remembers considerable resistance from the network, and in his biography of Ludlam, David Kaufman reports that ABC executives changed the plot of the episode at the last minute. As Charlie's rival romance writer, Ludlam was obliged not to play a woman, as the script originally prescribed, but to play a man playing a woman, along the lines of the hit movie *Tootsie* (1982).[34] The idea was that men who write romance novels must go to extraordinary lengths to appeal to women readers. Charlie prevails upon Madeline to don a blond wig and incarnate his nom de plume, "Crystal Love," while Ludlam's character, "Tiffany Knight," has only his own resources to draw on. The writing, especially for Ludlam, is exceptionally sharp, but the funniest scene in the episode—in which Ludlam's character, still in drag, critiques Madeline's "Crystal Love" and instructs her on how to walk like a woman—didn't make it into the broadcast.[35] At this remove, it's anyone's guess whether the scene was cut for time or for content.

"Play Crystal for Me" might have steered *Oh Madeline* to a more artistically satisfying path, but it didn't. The last episode, "A Little Fright Music," aired on March 13, 1984, and while it gave Madeline the chance to work again with Brandon Maggart, it hardly pushes any boundaries. Stage fright has been a staple of sitcoms for as long as the form has existed. Ralph Kramden got it when he appeared in a television commercial; Little Ricky Ricardo got it when he played drums with a student orchestra.

Had *Oh Madeline* survived, Lobue believes the comedy would have gotten broader, not smarter, "and Madeline would have been asked to do more and more zany, physical things. It would not have been fun, because she rebelled toward the end. The ratings were slipping, you're on that boat, and it's sinking. Those of us behind the camera move on to the next project. But the stars are visible, and they take the fall." Nevertheless, *Oh Madeline* made a lasting impact on Carsey and Werner's next show, *Cosby*, where they stayed true to their vision—and they recycled the *Oh Madeline* sets.

37

Aftermath

City Heat, Ludlam, and Beyond (1984–85)

TWO DAYS AFTER THE FINAL EPISODE OF *OH MADELINE* AIRED, MADELINE won the People's Choice Award as the favorite female performer on a new TV program. "That looked so light when the other people had it," Madeline remarked when she picked up her award at the podium. Alluding to the public opinion surveys that determine the awards, she expressed gratitude for the connection she'd established with audiences by "portray[ing] something about a woman which most of the time is amusing." In a career, she said, actors can become overly concerned with the opinions of critics and producers, thus losing sight of their connection with the audience. "So I'm very grateful that you've acknowledged me this year, so that this will remind me of that, when the other opinions vary—as they do, you know." The audience laughed, but Madeline, aware that this would be her valedictory speech, continued with a few words about the challenge of working in television, and she thanked Carsey, Werner, and Mandabach, and "those people at ABC who have been so supportive." There was not a trace of irony in her voice.

Victory at the People's Choice Awards afforded her the singular chance to pose for press photographs with the winner of the award for favorite male performer on a new TV program, Mr. T of *The A Team*. She earned one other token of recognition for *Oh Madeline*, a Golden Globe nomination as best actress on a musical or comedy series, but lost to Joanna Cassidy for her performance in another short-lived show, the cult favorite *Buffalo Bill*.

A few months later, Madeline went back to moviemaking, reuniting with Burt Reynolds for *City Heat*, which co-starred Clint Eastwood. An old-fashioned crime caper set in 1933, it's something like *The Sting*, but liberally splashed with modern violence. Bullets and punches fly, and vintage cars are destroyed at a furious rate. Reynolds plays Mike Murphy, a fast-talking gumshoe and retired policeman who must rely on his former partner, Lieutenant Speer, played by Eastwood. Longtime friends, both actors got their starts in TV westerns, and for a long time their careers followed similar trajectories, action movies interspersed with comedies.

City Heat played Reynolds and Eastwood off each other in something more than time-tested "buddy picture" fashion. They bicker like old lovers, to the point that Murphy's beleaguered secretary, played by Jane Alexander, pointedly asks each, "Why do you both go at it so hard?" The script consciously evokes the dynamics of films from the 1930s, in which a gangster interacts with his best friend, who is either a cop or a Catholic priest. Blake Edwards, who had directed the recent hit *10*, wrote the screenplay, originally entitled "Kansas City Blues," and signed on to direct. According to Reynolds, Eastwood nixed Edwards and proposed that Richard Benjamin (fresh from the success of *My Favorite Year* and *Racing with the Moon*) replace him.[36] Without Edwards, *City Heat* became "a pitch that was a little gone awry," Jane Alexander remembers. She signed on purely for the chance to work with Eastwood. Today she doubts that even he, as a director, could have made the movie work.

A last-minute addition to the cast, Madeline replaced another actress at Reynolds's suggestion. She plays Caroline Howley, a spoiled socialite who's sleeping—and falling in love—with Mike Murphy. A glamorous foil to Alexander's levelheaded character, Caroline becomes a plot device when she's kidnapped by gangsters. Caroline plays the stereotypical damsel in distress just long enough to break a vase over a thug's head in time-honored fashion, but her overarching concern is getting Murphy to admit that he loves her. It's not much of a role, but from Madeline's perspective, it had several advantages. *City Heat* meant a short shoot and fourth billing in a likely hit opposite two of Hollywood's biggest stars. She spent most of her time in a cleavage-exposing white satin negligée and a curly blonde permanent wave, and she looks slim and sexy—not bad for a woman who turned forty-three several months before shooting started.

The movie also gave her the opportunity to reconnect with Reynolds and to share a bedroom scene with him, as well as an extra reason to participate in a television special with him. Her crush hadn't abated much, if at all, but his name appears nowhere in her appointment book during the weeks of filming *City Heat*. He'd been severely injured during the movie's first fight scene. In pain and on medication, he lost fifty pounds during the shoot and contended with the after-effects of his injury for years.

Madeline also looked forward to working with Alexander, whom she knew socially, but the two share only two scenes and didn't see much of each other on the set. They discussed costumes and makeup for the movie, and Alexander recalls that Madeline wanted certain changes and got them. Calling her "the most professional person I ever worked with," Alexander observes, "Madeline was very good at knowing what she wanted, how she wanted to look, and how she looked best. . . . She would get what she needed. And I really admired the way she went about it." The two would work together closely, and for much longer, in *The Sisters Rosensweig* eight years later.

Opening on December 7, 1984, *City Heat* performed modestly at the box office, taking in $38,300,000. The film earned back its budget but fell short of the blockbuster expectations based on the two leads' drawing power. The movie does offer some pleasures, notably in the contrast between the two stars: Reynolds cracks wise, while Eastwood barely speaks; Reynolds winds up in the thick of almost every fight, while Eastwood stands back until directly provoked. For action fans, there's a third icon, Richard Roundtree (*Shaft*). But the clash between comedy and violence is difficult to reconcile, and *City Heat* is difficult to enjoy.

• • •

Madeline's artistic flirtation with Charles Ludlam hadn't ended. In New York on March 11, 1984, she attended a performance of his play *Galas* (in which he played an opera singer based on Maria Callas). He told her that he wanted to return the favor she'd done him. Now that she was unexpectedly at liberty, he offered her the role of the female psychiatrist in his play *Reverse Psychology*, a comedy less outrageous than his other works. However, Black-Eyed Susan remembers, Madeline said she'd accept only if Ludlam appeared in the show with her. He preferred to work on other projects instead, anticipating that *Reverse Psychology* would in effect become *her* project. She declined. She'd admired Ludlam's work with the Ridiculous Theatrical Company but hadn't followed it devotedly over the years. Black-Eyed Susan says that only after several trips to the theater did Madeline admit she finally understood what the troupe was trying to do. She did become at least enough of a member of Ludlam's gang to win an introduction to photographer Peter Hujar. A Ridiculous fan who took a series of photos of the troupe, Hujar also took a memorable portrait of

Madeline herself, expressing a profound, even startling melancholy. It's one of those moments when the camera sees in a subject what the eyes alone can't.

Astutely, Madeline judged that joining Ludlam at the Ridiculous—which by then had moved to a permanent home in a basement off Sheridan Square—might broaden his audience somewhat as her fans discovered his work. But to bring him to even greater attention, she needed to try to incorporate his sensibility in her more commercial world, much as she'd done in *Oh Madeline*. She wanted to bring him uptown.

Opera had long been a source of fascination to him, as several of his plays testify. Matthew Epstein, another of Ludlam's friends, began to dream up projects in which Madeline and Ludlam might work together. He hit upon another Offenbach operetta, *La Grande-Duchesse de Gérolstein*. For Ludlam, who revered Molière, a farcical French comedy seemed like a good fit, and for Madeline, who found high-lying music increasingly daunting, the vocal line (usually sung by mezzo-sopranos or mature sopranos) might prove congenial. And the character of the Grand Duchess, who's almost psychotically mad for men in uniform, suggested comedic possibilities that she might exploit brilliantly.

Long Beach Opera expressed interest, and after talking with Ludlam, Michael Feingold began to prepare English translations for several of the arias. The combination of Epstein's impeccable credentials at Santa Fe Opera and Madeline's work with the Festival Theater suggested another possible venue, and the pianist Earl Wild already had been lobbying Santa Fe Opera's founder, John Crosby, to find something for Ludlam to do there. (He wound up directing Henze's *The English Cat* [1985] and Strauss's *Die Fledermaus* [1986].)

On the afternoon of Saturday, January 12, 1985, Feingold came to Madeline's apartment with a pianist to audition three numbers. Endowed with a pleasing baritone, he did his best, "in my very apologetic fashion," he remembers. "Oh, they're wonderful, that was really well done," Madeline told him. "But I don't know if this is really right for me." With a smile, she added, "I think *you* should do it."

About a week later, Feingold's agent called to say that Madeline was no longer involved with the project. By the time he gave up, he'd been through four directors and three prima donnas, including Brenda Boozer, Robert Klein's wife at the time. "I think I never actually got a contract to sign," Feingold says, "and I don't think I ever got paid, and I don't think I ever did all of the work." As for Madeline, "The moral of the story is, she should have just sung opera, and she would have been great."

Whatever the hopes for *Grand Duchess* or for any further collaboration between Madeline and Ludlam, they couldn't last long. He had contracted HIV, and although he held off getting tested, Black-Eyed Susan is convinced that he knew he didn't have much time left. He died on May 28, 1987. Several weeks later, Madeline spoke at his memorial service.

Madeline did return briefly to the New York stage for the first time since *On the Twentieth Century* in the gentlest way possible: a twenty-two-performance run of Donald Margulies's *What's Wrong with This Picture?*, at the Manhattan Theater Club from January 29 to February 23, 1985. Judy Graubart's husband, Bob Dishy, co-starred, and Claudia Weill directed (this was a rare occasion when Madeline worked with a woman director). Presented as a workshop, performances were closed to the press, and the play gave Madeline a chance to confirm that her reputation in the theater community hadn't suffered permanent damage. "I still brag that she appeared at Manhattan Theater Club," the company's artistic director, Lynne Meadow, says.[37]

38

The Black Widow

Clue (1985)

"FLAMES! FLAMES ON THE SIDE OF MY FACE!" MADELINE'S MOST-QUOTED line from *Clue* doesn't appear in the shooting script and came as a surprise to the director and her fellow cast members—and quite possibly to Madeline herself. Although a box office disappointment in theaters, the movie has grown in popularity through cable television and home video. Only her work with Mel Brooks has done more to define Madeline in the public imagination. And it all started with a board game.

Invented during World War II by Anthony E. Pratt, a British law clerk, Cluedo (as it's called outside North America) takes the ingredients of the classic English country house murder mystery, adds dice, and asks players to deduce the murderer, the weapon, and the room in which Dr. Black (or, in North America, Mr. Boddy) breathed his last. Originally, simple pawns represented the "characters," whose personae were suggested by the color of each piece and even the most cursory reading of Agatha Christie. The game doesn't depend on role-playing, but it's more fun if you do channel English character actors as you move your pawn through the conservatory and the billiard room. In a sense, people had been playing Mrs. White ever since 1949, long before Madeline got the chance.

Surely inspired by the success of *Murder by Death*, producer–director John Landis optioned the film rights to Clue, braving the mockery of the press and public as he pursued what he believed was a surefire marketing gimmick. Like the board game, the movie would have different endings, and he expected that audiences would see the picture several times in order to see every permutation. At first, Landis planned to write and direct *Clue*, but he found himself drawn to other projects. He was editing Michael Jackson's "Thriller" video and had two feature films in production when Jonathan Lynn, the latest in a line of writers, arrived in Hollywood to meet him.

An affable Englishman best known at the time as the co-creator of the BBC comedy *Yes, Minister*, Lynn had recently directed an adaptation of a French farce at the National Theatre in London, which led film producer Jon Guber to recommend him as a good prospect for *Clue*. Lynn made his first trip to Los Angeles and wound up writing his first Hollywood screenplay, set not in Britain but in America. In fleshing out the characters beyond mere colors and in rounding out the plot, he set aside Agatha Christie and turned to a period that fascinated him, the McCarthy era. Thus the *Clue* characters became Washington insiders, each with a dark secret, summoned to a New England mansion for a confrontation with Mr. Boddy, the man who's been blackmailing them. In the course of a dark and stormy night, the corpses pile up, and the characters frantically try to figure out whodunit—though ultimately "Communism is just a red herring."

Lynn previously knew only one member of the *Clue* cast. He'd grown up with Tim Curry, who plays the indefatigable butler, Wadsworth. He'd seen a few of Madeline's movies, and their mutual friend, Austin Pendleton, recommended her enthusiastically. "Mrs. White was not a particularly rewarding part as originally written," Lynn says, "and I expanded it wherever I could in the hope that she would commit to the film." It was Lynn's conceit that the character names are all aliases, assigned to them by Wadsworth, and those names don't correspond to the colors of the costumes. Mrs. White is the greatest departure from the board game. Traditionally, the character is a servant (variously a nurse, a cook, or a maid), but in Lynn's script she becomes a well-to-do widow, dressed in mourning black. And as the script reveals, she's a black widow in the metaphorical sense, too, having lost five husbands in suspicious circumstances. Michael Kaplan's costume for Madeline, a sleek black sheath and perilous stiletto heels, even manages to suggest a venomous spider.

Murders and marriages aside, Mrs. White comes as close as any of Madeline's major roles to capturing her true character. Mrs. White's polished exterior, emotional reserve among strangers, and distaste for bawdiness all find their equivalents in Madeline's life, as does the character's adroit use of wit to reveal surprising truths. Asked whether she misses her late husband, Mrs. White replies, "Well, it's a matter of life and death. Now that he's dead, I have a life." Thanks to Lynn's script, Madeline gets off a number of good lines, but she improvised her most memorable scene:

WADSWORTH: You *were* jealous that your husband was shtupping
   Yvette. That's why you killed him, too!
MRS. WHITE. Yes. Yes, I did it. I killed Yvette. I hated her *so much*—
   it—it—the—flames! Flames on the side of my face! Breathing—
   heaving breaths!

Whether prompted by Wadsworth's lapse into Yiddish (and an allu-
sion to her best-known role), or by nerves, or by design, Madeline's response delighted Lynn, and all these years later, he doesn't remember
whether he bothered to reshoot the scene with the original line ("Yes.
I did it. I killed Yvette. I hated her."). It's good luck that Martin Mull,
standing just behind Madeline during the "flames" speech, is an experienced improv actor who didn't break character when she went off on
her tirade. Really, he barely reacted, so there was no obstacle to using the
take. According to Michael McKean, Lynn shot Madeline's improvisation
more than once. Madeline "just went into a kind of fugue about hatred
. . . and each time was funnier than the last. I thought they could have
strung a bunch of them together, because they had plenty of cutaways
of all of us going, *What the fuck is she talking about?*"[38] But Lynn used
only one take, and the scene appears in only one of the three endings
released.

Lynn wasn't particularly familiar with the work of the rest of the
cast, but he assembled a team of many of the best-loved comic actors in
America at the time: Mull, McKean, Christopher Lloyd, and Lesley Ann
Warren, a last-minute replacement for Carrie Fisher. Seemingly inde-
structible—though the universe did keep on trying—Eileen Brennan had
only recently returned from the Betty Ford Clinic to treat an addiction
to painkillers following a horrifying traffic accident in 1982.[39] She worried that she wouldn't be able to keep up with "all that running," but
she manages bravely as the garrulous Mrs. Peacock. Fans of these actors
must wish they'd been on the set, too, but in some ways shooting *Clue*
was the opposite of shooting *Yellowbeard*, despite the similarities between
the first-time directors and loony ensemble casts. "I don't recall much
clowning around between takes, if any," Lynn says. The complexity of
the shoot, especially the lighting set-ups, required the full concentration
of the cast, and he'd instructed them to deliver their lines at breakneck
pace, using Howard Hawks's *His Girl Friday* as a reference.

Brennan had looked forward to seeing Madeline, but now when they
got together after work, Madeline would say little, then leave abruptly.
"Something would happen," Brennan said. "She wouldn't talk to me.

She knew it. I would just go home." Soon enough the two stopped trying to see each other off the set. They had drifted apart, but the reasons had to do entirely with Madeline's psychology. She had tried so hard to insulate herself from unpleasantness for so long, but seeing Brennan forced her—whether they talked about it or not—to confront the violent, painful reality of her accident. Near the end of her life, however, Brennan still wasn't sure whether the reason for the distance between them lay with Madeline's personality or perhaps with some fault of her own, and the memories seemed painful to her. "She was a unique person and people wanted to love her and be with her," Brennan said. "But that wasn't what she did."

Lynn remembers a more generous spirit. His eleven-year-old son worked as a runner on the set, and for the wrap party, he dyed his hair red, green, and purple. Other people stared at him, but Madeline "complimented him on it and danced with him for much of the evening. As he was a total fan of hers, he was thrilled. So was I, of course."

In the finished picture, each of the three endings has its merits and boasts a prodigious performance from Curry, who dashes around the set reenacting the crimes, at one point dragging Madeline off her heels and face-first up the stairs. But this kind of mayhem wasn't payoff enough for moviegoers to see the movie three times, and in smaller markets, only one ending was available. Picking which ending to see proved difficult. As Roger Ebert reported in the *Chicago Sun-Times*, even Paramount didn't know which was ending A, or ending B, or ending C.[40] "The multiple endings were a terrible idea," Lynn says now. They had a "reverse effect: people didn't know which ending to choose, so they didn't go at all. This problem was compounded, I think, by the thought that if the filmmakers don't know how to end the film, why should people bother to go see it?" Further burdened by bad reviews, the film fell just short of earning back its $15 million budget.

Ebert may have been the first to suggest that *Clue*, as a relatively short film, would fare better if all three endings were included in the final cut. For viewers at home, the fun of watching all the endings proved the movie's salvation. The same was true of the smuttiness that Janet Maslin disparaged in her review in the *New York Times*.[41] For generations of kids watching cable and home video, *Clue* would seem daring and grown-up, yet unthreatening. "It was a surprising twist when the film gradually developed the enthusiastic following that it has today," Lynn says, adding that he receives more fan mail about *Clue* than about any of his other work. "I don't know why it was so reviled then, and I don't know why it is now so loved."

Over the next five years, Madeline would make only two movies, and both were animated features to which she lent her voice alone: *My Little Pony: The Movie*, a spin-off of a popular line of toys and its companion television series; and *An American Tail*, Stephen Spielberg's attempt to retell the experience of turn-of-the-century Jewish immigrants through mice, as animated by Don Bluth. In the latter, using a German accent that sounds more like Eva Gabor's Hungarian, Madeline plays the aristocratic Gussie Mausheimer, leading a crusade against the bigotry of cats. According to some critics, she stole the show.[42]

39

You'd Be Surprised

Chameleon (1986), "Wanted: The Perfect Guy" (1987),
and *Mr. President* (1987–88)

ONCE AGAIN, MADELINE TURNED TO TELEVISION. AT ALL TIMES, HER
goal wasn't merely to jump-start her acting career, but also to find a reliable source of income. She continued to support Paula, and the failure
of *Oh Madeline* didn't discourage her entirely. Several of her colleagues
were now flourishing in the medium, notably Carsey and Werner. And
in 1985, Cybill Shepherd, who quit acting altogether for several years,
rebounded with *Moonlighting*. Madeline's next forays wouldn't prove so
successful.

In 1986, she shot *Chameleon*, a pilot for ABC, playing Violet Kingsley,
who lies her way into jobs and relationships, then tries to lie her way out
of the predicaments that ensue. In the first scene, she pretends to be a
food critic in order to get a better table at a restaurant—though her lunch
partner, who happens to be her mother, Hannah (Nina Foch), instantly
blows her cover. Foch, a respected acting teacher, had graced such films
as *An American in Paris*, *The Ten Commandments*, and *Spartacus*. Considering how often Madeline's own mother complicated her plans, the premise of *Chameleon* may have made her uncomfortable, and casting a strong
actress in the role of Hannah wouldn't have made matters easier. In fact,
Madeline recommended several other women for the part, but all her
suggestions went unheeded.

As the pilot episode proceeds, Violet goes to a local television station
to urge the consumer reporter to investigate the diet clinic Hannah has
been frequenting. When the receptionist (Priscilla Morrill, of *The Mary
Tyler Moore Show*) steps away from her desk, Violet takes her place. Thus
ensconced, she regales a visitor with outlandish tales about the station
owner, only to discover that the visitor and the owner are one and the

same (Henry Jones, of *Phyllis*). Amused, he tells her to investigate the clinic herself, and she does so, disguised in a fat suit and using the name Miss Arbuckle. Though Hannah once again exposes her daughter's imposture, Violet nevertheless obtains incriminating evidence. By the end of the episode, she's hired to perform off-camera investigations, and she's discovered a new purpose in life.[43]

As sitcom pilots go, *Chameleon* isn't bad, but its characters are rounded primarily because we're familiar with the actors' other work. Such promise as the show delivers comes from the talent assembled, including the executive producer and scriptwriter, David Lloyd, who'd worked as executive story editor on *The Mary Tyler Moore Show* and *Taxi*, and director John Rich, an industry veteran. For her part, Madeline offers an assured, charming performance, but off-camera, she was miserable. In general, she felt that no one was "receptive to my ideas." In particular, she claimed that Rich disrespected her, accused her of "star tactics," and threatened her with unnamed "consequences."[44] She immediately asked her lawyers to get her out of her contract, and they helped her draw up a letter of complaint. Before they could proceed, however, ABC dropped its plans to pick up the series. *Chameleon* aired only once, as part of a summer replacement series, an anthology of failed pilots.

More happily, Madeline took a role in an *ABC After-School Special* called "Wanted: The Perfect Guy," which aired the next year. Billed as a "special guest star," she plays Ellie Coleman, the divorced working mother of a teenage son, Danny (Ben Affleck), who schemes with his best friend (Pam Potillo) to find her a suitable boyfriend. Without telling Ellie, they place a personal ad in the newspaper, but she's furious when she finds out the truth. Ultimately, Ellie has an epiphany much like the one Danny had at the beginning of the movie. Looking around her, she sees couples everywhere, and realizes she's alone. "Fate has a funny way of playing with us sometimes. What am I saying, sometimes? *Most* of the time!" Ellie tells her son as she sets out on a date with the man he found for her (Keith Szarabajka).

Produced by Joseph Feury and directed by Catlin Adams, "The Perfect Guy" won Madeline a Daytime Emmy, and introduced her to Jonathan Sheffer, a composer and conductor who provided the film's score. It was the start of a lasting friendship. Sheffer recalls that he actually suggested Madeline for the film in the first place. Feury liked the idea well enough but doubted Madeline would accept a made-for-TV movie—much less an *After-School Special*. What Feury didn't count on was her desire for work and income. The result is one of Madeline's subtler performances onscreen, and even when she's given funny lines or comic business (sitting on a scoop of ice cream, for example), she's grounded and credible.

In several relatively long speeches in Mary Pleshette Willis's script, we see that Ellie tends to ramble when she's nervous—a trait shared by many of Madeline's characters—and she frequently reenters the room to resume a speech we thought she'd finished. The character is weary of single life, of dating, of work, of raising a kid on her own, but she reserves a tenderness for her son at all times. We see this side of her most clearly in a nighttime scene, when Ellie visits Danny's room and discovers the responses to his personal ad. She doesn't read them, and he covers by telling her he's trying to write a love letter. Lying on his bed, Ellie describes the kind of man she finds attractive. She tells Danny goodnight, but returns a moment later. "Everything all right? You're acting weird. Clean up your room sometime, okay?" She's a mother as seen through a child's eyes, and yet she is, as she asserts at one point, "a very nice person and very cool."

The Daytime Emmy Awards are generally considered less competitive and less prestigious than their prime-time counterparts, and Madeline's nomination surely got a boost from her status as a well-known movie star. Yet the other nominees for outstanding performer in children's programming were all accomplished performers: LeVar Burton, Ruth Buzzi, Adolph Caesar, and Paul Reubens. If anything, the Emmy helped persuade Madeline that television still welcomed her.

She made occasional appearances on television specials during this period, and one, an all-star gala at Carnegie Hall in celebration of Irving Berlin's centennial (broadcast in 1988), warrants particular mention. The song selected for Madeline was "You'd Be Surprised." An airy comic number from early in Berlin's career, it concerns an unprepossessing boyfriend: He may not look like much, "but when you get him alone, you'd be surprised." At first, Madeline balked at the choice. Yet again, she felt she was being pigeonholed as a comedian, whereas she'd hoped to field an assignment more suitable to a leading lady—as she'd done at a Gershwin gala not long before.[45] The producers insisted, Madeline relented, and the result is one of the finest musical performances she ever recorded, a mini-masterpiece of comic timing and lyric poise, grounded in specific characterizations of gesture and accent. As an artist, she had arrived at a point where she could deliver exceptional work even with material in which she had limited confidence.

• • •

At least Madeline's unhappiness with *Chameleon* hadn't damaged an important professional connection. That show's creator, David Lloyd, was also one of Johnny Carson's favorite writers. In 1987, Lloyd, with Gene Reynolds and Ed. Weinberger, created a new sitcom, *Mr. President*, for Carson's production company. Starring George C. Scott as Sam Tresch, the president of the United States, the series premiered on May 3. It was one of the first programs on the fledgling Fox Network, which had begun prime-time programming only a few weeks before—and only one night per week.

The show represented an unusually bold venture. Just two years earlier, ABC cancelled its own White House series, *Hail to the Chief*, after only seven episodes. Like its predecessor, *Mr. President* would strive to mix comedy and drama, the personal and the political, but it's a difficult balance to achieve in a short amount of time. As critic Tom Shales observes today, Fox hadn't yet found its style, but even so, *Mr. President* made an odd follow-up to the network's early hit, the raunchy *Married . . . with Children*. "The sensibilities were incompatible," Shales says. "*Mr. President* wasn't particularly dirty. It was a civilized show: it could have been on NBC or CBS, which is why it probably shouldn't have been on Fox." And viewers had difficulty accepting the idea that Scott, best known as a dramatic actor, could be funny. Even Scott had doubts. One day Maddie Corman, who played his teenage daughter, asked why he was doing a sitcom. "Alimony," he replied.

The producers surrounded Scott with first-rate talent, including Lloyd and Weinberger, another veteran of *The Mary Tyler Moore Show* and *Taxi*. Reynolds had worked on *M*A*S*H* and *Lou Grant*. Director Marc Daniels helmed the earliest episodes of *I Love Lucy*. One of the most reliable foils in television, Conrad Bain, played the chief of staff, and Tony-winning actress Carlin Glynn (fresh from screen roles in *Sixteen Candles* and *The Trip to Bountiful*) played the first lady, Meg Tresch. But Scott often clashed with Weinberger. When Scott was unhappy, most of the cast and crew gave him a wide berth, while Glynn tried to play peacemaker.

A show in search of itself, *Mr. President* often failed to strike the right tone and soon switched from a single camera and no laugh track to three cameras and a live audience. "I didn't feel like, even at the time we were doing it, that we got into the groove," Corman says. "We had some stops and starts. George had health issues in the middle [of production], we had cast changes, we had format changes." As Fox announced that *Mr. President* would lead off the network's second night of programming, Saturday, the producers decided to place more emphasis on comedy—and wrote Glynn out of the series, a decision Corman calls "devastating." Glynn was universally loved on the set and a surrogate mother to Corman. "But if the show wasn't working, there's only one person who was replaceable." Bringing in Madeline made sense. On a show that consistently struggled with the perception that George C. Scott in a situation comedy was a contradiction in terms, Madeline's brand-name recognition proved valuable. Just as casting another actor to play opposite her in *Oh Madeline* might have relieved her of the pressure to make the show a hit, so casting Madeline in *Mr. President* relieved Scott. Another star could at least share the burden.

In a two-part episode, "Dear Sam," Meg Tresch does something no first lady has ever done: She leaves her husband. And with all the might of the presidency at his disposal, Sam can't find her. At a press conference, he announces that he'll meet her at a diner in her hometown, but she doesn't show up. The first part concludes as Sam sits alone in the diner—or as alone as a president can be, surrounded by his chief of staff and a Secret Service detail.

Walking into this scene, Madeline starts the second episode. She plays Lois Gullickson, Meg's sister, who has seen a news report and come to check on Sam. From the start, she sounds like Madeline. "I've known Meg ever since I was born," Lois tells Sam. "She's always been willful. She's selfish. She's spoiled. I never thought she deserved you, ever. Well, I've told you that before."

Sam pauses. "You never said that," he replies.

"Oh," says Lois. "I meant to. I probably didn't because you always seemed so—I don't know. What's the word? Happy."

Faced with the prospect of single parenthood, Sam tells Lois that he's worried about his children, and she offers to come to Washington "for a few days." Shortly thereafter, she enters Sam's office ("It really is oval, isn't it?" she says giddily). When Lois has a long phone conversation with Meg, we learn that Meg isn't coming back. The scene is actually a monologue, delivered as Madeline lies on a bed, much like a teenage girl chatting on the phone with her sister. Lois can't understand why Meg would leave. Ultimately, Lois confesses that she's long been in love with Sam, and when he asks her to move in and take on the duties of official White House hostess, she's ready to agree even before he's phrased the question.

Corman describes "Dear Sam" as especially difficult to act in, and the abrupt shift affected Madeline and Scott, as well. As the series continued, there would be few references to Meg Tresch, and Lois's crush on Sam didn't come into focus in the ensuing episodes, revealing itself more in the playing than in the writing. If the series ran for a few years, the producers intended to pursue a relationship like Sam and Diane's on *Cheers*, though uncertainties about Scott's health meant that long-range planning was difficult. "Nobody knew how long we'd be on and what the trajectory of the show would be," Corman says. "We changed many times—my age changed many times. But I think they really just were hoping that Madeline would . . . make the show light and funny, which she absolutely did, 100 percent."

From her first entrance in *Mr. President*, Lois Gullickson is in many ways an archetypal Madeline Kahn character, to such a degree that one wonders whether the producers considered anyone else for the role. She certainly reflects the image of Madeline that talk show hosts (including Johnny Carson) liked to highlight. Lois is bright but ditsy, loquacious, impractical, nervous. This may not have been the image Madeline preferred, but it was the sitcom equivalent of the song "You'd Be Surprised." Audiences found the material amusing, and she knew precisely how to play it. To some extent, Corman says, Madeline kept playing Lois even when the cameras weren't rolling: "She was on her own wavelength."

Years later, playing second banana to another commanding star on the sitcom *Cosby*, Madeline would say that she'd finally found the professional home she'd been looking for. *Mr. President* provided her with a foretaste of that experience, and it reifies much of Caryn Mandabach's analysis of her as a character actor who was more comfortable opposite a strong lead. Superior scripts don't entirely account for the ease and wit in her performances in *Mr. President*, qualities she hadn't displayed in *Oh Madeline*. Above all, her teamwork with Scott offers a marked contrast to her work with James Sloyan. Lois amuses Sam, as Madeline never amused Charlie.

Whereas Glynn tried to ease the tensions on the set, Corman says, Madeline appeared to take no notice of them. Instead, "she showed up and created her own energy." Scott "lit up" around her, and she brought out "a silliness in him that I certainly hadn't seen," Corman remembers. "It was very easy to tiptoe around him. I loved him, but he was a very moody and sometimes an intimidating presence. But that didn't affect her in any way. . . . She was this otherworldly being in our presence, and there was no way you could remain in a bad mood for long. And George adored her, which made all of our lives better."

As a young actor working with distinguished older colleagues, Corman paid close attention, and she's carried the lessons—as well as a flawless Madeline Kahn impression—into adulthood. No matter what else was going on—whether ratings or alimony or arguments with the writ-ers—Madeline, Scott, Bain, and Glynn were committed to their work and "never phoned it in." Corman's parents were fans of Madeline, and as a result, "she had been in my world for a long time," Corman says. "But to be up close and personal was exciting, week in and week out." At table reads, she found herself endlessly surprised by the laughs Madeline found in the dialogue. Even with the script before her, Corman says, she couldn't anticipate Madeline's delivery. And she appreciated the way Madeline approached her as a professional, saying, "That was exciting! How did you do it?" when she did well. Madeline complimented her especially when Corman found the comedy in her character, which en-couraged her to focus on her acting, rather than on pratfalls or silliness.

They shared the name Madeline, an interest in clothes ("I *need*! That *hat*! *Where*? Did you *get*? That *hat*!"), and the bafflement of New York-ers transplanted to the alternate dimension that is Los Angeles. Corman remembers an earthquake in 1988: When she called to ask whether the studio would close that day, the production manager replied, "Oh, please, the only phone calls we got were from you and Madeline Kahn." After rehearsal had been underway for about an hour, Madeline stopped. "*Peo-ple*!" she exclaimed. "*People*! There has been *an earthquake* no one seems to have *noticed*. But there was *an earthquake*, and *I* am *going* to *scream*." She screamed for a few moments, then stopped. "All right, we can go back to work now."

Both "Wanted: The Perfect Guy" and *Mr. President* meant that Mad-eline was working closely with child actors for the first time since *Paper Moon*—at precisely the moment she became an aunt. Jef Kahn and his wife, Juliette DeFord, welcomed their daughter Eliza into the world in 1987. "Both Madi and Paula were beside themselves," Jef remembers. "They were like two little old ladies, they were so happy."

In a sense, Madeline's relationship with Corman was a rehearsal for her role as Eliza's aunt. As the years went on, Madeline strove to instill in her niece a certain idea of femininity, "what it means to be a woman. She succeeded in her task," Jef says. "Eliza is amazingly imprinted with Madeline. She has so many of the same expressions and gestures." When Madeline came to Jef's home in Charlottesville, she and Eliza would lie in bed and talk in the mornings. Often, they'd go on excursions together, shopping for shoes or taking in a Jennifer Aniston movie. "She knew how to get to Eliza," Jef says. "It was beautiful to watch."

• • •

In principle, *Mr. President* might have been an effective fusion of two time-honored sitcom traditions, domestic and workplace comedies, with extra humor deriving from the fact that, in this case, the home and the workplace happened to be the White House. It's one thing when a father can't stand his son-in-law; it's something else when the father is president—or so the premise maintained. In practice, however, the comedy proved challenging to producers, writers, and cast. Unlike *SNL*, the show couldn't rely on up-to-the-minute topicality, and any political satire was kept to a gentle, generalized minimum. Certain kinds of broad comedy weren't suitable to Scott, and even Madeline's meddlesome character could be deployed in only so many ways. As several shows proved in the years since, the *idea* of a White House sitcom may be funniest thing about a White House sitcom.

Madeline appeared in fourteen episodes of *Mr. President* before the series was cancelled in 1988. Nothing about the experience dispelled her perception of the precariousness of series television. It seemed like steady work with a huge audience, but there were no guarantees, even when you worked with the top names in the business. And if Carlin Glynn could be written off a struggling show, so too could Madeline Kahn.

Always insecure, Madeline now began to fear that her career was finished. She made television commercials for Diet Coke and Michelob Light beer, figuring "she'd better go ahead and make the money while she was still worth something," as her brother put it. In 1988, the Beef Industry Council hired her for a fifteen-second promotional spot for its "Beef: Real Food for Real People" campaign. Casting about for more options, Madeline returned to the idea of a one-woman show that she would call "Kahn-cepts," but she never got farther than selecting musical numbers from among Laura Nyro's greatest hits and her own ("The Moment Has Passed," "Das Chicago Song," and of course, "I'm Tired"). At one point during this period, Madeline phoned Jef at his farm in the Blue Ridge Mountains. She'd helped him to buy the property, where he'd built a house, using skills he'd learned at Twin Oaks. Now she wondered whether he and Jules would mind if she sold her apartment, built a cabin somewhere on their place, and came to live there. "Her insecurities were always there, even when she was successful," Jef says. "They were almost like a virus, like herpes: You can always have it without symptoms." Once he reassured her that "she had a place to fall," she thought through the idea more carefully and realized she was too much a New Yorker to live anywhere else, least of all a farm. "She loved coming down here, but it was more like a scene from a '40s jungle movie with a safari hat," Jef says. Over the years, she grew more comfortable on the farm, "But New York was home. Manhattan was home."

Paula Kahn, however, came to a different conclusion. Once and for all setting aside her dream of becoming "a professional star," she determined to leave California and to focus on her granddaughter. Madeline bought her a house in Charlottesville, and Paula "proceeded to make our lives more challenging." By "our," Jef means not only himself, his wife, and his daughter, but also his sister.

40

Back to Broadway

Born Yesterday (1988–89)

IN NEW YORK ON JUNE 15, 1988, BERNARD WOLFSON DIED OF LUNG cancer, though he'd given up smoking some twenty years before. Madeline visited him often as his health declined, and she did so every day during the last week of his life. Illness didn't dampen Bernie's spirit. "He was joking when they put him into the hospice at Sloan-Kettering—he was joking even then," Robyn Wolfson says. "Up to the end, that's just what he did." He was buried on June 17, following services at the Frank Campbell funeral home in Manhattan.

Madeline continued to see Robyn and Marti from time to time, but without Bernie's presence to anchor them, drift set in. "She was busy, I always understood that," Robyn says. "I did try reaching out to her over the years, but again, she was either in New York, busy, or in California, busy. And I understand." Without having grown up together, as Madeline and Jef did, and without much opportunity to get to know each other, maintaining any kind of relationship meant a concerted effort for both half-sisters. Neither knew how little time they had. It was easier for Madeline to keep up with Marti, who continued to live in New York and who was available for the occasional date, like the lunch they shared just three months after the funeral. Keeping in touch with Robyn that year meant only a phone call on December 7.

Six days after Bernie's funeral, Madeline lunched with playwright Garson Kanin, who had been looking for the right actress to revive his comedy *Born Yesterday*. For a long time he had hopes for Bernadette Peters, but he couldn't build a supporting cast around her. In Madeline, he believed he'd found what he was looking for. One of the biggest gambles of her career, *Born Yesterday* would mean her return to a commercial Broadway stage for the first time since *On the Twentieth Century*. Before arriving in New York, there would be a national tour, something Madeline had never done and sometimes disparaged. The rigors of travel would compound the demands of eight shows a week in seven cities before opening on January 29, 1989.

And the play itself is old-fashioned, "a pretty old duck," as Kanin admitted. The plot concerns Harry Brock, a junk dealer who's made a fortune during World War II and now, in 1946, has come to Washington to push for legislation that will permit him to corner the scrap market in Europe. Crude though he is, he realizes that his mistress, a former showgirl named Billie Dawn, lacks the cultivation and social graces that would make her an asset to him in the capital. Instead, she's a liability who doesn't know what the Supreme Court is. Brock hires Paul Verrall, a reporter from *New Republic* magazine (of all places), to give Billie a crash course in history and politics. Under Paul's tutelage, Billie sees Brock for who he is and exposes his shady dealings. Inevitably, she and Paul fall in love.

For Madeline, the biggest gamble was Billie's indelible association with Judy Holliday, who created the role on Broadway and on film, winning an Oscar for her performance in 1950. Because of the film, Holliday still effectively owned the role of Billie long after her death in 1964. And Billie—pretty, sweet, yet feistier and more intelligent that she appears to be—influenced most of the roles Holliday played after *Born Yesterday*. Madeline saw herself as a very different type, "more hard-edged" and more like other women of her generation, who had reaped the benefits of feminism, "just more incisive people. Maybe more aggressive."[46] Madeline hoped to put a more contemporary spin on her interpretation. But above all, the chance to develop a character over the course of a couple of hours, and to be the center of attention once again for an entire play, proved irresistible. Kanin encouraged her, and as *Born Yesterday* moved forward, he took unabashed delight in her performances and personality. On the eve of opening night in New York, he told the *New York Times*, "I'm not speaking ill of the dead, but if I had a choice between the original production and this one for a New York presentation, I'd choose this one. This girl has got sex."[47] Introducing Madeline a few months later at graduation ceremonies at the American Academy of Dramatic Arts, Kanin declared that, in all the many productions he'd seen, the role of Billie had never seemed "as magical, somehow, as enchanting."[48]

His enthusiasm notwithstanding, Madeline struggled to fit into a part that had been tailored to Holliday's measure, and her work was complicated by the similarity between her own sometimes babyish speaking voice and Holliday's. Both grew up in Queens, and to some, they even looked alike. But Madeline "gradually creates an interior presence that is just right for the needs of the play," Walter Kerr wrote in the *Times*. "She is attractively sensual . . . [a]nd, behind Billie's accumulated shellac, you hear and feel an intelligence that is both wistful and tough-minded steadily stretching its wings."[49]

On tour, Madeline received some of the best reviews of her career, and critics rhapsodized about her performance, most singling out her comic business in the play's centerpiece, in which Billie and Brock (Edward Asner) play gin rummy. Several admired the way her Billie walked, as if wearing a showgirl's headdress. All praised the subtlety and wit of her characterization. Headlines like "The Kahn Festival" (*Washington Post*), "Madeline Kahn steals show in 'Born'" (*Denver Post*), and "Asner and Kahn a delight in 'Born Yesterday'" (*Boston Globe*) followed them on the road. Madeline's work in Brooks's movies left one Colorado critic unprepared "for the polished, highly inventive—and equally comic" portrayal of Billie.[50] After the show opened on Broadway, Mimi Kramer wrote an astute appreciation in the *New Yorker*: "That her approach consists largely in humanizing the character should not be surprising: acting the part of a brainless sexpot—and acting it well—is Miss Kahn's forte, but she herself came on the scene, and rocketed to stardom, giving the figure of the kept bimbo a realistic aspect." In Madeline's hands, the script was "funnier than Holliday's performance gave it credit for being," though every other part of the production was "a disappointment."[51]

For me, Madeline didn't entirely succeed in making the role her own in the matinée I attended during the play's Broadway run. She did make Billie tougher and smarter, less a victim than she was in Holliday's performance onscreen, but there are simply too many traces of Holliday in the script—as Madeline herself knew. "There's definitely . . . a ghost," she told the *Washington Post*. But, she said, "if the playwright asked me to do this, wouldn't I have to be a fool in this lifetime to turn it down?"[52] Billie was "a role with some dimension to it." As she told *Interview* magazine, it constituted her "first hearty meal after living on scraps. Was I starving. I can't lie—everyone's memory of Judy Holliday is a concern. But I'm not going to worry."[53]

Holliday wasn't the only specter Madeline had to contend with. The other was Lily Garland, and Madeline was determined to make her Broadway comeback offset the debacle of *Twentieth Century*. Arriving at the first rehearsal for *Born Yesterday* in Cleveland, Charlotte Booker was advised not to mention that she was Madeline's understudy. Booker proceeded to read her own part, that of the Manicurist, but during the first break, Madeline found her in the restroom. "You're my understudy, aren't you?" she said. The other women cleared out, but Madeline wasn't spoiling for a fight. "Look, I don't know what's gonna be funny and what's not gonna be funny," she said. "I know I'm not Judy Holliday. And I've had trouble with understudies in the past. Can we just say that we're working on this together?"

Booker was charmed. "Well, yes, that would be a wonderful thing to say!" she thought. When Madeline alluded to "the history here," Booker thought she meant Jean Arthur, who was replaced by Judy Holliday before the premiere of the original production. But Holliday wasn't the understudy. Madeline was talking about Judy Kaye, and she meant to warn Booker that she'd get no opportunity to outshine her. "We did the show for almost a year, and she never missed a show," Booker says. "I was the only understudy who didn't go on."

In rehearsal and every performance, then, Booker watched Madeline develop Billie's character. Madeline worried that she was too old for the role, and she seemed "cautious," Booker says. "She played everything very close to herself, nothing broad." When she did get a laugh during rehearsal, "she would look up as if they were laughing at her. She was very protective of her process."

"I start with the text," Madeline told the *Washington Post*. "Stay right with it, study it meticulously and deeply until you can picture someone who would say these words, what sort of person is this?" Billie's ignorance, for example, is "not even funny. How am I going to believably— and I have to believe in it myself—construct someone who will not only be believable to me but who will also be funny? Who has agreed to live a life with no prestige, no status, no position. It was quite a job, a nice challenge."[54] Because of her feminist sensibilities, she rejected the "dumb blonde" aspects of the comedy, and she looked forward to acts 2 and 3, when Billie asserts herself. Even Billie's elaborately upswept ringlets helped Madeline feel "uncomfortable," the way the character does. She was "adorned and far from her natural self," Madeline told the *Times*.[55]

Madeline tried not to emulate Judy Holliday, "but the trap is that you kind of have to," Booker says. The script's built-in limitations also affected Asner's performance, described by the *Washington Post* as "loud and blustery." New York critics were even tougher on him.[56] (Recalling Frank Rich's review in the *Times*, Asner wonders, "Could he have been any meaner?") Though *The Mary Tyler Moore Show* was taped before an audience, several critics suggested Asner's years in television had spoiled him for stage work, much as Madeline was sometimes dismissed as "just a movie star." Asner's great gift as an actor is his gradual revelation of warm, decent qualities in outwardly unsympathetic characters, but to make Brock sympathetic would unbalance the play, and the script simply doesn't offer such opportunities. Asner tried not to let the reviews discourage him, and he takes pride in the work he continued to do during the play's run. When the show closed, Kanin told him he was the best Brock yet. Asner had played Brock once before, in summer stock in 1973, but Gregory Jbara, playing two small roles in this production, says Asner didn't seem to trust the material. When he did find an effective bit of business, he'd almost immediately begin to overdo it. In the scene where Brock discovers that Billie has betrayed him, he considers having her killed. Asner poured a drink and slowly, softly moved the glass as he thought. "There was no sound but the ice as it was tinkling," Jbara says. "It was absolutely fabulous and brilliant. . . . But over time, the subtle glass tinkling was like a maraca in his hand."

While Asner struggled with his characterization, he was playing opposite Madeline, and, as she told the *Washington Post*, "A lot of my acting choices have to do with the fact that I'm working with Ed Asner." She said this neutrally ("Now if he talks to me in a certain way, then [Billie has] lived with him for nine years, and I feel comfortable, so I talk a certain way, too"), but Asner's process was necessarily part of Madeline's, and it added to the challenges she faced.[57] For example, the play's most important scenes depend entirely on Billie's physical interactions with Brock and require a high degree of coordination between the actors. The gin game that concludes act 1 isn't merely comic, it also paves the way for her to turn away from him by making it "obvious that they have nothing whatever to say to each other," as Kanin's detailed stage indications prescribe.[58] The climax of the play comes when Brock strikes Billie, forcing her to sign several legal documents he needs—and ensuring that she'll leave him almost immediately. On Broadway, the gin game went beautifully, with Asner developing a long, slow burn with genuine craft and discipline, while Madeline airily toyed with her cards and with him. But at least on the occasion I saw the show, Asner overplayed the slap in act 2. As other critics agreed at the time, it was Madeline's acting, not his, that made the scene work.

Offstage, Madeline got even less support, though she needed it because, as Asner remembers, "We were in trouble from the beginning." The revival originated with Josephine R. Abady, artistic director of the Cleveland Playhouse, which would be the first stop on *Born Yesterday*'s long road to Broadway. The year before, Abady had enjoyed success in New York with Tom Griffin's play *The Boys Next Door*, following an initial run at the Berkshire Theatre Festival, where she was artistic director at the time. With Theodore Mann, she would later serve as co-artistic director of Circle in the Square, a highly regarded New York repertory company. But with *Born Yesterday*, with two powerhouse stars onstage and with the playwright (and original stage director) looking over her shoulder, she was evidently out of her depth. While Asner speaks only generally of a production that wasn't working, Jbara recalls that the older actor "was unable to take direction from a female director," and that Abady didn't prove adept at handling Madeline, either. Before *Born Yesterday* made the move to Broadway, the producers eased Abady aside in favor of John Tillinger, who arrived in Washington on opening night, November 2. Rehearsals continued on days when there was no matinée, but with Tillinger in charge. Because of the participation of the Cleveland Playhouse, Abady herself was a producer of the show, and she retained the director's title through the end of the run, while Tillinger received billing as "production supervisor."

Then Jack Gilpin lost the role of Paul Verrall, to be replaced by Daniel Hugh Kelly, best known for his work on the ABC soap opera *Ryan's Hope*.[59] But the arrival of new talent didn't eliminate the show's troubles, and Booker felt that "Madeline never really got to do what she wanted to do. But for that matter I don't know if anybody ever got their footing." While Kelly and Madeline hit it off during rehearsal, Asner found them "unmindful," giggling behind his back. ("I turned and wheeled and glared, and it stopped," he says.) Tillinger was at times unsupportive, too, and Asner saw little difference between his directorial approach and Abady's, "Just trying to get the trains running on time was his main purpose, I think. . . . The interesting thing is that, opening night, Tillinger was heard to apologize to a couple of friends to the effect that 'You really can't do a lot when you take over for someone.'"

Madeline and Asner didn't get along, he admits. "She was a strange duck. I suppose I was steeped in my own insecurity and problems. I should have asked her to dinner, which I never did. I think I probably was in awe of her, and I figured I would merely execute as best I could— we never fought." He remembers one sign that she might not like him, a joke that she told during a question-and-answer session at a benefit. Asked what it was like to work with Asner, Madeline replied, "It's like being with a 600-pound gorilla." "I didn't know what it all meant," Asner says, and he didn't ask.

In fact, Madeline's personality clashed with his to a far greater degree than he realized. Although Booker and Jbara laud him as an actor and a mensch, Madeline complained to her friends and family of "inappropriate" behavior. The low point came at a Russian restaurant in Denver, when Asner began to roughhouse with Madeline in front of several other members of the company. If he'd realized how far he'd gone, Asner would have been mortified. Madeline said nothing to him, and she made no formal complaint. Instead, she froze him out altogether. Asner "didn't have an edit button," Jbara says. "So I would imagine that if Madeline had a certain template for what's appropriate for innuendo or behavior, or how women are to be treated in the workplace, it's quite possible that it may have tested her boundaries." "She definitely had a sense of decorum and *comme il faut*," Booker says. In this case, Madeline's dignity required her to avoid making a fuss. But the damage was done, and she gave Asner no chance to make amends.

With other cast members, Madeline let down her guard only gradually. Jbara observed "a definite evolution of her willingness to show a zaniness and an appreciation of life that definitely became more prominent over the time we did the play, both in rehearsals and also socially, after performances." Only after opening night in Denver did she go out with him and a few other actors, dancing in after-hours clubs. One club had a cage for go-go dancers. When Jbara climbed into it, Madeline cheered and called out, "Take off your shirt!" "For me as a guy, it was a little bit of living a fantasy," he says. "I did have a mad crush on her."

During the pre-Broadway run, Madeline's Diet Coke commercial first aired. Though Jbara has gone on to success on television and on Broadway (winning a Tony Award for *Billy Elliot* in 2009), at the time of *Born Yesterday* his primary income came from acting in commercials. The day after he saw the Diet Coke ad, he commended Madeline backstage at the Shubert Theater in Boston. She stopped short, then wheeled around. "Is that supposed to be funny?" she asked. "By her reaction, it was as if I'd said, 'Boy, you really sold out, doing a TV commercial!'" Jbara remembers. He assured her that he sincerely thought she'd done good work, and that he saw no shame in the job. He'd gotten a glimpse of her discomfort with some of the professional choices she'd made in order to support Paula.

Born Yesterday generated extensive press coverage for Madeline, as well as gratifying responses from audiences across the country, as people who knew her only from movies came to see her perform live. She also got a Tony nomination, proof that she'd moved beyond *On the Twentieth*

Century and that the theater community still valued her. But her happiness about the nomination was overshadowed by the death of Gilda Radner from ovarian cancer, on May 20. On June 4, Madeline lost the Tony to Pauline Collins (reprising her London triumph in *Shirley Valentine*). With no other nominations—and thus no wins—*Born Yesterday* closed one week after the awards ceremony, after 153 performances.

41

At First Glance

John Hansbury

WHEN COMPOSER JONATHAN SHEFFER'S BIRTHDAY ROLLED AROUND IN 1989, he invited Madeline and their mutual friend Gail Jacobs to a party given in his honor. There, Madeline was introduced to John Hansbury, and both Jacobs and Sheffer remember watching in amazement at the result, which was like a scene out of a movie. From the moment they met, Madeline and John monopolized each other, ignoring everyone else at the party. It was the beginning of the last romantic relationship of her life. "And let me tell you," Jacobs says, "he was a good-lookin' guy."

Madeline hadn't been this serious about a man in years. Hansbury had several advantages over other men that she dated. For one thing, he actually liked her sense of humor, rather than being put off by it. And her celebrity amused him. He remembers an encounter with actors Emma Thompson and Kenneth Branagh who, much to her astonishment, began to reenact Madeline's more famous scenes. On another occasion, arriving late to the Kentucky Derby, they were introduced to Oscar-winner Rod Steiger, who gushed, "I wouldn't leave until I'd met you." Hansbury urged Madeline to relax around less-famous fans, too, and he encouraged her to consider roles that would permit them to travel to interesting places. A shoot in New Zealand, for example, would make it easy to visit Bali, where he had friends who could put them up. The result, in 1992, was Madeline's only trip, to Asia, which included stops in Hong Kong and Thailand. Now an attorney but trained as a painter, Hansbury appealed to Madeline's natural inquisitiveness, and he introduced her to contemporary art, taking her to galleries and museums.

Hansbury characterizes himself and Madeline as "children of the 1960s" who weren't interested in conventional commitments. She'd told *Village Voice* columnist Arthur Bell in 1973 that marriage "was once an ideal, but I no longer have any ideals."[60] She and Hansbury didn't move in together. She was as firmly ensconced in her apartment on Park Avenue, he says, as he was in Greenwich Village, but they fell into a comfortable pattern of weekends, parties, and vacations together. The ease she felt with him can be seen in pictures he took of her in front of European monuments. She mugs and clowns, she's relaxed and happy.

Striking the right balance between "separate lives" and intimacy sometimes frustrated Madeline. After several years she remarked in her notebook that they sometimes seemed more like brother and sister than like romantic lovers. Yet she congratulated herself for not trying to change him, and she credited her years in therapy for the strength of their relationship.[61] Hansbury gave Madeline an emotional foundation—and perhaps even the springboard she needed to revive her career once and for all.

PART IV

The 1990s

MADELINE'S FINAL DECADE SAW A REFINEMENT OF HER SKILLS AND A growth in her confidence as an artist. Though her movie career dwindled to almost nothing, in her last film, *Judy Berlin*, she turned in her finest screen performance, a subtle blend of humor and heartbreak. Her efforts onstage and on television, too, culminated in superior work in *The Sisters Rosensweig* and on the show *Cosby*. As she matured, it seemed that her personal life would similarly rise to new challenges. The greatest of these, however, she could not overcome.

42

The Trouble with Auteurs

Betsy's Wedding (1990) and *Shadows and Fog* (1992)

SO OFTEN, MADELINE SEEMS TO HAVE TAKEN PARTS IN ENSEMBLE pictures almost as insurance. Her next movie, *Betsy's Wedding*, found her amidst another all-star cast, yet this time she got lost in the crowd. Alan Alda, who wrote and directed, intended a personal statement about love and family, tradition and change. The Hopper family, like his own, is Italian on the husband's side, Jewish on the wife's, and like the character he plays, he's the father of two daughters. *Betsy's Wedding* might have been a sweet, observational comedy, but it's hijacked by a subplot with broader comedic potential: the budding romance between a gangster (Anthony LaPaglia) and Betsy's older sister, a police officer (Ally Sheedy). The Betsy in question (Molly Ringwald) seems almost an afterthought. Her preparations for the wedding are sketched in sporadic bursts, and her conflicts are resolved hastily. Though Madeline plays the mother of both sisters, there's scant room for her in the gangster plot, and she suffers through long spells with little to do.[1] The movie seems especially disappointing when one considers the squandered opportunities for interplay with such inventive comic actors as Catherine O'Hara and Joe Pesci. Even Madeline's work with Alda himself fails to rise to the level he achieved with Carol Burnett in *The Four Seasons*, his best film (1981).[2]

Behind the scenes, and beginning with the first read-through, Madeline and Alda failed to establish a rapport. "She may have rubbed him the wrong way," says Carol J. Bawer, a production assistant on the film. "Alan likes to say he's giving everybody the freedom to do what they want, but he's got an idea in his head. When he's writing and directing, he knows what he wants on the screen, and that's what he wants from the other actors." That wasn't Madeline's preferred way to work, and Alda's own preferences didn't stop others in the cast from trying to advise him. "All these huge actors, very opinionated, colorful, and larger-than-life, so many creative minds in one room," Sheedy says. "[E]verybody [thought he] knew how that movie should be shot. . . . I could see that Alan was worn down and needed to go to sleep for six months." Later, Madeline's cousin Sarah Kahn asked what working with Alda was like. Madeline answered with an imitation: "No, no, no! Me, me, me!" She wasn't being mean, Sarah says, but rather suggesting that "it was about him and his needs and his desires, that she had no time for [and] it was clear that if another opportunity arose to act with him, she might look elsewhere."

Following the read-through, rehearsals, costume fittings, and a few location shoots in New York City, the production moved to North Carolina, which doubles for Long Island in the film. There, Madeline had more opportunities to interact with Alda, and their lack of rapport posed problems that came to a head while shooting a bedroom scene. In one sequence, the stressed-out father of the bride dreams he's wrestling a tiger, only to discover that he's in bed, wrestling his own wife. For the scene, both Madeline and Alda wore pajamas. She felt vulnerable, and the force he used surprised her. On the few occasions when she'd played a scene with even mildly sexual roughhousing, she'd worked with actors she knew well and trusted as friends, such as Peter Boyle and Gene Wilder. Alda was different. After the first take, Bawer remembers, Madeline asked to be excused for a few minutes and tried to compose herself, without saying what was wrong. She resumed the scene, but at the end of the day, she asked a producer to have a word with Alda.

The next day, having been asked to "tone it down" because Madeline was uncomfortable, "He didn't," Bawer says. "After that, she just went through the motions and finished the movie. . . . She felt he wasn't listening to her as an actor." After the bedroom scene, Bawer frequently acted as a go-between, and Madeline began returning to New York on weekends, rather than remain with the crew at the hotel in North Carolina (where in any case she had to spend a great deal of time waiting by the telephone, because of weather delays). Though she grew close to Sheedy, Madeline didn't complain about Alda. Madeline was "very private and circumspect," as well as respectful of her younger colleague's need to maintain a good relationship with Alda for artistic purposes, Sheedy says. "I was playing her daughter, who loves them both. She was also extremely creative and so completely committed to whatever your acting process was."

Taking long walks together when the weather permitted, Sheedy found Madeline a good listener, "But she had so much more to tell me than I had to tell her." Madeline gave her "little hints about her life," and even talked about her relationship with John Hansbury. Madeline made Sheedy feel trusted and special, yet "It was very difficult for me to get over the being-dazzled-by-Madeline thing. She was a dazzling person, you know?" They couldn't go anywhere without Madeline being recognized. Sheedy had been a fan since girlhood and made a point of sneaking the *On the Twentieth Century* cast album into the makeup trailer so that LaPaglia could listen—after Madeline left the vicinity.

Madeline hated long shoots, and the bad weather prolonged a difficult experience. Her appointment book for the fall of 1989 shows that rehearsals began on October 9 and lasted at least one week. She filmed her first scene on October 24 and flew to Wilmington to begin remote shooting six days later. With only brief breaks, she was still filming up to the end of the year, and to celebrate Thanksgiving properly, she invited Hansbury to fly down for the holiday. He made a few visits, his first to a movie set. He found Sheedy and Ringwald charming, and he made an excellent impression on Bawer, confirming Madeline's belief that her new boyfriend was extraordinarily comfortable with her professional life.

Betsy's Wedding also reunited Madeline with Julie Bovasso. If any differences lingered between the two after *Boom Boom Room*, Sheedy saw no sign of them. Back in New York, Madeline and Bovasso met for dinner one night, and afterward Madeline attended a few acting classes at Bovasso's studio, bringing Sheedy along for the first. Watching Bovasso's "volcanic" emotional range, Sheedy says, "I was scared of her. Madeline *loved* her." Their acting styles were very different, Bovasso "huge with her gestures, physically expressive," while Madeline was "tiny" and "detailed," Sheedy says. "She worked very internally, she was subtle."

Madeline would need grand gestures onstage in the next few years, but her next theatrical assignment required hardly any movement at all. A. R. Gurney's *Love Letters* involves only two actors, a man and a woman, who sit at a table and read aloud from correspondence between upper-middle-class Americans written over a fifty-year span. John Tillinger directed Madeline alongside Victor Garber during a two-week run in Toronto, in June 1990. Tillinger had directed the original production and the New York premiere, as well. Inexpensive to produce and requiring minimal rehearsal, the play quickly became a success on "dark nights" at the Promenade, and big-name duos cycled in and out of the production.

Garber, who performed *Love Letters* in New York as well, describes the play as best suited to such limited engagements, rather than long runs. "I was stunned that she wanted to do it," he says, "but we had a great time."

Once again, Madeline's inventiveness amazed him, but in *Love Letters*, as opposed to *Blithe Spirit*, he had the script in front of him whenever she threw him off track. Toronto critics understood Garber's occasional hesitation to mean that he was stumbling over his lines, but they praised Madeline's "particularly vibrant and self-assured performance," especially her adroit handling of her character's transitions from girlhood to middle age and from depression to alcoholism.[3] This was the kind of "dimensional" acting she seldom got to do, and working with Garber and Tillinger (under more relaxed circumstances than in *Born Yesterday*) made the experience thoroughly happy for her.

• • •

As disappointing as *Betsy's Wedding* had been, a greater one was on the horizon. *Shadows and Fog*, Woody Allen's homage to Franz Kafka and the great films of German Expressionism, would be released in 1992. Madeline had yearned to work with Allen, a director who consistently wrote sophisticated roles for mature women, in pictures good and bad, at a steady rate of one per year. *Shadows and Fog* was her first opportunity to work with Allen—and her last. For a scene at a carnival, Allen cast Madeline as the "Bear Lady," and called her to the set for at least two days of shooting, January 18 and 24, 1991, according to call sheets that she kept afterward. Her time on the set coincided with a visit from a reporter from the *New York Times*, and in a news feature about the historic Astoria Studios, Diane Ketcham observed, "Long Islanders don't have to go to Hollywood to be in the pictures." Ketcham cited a set dresser from Freeport and "Madeline Kahn, the actress and Hofstra graduate who was recently wearing a period costume with a hat that looked like a pizza pie."[4]

As was usual for visitors to Allen's sets, Ketcham was told nothing about the new movie, apart from the names of a few actors ("Mia Farrow, Jodie Foster, Madonna, Miss Kahn, John Malkovich and Lily Tomlin"). Looking at the décor, she guessed the movie must be set "in the late 1800's in France," but added, "That could not be confirmed. Trying to obtain information on an unfinished Woody Allen movie is like trying to obtain a casualty count from the Iraqis." Ketcham would be one of very few witnesses to Madeline's participation in *Shadows and Fog*, since the Bear Lady was cut from the finished film.

43

An International Guest Star

Avonlea (1991), *For Richer, for Poorer* and *Lucky Luke* (1992), and
Monkey House (1993)

DESPITE HER EAGERNESS TO WORK, MADELINE CONTINUED TO BELIEVE that accepting guest roles on American television series would limit her appeal. In hindsight, she was probably wrong. A few select appearances on better shows would have afforded her big audiences and the luxury of good writing, benefits she reaped in few other projects at the time. High-quality programs like *Cheers, Murphy Brown, Evening Shade* (Burt Reynolds's gently quirky sitcom, which was a playground for good actors), or any of the thriving Carsey-Werner shows, represent missed opportunities for Madeline, casualties of her professional judgment. Yet she did sometimes bend her rule for TV movies and for international productions, and in the early '90s, she signed on for four relatively quick gigs, all of which treated her as a "very special guest star."

Her first stop was Ontario, for an episode of the CBC series *Road to Avonlea* (or simply *Avonlea*, as the Disney Channel called it). Based on the work of Lucy Maud Montgomery, the series grew out of a beautifully crafted television movie, adapted from *Anne of Green Gables* (1985). While Anne is something of a national heroine, audiences far beyond the Canadian border also embraced the show. A slew of awards followed, as did a boom in Montgomery's book sales, three more films about Anne's adventures, and *Road to Avonlea*, which is based on Montgomery's many other stories about Anne's fictional home on Prince Edward Island. Produced 1990–96, the series skewed to younger audiences and at the start featured the child actor Sarah Polley. Polley plays Sara, a wealthy girl from Montreal who, after her mother's death, moves to live with her maternal aunts in Avonlea, where she becomes involved in the lives of the townspeople. In Madeline's episode, another relative returns to town after a long absence: Sara's cousin, the celebrated actress Pigeon Plum-tree, whose beauty, fame, and selfishness soon create trouble, derailing the wedding engagement of a farmer who's besotted with her. At last, a word from Sara makes the fundamentally good-hearted Pigeon see the error of her ways, and together they steer the farmer back to his fiancée.

Madeline obviously relished Pigeon's comically grand manner, and there's the added interest of seeing her work with young Polley (now an acclaimed filmmaker), revealing not merely comfort, but complicity with a child actor. Montgomery's stories depict young heroines who are intelligent and unafraid to speak their minds. These traits resonate for innumerable women and girls—Madeline included—and they account for the enduring popularity of Montgomery's books and their television adaptations, long after other fiction from the period has been forgotten. While *Avonlea* didn't maintain the extraordinarily high level of quality shown in the first films, Madeline's elegant costumes are unquestionably becoming, and the script, while simple, is great fun. Polley somewhat re-sembles the young Eliza Kahn, and you can almost see Madeline think-ing, "Won't Eliza enjoy watching this!"

A more demanding, decidedly less glamorous role in the made-for-TV movie *For Richer, for Poorer* (HBO) found Madeline playing a homeless woman opposite Jack Lemmon. Just working with Lemmon was a good omen. A popular and gifted actor, he was also a generous co-star with a track record of making his onscreen partners look good. Writer Stan Daniels and director Jay Sandrich both made important contributions to *The Mary Tyler Moore Show*, and both had connections to *Oh Madeline*'s producers, Marcy Carsey and Tom Werner. Something of an urban fairy tale, *For Richer, for Poorer* wants to be a comedy, though it contains few jokes. Lemmon's self-made millionaire grows weary of his son's insou-ciant indolence, and in response, sells his business and gives away his money. When even that doesn't spur the son to act, Lemmon is left with nothing. He contemplates suicide, but Billie (Madeline) talks him out of it. As he relates his story to her, we see it acted in flashbacks, with Talia Shire as his wife, Joanna Gleason as his mistress, and Jonathan Silver-man as his son.[5]

Weather-beaten and suntanned, wearing a battered hat and a man's jacket and trousers, Madeline's character, Billie, is nevertheless romanti-cized. "Madeline didn't want to be dirty, she didn't want to be messy," ex-plains Carol J. Bawer, who was on the *For Richer* set, where her mother, an extra, played another homeless woman. Madeline "wanted to have some class," Bawer says. "She wanted to portray [Billie] as someone who was confident in herself and not giving up. She didn't want to come across as a victim or as *less* because of her situation." It was an unfortunate marriage of armchair liberal sensibilities and her persistent desire to look pretty, and on location in Los Angeles, Bawer says, Madeline realized that the real homeless nearby didn't resemble Billie. In a review, the *Los Angeles Times* described Madeline's performance as "the most fatal element . . . [a] straight-outta-Hollywood street person."[6] But Daniels's script is hardly blameless. Billie is merely a device in service to the main character, existing only to help him get his life back on track. She functions much as a psychoanalyst—or a fairy godmother—might. But she gets off a few good lines, and even in 1992, long before HBO earned its reputation for prestige vehicles, *For Richer, for Poorer* helped to elevate Madeline's profile, exactly as she hoped. The cover of the *New York Times* television magazine for that week shows Lemmon with a *very* unglamorous Madeline. She sent a copy to Paula and wrote across the top of the cover page, "Ma—A cover girl at last."

Madeline next returned to Santa Fe to work in Terence Hill's short-lived television series, *Lucky Luke*. Adapted from the comic books by the Belgian artist Maurice de Bevere (under the nom de plume Morris) and the superlative French writer René Goscinny, *Lucky Luke*—an affectionate lampoon of American cowboy movies—depicts the adventures of a laconic sheriff in a small western town. In the episode "Midsummer in Daisy Town," Madeline plays Esperanza, a Gypsy fortuneteller whose love potion actually works—much to her surprise. A Shakespeare-themed farce ensues, and soon Luke (Hill); his romance-starved girlfriend, Lotta, the saloon keeper (Nancy Morgan); Betty Lou, a shy seamstress (Julie Hagerty); Luke's arch-nemeses, the four Dalton Brothers; and even Luke's horse, Jolly Jumper (voiced by songwriter Roger Miller), fall under the potion's spell. The mismatched lovers flee to the forest, where Luke manages to sort out the mess.

A veteran of spaghetti Westerns, the Italian-born Hill saw *Lucky Luke* as an opportunity to capitalize on his fame while providing work for his son, who would have played Billy the Kid but who died before production began. Only eight episodes were shot (in English, then dubbed into Italian), and Hill insisted on filming at the Bonanza Creek Ranch, near Santa Fe, rather than in Spain, as his European backers proposed.[7] The prospect of returning to a place she loved and spending time with Ginny Kahn—and getting paid for it—appealed to Madeline, and she thoroughly enjoyed herself. She plays Esperanza with a parrot on her shoulder, a bangle on her forehead, and a purposefully vague Mittel-European accent on her lips. She was working with an Italian crew, and it comes as no surprise when she starts singing an Italian aria. "Midsummer in Daisy Town" reunited her with Ron Carey, who plays Joe Dalton, and in her scenes with Hagerty, Esperanza's cynicism plays in perfect counterpoint to Betty Lou's glorious naïveté. Their work promises the birth of a terrific comic team, and indeed, the characters ride off together at the end of the episode. Although Madeline and Hagerty would co-star in *London Suite* in 1996, they share no scenes in that TV film, and this was as much of their partnership as we'll ever get.

In 1993, Madeline appeared in one episode, "More Stately Mansions," of the Canadian TV series *Welcome to the Monkey House*, based on an eponymous collection of Kurt Vonnegut short stories. Madeline's experience in the show redeemed the disaster of *Slapstick* in many ways. Vonnegut served as host for the series, and he praised Madeline as "a superb actress" who "added touches . . . [that] made the character come totally alive. I'm honored that actors and actresses of that degree of talent can respond to my material."[8] At the helm of "More Stately Mansions" was Brad Turner, who had recently directed three episodes of *The Ray Bradbury Theater* and one episode of *The Twilight Zone*, good preparation for the tricky material in "More Stately Mansions." Madeline plays Grace Anderson, a woman with exquisite taste and boundless enthusiasm for redecorating; her neighbors are surprised to find that she and her husband (Stuart Margolin) have lived in squalor since he lost a fortune in the stock market. Grace falls ill, and while she's in the hospital, her husband inherits money, which he uses to create the home of her dreams. But when she returns, she reacts in ways that nobody anticipated—more O. Henry than Rod Serling, perhaps, but close enough.

Madeline gives an unusually physical performance, dancing across rooms as she describes the beautiful objects she wants to place in them, and her careful diction and always musical speech give viewers reason to believe, as the neighbors do, that Grace must be a wealthy aristocrat. As the episode continues, however, it becomes clear that decoration isn't a hobby, it's an obsession, and Grace is something close to a nutcase. Yet Madeline plays the role subtly, as Grace's delicacy turns brittle, then cracks. Margolin (best remembered from *The Rockford Files*) underplays beautifully. A small gem, "More Stately Mansions" exemplifies the kinds of opportunities Madeline sacrificed to her determination to avoid becoming a too-familiar presence on television.

44

Calling on Dolly

Hello, Dolly! (1992)

IN FEBRUARY, 1992, MADELINE PARTICIPATED IN A READING OF A NEW play by Wendy Wasserstein at Lincoln Center Theater, and everyone from the playwright to Paula Kahn urged her to sign on for the production, slated to open in the fall. True to form, on May 13, 1992, Madeline committed to a short-term theatrical engagement to make sure she was ready for the more prominent gig. Jerry Herman's *Hello, Dolly!* would be her last fully staged musical comedy, and at first glance it may look like a fool's errand: a three-city tour of enormous outdoor theaters in the summer heat, with limited rehearsal time, in an iconic role written not for lyric soprano but for Broadway belter. Madeline hadn't appeared in a musical since *Amerika*, a decade earlier, and though she'd done summer stock, those engagements didn't require touring; only for *Born Yesterday* had she embarked on a multi-city, quick-stop tour. She told friends that she signed up for *Hello, Dolly!* precisely because it meant a new experience for her—even as she told her director, Lee Roy Reams, that she took the job for the money. Paula was yet again racking up bills.

"*Hello, Dolly!* is an old warhorse, but I had never seen it, so I came with no preconceptions," Madeline told *Theater Week* in 1993. She returned to the source play, Thornton Wilder's *The Matchmaker*, basing her interpretation on those of Ruth Gordon and Shirley Booth, rather than on "all those musical ladies, some of whom camped it up. I treated it as a regular straight role, with music added."[9] She went so far as to ask John Hansbury, a practicing attorney, to introduce her to some of his clients from Yonkers, so that she could get the right accent (for example, referring to Ephraim Levi not as "my husband" but as "m'husband"). Only after watching Booth in *The Matchmaker* did she begin work on the songs.

Madeline and John Schuck, a versatile character actor, had already been cast when producer Chris Manos hired Reams, whose credentials were impeccable. Reams had worked with the original Dolly, Carol Channing, first in *Lorelei*, in 1974, then again in her first Broadway revival of *Dolly*, in 1978. The *next* time Channing played Dolly on Broadway, in 1995, Reams himself directed her. By the time he met Madeline, Reams had also directed the French premiere of *Dolly*. And in 1980, he'd starred in *42nd Street*, working with director Gower Champion, producer David Merrick, and book writer Michael Stewart (all three had performed the same duties in the original *Dolly*).

The week of June 1, Reams and composer Jerry Herman met Madeline for the first time, at Herman's townhouse in Manhattan. "Jerry was very excited, because she had all the necessary skills and was also really a singer," Reams remembers. When she walked in, he was struck by her "mass of thick red curly hair" and her "classic-looking face," which he knew would read well onstage. "She was charming, and we hit it off." But at the outset, Madeline announced, "You know of course I'm little and I'm not Carol Channing." "Nor would anybody want you to be Carol Channing," Reams replied. Pointing out that "Ruth Gordon was even littler," he said, "Dolly is big on the inside."

Reams began to outline the character in terms that appealed to Madeline. Dolly Gallagher was Irish and probably worked in a factory when she met Ephraim Levi, a merchant with an outgoing personality. Because he gave his customers credit, he left her with outstanding bills when he died. As a woman in turn-of-the-century New York, Dolly had few options and "did whatever she had to do to make a buck," as the opening number, "Call on Dolly," reveals. "At this point," Reams says, "she's getting older, and she's tired of living hand-to-mouth. She had to sell her husband's business, because she couldn't keep it. Basically, she was probably this shy Irish girl, but she adopted the ways of her husband to survive." Just four months away from her fiftieth birthday, Madeline heard echoes of her own story—and Paula's—in Dolly's, as well as currents of seriousness she found essential to establishing the "truth" of her characters. However, Reams warned her, with only ten days to rehearse, there wouldn't be time for "a lot of discussions to find things."

Madeline flew to Atlanta on June 17 to record a TV commercial for *Dolly* before flying to Charlottesville to spend time with Jef and Eliza. Then it was back to New York and a July Fourth weekend on Fire Island before returning to Atlanta on July 9. Rehearsals began on Saturday, July 11. Reams began by staging the dinner scene from act 2, which contains a great deal of business between Dolly and Horace; he'd learned in Paris that this way, the leads could practice on their own while he worked on other scenes, making profitable use of limited time. Working with the props can even help the actors playing Dolly and Horace to learn their lines, Reams says—though he notes that Madeline was off-book already by the time she got to Atlanta.

Madeline's determination became clear at once. She wanted the director to respect her habitual process of finding a character, despite the limitations on rehearsal time and the conventions of a musical so well known that many actors manage to play it perfectly well almost by reflex. Reams indulged her to a degree, though he says he had to remind her not to overcomplicate the role: "It's not Chekhov. You have to have that kind of simplicity, and to play the intent." Certain conventions of *Dolly* vexed Madeline. For any business that she considered "shtick," Reams had to supply her with motivation, and he had to coax her to turn to the audience whenever Dolly addresses her late husband, though from the first scene Dolly frequently breaks the fourth wall. Despite her recent work with Julie Bovasso, "She wasn't comfortable doing *big*," Reams says. "She was an intimate actress." Reams showed her "how to be larger-than-life."

Hello, Dolly! contains no moment larger than the heroine's triumphant return to the Harmonia Gardens, an occasion celebrated by the title number, and, ever since Champion's original production, staged as a grand promenade along a passerelle or ramp projecting over or beyond the orchestra pit and into the house. Arriving at Atlanta's Theater of the Stars, Reams wanted to stage "Hello, Dolly" right away—and Madeline got her first glimpse of the ramp. Roughly three feet wide and skirting the edge of the orchestra pit, it looked precarious. To allay her fears, Reams walked with her the first time. But she still felt uncomfortable. "I can't walk like this, like 'Here Comes Miss America,'" she told Reams. He explained that Dolly is greeting people she knows in the restaurant, and he rattled off specific names, other characters she could visualize, instead of merely waving at the audience. She even found a feminist subtext in Dolly's kiss-off to Horace, "So Long Dearie," making a political statement in a show that depicts an era when women couldn't vote. "It was wonderful to see her discover Dolly and to feel free enough onstage not to feel insecure, and stop worrying about it," Reams says.

Musically, the part wasn't ideal for her. Herman's score is available in several keys to accommodate the vocal demands of different Dollys (including the non-belter Mary Martin), but Madeline, like many another middle-aged soprano, worried about her upper register. To those accustomed to hearing her in lyric roles of greater musical complexity, her trained voice makes one realize how much Dolly's songs depend on a big, brassy belt to put them over, and Madeline simply didn't have one. At the same time, her insistence on lower keys deprived listeners of the pleasures of her upper register. But she effectively reduced the risk for herself, and Reams describes her as "very secure about singing."

The technical rehearsal was completed in a single night (from 3:00 p.m. to midnight on Monday, July 20), "which was herculean," Reams says. Although the rest of the cast wasn't in costume, Madeline wore hers, to learn when and how to change. She never heard the orchestrations played until a run-through on the afternoon of opening night, July 21. That night, when a young actor forgot his line in the first scene, Madeline ad-libbed, "Ah! Don't say a word, Mr. Kemper! I know what you're going to say: You want to know why. Well, let me tell you why!" Delighted, Reams ran backstage at intermission to congratulate her. "That's the way she worked," he says. "She'd get into the scene and she listened."

During rehearsals and after hours, Reams and Madeline spent a great deal of time together. "We're about the same age," he says (in fact the difference is just a little more than one month). They became friends, and at one point, Madeline told him, "Before I knew what was what in show business, you're exactly the kind of man I used to fall in love with." Even today, he describes their relationship as "a love affair, without the sex. We were mad for each other, and it was a good combination of people."

Schuck has told author Richard Skipper that he didn't feel Madeline came fully into the role until the end of the run in Atlanta.[10] It seems that Madeline needed a few performances to persuade her of something that everyone in the *Dolly* company had been telling her: Audiences were coming to see a star named Madeline Kahn.

From Atlanta, the production moved to the Municipal Theater Association of St. Louis, better known as the Muny, an amphitheater that Reams describes as "Ten thousand people on a hillside, in the heat!"[11] Madeline flew out on Monday, July 27, without a break from the final Atlanta performance; the show opened in St. Louis the same night. Reams didn't join them, and the next morning Madeline called him to report a few changes. In the "Motherhood March," she had interpolated "Ah! Sweet Mystery," getting a huge reaction. "But it's all right!" Madeline assured him hastily. "It was a song of the period!" Reams was laughing so hard he barely heard her. "Everything you told me to do gets a laugh every night," she told him. "I've never had that kind of confidence before, and it's wonderful." She even grew more comfortable with her fans. When one young male admirer at the Muny gushed how much he loved her, Madeline didn't miss a beat. "Oh, really?" she said. "And how long have you been a homosexual?"

A fuzzy archival VHS recording of one performance in St. Louis reveals a relaxed, radiant star, connecting with a public far from New York and Hollywood, and having a great time doing it. Schuck delivers a winning performance as Horace, blustering lustily and giving Madeline plenty to play off of. And to top it off, she looks smashing in her gowns.

Dolly ended its St. Louis run on Sunday, August 2. The next day, Madeline flew to Kansas City, rehearsed again in the afternoon, and opened that night at the 7,958-seat Starlight Theatre. Days off seem to have been anathema to the producers, and the *Dolly* cast rehearsed and/or performed every day between July 11 and closing night in Kansas City, August 9. According to Madeline's appointment book, Kansas City was "<u>HOT</u>" throughout closing weekend, too. Nevertheless, she told Reams, "I'm having the best theatrical experience of my life playing this part."

Reams regrets that she didn't capitalize on the experience. Relatively few people saw her in *Dolly*, and her only other appearance in musical comedy was the one-time-only benefit performance of Sondheim's *Anyone Can Whistle*, in concert in 1995. A reading of Herman's *Dear World* with the Roundabout Theater in 1998 was her last theatrical outing of any kind. A number of other vehicles would have suited her vocally and appealed to her tastes: Weill's *Lady in the Dark* or Rodgers and Hart's *Pal Joey* from the classic repertoire; *Into the Woods* or almost anything by Sondheim in the modern rep. Indeed, Madeline's beautifully nuanced performances of "Bewitched, Bothered, and Bewildered" at an AIDS benefit (1997, under Fred Barton's direction), and "Getting Married Today" at a Sondheim gala (1992) can be construed almost as auditions—especially in the latter case, with the composer sitting in the audience.[12]

But musicals still involved enormous psychological and practical complications for Madeline. *On the Twentieth Century* was almost universally viewed as *her* failure, and it had long since become Broadway legend. She'd redeemed herself only after phenomenal effort, and she hadn't banished fears about her ability to deliver consistent performances eight times a week. Singing had always reminded her of Paula, increasingly a source of concern, and Madeline was at an age when most lyric sopranos begin to think about retirement. With musical comedy as with opera, it's possible that an attractive engagement might have persuaded her, but television and film yielded concrete offers. She would manage to apply elsewhere—immediately, and close to home—some of the lessons she learned on the road with *Hello, Dolly!*

45

Simply Gorgeous

The Sisters Rosensweig (1992–93)

AS MADELINE TURNED FIFTY, SHE RECEIVED ONE OF THE BEST BIRTHDAY presents anyone could have given her: Wendy Wasserstein's *The Sisters Rosensweig*. "I have known many actresses whose career opportunities diminished because they made the grievous error of growing older," Wasserstein wrote in the preface to the play, published in 1993. "Therefore I deliberately set out to write smart and funny parts for women over 40." Recalling the first preview, just days before Madeline's birthday, Wasserstein explained,

> To my mind, *The Sisters Rosensweig* was my most serious effort—a one-set, non-episodic play, complete with unities of time, place, and action, deliberately set on the eve of a momentous historical event, and even with the pretense of echoing those three far more famous stage sisters who yearned for Moscow. But just five minutes into the first act, the audience was rapidly chuckling, and by the time Dr. Gorgeous entered in her shocking-pink fake Chanel suit and vinylette Louis Vuitton luggage, they were convulsed with laughter. André [Bishop] tapped my shoulder. "Wendy, what is happening here? I've never seen anything like this."[13]

Very few people had. Madeline played Georgette "Gorgeous" Teitelbaum, the middle Rosensweig sister, and audiences responded to her with laughter and much more, as the play charged through previews, a smash-hit run at Lincoln Center Theater, and a transfer to Broadway. One of the most significant artistic achievements of her career, *The Sisters Rosensweig* brought Madeline widespread recognition that—no matter how funny Gorgeous might be—her talents extended far beyond comedy.

If the playwright was at first surprised by the reaction to Madeline's performance, the play's director, Daniel J. Sullivan, says that's in part because Bishop, then artistic director of Lincoln Center Theater, tended inadvertently to make Wasserstein nervous during previews. Beyond that, Wasserstein's closeness to the material made it more difficult for her to anticipate how her play would affect others. Minutely concerned with character and larger questions of identity, much less concerned with conventional notions of dramatic conflict, the script contains a number of autobiographical elements. Like the eldest Rosensweig sister, the late Sandra Wasserstein Meyer was a twice-divorced cancer survivor, a top executive with a multinational bank who lived for a time in London. Like the youngest, Wendy, who died in 2006, was a writer, single, and prone to emotional entanglements with gay or otherwise unavailable men. The middle sister, Georgette "Gorgeous" Wasserstein Levis, focused on her husband and children, and lived in New England. (Their brother, Bruce Wasserstein, was a successful financier who died in 2011.) All of them grappled as adults with the expectations of their mother, Lola Shleifer Wasserstein, just as the three Rosensweig sisters—Sara, Gorgeous, and Pfeni—view their lives through the perspective of their mother, Rita, who has died before the play begins.[14]

Madeline had considerable reservations about the venture. Apart from her usual ambivalence about new projects, she worried that she'd been asked to read for *Sisters* only because of her reputation as a comic. She saw Gorgeous depicted in the script as a stereotypical suburban yenta, designed to be treated with condescension and played for laughs, and she wasn't interested in that kind of characterization. "I think it may have to do with the fact that I'm a Jewish woman, and I'm very sensitive to doing stereotype sketches of Jewish women," she told the show's stage manager, Roy Harris, in a long interview in 1993. "And, right off the page, I thought that the role of Gorgeous had the danger of being that. When I first read it, I couldn't imagine a real individual saying those words unless she was campy. And I didn't want to come to Lincoln Center, be in a new play with all these talented people, and be the campy one." For the reading in February, she based her characterization ("a surface version," she called it) on women she'd known "who are very likable, very intelligent, but do have some of these stereotypical qualities."

Afterward, people came up to her saying, "You were so funny. You have to do this part." "I was? I do?" Madeline thought. After reading again for Wasserstein and Sullivan, this time focusing on Gorgeous's more serious aspect, "mostly I decided to play Gorgeous because everyone thought I should do it," she told Harris. "I take my cues from the universe, too, not only from inside myself."[15]

Gorgeous was "a part that calls for dimensions I have never used before," she told the *New York Times*. "The comedy is there. But underneath it is a real burden this character carries. The way she carries that burden, the way it is revealed and what it takes to reveal it—well, I can only do that now because I have grown as an actress and a human being. I couldn't have done this when I was younger because I just didn't have the compassion. Unfortunately, it seems to come with age."[16]

Wasserstein's association with Bishop dated back to his tenure at Playwrights Horizons, where he produced the plays that immediately preceded *Sisters Rosensweig*: *Isn't It Romantic?* (1983) and *The Heidi Chronicles* (1988), the latter directed by Sullivan. *Heidi* went on to Broadway, winning the Tony Award for best play and the Pulitzer Prize for drama in 1989.[17] Coming after that success, *Sisters Rosensweig* is unevenly written, it must be said, and the character of Pfeni, the author's stand-in, is especially undeveloped.

Set in August, 1991, on the eve of the fall of the Soviet Union and at the height of the AIDS crisis, the play unfolds in Sara Goode's London sitting room. Sara's fifty-fourth birthday is the occasion for a family reunion. Played by Jane Alexander, she guards her emotions and conceals her heritage; her seventeen-year-old daughter, Tess (Julie Dretzin) can scarcely persuade her to talk about her past for a school project. Pfeni (Frances McDormand at Lincoln Center, Christine Estabrook on Broadway) yearns to address serious international subjects but writes travel features instead. She's having an affair with Geoffrey (John Vickery), a bisexual British stage director. Gorgeous, the busybody, has doubts about the relationship, telling Pfeni, "I know you can't judge a book by its cover, but sweetsie, you're at the wrong library altogether." Geoffrey has invited his friend Mervyn Kant (Robert Klein) to join the party. Gorgeous promptly suggests that he marry Sara—and he's very much attracted to her. But Mervyn is as up-front about his Bronx–Jewish origins as Sara is detached from her Brooklyn–Jewish ones. Seeking any kind of identity, Tess has gotten involved in Lithuanian politics and is preparing to fly to Vilnius. Geoffrey realizes, "I miss men," and he leaves Pfeni. After resisting Mervyn, Sara falls for him but tosses him out the next morning. By the end of the play, he's persuaded her to give love a chance, and at last Sara is ready to do for Tess what she's refused to do all along: sing a song from her youth.

On the page, the role of Gorgeous does initially seem to be as shallow as Madeline feared. Only gradually does the reader realize that she's the only sister who's in touch with herself and fully conscious of the people around her. Gorgeous has come to London to lead a tour for another sisterhood, the women from her synagogue in suburban Massachusetts. She paints her circumstances rosily: her wonderful husband and children, her faith, her "funsy" job as the host of a radio advice program that justifies calling herself "Dr. Gorgeous." But at last she breaks down, admitting that her husband lost his job two years earlier, and she wears designer knockoffs because she can't afford the real thing she so dearly craves.

In the next scene, the women from her synagogue reward Gorgeous with an authentic Chanel suit and all the accessories. With infectious delight, Madeline dressed up in full view of the audience. "I haven't been so happy since the day I found out I made cheerleader and I knew Sara didn't," Gorgeous exclaims (Madeline made a gesture to keep from getting a laugh after "cheerleader"). Seconds later, she announces that she's going to exchange the entire ensemble for cash: "Sweetsie, somebody's got to pay for tuition this fall, and better Chanel than Henry or me." Madeline made this sacrifice so poignant that the audience gasped aloud at every performance.

"There are certain actors who are so right for what they are doing that it would be very, very hard for them to make a mistake," Sullivan says. "This is true of Madeline in that role. She was just a kind of perfect fit, like the dress itself."

For Madeline, this performance required getting under the skin of a character who resembled her only slightly. Both she and Gorgeous were Jewish, but in life Madeline hewed closer to the character of Sara, who has become more British than the British, complete with a London home and a posh accent. (You'd never know Sara was Jewish—and Alexander isn't. Neither are the two actresses who played Pfeni.) Gorgeous, along with Mervyn, forces Sara to recognize her Jewish identity, and for Madeline, the play was a means of reflecting on her roots. To light the Sabbath candles in act 1, scene 2, she consulted a rabbi to ensure she performed the ceremony correctly. Hers hadn't been an observant household, but now Paula put her in touch with friends in Charlottesville who advised her further about Orthodox traditions. They videotaped the candle lighting ceremony so that she could study it at home. Wasserstein brought a rabbi to rehearsals, and Sullivan learned the ceremony, too, so that he'd be able to help Madeline and other actresses who might play Gorgeous in the future.

The greatest similarity between Madeline and Gorgeous, Alexander observes, is love of fashion. Beyond this, however, the contrast could hardly be greater. Unlike Gorgeous, Madeline was childless, single, and never a middle sister. Whereas Gorgeous tries to circumvent her mother's definition of happiness, Madeline strove to live up to Paula's definition of success. Paula wrapped herself in a cloak of personal mythology, as Lola Wasserstein did, but Lola (and Rita Rosensweig) talked about family. Paula's stories began and ended with herself. Gorgeous follows a geographic trajectory, from New York to Massachusetts, the opposite of Madeline's own. Nevertheless, the actress understood the character—perhaps even better than the playwright did.

Sullivan says it wasn't really a case of indulging Madeline's desire to play Gorgeous seriously. "That kind of thing has always been her comic forte. She always came to a thing with great earnestness and seriousness, and that's why it was funny. That's in all of her work." "Reality didn't prevent her from being hilarious," says Bishop, whose title is now producing artistic director of Lincoln Center Theater. "Madeline didn't think the play was funny at all. She worried that the audience was laughing *at* her." Sullivan, too, remembers "that wonderful innocence of 'Why are they laughing?' That would often happen in rehearsal. She would say something entirely seriously, but because of her manner, everyone would laugh. There was that—one would think clueless, but perhaps clueless on purpose—'why are they laughing?'"

At first, the playwright asked the same question. Far from having conceived of Gorgeous as a caricature, or of the play as a broad comedy, Wasserstein "thought the same thing about the play that Madeline thought about the role," Bishop suggests. Sullivan says, "Because Madeline's performance was brilliant, with a good deal of hysterical laughter, it could be the *nature* of the laughter that surprised Wendy. I know she considered the character comic, and she is a comic masterpiece, only because she is very, very real." Madeline made Gorgeous real not by "ennobling her," Sullivan says, but by focusing on "this character's sorrow for what has happened to her and to her husband, trying to keep the heart up. That was the soul of the performance." "The temptation was, Wendy wrote jokes in there and she wanted them done," Robert Klein says. "She wound up getting laughs, but Madeline was on the ball all the time that this woman not be a clown, not be a buffoon. Her instinct was right." As a result of her approach, Gorgeous's revelation in act 2 was "all the more touching," Klein says, "and even then, she didn't play it like a wimp; she played it angry. She had a great gift."

"She behaved and worked like someone who was a Method actor, but she was a comic," Bishop says, still fascinated by her process. "Everything was real," Dretzin says. "Everything was funny. She couldn't say a line that didn't sound truthful."

"I am not, in general, a funny person," Madeline told the *New York Times*. "From inside where I live, I feel like I just perceive events in a certain rational way. I often find it sad or poignant, and it may not make me laugh a bit. But I don't mind inventing a portrait that allows others to laugh if that's what they want to do."[18]

The Sisters Rosensweig would prove a happier experience for Madeline than almost any other she'd known in the New York theater, and much credit is due the cast. "They're all theater people, you know, so there was no bullshit," Dretzin says. "Everyone was excited to get down to work and get to know each other. I was the least experienced, and I'm sure I was the most terrified." Madeline tried to encourage her, she says, sharing stories of her own work experience and praising her after a good performance. It was the beginning of a close friendship. According to Dretzin, Blythe Danner and Gwyneth Paltrow were originally considered for the roles of Sara and Tess, but when Paltrow signed on for a movie, Danner backed out. This cleared the way for Dretzin, who, assuming she wouldn't get the part, had been ready to start graduate school. Wasserstein and Sullivan took Jane Alexander to lunch, then gave her the play to read. "I loved it from the beginning," Alexander says. "I think Wendy always was writing romantic comedy. Even if the romance was about feminism or about women bonding, it was a romantic comedy—to me." She was especially pleased to be working with her onstage sisters, and the presence of so many comedians—John Vickery, as well as Madeline and the "always delightful" Klein—kept spirits high.

A quarter-century after *New Faces*, Madeline and Klein were a seasoned team. During rehearsals, Klein says, it was he who made her laugh, "like George Burns had this power over Jack Benny." Onstage, "I became her willing and delighted straight man. You know, for a comedian to be a straight man! And sit there for five minutes and watch the audience fall off their seats while I handed her gems. She was there every night, on the money." "Over the course of the run, she never gave less than 95 percent," agrees Roy Harris. Describing Madeline as "luminous," he was impressed by her seriousness, as was Dretzin. "I think often people expect brilliant comediennes like her to be extroverted, loud, always 'on,'" Dretzin says. "[C]ertainly there are performers who are like that. But Madeline was the opposite: quiet, gentle, thoughtful, serious, and then she'd come in with some ridiculous voice or hysterically funny little jab, and you would suddenly be reminded that you were talking to . . . Madeline Kahn."

The only dark cloud in the company hovered over McDormand, who had trouble finding Pfeni's character. "She just didn't feel she was right for the role," Sullivan explains. "It's a very difficult part. In all cases, when you're really playing the author, there's a terrible burden there." He found it difficult to help her. Wasserstein seemed to presume that her "sadness" was dramatic and that audiences would automatically identify with her stand-ins. McDormand strove to keep from letting her problems spill over into the rest of the production, then left the company shortly before the end of the Lincoln Center run.

Sharing a dressing room at Lincoln Center, all four actresses bonded, and they were thrilled when many of the design houses cited in the play sent them samples. As show time neared, however, Madeline preferred (like most actors) to concentrate and to prepare in silence. "I tend to be, unfortunately for other people, a little too talky in a dressing room," Alexander says. "I'm more easy; my preparation after a while is nil. It's kind of—walk onstage. But Madeline was so gracious about me, and she would just very quietly say, 'Jane, I think we should be quiet now!' But she never got upset with me, and I think back and I say, 'Wow, she was really a trouper.'"

During the Broadway run, the Clinton Administration approached Alexander with a view toward naming her chairman of the National Endowment for the Arts, which had been embattled during the two previous, Republican administrations. Alexander couldn't discuss the matter until the White House officially announced her appointment. "The one who was most delighted in the whole company was Madeline," she says. "She was really excited about it, and she laughed and said, 'Jane, how did you keep this such a secret?' She gave me a gorgeous, huge silk scarf that had horseshoes on it for luck."

Remembering Madeline's performance, Alexander says there was never a time when she worried that Gorgeous was stealing Sara's thunder, "because it doesn't work like that, when you're onstage with a great comedian. I know about that, and my comedy is very different than Madeline's—I'm known as a dramatic actress." The play itself was "a careful balance between comedy and drama. I was carrying the dramatic part of it." Still, she says, "There was something about Madeline and me together that was funny," and she cites the scene in which Sara comes downstairs the morning after sleeping with Mervyn. "Everybody's there in the living room, it's a dead pause, and Madeline says, 'So, how was it?' I look at her, a slow burn, and it's the longest laugh I've ever heard in the theater that I've been involved with."[19]

The Sisters Rosensweig opened at the Mitzi Newhouse Theater at Lincoln Center on October 22, 1992, but the production didn't meet with universal favor, and Wasserstein's play sustained palpable blows. *Newsweek* was especially tough, and *Variety* called the play "a stunningly mean-spirited affair," complaining that the sisters "don't seem to have issued from the same species, let alone the same womb." Madeline is scarcely mentioned in either review.[20] The *New York Times* was more encouraging, its review a portent of box office success. "The play offers sharp truths about what can divide relatives and what can draw them together," Mel Gussow wrote. "For Ms. Kahn, Dr. Gorgeous . . . is the choicest of roles. Restlessly changing her costumes and interrupting conversations, she is a delirious combination of extravagant plumage and native intuition."[21] In *Time*, William A. Henry III wrote, "Wasserstein is interested in serious issues . . . [b]ut in form and uproarious dialogue the play is a commercial comedy. On that level, *Sisters* is a delight and is exquisitely performed, especially by Kahn as the ditsiest, daffiest and ultimately most devious of this matriarchal clan."[22]

Buoyed by Wasserstein's reputation and building word of mouth about Madeline, *Sisters Rosensweig* hardly needed the critics. And as the run continued, a consensus grew: Madeline was giving a not-to-be-missed performance. Michael Specter's profile in the *New York Times* reflects that evolving perspective: "[C]ritics have nearly universally praised Ms. Kahn in this role, not only for her ability to bring down the house with the flick of an eyebrow, but for the streaks of sadness she lays on top of the laughs." And he quotes David Richards's *Times* review of the Broadway transfer: "She can make the most innocent utterances seem like the wildest of non sequiturs. She winds up stealing everybody's thunder."[23] The play was a smash hit, selling out at Lincoln Center. Friends and family came; it meant a lot that Ginny Kahn, with her high standards and cultivated tastes, expressed enthusiastic approval. Even Hal Prince and Peter Bogdanovich came and found much to admire. "You got laughs where there aren't any," Bogdanovich told her. "She would say something like 'But,' and it got a laugh," he remembers. "I'm serious. I'm sitting there, and she'd say something, and the audience would scream, and I'd say, 'That's not a funny line, that's just Madeline's reading.'"

Lee Roy Reams brought Carol Channing backstage after seeing *Sisters Rosensweig*. "You know of course I could never have done this play without having worked with you last summer," Madeline told them. "For the first time, I had confidence. When I put on that Chanel suit, I was Dolly on the ramp."

At the Newhouse, *Sisters Rosensweig* was performed in a modified three-quarter round. After retooling for the Barrymore Theater's proscenium stage, and after bringing Christine Estabrook into the cast, the play transferred to Broadway. That move made the show eligible for Tony nominations. It was a competitive year. Klein didn't even receive a Tony nomination for *Sisters Rosensweig;* the prizes for actors in a play went to Ron Leibman (lead) and Stephen Spinella (featured) in *Angels in America.* Everyone assumed that Alexander would be nominated for best leading actress in *Sisters Rosensweig,* with the support of the producers. After all, the role of Sara is central, and no one disputed Alexander's status in New York theater. She won the Tony for her Broadway debut in *The Great White Hope* (1969), and before *Sisters Rosensweig,* she'd been nominated four more times as best leading actress in a play, most recently in 1992. But this left Madeline's status in question. If Alexander was the leading actress, did it necessarily follow that Madeline was a featured actress? Other award nominations that year reveal the uncertainty. For the Drama Desk Award, Alexander was nominated as outstanding actress (and won), and Madeline was nominated as outstanding featured actress (and also won). At the Outer Critics Circle Awards, Madeline and Alexander both received nominations in the best actress category, and Madeline won.

The potential box office impact of Tony Awards came into play, too. If Madeline vied for featured actress, that might mean that both she and Alexander would win Tonys and give the producers an extra prize to publicize. But if both were leading actress nominees, then—barring the unlikely possibility of a tie—only one could win, or they might cancel out each other's votes. Bishop left the decision up to the actors, according to his longstanding policy, and Alexander also left the decision to Madeline. Wasserstein, however, made her position clear. *The Heidi Chronicles* had earned her three major theater awards (Tony, Drama Desk, and New York Drama Critics) and a Pulitzer Prize, and now that she faced the juggernaut represented by Tony Kushner and *Angels in America,* she wanted to exceed *Heidi*'s tally, one way or another. As far as Madeline was concerned, this was hardly the self-serving demand of a celebrated writer, but the completely understandable desire of a colleague and friend. Madeline discussed her options with other close friends and family, including Gail Jacobs and Gerri Gerson. The confidence she'd been developing since *Born Yesterday* and *Hello, Dolly!*—not only as an actor but also as a star—now bloomed.

"You know, they come to see me," she told Gerson. "I have the plum part."

"What do *you* want?" Gerson asked.

"I want best actress," Madeline replied. She told Bishop of her decision, and once the nominations were announced, "I never doubted for a minute that she would be the one," Alexander says, sounding pleased and rather proud of Madeline, "so I never had any problem with that."[24]

Immediately, Madeline booked a trip to see Gerson, whose husband, Sam, was CEO of Filene's Basement. "She didn't seem to shop that well in New York," Gerson remembers. "She wasn't her own best advocate when it came to things for herself. She wasn't an asky person." Gerson always offered advice and retail contacts, but in the end, one of her friends lent Madeline a simple yet sparkling black gown. "You know, you need a certain glitz and a certain look when you're onstage," Gerson says, "because it doesn't show if it's just a lovely sedate little thing. It has to have some *pow* to it."

On June 6, 1993, the night of the forty-seventh annual Tony Awards ceremony at the Gershwin Theater, Madeline joined Alexander and Klein in a brief excerpt from *Sisters Rosensweig*, presented as if at a rehearsal or audition, with the actors in street clothes and seated at a table. A stage manager (who was not Roy Harris) set the scene. Madeline got off a couple of her surest-fire laugh lines, including "You've heard of Dr Pepper? Well, I'm Dr. Gorgeous." But the big event was yet to come. Madeline's friend Lily Tomlin, herself a two-time Tony winner, presented the award for best performance by an actress in a leading role. Entering to applause, Tomlin called a return to New York theater a homecoming, "So I must say it is with great family pride that I announce the nominees." The family theme persisted as Tomlin read the names: "sisters" Alexander and Madeline; Lynn Redgrave for her autobiographical one-woman show, *Shakespeare for My Father*; and Redgrave's niece, Natasha Richardson, for a revival of O'Neill's *Anna Christie*. Tomlin's introduction turned out to be prescient. As joy transformed her features, she opened the envelope, then clutched it to her heart and said, "And the Tony goes to the person who gave me my first job at the Upstairs at the Downstairs by writing a note to the producer because she saw me at the Improv: Madeline Kahn, *The Sisters Rosensweig*!"

Revealing the extra "pow" of her gown—a hem-to-thigh slit up the skirt, visible only when she walked—Madeline hurried to the stage and embraced Tomlin. "Thank you so much for this recognition of my work," she said. "To be named among such fine actresses, for work labeled as comedy, is I'm sure a rare privilege. But then again, this comedy is laced with hidden meaning, thanks to Wendy Wasserstein. And thank you Wendy and Lincoln Center Theater, André and Bernie [Gersten], and especially Daniel Sullivan, for choosing me to bring this woman to life and for making sure that she is an individual . . ." The orchestra began to play her off. Madeline wasn't finished making her point, one that had been of paramount concern to her since *Sisters Rosensweig* first came her way. Without skipping a beat, she continued, " . . . not a stereotype of a Jewish woman. Thank you to my entire cast, especially Jane and Robert, true champions. And Mom, you're always right!"

Tomlin wasn't the only friend on Madeline's mind that night. Around midnight, Lee Roy Reams's phone rang. No sooner had he picked up than Madeline said, "I called my mother first." Gerson called and left a message on Madeline's answering machine just minutes after Madeline received the award. "I wanted to be the first," she says. "The next morning, she called, I picked up the phone, and she just . . . ." Here, Gerson lets out a little scream.

"As far as I can tell, your winning that Tony is about your future work," Roy Harris told Madeline. "People will finally see—and too bad it took an award to do it—what a fine dramatic actress you are. The Tony will give you a new kind of clout."

"And who knows what that will mean?" Madeline answered.[25]

Yet even at Lincoln Center, Madeline was still associated with comedy. Urged on by their mutual friend Gail Jacobs, André Bishop mulled over potential projects for Madeline, with *The Matchmaker* a strong contender. "For all her brilliance, I don't know how versatile she was," he says now. "She was a great actress and a great persona [but] she was not that easily castable. You wouldn't cast her as Gertrude in *Hamlet* or Medea, though she would be interesting."

Madeline would never return to Lincoln Center or to Broadway in a full production. And yet, more than any other project, *The Sisters Rosensweig* confirmed her comeback from *On the Twentieth Century*. Her performance as Gorgeous earned her vast acclaim, and it reminded the press and audiences alike of her range as an actress. The role not only proved her popularity, it reinforced it, by linking her more closely to Jewish Americans, who now embraced her as never before. (After all, for theater groups from Jewish organizations, *Sisters* was a natural choice.) The success wasn't enough to calm Madeline's insecurities entirely, but she proceeded through the 1990s with greater confidence—and a few superior gigs.

46

The Mother of All Lawsuits
(1993)

PAULA KAHN WAS RIGHT ABOUT *SISTERS ROSENSWEIG*, BUT BY NOW her mental deterioration had become an inescapable reality, not conjecture. Nearly five decades after she filed suit against her own father, she filed one against Madeline in a dispute over the house in Charlottesville. Though Madeline had paid for the house, Paula insisted that the title be transferred to her, and "weirdly" (as Madeline described it) she accompanied the attorney's letter with an old photo of her holding baby Madeline. At the same time, Paula filed another suit against Jef, claiming that he wasn't allowing her to visit Eliza and boldly charging into the still new territory of grandparental rights. Although she dropped both suits, the siblings had to consult an attorney, and as Madeline wrote in her notebook, the suits constituted "an undeniable 'ACT' which among other things let the truth in." The dispute marked a sharp change in the way Madeline approached her mother. She described Paula as "delusional, probably paranoid schizophrenic." The lawsuit represented an "episode," she wrote. "But wasn't her first episode really when she left the whole family [in Boston] and came to NYC with me, and me having no one[?]"[26]

Jef had long felt that Paula needed limits and boundaries, and now Madeline agreed. "We really cut the cord finally," Jef says. Joining forces made it more difficult for Paula to "triangulate" or manipulate them. They waited for her to make the next move. Remarkably, it didn't occur to Paula that her children might be upset with her; she began phoning Madeline as if nothing had happened. Madeline screened the calls, but at last she drafted a letter.

Dear Mother,

. . . I do feel somewhat at a loss in expressing myself to you after the shock of receiving letters from your attorney (to all that followed). I'd be reticent about communicating with anyone who did that to me—perhaps even more so because it wasn't just anyone, but my mother. I do not deserve that and don't know when or if I'll be able to be spontaneous and un-self-conscious with you again.

Even so, or "beyond our differences" as you call it, I do not wish you any harm. I hope you are well and free from pain. I assume you are (and) flourishing in your activities. I hope (they are/your life is) bringing you gratification and nourishing friendships. I am well.

Always love,
Madeline

She went through several drafts, Jef believes; this is the version she showed him. In her notebook, Madeline expressed anxieties over the "role reversal" and the need to exercise power over Paula. She questioned why she felt obligated to care for her mother, when no reasonable obligation existed after years of Paula's manipulation. "When did I stop loving her? And why[?]," she asked, answering herself with the next line: "She stopped talking to me in the same way." A few days later, she wondered, "Am I liberated or just mean[?]" She tried to see herself as a "good person doing one's best with a *sick* and *twisted* woman," but instead returned to the image of a "beaten victim."[27]

At last Madeline suggested that Paula come to New York, but insisted that she couldn't stay at the Park Avenue apartment. Paula took the train, arriving at Madeline's door without a suitcase. She'd left it outside the restroom, she said, and someone had taken it. With no other choice, Jef says, "Madi runs to the rescue. This was Paula's way of getting back in." Meanwhile, Madeline started to sketch ideas for a comedy act, "The 50-year-old daughter and the 70-year-old outlaw," the flip side of Paula's *A Little Off-Broadway*. To play the role of Freda/Paula "truthfully would require such meanness, hostility toward a young woman you're in love with," she observed. "My retribution could be standup." However, she added, "We must ask ourselves—is this funny?"[28]

47

Mixed Bags

Mixed Nuts (1994) and *Anyone Can Whistle* (1995)

FOR MADELINE, *SISTERS ROSENSWEIG* MEANT SHARING HER SUCCESS with her old friend Robert Klein, and making a new friend in young Julie Dretzin, who in many ways came to fill the role of niece in Madeline's private life, as she'd done onstage. John Hansbury got along well with Dretzin, too, and the three went out together often after Madeline left *Sisters*. "They were consumed with my romantic life," Dretzin remembers, "always wanted to make sure I was dating someone and someone who they liked!" And Hansbury "adored" Madeline, "which was lovely to see."

Together, Madeline and Klein tried to seize the *Rosensweig* momentum with *Mixed Nuts*, a film by Nora Ephron released in 1994. An American remake of a farcical French hit (*Le Père Noël est une ordure*, or "Father Christmas Is a Shit"), *Mixed Nuts* is a mess that nevertheless finds defenders among Adam Sandler's fans (it's one of his first pictures). Madeline plays Mrs. Muchnik, a crisis counselor at a suicide prevention hotline run by Steve Martin. Working with Rita Wilson, Tom Hanks's wife, made Madeline realize "there's no one 'behind' me"—certainly not a husband and not even her agents, who could have cut her a better deal, she believed, since Ephron's sister, Delia, told her that no other actress had read for the part. In her notebook, Madeline wrote of feeling "insecure" and "sabotaged" as shooting began, and she worried about working with a cast of such varied acting styles, ranging from Sandler's insouciance to Liev Schreiber's intensity.[29]

Remarkably, Madeline comes up with a winning performance. Though Mrs. Muchnik is supposed to be an object of mockery—a sexually frustrated killjoy, exactly the sort of role she had set aside after Eunice Burns—Madeline consistently finds moments in which to shine. An extended sequence in which she's trapped in an elevator is at once real and funny, and she lets her hair down near the end of the picture, by which time she's been revealed as pretty, sexy, and fun in scenes with Klein that benefit from their quarter-century of chemistry. "I guess we were a thing in casting people's eyes," Klein says. "As an actor, I resented having such a small part, but I didn't resent getting so much money for it. They kept delaying things and leaving equipment on the boardwalk in Venice, [while] Sven Nykvist [kept] looking at the sun, hung over from a party the night before." Once again, Madeline invited Hansbury to join her on location, and he, too, remembers long waits between takes on cold nights, shivering in the van and quaking with laughter at Sandler's improvised routines. In her determination to line up better support, she soon changed agents, too, after losing a role in a Broadway revival of Cocteau's *Les Parents terribles* (billed as *Indiscretions*) in 1995.

Madeline had long supported a number of charities, her sympathies for the less-fortunate being exceptionally keen, Hansbury says. Mostly, she made donations privately, but in the 1980s, she began to lend public support to AIDS charities, as the epidemic sliced through New York. Her most important contribution to the cause was her performance in a 1995 concert staging of Sondheim's *Anyone Can Whistle*. Both ticket sales on the night of the show and a cast album would raise funds for the Gay Men's Health Crisis. The project was a worthy vehicle, surely, yet it was also a daring choice for Madeline—for a number of reasons.

The first reason was artistic. The book for *Anyone Can Whistle*, by Arthur Laurents, is fatally convoluted, and Madeline, with her astute critical perceptions, disliked it. Sondheim's songs are difficult, based on tricky rhythms and building on dense lyrics that must be projected with precision. The consensus after the concert at Carnegie Hall was that Madeline hadn't rehearsed enough in the role of Mayoress Cora Hoover Hooper. And indeed, she missed a cue in "The Cookie Chase" and had to ask conductor Paul Gemignani to start over. (Her entrance, in "Me and My Town," and her dance routine in "I've Got You to Lean On" earned thunderous applause, however.)

The second reason was psychological. Walter Willison, taking part in what was billed as "an all-star chorus" (each member of which had a Tony nomination) believes Madeline was thoroughly intimidated. She knew that the nature of the concert guaranteed an audience composed of the most discerning Broadway fans. The narrator for the evening was Angela Lansbury, who originated the role of the Mayoress and who declined an invitation to reprise the part for the concert. Watching Madeline in rehearsal, Lansbury is said to have remarked, "I should've played it after all." Also starring—and sharing a duet, "There's Always a Woman," with Madeline—was Bernadette Peters, by this point the idol of Broadway musical fans. Both Lansbury and Peters could be confident of the approval of Sondheim, who'd written entire shows for them; Madeline had no such insurance. Taking many by surprise, Scott Bakula flew in from shooting the TV series *Quantum Leap* to play Hapgood, the male lead. Singing with suave authority and looking like a grade-A hunk, he brought down the house. But his success only compounded Madeline's fear that she was the weak link. Gemignani tried to reassure her, but he says, "She wanted to be great and never wanted to do something when she could not be at the top of her game."

When Willison approached Madeline after a rehearsal, she seemed hardly to recognize her old friend. They'd been through so much together: Danny Kaye, Paula's one-woman show. He'd even taken part in the saga of Peter and Cybill, since he was supposed to play a lead in Bogdanovich's Rodgers and Hart project. Yet now Madeline was cold, distant, perhaps even disoriented. The reason seems clear enough: At this point in Madeline's life, even Willison couldn't penetrate her densely woven anxieties. Forever sensitive, she knew already that she wasn't making a good impression on people like Lansbury, possibly on Sondheim himself—and ultimately on the audience. And to make her New York musical comeback with limited rehearsal in a difficult role made it almost impossible to live up to her own exacting standards.

After *Anyone Can Whistle*, Madeline wrote in her private notebook:

I don't really like winging it—I'm not brassy naturally, I don't "sell it"! So, this BENEFIT THING is really not my area, esp. when the part is imperfect. I would've needed more time, in the theatre, etc., off book, etc., to do a decent job on the role. Well—one reason I did it was to learn; to experience what I like and where I belong. The results will surely be the evidence and feedback that I asked for. Do I want to feel that I should pursue musicals? (Maybe Noël Coward) Of course when I could fool around and have fun—it was good, and I did get better as the evening went on and I got used to the space. After all I opened the show.

Why do you feel—"it's all over" when it rarely is . . . ?

48

Idle Tongues

New York News, Saturday Night Live, For Love Alone, and
London Suite (1995–96)

MADELINE APPROACHED *NEW YORK NEWS,* THE VEHICLE FOR HER RE-
turn to series television, with trepidation. "She felt she probably would
have only one more television show in her, and she wondered whether
that was it," her agent at the time, Bill Butler, recalls. "If that show went
five or six years, she knew that she was in her last very fertile period,
and she was aware of that." Part of her concern, he says, was that while
she still felt "hotsy-totsy" (the word she used), she'd noticed that other
people didn't always agree with her assessment. But Nan Chase, gossip columnist for the *New York Reporter,* wore nice clothes and looked
pretty. Madeline might be playing a middle-aged character role, but
amidst the gritty surroundings of a tabloid newsroom, she was downright glamorous.

Intended as *"E.R.* at a newspaper," as Butler puts it, *New York News*
featured Mary Tyler Moore as Louise Felcott, the paper's editor-in-chief.
Most episodes contained some comedy, but this was drama, and while
the show did put Moore back in a newsroom, this one was nothing like
the WJM studio in *The Mary Tyler Moore Show* (or, for that matter, the
Chicago newspaper setting of the short-lived *Mary* [1985–86]). *New York
News* more closely resembled two previous shows produced by MTM En-
terprises: *Lou Grant,* particularly in the newspaper setting and in many
of the characters, and *Hill Street Blues,* with its overlapping plot lines and
urban ambiance. Louise Felcott seems like a mixture of *Lou Grant*'s Mrs.
Pynchon and Lou himself, though she is decidedly less amiable than
either: Felcott's nickname is "the Dragon." Audiences and critics alike
found Felcott not merely tough but unsympathetic. The result was bru-
tal reviews that made the star less of a draw for a show that had barely

gotten on the lineup in the first place. Almost immediately, Moore began trying to get out of the show, putting *New York News*—and Madeline's job—in jeopardy.

As Nan Chase, Madeline reaped most of the scripts' funniest and most effective lines. Faced with staff cuts in the pilot episode, Nan tells her hard-news colleagues, "If anyone at this paper is expendable, it is all of *you.*" *Entertainment Weekly* praised her for her "shrewd embodiment of a haughty gossip columnist who has the cheerful gall to rag on Liz Smith," while the *New York Times* singled out Madeline's "maniacal relish."[30] The *San Francisco Chronicle* observed that co-star Gregory Harrison "may dominate the narrative, but as usual Kahn manages to commit larceny."[31] However, Tom Shales of the *Washington Post* found nothing to admire in Madeline's "bossy and blabby" character.[32] Subsequent episodes showed Nan almost in her own orbit, not only in the comic nature of her scenes but also in her spiritual and physical isolation from the other characters. Often, it seemed that Nan and Madeline were in another series entirely.

Although in her own career Madeline had been mostly spared the ire of gossip columnists and entertainment reporters, and though she had more often found champions like Rex Reed and Shaun Considine, she hadn't developed much sympathy for the fifth estate. "I experience the press as this large clump . . . ," she told the *Ogden (UT) Standard-Examiner.* "[I] don't think of them as individuals. So it will be interesting to me to try to find the inner life and find the individual underneath the person who's doing the reporting that I often feel uncomfortable with."[33]

"BOY, did I stumble into this," Madeline wrote in her notebook. She hadn't expected the "queen" treatment accorded to Moore, whose return to television became the primary focus of publicity for the show. Madeline found the scripts "boring, i.e. conservative . . . yesterday's news," and as for Nan Chase, "the character IS NOT THERE on the page—NO CHARACTER—and not enough [screen] time" to develop the role. Once again Madeline worried "that I'm only meant to be funny," but this time she complained to the producers. Soon she saw results: "I like Nan also for the facts = she is WORKING, SUCCESSFUL, fit, single."[34]

The character remained underused, however, and Madeline believed that Moore's looming departure meant that Nan, too, would be phased out, since so many of her strongest scenes are those in which Louise and Nan, the senior women in the newsroom, commiserate in the restroom. The off-screen rapport between Madeline and Moore is reflected in their playing, and their scenes offer an intimate glimpse of a bond between women in the workplace that was, in its way, as revelatory as the dialogues between Mary Richards and Rhoda Morgenstern, friends who bonded outside the workplace. For a few minutes, at least, Louise could be sympathetic and Nan could be sensible—and viewers got a welcome respite from the churning plots that focused on the other leading characters, played by Harrison and Melina Kanakaredes. Even if *New York News* could have survived without Moore, her absence would have deprived the show of its most effective material.

CBS cancelled *New York News* with half the season's episodes completed. The final episode appeared on November 30, 1995, leaving five more episodes unaired.[35] The show's untimely demise didn't in itself diminish Madeline's reemergence. Oliver Stone's *Nixon* would be released in December 1995, and the new movie, which featured Madeline in a cameo role, gave the producers of *Saturday Night Live* a reason to sign her for her third and final appearance as host (substituting for another star who'd had to drop out, as Bill Butler recalls).

By the time Madeline got to Rockefeller Center, on December 16, 1995, her *Mixed Nuts* co-star Adam Sandler had been fired, as had cast member Chris Farley. Despite pressure from NBC executives, the transition from the kind of frat house humor championed by Sandler and Farley had barely begun. Neither the show's idea of comedy nor the show itself was what it had been in the 1970s—or even the year before. Punch lines relied heavily on name-calling, and if referring to a politician's husband as "fat" got laughs from the studio audience, why bother writing sharper material? Madeline's second sketch demonstrates the laziness of the writing. "Leg Up," a talk show about dance hosted by Ann Miller (Molly Shannon) and Debbie Reynolds (Cheri Oteri), quickly devolves into a vulgar discussion of the sex lives of aging dancers, as they interview a legendary Russian ballerina (Madeline). There's scant indication that any of the writers had ever seen a ballet or an MGM musical, or that Oteri had ever seen or heard of Debbie Reynolds.

Madeline's first sketch is stronger: Bickering picnickers, husband and wife, are being carried off by a gigantic bird. We see only the bird's claws gripping Madeline and cast member David Koechner in mid-air, as the couple reviews how they got into this mess. The gimmick is that each repeats, with heavy sarcasm, things the other ostensibly said earlier in the day. ("There's a good spot, Nancy, up on top of that hill, in that big, round ball of hay!" "Stop running! It can't see you when you stand still!") In Madeline's only other sketch, she plays a dissatisfied customer in an antique shop run by two impossibly fey men in eighteenth-century costumes (recurring characters played by Koechner and Mark McKinney).

The shop owners are too outlandish to be funny, but Madeline delivers a nicely scripted speech as she tells them off.

What's most striking, especially to anyone who has seen Madeline's first guest-hosting gig, is that the material she was given in 1995 is so generic. Virtually any woman could have been cast in these sketches, and no one would know the difference. Madeline brings a few assets: She knows how to deliver a sarcastic line, she can do a Russian accent, and she can play an elegant, middle-aged lady. But dozens of others (presumably including the host she replaced) could have done the same. At least in Madeline's opening monologue, she's given some personal material, a self-deprecating account of her eighteen-year wait to host the show again: "But 1978 passed, you know, and um, no phone call from the show. Anyway, uh, '79, 'kay? . . . Then came the '80s—the entire '80s, actually. And then the '90s arrived, and it seemed very promising, you know, what with the miracle of fiber optics and so on." When the phone rings in 1994, Lorne Michaels's office is looking for Madeline—Madeline Stowe. Finally, Madeline has the chance to perform the song she's been rehearsing since 1978. In reality, it's one of her party tricks, singing Clarence "Frogman" Henry's "Ain't Got No Home" in three distinct voices. The song doesn't compare with the abundant musical material she had in her earlier appearances, but it's recognizably Madeline Kahn.

Behind the scenes, the show was in trouble. It had narrowly escaped cancellation the previous season, its twentieth. Longtime producer James Downey had been fired, and only five cast members returned for the twenty-first season. While the writing may have gotten away from its reliance on frat house humor, Downey identifies 1995 as the year that *SNL* "became very much a performer's show . . . enforcing the idea that 'the cast isn't here to bring to life the writer's notions; the writers are there to supply material for the characters that the cast already does.'"[36] This background helps to explain why Madeline's material is so weak, and why the episode as a whole is so disappointing. The only sketch that lands squarely is a mock TV commercial, presented by actor Sam Waterston, that urges the elderly to purchase insurance against robot attacks—and Madeline isn't in it.

Four days after that final gig on *SNL*, Oliver Stone's *Nixon* opened. As Martha Mitchell, Madeline doesn't look like the woman she's playing, but she captures Martha's essence—or anyway, what many Americans perceived her essence to be. As the wife of United States Attorney General John Mitchell, Madeline has only two brief scenes, and she isn't seen at all until nearly forty-five minutes into the "director's cut" of the movie, released for home viewing. Madeline makes a vivid impression, however, as a garrulous Southern matron, with an accent not unlike Trixie Delight's. She knows how to hurt Nixon, as well as her husband, and she has no qualms about doing so. So much of the rest of the rest of the movie is intensely dramatic, or surreal, or lugubrious, that Madeline's performance has the effect of comic relief, though one comes to realize that nothing she does is funny. It's delicate, almost surgically precise work.

Stone had scored a hit four years earlier with *JFK*, dramatizing an unprovable conspiracy theory. For *Nixon*, Stone again assembled an impressive cast, which managed to evoke figures many in the audience remembered well from newspapers and television. This time, however, the most provocative aspect of Stone's work is his sympathetic treatment of the disgraced former president, who died in April 1994. Since Nixon still has his admirers, the director's generosity toward his subject isn't universally viewed as a flaw. Faced with a large cast and limited column inches, not every critic mentioned Madeline, but Mick LaSalle of the *San Francisco Chronicle* ended his review by saying, "Madeline Kahn appears all too briefly here as Martha Mitchell; she should have played Pat"— which of course she'd done on *SNL* nearly two decades before.[37]

Madeline almost didn't get to play Martha. Diane Ladd had been the leading contender to play the role, but she was unavailable. Madeline's performance is as good an example as any of her late-career work. No longer burdened with much if any responsibility for the box office success or failure of the projects she took on—and freed from the demands of broader comedy made on her in so many of her earlier movies—she has the skill and talent to etch deft portraits using minimal means. She's often funny, but even when the writing is substandard, she builds her humor on a solid foundation of character, and she knows how to deliver any line to make it register effectively. Looking back at her performances in these years, the possibilities seem limitless. But she was a mature woman now. Though she lent her voice to Pixar's *A Bug's Life*, in 1998, *Nixon* marked Madeline's last onscreen appearance in a major studio release.

Having played Nan Chase probably made another assignment easier for Madeline: playing another New York gossip columnist in *For Love Alone: The Ivana Trump Story*, a TV movie that aired on CBS on January 7, 1996. An adaptation of a roman à clef written by the ex-wife of Donald Trump, *For Love Alone* plays with the audience's presumptions about the Trumps' marriage, dramatizing known incidents while keeping the heroine ever-admirable and blameless.[38] The only leaven in the melo-drama comes from Madeline, playing Sabrina, first the heroine's an-tagonist, then her ally. Making astute use of her character's enormous, black-rimmed eyeglasses, Madeline recalls Edna Mode, the diminutive costume designer in Pixar's *The Incredibles* (2005). In one of the movie's rare visually telling sequences, Madeline appears in the background of a shot, rising from behind a bank of potted flowers while she eavesdrops—like an owl spying on mice in a garden. She didn't impress the critics ("equally uninspiring," wrote Lisa D. Horowitz in *Variety*, while noting the similarity to Nan Chase), but she got a paycheck.[39]

The same year, Madeline took a more substantial role in a TV movie, *Neil Simon's London Suite*, opposite her *Harvey* co-star Richard Mulligan. Playing a widow who engages in "shopping therapy" rather than fac-ing her loneliness, Madeline recalls a better-dressed Mrs. Muchnik from *Mixed Nuts*. Now that she was middle-aged, and not at all a saucy wench, she was on the brink of being typecast as something of a prig who was funniest when rattled. The writers of her next project would do little to change that image.

49

Do You Love Me, Pauline?

Cosby (1996–99)

WITH MADELINE'S FOURTH TELEVISION SERIES, SHE FOUND ARTISTIC and personal satisfaction at last. Yes, weak scripts posed a problem again, but this time she was working with Bill Cosby, an incorrigible impro- viser whose riffs were superior to anything most writers could devise, and who gave her ample room to join him. When his producers, Marcy Carsey and Tom Werner, cast her in the role of Pauline Fox, the wife's sidekick in their new sitcom, they played to Madeline's strengths—once again applying the lessons they'd learned from their mistakes in *Oh Mad- eline*. Caryn Sneider Mandabach joined the team again, too. Madeline was among friends, and Cosby's arrival at CBS was heralded as noth- ing less than the salvation of the "Tiffany Network," after an erosion of audiences and the humiliating loss of NFL football and several affiliate stations to Fox. Though triumph was hardly guaranteed, the welcome could not have been more propitious.

Since the finale of *The Cosby Show* in 1992, Bill Cosby had hosted a syndicated game show, *You Bet Your Life*, and, on NBC, *The Cosby Myster- ies*. Neither show had anything like the impact of his previous prime- time juggernaut, and therefore was nothing like the national platform to which he'd grown accustomed. Now, hoping to replicate his earlier success, he turned again to Carsey and Werner, and when NBC passed on the new series, CBS snatched it up. Based on the British series *One Foot in the Grave*, *Cosby* is centered on Hilton Lucas, a cantankerous sexagenarian in Queens who is laid off after working thirty years as a baggage handler. His wife, Ruth, isn't entirely pleased with this development, either, but she manages to keep her sense of humor—thanks in part to her friend Pauline.

Phylicia Rashad, the onscreen spouse from *The Cosby Show*, played Ruth, and her ease with the star transferred seamlessly to the new program. The Lucases are less huggable than the Huxtables, and far more conscious of decline and mortality. The sharper, sassier humor now at play inspired both actors to deliver loose, witty performances. As Hilton, Cosby sometimes breaks the fourth wall, addressing the camera, while launching his ad-libbed "rants" (as Carsey called them) more freely than was possible when he was working with a supporting cast composed of children who couldn't always keep up with him or return to the script when he was ready. Precisely because Rashad knew how to "catch" his improvisations, Cosby told the press, she prevailed over Telma Hopkins, the actress originally cast as Ruth. As for Madeline, "I have to catch *her*," Cosby told Charlie Rose in 1996. "She knows that she can do this to me," he explained, mashing his face, "and I couldn't care less. She can do *that* to me," mashing his face a different way, "I couldn't care less. She knows that she's got somebody that she can come to and roll 'em over and push."[40]

In a preview feature for the *New York Times*, Lawrie Mifflin noted, "While Ms. Rashad plays the patient foil, Ms. Kahn matches Mr. Cosby raised eyebrow for raised eyebrow in the mugging department. Their melocomedic exchanges have had audiences hooting at the Thursday night tapings."[41] Throughout the series, Pauline and Hilton would engage in tart but affectionate teasing that Cosby insists was never inappropriate, because Hilton knew too well that Pauline and Ruth were not only friends, but also business partners in a flower shop/coffee house. But Hilton is unstoppable. Throughout the series, whenever Pauline leaves the Lucas home, he asks, "Do you love me, Pauline?" "I do," she replies in the pilot episode, adding after a pause, "but I don't show it." As the series went on, each iteration of Hilton's question would elicit a fresh response from Pauline: "When two people have what we have, there are no words," and so on. In the most elaborate of these exchanges (in the first-season episode "Social Insecurity"), Hilton has undergone a near-death experience, about which Pauline questions him avidly. At last he tells her that he saw *her* in the afterlife, and that, as she ascended to heaven, he called up to her: "Do you love me, Pauline?" With a smile, Pauline interrupts him to answer, "I'll get back to you on that!"

Cosby insists that Madeline improvised every one of Pauline's "Do you love me?" comebacks, and he compares the experience to playing jazz. "If I was a drummer, and she was playing tenor saxophone, then I would do something, change the rhythm on her, and look right at her, and make her come to the moment with that honesty that she had—it's called ad-lib, by the way—and every time, she was always brilliant." He particularly admires her body language in these scenes, and he laughs as he recalls the way that Madeline's Pauline would be "bowing, almost *bowing*, begging to get out of this. She was not of a character to just say to him, 'Shut up.' Her head would go down, and she would start this stepping backwards, and then out would come—and they were all ad-libs."

For most of her career, Madeline preferred to improvise within a script, that is, to ad-lib the interpretation, not the jokes. ("Flames!" in *Clue* is a notable exception.) She told a reporter for the *Washington Post* that she'd never before been involved in a project so "free-flowing." Cosby gave her the impression "he was determined to break through typical sitcom barriers. He wanted to let the show form itself, as opposed to sticking to format. . . . The spoken word is much more important than the written word."[42] As Madeline diplomatically suggested, however, one reason to resort to ad-libs was that the scripted material wasn't top-notch, an assessment with which critics generally agreed.[43] Cosby was dissatisfied with the writing for Pauline's character in particular. As he saw it, Madeline was an attractive, intelligent, successful woman, while Pauline was naïve, uptight, lonely, and a bit desperate. If the character we see retains her dignity, he says, that's because Madeline understood Pauline better than the writers did.

Pauline is "an innocent, has a certain naïveté that's necessary to survive and come through vibrant and independent," Madeline told the *Washington Post*. "She is able to hold her own among people who are not similar to her at all." Perhaps thinking of the script problems, and almost as a warning, Madeline continued, "If Pauline were approached without delicacy and sensitivity, we'd hit some snags. We'd get an edge—perhaps even a certain truthfulness—but not humor."[44]

The writers were "very, very impatient with whatever character they wanted to give her," Cosby says. With great writers, any series Madeline was in "would have been a hit. When you reach . . . to the next level down, and get to writers who *want* to be funny, but don't have the genius of better writers, then you have people who will give a genius like Madeline things to say that are very, very—*negatively adolescent*." The writers understood Madeline's potential, he believes, "Yet they kept writing things that were sexually oriented, driven, in a kooky, weird, unsatisfied-woman behavior." Cosby told the writers, "She is not a woman who is unhappy in a love affair. Make her a woman that other women should in fact be laughing *with*, because she believes in herself." But

Cosby, an executive producer of the show, remained "very respectful . . . and very tolerant" toward the writers, to a degree that at one point infuriated Rashad, as she recalled in an interview.[45] After all, here was a man who knew comedy, and it was his show, besides. When the writers brushed off one of Cosby's suggestions, Rashad demanded, "Did you hear what he said?" Cosby promptly apologized for her outburst. "Okay, I got it," Rashad said to herself, "they're related to somebody in the network. That's what it is."

What Rashad saw as Cosby's "tolerance" did have its limits, and he remembers reading over one of Pauline's typically rambling monologues. He asked that the speech be overhauled or cut, but on the day of taping ("'A' Day," he calls it), he found Madeline on the set in front of the studio audience, performing the scene as originally written. "It was about sex, and it was *not* funny. It had *no* dignity," Cosby recalls. "The lone [recurring] white actor, they give degrading, beneath her character and her ability, trash-monologue lines to." Cosby gave the scene a chance, saw that the audience wasn't laughing, and called out, "Stop it! This is not funny."

There were women on the writing staff, but nobody provided Madeline with the kind of material Cosby wanted. He suggests that the entire staff had trouble writing for women characters. He marvels that any comedy writer could walk out of a Brooks movie not wanting to write scenes for Madeline. "These writers are spoiled, in a sense, because they can push a button [in the editing room], and there's laughter coming into the [audience's] living room," Cosby says. "No one is laughing, just your TV set. Which I've always thought was amazing, because you could turn on [an unfunny] sitcom—is your TV set laughing at you? You get a paranoia."

As the seasons progressed, the writers would move to find a suitable love interest for Pauline—other than the elderly, overly frisky man (Red Buttons) who is her blind date in the episode "My Dinner with Methuselah" (Season 1), or the younger, ineffectual employee (Michael Bergin) at the Flower Café, whom Pauline finds too attractive to fire in the episode "Old Yeller" (Season 2). By then, however, it was too late to develop either a new character or Pauline. Madeline was already very ill.

Still, *Cosby* provided a showcase for Madeline. Pauline often sings, many of her long speeches are quite funny, and her pratfalls offer fertile ground for Madeline's improved ease with physical comedy. In the pilot episode, Pauline believes Hilton has tried to commit suicide by taking an overdose of sleeping pills. Tiny Madeline slings the arm of former Temple

University fullback Cosby over her shoulders and pushes and throws him around the stage. "I'd give anything to see that scene again," says Lily Tomlin now. (The show hasn't been released on home video, though it recently became available for streaming over the Internet.)

Cosby describes the characters Ruth and Pauline as "separated at birth," and Rashad stoutly defended the friendship between a black woman and a white woman: "[I]f we actually step outside of this little bubble that seems so much bigger than it is, people are living like this all the time." Throughout his career, Cosby has striven to show audiences that people's similarities are more important than their differences. But because Madeline was the only white actor in the regular cast, many episodes do play on the notion of Pauline being a "fish out of water" (a description Madeline used), finding comedy in the way she tries to sing like Patti LaBelle, for example, or in her initially clumsy attempts to "throw shade" (to trade humorous insults) with Hilton. In general, however, *Cosby* depicts a harmonious, multicultural community. Pauline feels herself so much a part of the Lucas family that, in a memorable confrontation with a bank officer who's refused a loan for the Flower Café, Pauline cries, "It's because we're black, isn't it?"

In other scenes and episodes, Madeline capitalizes on her uptown girl gentility, almost as a way to combat that portion of the material that Cosby considers undignified. The prospect of a visit by President Clinton sees her artfully trying to finagle an invitation. When that effort fails, she pops up anyway, dressed to the nines. In another episode, when Hilton informs her that a bat has been removed from the house, Pauline says all the right things—with a double edge: "Well, there is no shame connected to any of this. And it does not mean that you have a filthy home. In fact—because, you know, I would eat here *any* night of the week." But she can't control her grimaces of revulsion as she beats a hasty retreat. When Pauline and Ruth host a poetry slam at the Flower Café, Pauline doesn't know at first how to react to the angry, minimalist (and comically bad) poetry she hears. Soon enough, she's donning a black leather jacket and sunglasses, and she slams away. "To use a musical term, I'm a counterpoint here," Madeline told the *Washington Post*.

"When I heard that Madeline Kahn was in the show, I thought, 'I'm gonna work with Madeline Kahn! Oh, boy, I've arrived!'" Rashad said. "That's what I really thought: 'I have *arrived*.' . . . Nobody like her, anywhere in the universe!" No matter how small a part Madeline had in a given episode, Rashad remembered, she would rehearse at length in her dressing room. "What she would do was move to the center of the thought that made those three lines significant." The reason Madeline worked in her dressing room was that her fellow cast members were less keen on rehearsals. For her, these were the equivalent of multiple takes in a movie, or the variations she'd try when acting onstage. Rashad assured her that the extra practice wasn't necessary. "I could see that this was a real dilemma for her," she said. Then one day Madeline told her, "I've got it now, I've got it, you've just got to [grab] that throat and just go for it."

Madeline was in her element, and soon she was telling her colleagues, family, other friends, and the press that she'd found the professional berth she'd been seeking. She may have winced when Cosby, observing the kind of reactions that led people like Merv Griffin to think Madeline was "kooky," started to call her "Space," but clearly her colleagues appreciated her. Cosby described the show as "a family"—with the understanding that, at all times, *he* was the head of that family.

Because stations in some markets had changed their network affiliations, CBS was now vulnerable to ratings competition. Viewing patterns had changed and *Cosby* skewed too old demographically to be the kind of hit *The Cosby Show* was, but early ratings were strong. With *Murphy Brown*, *Cosby* anchored "Big Comedy Monday," one of CBS's better-performing nights. In its initial season, the series won its timeslot and finished as the network's leading comedy. While comparisons to the earlier series were inevitable, *Cosby* nevertheless found a following and a measure of critical acclaim—with extra praise reserved for Madeline. "Kahn gives her dull lines bright, off-kilter readings," wrote Ken Tucker in *Entertainment Weekly*. "Oddly enough, Hilton and Pauline's relationship—wary, but a little flirty—is more interesting than Hilton and Ruthie's . . . ."[46] In the *New York Times*, John J. O'Connor wrote that Pauline was "the character that gives *Cosby* just the extra bit of edge that it needs," and noted that Madeline had "refined deadpan sarcasm into an art form."[47]

• • •

Satisfaction with her work gave Madeline some of the strength she needed to face two crises at home. The first was her mother's decline. Paula Kahn was still living in Charlottesville, near Jef and his family. In her basement, she had opened an acting school for children. This enterprise violated both zoning laws and the fire code, but Paula didn't care. Her brother, Ted Barry, sensed "obsessive plans" for Jef's daughter, Eliza, and wondered whether Paula was "trying to groom another Madeline."[48]

Paula gave Eliza private music lessons and enrolled her in the acting school, making no secret of her connection to Madeline as she publicized the classes. "She did teach me a lot," Eliza says. "She was a good teacher, not too harsh or strict." Periodically, the children would perform for their parents in plays written by Paula, who also created beautiful costumes for her pupils.

At one such performance in 1997, Paula was still attending to last-minute details long after the show was supposed to begin. Meanwhile, the parents sat impatiently in the airless basement. At last, little Eliza gave the signal to start. Paula lost her temper and began to berate her granddaughter. In tears, Eliza phoned Jef and Jules and asked to go home. She never wanted to go back, she said. For a full year, she and Paula didn't see each other, and Paula didn't ask to see Eliza. The other parents removed their children from the school.

Then Paula—now seventy-three years old—fell and injured her shoulder. Madeline went to Charlottesville, where she and Jef met with their mother and gently urged her to move from her four-level house to a single-story home. Paula refused, hurling insults at them, then running to phone her brother and other people who, she believed, might "rescue" her. Everyone refused; Ted went so far as to tell her the single-story home seemed like a good idea. Once again, Paula tried to sue her children, and Madeline and Jef staged "a mini-intervention," Jef remembers. He checked her finances, discovering high debts, "sketchy stuff with insurance companies," and other signs of erratic behavior.

Madeline had always resisted looking too deeply into her mother's behavior, no matter the provocation, but now she was forced to do so. Such scrutiny meant coming to terms with the ways Paula treated her, and confronting a great deal of unpleasant history. For some twenty years, she'd kept her personal notebook. (That there's only one suggests not only how meticulous Madeline was, but also how seldom she wrote.) She returned to it now. Her observations about her relationship with Paula probably spring from sessions with a therapist, but all are insightful. To cite one example:

Guilt: why do I have it and what does it look like.
She did not see your needs as separate from hers. You learned that her needs were your needs. To deviate from this is wrong.
To have your own needs, which may not please—GUILT. You're bad for leaving.[49]

Madeline also wrote to Ted Barry, who replied with a long letter.[50] From her few marginal notes on that letter, one sees that Madeline always been led to believe that Paula had thrown out both Bernie and Hiller, when in truth it was they who walked out on her. It was her behavior, not theirs, that led to the divorces. For the first time, too, Ted shared his solution to the mystery of the matching four hundred-dollar "loans" that engendered so much resentment between him and Hiller.[51] Madeline even began to analyze how her relationship with Paula might have affected her career choices. She writes of watching *Gypsy* and realizing for the first time why she'd shied away from that ultimate stage mother, Mama Rose: because she identified with Louise, the daughter who becomes a star.

It's hard to know what use Madeline might have made of her new understanding. According to many of those who knew her best—including Jef Kahn, Gail Jacobs, and John Hansbury—Madeline had come close to an epiphany several times before, and each time turned away from it. As Hansbury put it, "She willingly let Paula pull the wool over her eyes," and Paula, for her part, had grown proficient in stirring up trouble or getting into a jam whenever she sensed Madeline might lose patience with her. Now Madeline had the chance to focus on her past. But her time was already short, and her second personal crisis was imminent.

50

Enlightenment in the Dark

Judy Berlin (1999)

IN ERIC MENDELSOHN'S *JUDY BERLIN*, MADELINE AT LAST FOUND A movie role that went beyond the "sketches" or "bits" that she had complained of for so long. She plays Alice Gold, a Long Island housewife who, during a solar eclipse, begins to see her own life more clearly. Madeline set aside many of her hang-ups for the movie, her first and only independent film, and she abandoned some of her usual safeguards. *Judy Berlin* is shot in black-and-white, which she had always found unflattering, and she plays a far from glamorous, unsexy, middle-aged mother and wife. Yet her sympathy for Alice Gold is unmistakable—remarkably so, given her status as an unmarried, childless actress—and when, as Alice, as she wanders about her neighborhood in sneakers and a down jacket, she's irresistibly cute and, in her emotional fragility, quite beautiful after all.

Judy Berlin begins in the Long Island home of Alice and her husband, Arthur (Bob Dishy). Their son, David (Aaron Harnick), a screenwriter just turned thirty, has recently come home in a deep depression after a sojourn in Hollywood. Alice tries relentlessly to cheer him up. For her, light conversation—even the one-sided variety—is a refuge from unpleasantness. Then a random encounter with a high-school classmate, Judy Berlin (Edie Falco), sparks David's interest. An aspiring actress as upbeat as David is glum, Judy is preparing to leave, this very day, for Hollywood—or, as she calls it, with expertise apparently derived from watching *Entertainment Tonight*, "the Coast." Neither is aware that David's father and Judy's mother, Sue (Barbara Barrie), a teacher at the elementary school where Arthur is the principal, are on the brink of an affair; Arthur and Sue barely know it. With this situation in place, the sky grows dark in the middle of the day.

The eclipse goes on until the characters begin to wonder whether something has gone wrong. For Alice, it's the end of the world—and also its remaking. After a lifetime of hiding behind barriers of chatter, she realizes that none of her relationships is quite what she thought it was. A friendly visit with a neighbor (Carlin Glynn) serves to expose the miscommunication between them. Her housekeeper, Carol (Novella Nelson), tags along as Alice plays "space explorer" in the dark. But then it's time for Carol to go home; she's not Alice's friend and has a life of her own. Even Alice's therapist (Arthur Anderson) turns out to be less reliable than Alice believed, and when she sees her husband parked in front of the house at an hour when he should be at work, she understands— correctly, yet without knowing anything more—that he's leaving her.

A testament to the beauty of suburban ordinariness, *Judy Berlin* is imbued with great charm and a generous spirit, in which no one is what she seems on the surface. Lonely, embittered Sue feels passion and, more importantly, compassion. At age thirty-two, with adult braces, Judy may be an unlikely starlet, yet when David chances to see her in a TV commercial, her dreams seem plausible. And Alice is more aware, better attuned to her own feelings and those of others, than anyone might have guessed. Throughout the film, Alice recites the first lines ("I wish, I wish, I wish in vain, / I wish I was sixteen again") of a poem, completing it only at the end of the picture ("But sixteen again I'll never be / 'Til apples grow on a cherry tree"). It seems like a lament for lost youth, but instead it's the conclusion of a traditional ballad, known as "The Butcher's Boy" or "In Jersey City," in which a girl hangs herself when her lover is unfaithful. The verse Alice recites is part of the girl's suicide note.[52] It's as if, on a barely conscious level, Alice knows even at the beginning of the movie that her husband might leave her for another woman. In their first scenes together, Arthur scarcely looks at Alice, grumbles wearily in response to her chatter, and shies from her embrace. She may pretend not to notice, but ultimately we realize that she's missed nothing, she knows the truth.

Above all, *Judy Berlin* gives a moviegoer the clearest possible impression of Madeline's range and potential. Completely submerged in the character, she traces a gossamer thread between comedy and tragedy, as Jeffrey Seckendorff's cinematography catches the luminosity of Madeline's face and the minute flickers of her emotion. While there are elements of Trixie Delight and Gorgeous Teitelbaum in Alice Gold (the three share a need to talk and joke their cares away), Alice is more delicate than Trixie and less resilient than Gorgeous. Alice has less to occupy the empty spaces and hours of her life. In many ways, the role is a summation of Madeline's career, combining the lessons she'd learned in earlier work with the instincts and experience life gave her. By now, she knew how to find the sympathetic heart of a woman who might otherwise seem shallow, annoying, or ridiculous. While one of Madeline's least-known performances, Alice Gold is one of her finest, and it should have been the prelude to a new era in her work. The movie leaves you wondering what might have been.

Mendelsohn had worked as costume design assistant on six films with Woody Allen, including *Shadows and Fog*. His first film as writer–director, a short called *Through an Open Window* (1992), also offered a somewhat mystical view of life on Long Island, shot in black-and-white and starring Anne Meara, another actress less known for drama than for comedy.[53] That experience led him to believe that Madeline might deliver the "grit" he wanted. He'd written the role of Judy specifically for Falco, a friend since their college days at SUNY Purchase who hadn't yet been cast in *The Sopranos*. Surrounding her was what Mendelsohn calls "a little jewel box" of a cast: Oscar-nominee Barrie, Barrie's real-life son Harnick, and Dishy.[54] When Dianne Wiest withdrew from talks to play Alice, Dishy's wife, Judy Graubart, read for the part. But Dishy's casting gave Madeline confidence in Mendelsohn's taste and his ability to make a movie she'd be proud of. Graubart wound up with the small but (one hopes) consoling prize of a funny cameo as a schoolteacher. For Madeline and all the actors in *Judy Berlin*, Mendelsohn's script served as a highly effective lure, Barrie says, "so well written, and I think people do love to do good characters." Most of the scripts she sees are "junk stuff," "cheap commercial films that do *not* elevate the human spirit." *Judy Berlin* was something else.

Yet for Madeline, the prospect of making an independent movie was daunting, and Mendelsohn believes "her agents didn't know the landscape she would be walking on." She required more than the script and Dishy's good name to persuade her to sign on. She asked whether she would have a dressing room, car service, and a professional crew, but above all, she wanted to know his intentions for the role of Alice Gold. "I don't know anything about this world," Madeline told Mendelsohn. Her concern was much what it had been when Wendy Wasserstein wrote Gorgeous Teitelbaum: Would this production in any way mock a character that Madeline preferred to play as sympathetic? Meeting with her privately at her apartment, Mendelsohn assured Madeline, "There is no way in the world I am making fun of this person. I adore her. She is very close to my experience, not someone I am poking fun at."

Much of the development of Alice's character sounds like business as usual for Madeline: going through the script line by line, looking for "dramatic steppingstones" to help her find emotional truth. Mendelsohn had worried that she might be "shrill," but as soon as they met, he saw that "she wanted to get at the sadness of the character and her delight-fulness and her little-girl quality." The preliminaries were necessary to free up her imagination once she got to the set. Meanwhile, however, she emphasized the differences between her and Alice: "I'm nothing like this Jewish person, I'm from Boston." "It stuck with me," Mendelsohn says. "It seems like one of those insistent comments one makes to dis-tance oneself from the truth." And the truth was that Madeline was only technically from Boston, that she *was* Jewish, and that she'd grown up thirty-five minutes from Mendelsohn's home on Long Island. No, she'd never been a housewife and mother, but Madeline was trying to see as little as possible of Paula Kahn in Alice Gold.

Looking around her apartment, Mendelsohn sensed Madeline's aver-sion to "any kind of ugly, bumpy encounter," he says. "She wanted to float or rise above everything that was uncomfortable or ugly." He de-scribes her as highly sensitive, such that "a misapprehension, or the sub-tleties of human interaction seemed almost to pain her." It was as if she "had her nervous system mistakenly put on the outside of her body." Moved, he told her, "I can see just how hard it is to be you."

The serene detachment Madeline sought could be costly to maintain, and easily shattered, as Mendelsohn observed as soon as she arrived on the set, his parents' home in Old Bethpage, the first morning. She com-plained vehemently to the producer about the car service, though she was perfectly pleasant with the director. He saw at once that she was "terrified" that her professional standards wouldn't be met, not only by the driver but also by the crew, consisting largely of volunteers almost none of whom (including the producer and the director of photography) had any experience working on a feature film.

Later in the shoot, Madeline lashed out at Mendelsohn in a way pret-ty much unprecedented in her career. They'd begun filming one of the eclipse scenes at four or five in the morning, and Madeline had to deliver her longest speech. Arthur has driven off and Carol has left Alice alone, when she encounters her psychotherapist in the street in front of his house. He's far more anxious about the eclipse than Alice is. "Don't be afraid," she tells him. "I'm actually very good in emergencies, really. It's just the day-to-day things that give me a little trouble. Something like this happens, and I just feel that finally the rest of the world and I are speaking the same language." She reassures him, then walks away. Musing on the word "Wednesday," she unleashes a stream of fragile emotions: "The whole world crumbles and a thing like Wednesday that you thought you could depend on just vanishes, and I think of Arthur and the time that he got up in the middle of the night to get himself a glass of water, and without asking, he got one for me. Without asking." And so she wanders onward in the darkness.

Everyone was tired, Barrie had fallen asleep on the floor of the production office, and the sun would soon rise. "The tension that Madeline was throwing off was like nothing I've ever felt," Mendelsohn says. She later told him that Alice's isolation in the scene overwhelmed her, and that this unconsciously affected her behavior. He also believes that she wanted his help in achieving specific goals. But at the time, he felt "inarticulate," and communication between them faltered as shooting continued and nerves wore thin. At last, "She attacked me and just about everyone on the set."

After one take, Madeline turned to him and said, "How was that?"

"That was really great," Mendelsohn said, adding, "I want to go again, but it was great."

"It was *terrible*," Madeline replied, "and I did it on purpose, and *you* said it was great." She continued in this "immensely mean" vein, then left the set. The shoot ended without the director's knowing whether they had the scene.

The next day, Madeline called to apologize. By then Mendelsohn had seen the rushes and, although the sound quality wasn't what he'd hoped, he could reassure her that the scene had turned out beautifully. "Of course I forgave her," he says, "but [her outburst] was something I had never experienced before."

At other times, he saw a more familiar side of her. After four decades in comedy, she still didn't seem to know she was funny. After the first take—one of the interior scenes at the Golds' home at the beginning of the movie—the crew broke out laughing as soon as Mendelsohn called "cut." Just an hour or so before, she'd been furious about her car, but now, "Whatever iciness she had come in with melted," he says. "She was delighted." Mendelsohn had spent a year writing the script; on the set, Madeline's line readings didn't sound like what he'd imagined. But he often let them stand. As he saw it, "this woman has created an entire castle of Murano glass that is this character and this movie, and to break one column just to get a line right would be ridiculous."

Toward the end of the shoot, Madeline told Mendelsohn how much she'd enjoyed working with Dishy and how much his portrayal of Arthur reminded her of her father (he has no idea whether she meant Bernie or Hiller—or both, since both walked out on her mother). Madeline also loved working with Harnick, who found her fascinating and quite sexy. For him, the movie was "a harrowing experience," because his character is so depressed, a tough order for an inexperienced actor. Harnick hadn't acted since high school, and today, he says, he probably wouldn't take the job. When Mendelsohn first suggested that he read for *Judy Berlin*, he scoffed and told him to call Ethan Hawke instead. Harnick's first scene proved most difficult, "because I had to cry and yell—with Madeline Kahn, whom I had never met," he says. Yet he instantly admired "how good she is. So simple. Just *there*, and I'm emoting all over." "Madeline is the kind of actor where, before they speak, they vibrate with intensity as if they're a struck gong," Mendelsohn says. "There was no line, no gesture, no breath that wasn't going to be consummate, thorough, and throbbing with Madeline Kahn-ness."

The combination of no-frills indie production, late-night shoots for the eclipse scenes, and late-autumn weather ("January in November," Mendelsohn says) proved difficult for everyone involved. Although *Judy Berlin* is set during the second day of the school year, Madeline wore a coat, because she was afraid of the cold. Barrie, for her part, was still shivering some mornings when she came home to Manhattan. "It was torture!" she remembers. In the movie's final scene, Sue helps a retired teacher (Bette Henritze) with Alzheimer's find her way home in the dark. In the bitter cold, without even soup to warm the actors between takes, Barrie lost her temper as Mendelsohn kept retaking the last shot, a long pullback as the women walk away from the camera. "I kept saying to Eric, 'What's wrong with it? Why are we doing it over? I want to go home!'" Generally, however, she found Mendelsohn extremely effective, albeit, as he suspected, not always articulate. Giving direction, he'll "phumpher around," she says, yet he managed to convey his meaning. "You feel you would do anything for him," she says, and Madeline felt the same. "She really loved doing that part," Barrie says.

"The last day of her shoot, [Madeline] seemed like she was going to cry," Mendelsohn remembers. "She was so thrilled and thankful about the opportunity to have played, to have played *around*."

Judy Berlin premiered at the Sundance Festival in January, 1999, taking the award for best director of a dramatic film and a nomination for the grand jury prize. A New York premiere at the Museum of Modern

Art and a slew of foreign festivals followed, including Cannes and To-ronto. Mendelsohn won the Prix Tournage at Avignon and nominations for grand prizes at Deauville and Ghent. In the United States, *Judy Berlin* took the prize for best American independent film at the Hamptons International Film Festival, and a nomination for best film at the Newport International Film Festival. In 2000, the movie was nominated for three Independent Spirit Awards: best first feature, best cinematography (Seckendorf), and best supporting female (Barrie). Despite the acclaim, Mendelsohn and his producer, Rocco Caruso, had trouble finding a distributor; *Judy Berlin* wasn't commercially released until after Madeline's death, and in tribute to her, proceeds from the premiere were donated to the Ovarian Cancer Research Fund. National distribution followed a year later, in April 2001. Because of the extended rollout, reviews (while generally admiring) were scattered, compounding the challenge of finding an audience for a small, sensitive, black-and-white film.

To some degree, *Judy Berlin* is still searching for its audience—though not for lack of trying. In addition to entering the film in so many festivals, Mendelsohn and Caruso worked hard to promote the movie, and Madeline pitched in, though she was already undergoing treatment for cancer. She joined Mendelsohn for press interviews and attended the premiere at MOMA, where the director's mother complimented her on her hair. "To this day I don't know whether my mother knew that it was a wig," Mendelsohn says.

Immensely pleased with *Judy Berlin* and relieved of any pressure associated with making the movie, Madeline grew close to Mendelsohn in the last months of her life, speaking regularly with him by phone. He wouldn't direct another feature until 2010, with *3 Backyards*, also starring Edie Falco. He's got one muse, and she's Falco; it's anybody's guess whether he needed or could have handled a second. But it's tempting to think that, had Madeline lived, Mendelsohn might have been inspired to work with her again. Sensitive to her talent and her needs, he might have guided her to richer, more satisfying work. "She knew what greatness was," David Marshall Grant says, "and she struggled, because she believed she could never achieve it. So I was moved by how *proud* she was of her performance in *Judy Berlin*, succeeding as an actress in an independent film, that people could respect her. I remember her telling me, 'I'm so glad that happened before I died.'"

She told Mendelsohn that *Judy Berlin* "was going around like a satellite, and that, though she couldn't be there, it was traveling for her." Still, he wonders whether his first movie was truly worthy of her. "I was such an amateur, and she was such a pro," he says. "When she died, I felt as if I had let down all the people who expected one kind of thing from her, and that her last offering had to be my paltry film." But the one thing *she* wanted was to defy moviegoers' expectations of her, and Mendelsohn helped her to do it. As Bill Cosby has observed, cancer cut Madeline down "just when she was ready to break records."[55]

51

Loving Madeline

IN AUGUST OF 1998, ON VACATION ON FIRE ISLAND, MADELINE FAINTED.
A doctor examined her and suggested she'd merely had low blood sugar.
"I was worried something was really *wrong*!" Madeline said. But upon
returning to New York, she continued to feel bloated and uncomfortable. Her doctor, Bill Perlow, referred her to Peter Dottino, a specialist at
Mount Sinai. Dottino found elevated levels of CA 125, a protein released
by ovarian cancers. An ultrasound test proved inconclusive, so he recommended laparoscopy. He found that the cancer had spread throughout her abdomen.

It was time for Madeline to return to work on *Cosby*, but instead she
went immediately into surgery, where doctors "removed as much tumor
as they could see," Hansbury remembers. Afterward, he packed up cell
samples and sent them to California, where they would be cultured in
order to determine what form of chemotherapy would be most benefi-
cial. To his surprise, this procedure wasn't covered by Madeline's health
insurance—indeed, Hansbury found, it wasn't covered by most policies,
and no doctor he asked could explain this to him.

Ovarian cancer is the fifth-leading cause of cancer death among wom-
en in the United States, according to the Ovarian Cancer Research Fund.
If treated and detected early, there's approximately a 92 percent survival
rate. But very often it's not detected early, as most of the symptoms associated with its early stages are also associated with relatively common
ailments: bloating; pelvic and/or abdominal pain; difficulty eating or filling up more quickly than usual; urgency or frequency of urination—the
sorts of troubles most people wouldn't worry about.

At present, there is no accurate test for ovarian cancer. Blood tests
for CA 125 miss 50 percent of early-stage cancers, and levels of the protein can be elevated by other, benign conditions. The National Cancer

Institute doesn't recommend CA 125 tests for women at ordinary risk. Researchers have, however, identified certain other genetic markers, called BRCA 1 and 2, which are associated with breast and ovarian cancer, and on that basis, they are exploring reliable tests for ovarian cancer. According to Audra Moran, Chief Executive Officer of the Ovarian Cancer Research Fund, certain groups are associated with higher risk, and Madeline belonged to several of them. She was of Ashkenazi Jewish heritage; she never gave birth; she didn't consistently use birth-control pills; and evidently she carried the BRCA 1 and 2 genes. (A family history of breast or ovarian cancer is another indicator.)

Again, early detection is the key to survival. Most patients, however, are diagnosed only in advanced stages of the disease, at which point a mere 45 percent survive longer than four years. In 81 percent of all cases, the cancer has spread beyond the ovaries to the pelvic region. Recent research indicates that the cancer may actually begin in the fallopian tubes, and then move, but as Moran points out, these parts of the body aren't as accessible as the breasts, for example, and the only way to be sure is through surgery. "You don't want to over-operate," she says. Among researchers in the field today, "It's not that they're not looking for early detection, it's that they're trying to minimize risk." The other important trend now is toward personalizing treatments and understanding why, for example, some women respond well to chemotherapy in the first instance, but don't respond the same way in the event of a recurrence. Madeline's cancer was "very aggressive," Moran observes; it killed her a little more than a year after her diagnosis.

"With breast cancer, there are options, time to get a second opinion," Hansbury says. "With ovarian, there are no options. You must operate. Thereafter, you may have options."

Following her first surgery, Madeline underwent chemotherapy and returned to work. She told no one on the *Cosby* set about her cancer, though hair and makeup artists had enough clues to guess, and Mel Brooks remembers Cosby's telling him, "She's sick. We don't know what it is." Because of chemotherapy, Madeline now penciled in her eyebrows and wore a wig and false lashes until her own hair grew back. However, even those with suspicions respected her privacy as she continued to fight. "She didn't want to be pitied," Hansbury says. "She wanted encouragement and sustenance. I never told anyone unless she said it was okay."

Madeline immediately broke the news to Jef, who spent much of the subsequent months with her in New York. Her friends Gail Jacobs and

Carol Greenberg were told, too. A multi-talented, exuberant redhead, Greenberg is a physical therapist. She applied her skills to massage and comfort Madeline, while attending to the spiritual side, too, by taking Madeline to a Kabbalah class and to a holistic healer. Julie Dretzin joined the support team, as well, and she and Madeline went shopping for wigs.

Chemotherapy left Madeline's immune system suppressed, and she was constantly exposed to infections. Each proposed cancer treatment raised the question of her ability to withstand it. She underwent a total of three surgeries in addition to three rounds of chemo. Each time her hair grew back, she left it silver and cropped short. Photos from a summer stay on Fire Island in 1999 show her smiling and extraordinarily beautiful. "It wasn't about the hair," Hansbury says. "I never loved anybody as much as I loved her when she was bald."

Despite her illness, Madeline worked as much as she could, returning to *Cosby* for the third season and for the fourth, albeit for only four episodes. "When she became ill the first time, the illness was never discussed," Phylicia Rashad told an interviewer. "And she came back and we were very, very happy to see her. She just looked a little frail, but she was so determined to work. I think she might have come back sooner than she really should have. But she was determined to do that."[56]

Madeline told Robert Klein that *Cosby* was "the best job I ever had." Her longtime friend joined her on the series for a single episode, "A Very Nice Dance," which aired in February, 1999, and in which he plays a police detective and potential love interest for Pauline. "It was a nice bolt out of the blue," Klein says. He remembers thinking, "Maybe the part will float and they'll continue to do it." Cosby did his best to welcome Klein, offering him a bottle of his private-label wine and insisting that Klein's costume, a jacket, be made of "the most beautiful kid-glove leather." By this point, Madeline's health problems were an open secret throughout the studio. Klein says that, though she said nothing to him, he believes she already knew she wouldn't recover. "That's certainly the way she played it," he says.

Actor–director–choreographer Lawrence Leritz confirms that impression. In "A Nice Dance," he plays a policeman. Because his role included stunt work, he arrived at the studio early for extra rehearsal. He'd been a fan of Madeline since his boyhood, when he sent her a fan letter. He was looking forward to meeting her now, but as the rehearsal began, a stand-in read Madeline's lines, and she was nowhere to be seen. "In television, that's totally unusual," he says. "You put together an episode in one week. You go to rehearsals, and then you shoot. You're just *there*."

Privately, a friend in the production office told him that Madeline was too sick to come until the taping. "The set was not relaxed," Leritz says. "People were freaked out because they saw the writing on the wall. With Madeline dying, they knew the show was coming to an end in the near future." The next day, Leritz met Madeline in the hallway. He reminded her of the fan letter he'd written in 1971 and told her she'd sent him a picture and a nice letter. "You were lucky," she said. "I wouldn't do that today." She hugged him, and for the rest of the day, she smiled whenever she saw him. At one point she even confided in him, admitting she was sick. "I think I reminded her of the good days, when she was young," he says.

When Madeline returned for the fourth season of *Cosby*, Hansbury's encouragement gave her the confidence to dispense with wigs and appear with her own short silver hair. She got one last glamour role, playing a Russian femme fatale in the season opener (an elaborate dream sequence that spoofs Cosby's first TV series, *I Spy*), and in that and two other episodes, she throws herself into her work with something like her usual gusto. She's thin yet lovely, and hale enough to push Cosby on a rolling ladder in an episode set in a bookstore. But in the fourth episode she shot, "Book 'em, Griff-o," she's barely a walk-on. Madeline took another medical leave, and this time, she felt she had to say something to her colleagues. She went to Rashad's dressing room. "We never talked about what was wrong," she said. "It's happening again, and I have to go back. And I just wanted to be the one to tell you."

"Come back when you want to," Cosby told her—then locked her dressing room and handed her the key. She understood: As far as he was concerned, this wasn't goodbye.

• • •

Beginning with the first surgery, Hansbury arranged for private nurses to come to Madeline's apartment, allowing her to spend as much time as possible at home. Now friends and family began calling on her, and Madeline consented to see many of them, including Roy Harris and Betty Aberlin. "She was always made-up," David Marshall Grant remembers. "She couldn't stand for people to see her when she wasn't in control. That was distasteful to her." Cosby sent her gifts, and Eric Mendelsohn phoned often, ending each call with "I love you." "Which was difficult," he says. "She was so private a person. But I didn't want to be intimidated by that, I wanted to tell her how much I felt for her."

She found it more difficult to see—or to let herself be seen by—two family members. Paula wanted to come up from Charlottesville, and Madeline allowed her to visit the apartment, but not the hospital. "It wouldn't have been helpful," Hansbury says. "I tried to limit her burdens, to act as a gatekeeper. We wanted to preserve her strength to fight for her life." Madeline couldn't bring herself to let her twelve-year-old niece see her at all. Though her regret is palpable, Eliza now says she understands why her aunt felt this way. "She always tried to show me what it meant to be a woman, to be feminine," and sickness wasn't beautiful.

Other friends knew she was ill, but didn't know how to approach her. "I should have called her, I should have gone to see her," Lee Roy Reams says. "But I didn't know where her head was or what condition she was in. It's very hard to pick up the phone and say, 'Hi, Madeline, I hear you have cancer.' I didn't know how to handle it, so I didn't handle it. I felt guilty [but] I wasn't involved in her life as Madeline. I was involved in her life as Dolly." Robert Klein remembers, "She chose to go totally private. I heard some floating rumor somewhere, and by the time I knew anything, she didn't want to see anybody. It was the opposite with Peter Boyle: I sort of participated, and that was not pretty. Two of my oldest friends in show business, to die before their time. I don't get any wisdom out of it."

In October 1999, Madeline's accountants learned that the bulk of her pension from the actors' unions would go to taxes if not left to a spouse. Madeline was still single. Hansbury asked to be the one to discuss the matter with her, and he did. Thereupon, he got down on one knee and proposed. "I must be really sick," she answered.

"I should have asked a long time ago," he told her. Both believed she would recover. "She was going to fight," he says. "She never stopped."

But on her wedding day, October 10, she was too sick to leave the hospital. Mount Sinai had a priest, a rabbi, and a minister on hand, and Madeline and John chose the minister, a black Southern Methodist. Jef Kahn and Gail Jacobs attended, and Gail remembers Madeline's cold feet. "Am I making a mistake?" she asked. "Don't worry," Gail joked, "you can always get a divorce!"

Shortly thereafter, Madeline returned to her apartment. John tried to adjust to married life. "The nurses would say, 'Your husband's home,' or 'Your wife is okay,' and I'd think 'Who are they talking about?'" Whether at the hospital or the apartment, John and Jef took shifts, to be sure Madeline was never alone.

One day in November, the private nurses told John, "We don't think she should be here anymore," and she returned to the hospital. The private nurses came, too, since the doctors believed it would be helpful for Madeline to see familiar faces.

At last Madeline understood that she would have to release a statement to the press, and so the truth guarded by her friends and colleagues became public knowledge. "It is my hope that I might raise awareness of this awful disease and hasten the day that an effective test can be discovered to give women a fighting chance to catch this cancer in its earliest stage," Madeline wrote in a press release. "I would urge everyone to support the vital work being done by the Ovarian Cancer Research Fund."

Late in November, she was diagnosed with a massive tumor in her chest that suppressed her throat and made it difficult to speak. Doctors told John that they could operate on the tumor, but that surgery would impinge on the vocal cords. Dr. Dottino advised him that surgery would be only a temporary measure, but without it, she would die. "How much longer?" John asked. Not long, was the answer, and John said, "Don't do it. It would be too painful." "She lived about a week," he says. "They said she'd live 24 hours."

On December 3, around 4 o'clock, Jef Kahn and Madeline's friend Stephen Clark had been standing vigil. Madeline was unconscious, but a nurse said she might still be able to hear. Jef whispered, "I love you," and she squeezed his hand. When John came to relieve Jef and Steve, they went to get a cup of tea. Then Madeline made a strange sound. John said to the nurse, "'Is it now?' And she said it was. I told her I loved her. It was peaceful. And I'm glad I was there. I hope she heard me. I think she did."

Hansbury pauses, then rallies. "It was an honor to be with her," he says. "She was a great lady. She couldn't tell a joke, though. But she was very sweet."

Epilogue

AFTER MADELINE DIED, HANSBURY SPOKE TO THE PRESS OUTSIDE THE hospital. "We all suffered a great loss today," he said. "While we mourn her passing, we celebrate a full and wonderful life."[1] As the news spread, New York City seemed to stop short and gasp, "Oh, no! I loved her so much!" You didn't have to ask about whom people were talking. Some actors' deaths are taken almost personally by the public, and in the city, at least, Madeline's was one of these. At the time, I wondered whether she knew how people felt about her. Her friends and loved ones agree: She didn't.

Paula Kahn took Madeline's death hardest. "She'd lost her sparring partner," Jef says. Paula's own health declined rapidly. In 2001, after she collapsed in a restaurant, Paula was diagnosed with colon cancer—just as the city of Charlottesville declared that she had sixty days to bring her house up to code or see it condemned. Confined in the hospital and desperate to keep her possessions, she asked Jef to take charge, but he refused unless she agreed to grant him power of attorney. Entering the house for the first time in years, he discovered a mess. Paula had become a hoarder, making innumerable purchases from home shopping networks. Sorting through the accumulation, Jef filled two dumpsters with detritus. He sold the house, and Paula moved to an assisted living facility, where she lived until moving to a nursing home. She died there on June 11, 2012, five days after Hiller Kahn's death.

In the immediate aftermath of Madeline's death, the show *Cosby* prepared a tribute episode, "Loving Madeline" (December 29, 1999), that featured clips of her best scenes and a conversation in which the cast shared memories of her. At a memorial service at Lincoln Center's Mitzi Newhouse Theater on May 20, John Hansbury introduced a program that featured speakers Wendy Wasserstein, Stephen Clark, Robert Klein,

Phylicia Rashad, David Marshall Grant, and Peter Bogdanovich. Jonathan Sheffer, Christine Ebersole, John Cameron Mitchell, and Audra McDonald offered musical tributes. Joseph Feury's wife, Lee Grant, directed an *Intimate Portrait* documentary for the Lifetime channel that first aired in April 2001, narrated by Teri Garr, whose voice betrayed her grief. And in October 2003, Madeline was inducted into the Theater Hall of Fame (alongside Kevin Kline, among others). Her portrait hangs today in the Gershwin Theater on Broadway.

We're left with her work, and with questions about the paths she might have followed. The show *Cosby* completed its fourth season without her, then ceased production by mutual agreement between Cosby and the network. Had Madeline survived, the show might have run longer, and Cosby's pressure on the writers to improve Pauline's character might have resulted in the anticipated romance between her and the detective played by Robert Klein. Her commitment to the show would have jeopardized a return to the stage that was already under discussion in 1998, when she participated in two staged readings (one private, one public) of Jerry Herman's *Dear World* at the Roundabout Theater. An adaptation of Giraudoux's *The Madwoman of Chaillot*, directed by the company's associate artistic director, Scott Ellis, *Dear World* starred Chita Rivera in a role originated by Angela Lansbury. Madeline took the supporting role of Gabrielle, the Madwoman of Montmartre, with Debra Monk as Constance, the Madwoman of the Fleamarket. "In that trio, she absolutely set the tone," Ellis remembers. "I remember looking and thinking, 'That's where it needs to lie. The Madeline Kahn world.' Because it's such a wacked-out world to begin with. She brought her wackiness to it, with this firm belief in what she was saying and that what she was talking about was the truth." The public reading, on June 14, was her final theatrical appearance, thirty-three years after she made her New York debut in *Kiss Me, Kate*—and thirty-five years after *The Madwoman of Chaillot* led to the loss of her drama scholarship.

An extensively revised book by David Thompson and the stellar cast (also including David Garrison, Audra McDonald, and Mario Cantone) gave rise to hopes of a full production of *Dear World* at the Roundabout, though Ellis harbored doubts about the strength of the source material. Gabrielle has only one solo number, one duet, a quartet, and some ensemble singing. The less demanding yet rewarding assignment might have appealed to Madeline, as would the chance to work more with friends like Rivera and Monk. As Ellis observes, Madeline wouldn't have agreed to the second reading of *Dear World* if she hadn't enjoyed the first.

Had she participated in a full-blown theatrical production, she might have known—at long last—good luck in a musical in New York.

Marlena Malas, Madeline's last voice teacher, suggests that Madeline's operatic days were behind her, though she continued to work on Offenbach songs. Nevertheless, offers might have come her way. In 1995, conductor Patrick Summers suggested Madeline for the role of Orlovsky in a revival of *Die Fledermaus*, the vehicle for his Metropolitan Opera debut three years later. Casting Madeline "would have been pretty out there" for the Met at the time, Summers observes, and the idea went nowhere. Orlovsky is a short, comic role, highlighted by an undemanding aria, "Chacun à son goût," that would have suited Madeline. If the Met had made the offer, Summers believes she would have accepted it. In subsequent years, he took on leadership positions with opera companies in San Francisco and Houston, which presented several works with roles appropriate to Madeline's talents. Summers surely would have reached out to her. Recently, the Met has extended invitations to a few Broadway and "crossover" stars. Given conductor James Levine's admiration for her, Madeline might have made her debut after all.

Beyond opera, a wealth of other musical roles was still available to her—including those being written by her friend Michael Cohen. Enterprising producers might have cast Madeline as Liza Elliott in Weill's *Lady in the Dark*, or in the speaking role of Amanda Wingfield in Williams's *The Glass Menagerie*—after André Bishop produced *The Matchmaker* for her, of course. On film, Madeline surely would have tried to capitalize on her two final successes. Pixar's *A Bug's Life* (1998) featured her as the faded beauty, Gypsy, in a tender, almost melancholy performance that showed her range—and for once, she didn't have to worry about how she looked. She'd done voiceover work since the 1980s, and with the booming market for animated films, she'd have had opportunity to do more as the century turned. And she'd surely have sought roles as good as that of Alice Gold. The acclaim she received in response to *Judy Berlin* suggests that many people, both in Hollywood and in independent cinema, would have looked at her with renewed interest. John Cameron Mitchell wanted her for the film adaptation of *Hedwig and the Angry Inch*, and he might have created roles specifically for Madeline. Moreover, as she grew older, she had the potential to become an American Maggie Smith, and as much in demand as her British counterpart, with her expert timing and delivery. It's easy to imagine Madeline in an American *Downton Abbey* or *The Best Exotic Marigold Hotel*—or in *Arrested Development* or *30 Rock*. "I once said to her, 'You are the detached retina in the eye of American comedy,'" Joanna Gleason remembers. "There was always something off-center and wonderful about her."

Now it's left to her creative heirs to explore the paths on which she set out. It's notable that, unlike many other actors, Madeline did leave an artistic legacy. She was correct when she wrote that, by standing out, she "set an example for others."[2] Kristin Chenoweth, another diminutive dynamo with classical training, has enjoyed success on Broadway and television, and she cites Madeline as an inspiration as she takes on roles like Cunegonde and Lily Garland.[3] Another Broadway star, Kelli O'Hara, has pursued roles that are less comedic, but she, too, has classical training, and she was slated to make her Met debut in Lehár's *The Merry Widow* while this book was in production. O'Hara says she's inspired by Madeline's richly varied performing career. Young singers see Madeline the same way—whether they're like baritone Wes Mason, who performs both musical comedy and opera, or like Marjorie Owens, who sings the most demanding soprano roles. One finds many of Madeline's most devoted admirers among performers.

Another part of the legacy is "Stand Up for Madeline," an annual benefit for the Ovarian Cancer Research Fund, where John Hansbury serves as co-president of the executive committee. Launched by Hansbury and presented at Carolines comedy club in New York City, the benefit features a parade of performers doing something Madeline never did: stand-up comedy. "She was a pure actress; it's a different skill set from what I do," says Joy Behar, who, like Robert Klein, has participated in most of these events. Though Behar knew Madeline only slightly, she wanted to "Stand Up" not only for her, but also for Gilda Radner and for a friend who survived the disease. The cause matters. "Women are just at the mercy," she says. "There aren't even signs to tell you you have it."

Yet for Behar as for so many others, Madeline's most important legacy is her movies. "It's a contribution," she says. "We're still watching Bette Davis movies and Clark Gable and Cary Grant, all the great artists in the movies. She's part of that group. She's one of those people that you'll always see and think, 'That was wonderful.'"

That assessment would have meant a great deal to Madeline. For her, work was always the one sure thing, the constant in her life. Other people might lie, other people might leave. Even Madeline might fudge, insisting that she was 5-foot-3 when no one she knew believed it. But her characters were always predicated in *truth*, the word to which she returned again and again. We'll never know to what purposes she might have applied the truths she learned late in life—how her relationship with her mother might have matured, whether she'd even have wanted to continue performing. But we can see clearly that, growing beyond a childhood of anxiety and solitude, as an adult she created something enduring and solid, something that could be shared with others, though it remained uniquely hers. As Carol Kane observes, "There's nobody like her, is there?"

ACKNOWLEDGMENTS

Jeffrey Kahn has been an ideal partner in this biography, encouraging every avenue of inquiry, making available every resource he had, and helping me to piece together the many gaps in Madeline's records. After Jef and his family, no person has been more necessary to the completion of this book or more generous to its author than my beloved friend Kara Lack. I also thank my parents for their loving support, and Betty Aberlin and Walter Willison, whose encouragement and infinite helpfulness have guided me almost daily for seven years.

• • •

The Family:
Paula Kahn, Hiller Kahn, John W. Hansbury, Eliza Kahn, Jean Barry, Ted Barry, Virginia Lewisohn Kahn, Dan Kahn, Sarah Kahn, Juliette DeFord, Heidi Berthoud, Robyn Wolfson Larsen, Gerri Bohn Gerson, and Jenny Hopkins.

• • •

Friends, Colleagues, Critics, and Admirers:
Betty Aberlin, Rita Abrams Edge, Robert Allan Ackerman, Jane Alexander, Edward Asner, Evalyn Baron, Barbara Barrie, Fred Barton, Carol J. Bawer, Joy Behar, George Bettinger, Deborah Birch, André Bishop, Peter Bogdanovich, Charlotte Booker, Eileen Brennan, Mel Brooks, Scott Burkholder, Carol Burnett, Bill Butler, Black-eyed Susan (Carlson), Martin Charnin, Maris Clement, George Coe, Michael Cohen, Shaun Considine, Joan Copeland, Maddie Corman, Bill Cosby, John Cullum, Blythe Danner, Dorothy Frank Danner, Julie Dretzin, Scott Ellis, Matthew Epstein, Michael Feingold, Richard Fredericks, Joseph Feury, Victor Garber, Paul Gemignani, Joanna Gleason, Bette Glenn, Amanda Green, Carol Greenberg, Joel Grey, Jeffrey Haddow, Aaron Harnick, Roy Harris, Michael

Hayward-Jones, Marilyn Horne, George S. Irving, Gail Jacobs, Kristen Johnston, Michael Karm, Robert Klein, Kevin Kline, Arthur Korant, John Kramer, Miles Kreuger, Joey Landwehr, Lawrence Leritz, William Lewis, J. D. Lobue, Jonathan Lynn, Brandon Maggart, Marlena Malas, Caryn Mandabach, Wes Mason, Donna McKechnie, Lynne Meadow, Eric Mendelsohn, Audra Moran, Tiffany Nixon, Kelli O'Hara, Ryan O'Neal, Marjorie Owens, Thomas Pasatieri, Sheldon Patinkin, Joey Patton, Steven Paul, Bobby Pearce, Austin Pendleton, Maurice Peress, Harold Prince, Lee Roy Reams, Julius Rudel, Nicholas Sabato Jr., Chris Sarandon, Tom Shales, Ally Sheedy, Jonathan Sheffer, Cybill Shepherd, Rosie Shuster, Kenny Solms, Richard Stilwell, Teresa Stratas, Daniel Sullivan, Patrick Summers, Alan Titus, Lily Tomlin, Frederica von Stade, Gene Wilder, Walter Willison, Darren Keith Woods, and Mary Woronov.

• • •

Research Assistance:
I am profoundly grateful to Kevin Daly, my principal assistant. In a less official capacity, Elise Goyette and Michael Benchetrit also made heroic contributions, and Ashley Marie Piar helped to locate photographs and other archival material.

• • •

Invaluable Assistance:
Profound thanks go to my editors at the University Press of Mississippi, Leila Salisbury and Carl Rollyson, and also to John Langston, Valerie Jones, Steve Yates, Courtney McCreary, Anne Stascavage, Shane Gong Stewart, and the valiant, vigilant Lisa Paddock. My agent, Rob McQuilkin, has represented this book with persistence and ingenuity far beyond what I had any reason to hope for.

• • •

I am also grateful to Scott Frankel, Brian Kellow, F. Paul Driscoll, Scott Barnes, Rebecca Paller, Anne Midgette, Donald Arthur, Clifford Capone, Carol Kane, Emily Frankel, Aulay Carlson, Carolyn Weber and Dave Stein of the Kurt Weill Foundation for Music, David Kaufman, Eric Myers, Andy Propst, Eddie Shapiro, Claudia Dreifus, Barry Monash, Karen Kriendler Nelson, Elizabeth L. Dribben, Steven Bryant, Susan and Liz Wagner, Alan Arkin, Lucie Arnaz Luckinbill, Carol Lurie, Cristina McGinnis, Stephen Koch, Phyllis Newman, Rosemarie Tichler, Debra Monk, Ed Dixon, Jennifer Van Dyke, Amanda Jacobs Wolf, Glen Roven, Cort

Casady, Shelby Van Vliet, Maria Ciaravino, Ellie Koscheski, Dick Guttman, Sue Leibman, Jeff Berger, Sam Neuman, Richard Glatzer and Wash Westmoreland, Todd Hughes, Kara Johnson, Vivian L. Schneider, Julia Judge, Dennis Yslas, Mark Fischer, Dominick Mazza, Alex M. Stein, Holly Sklar, Christopher Hart, Michael Solomon and Washington National Opera, Andrew Patner, David Shengold, Joshua White, Mark Dennis, Anne Dennis, Richard and Carlene Ginsburg, Nathaniel Goodman and Gayle Baigelman, David Farneth and David Gilbert, David Kidd and Wendy Lawless, Joy and Randolph Partain, Dan Guller and Eric James, Janice Hall, Susan Graham, Joyce DiDonato, Joyce Castle, Dan and Jean Rather, Lisa Gilford, Linc Madison, Konrad Will, Jonathan C. Feldstein, Fredd Tree, Melia Bensussen, Bernard Boutrit, and Patrick McDonald.

NOTES

INTRODUCTION

1. MK personal notebook.

2. Alan Arkin, *An Improvised Life* (paperback edition, Da Capo Press, Cambridge, MA, 2011).

PART I

1. Madeline Kahn (MK), Speech to the American Academy of Dramatic Arts, New York, April 17, 1989. Transcript from MK personal files. Hereinafter "AADA Speech."

2. Letter from Ted Barry, September 18, 1998. Capitalization in the original. MK personal files, used with permission.

3. *After Dark*, "The Kaleidoscopic Madeline Kahn," Shaun Considine, July 1973. This article was the first feature on Madeline in a national publication.

4. MK personal notebook.

5. AADA speech.

6. "The Kaleidoscopic Madeline Kahn."

7. MK personal notebook.

8. Court documents pertaining to the Mexican divorce and the alimony case found in MK personal files.

9. Roy Harris, *Conversations in the Wings: Talking about Acting* (Heinemann Drama, Portsmouth, NH, 1994).

10. AADA speech. Subsequent quotations pertaining to Hofstra also derive from the speech, unless otherwise noted.

11. Madeline's serious monologue, she remembered, was "something by Saroyan."

12. The announcement of a performance of Mozart's *Requiem* in her senior year, on March 14, 1964, seems to be the first time Madeline's name appeared in the *New York Times* (*NYT*), along with those of other "student soloists."

13. *NYT*, "Woses Are Wed, Madeline's a Wow," March 24, 1974. Puccini's Manon is an extremely demanding vocal role. Massenet's Manon features elaborate but lighter music, and it might reasonably have found its way into Madeline's early repertoire.

14. MK personal notebook.

15. David Kaufman, *Ridiculous!* (Applause Books, New York, 2001).

16. AADA speech.

17. MK personal notebook.

18. *Live from the Met*, PBS, Metropolitan Opera, January 3, 1985. Transcribed by the author.

19. *Newsday*, "Suddenly, She Had a Fine Voice," Mona Sarfaty, July 10, 1969.

20. Geiss, who died in 2011, went on to write for *Sesame Street* and the animated films *The Land Before Time* and *An American Tail*, in the second of which Madeline plays Gussie Mausheimer.

21. AADA speech.

22. *NYT* review, May 13, 1965. Madeline isn't mentioned in the article.

23. James Gavin's *Intimate Nights: The Golden Age of New York Cabaret* (revised and updated edition, Backstage Books, New York, 2011) has been an invaluable resource in my research for this chapter. Quotations from Madeline and from Dixie Carter come from Gavin's book, unless otherwise noted.

24. Produced in house, the record albums of Madeline's Upstairs revues are collectors' items today. Some tracks have made their way to YouTube and other Internet sharing sources.

25. *NYT*, "Upstairs at Downstairs Aims at 'Mixed Doubles,'" Sidney E. Zion, October 25, 1966.

26. Among Paula's credits, there's some overlap with Madeline's, and thus greater credibility. Notably, both listed study with Patricia Neway. An operatic soprano, Neway earned fame on Broadway in Menotti's *The Consul* and as the Mother Abbess in the original cast of *The Sound of Music*. Paula also listed summer-stock credits with producer Jay Harnick, whose wife and son co-starred with Madeline in *Judy Berlin*.

27. As an industrial short, *A Song of Arthur* isn't listed among Madeline's credits at IMDb.com. The film came to light when Hoffman posted it on YouTube in late 2013. It can be found at https://www.youtube.com/watch?v=H6VvCVkKWDo.

28. "The Kaleidoscopic Madeline Kahn."

29. *NYT*, "Theater: 'New Faces,'" Clive Barnes, May 3, 1968.

30. Ibid.

31. Mel Brooks contributed material to *New Faces of 1952*.

32. *NYT*, "Broadway Goes All the Way to 7th Ave. for a Touch of Chic," Enid Nemy, April 13, 1968.

33. Miles Kreuger's liner notes are reprinted in the compact disc edition of *New Faces of 1968*, DRG Records, 2005.

34. A great year for Bergman parodies, 1968 also saw the publication of Woody Allen's short play *Death Knocks* in the *New Yorker* issue of July 27.

35. "Suddenly She Had a Fine Voice."

36. "Madeline Kahn: Too Pretty to Be Funny?" Rex Reed, syndicated column, published April 7, 1974. Also collected in *Valentines and Vitriol* (Delacorte Press, New York, 1977).

37. *The Tonight Show with Johnny Carson*, January 8, 1986, author's transcript. Found on YouTube at http://www.youtube.com/watch?v=DZYw6M3O4BM.

38. I assisted Dan Rather on several appearances on *Late Night with David Letterman* in the 1990s. Rather would spend hours on the phone with producers for the show; only rarely did Letterman even allude to the prepared material. Letterman's approach proved stressful for everybody concerned, except perhaps the host himself.

39. *Charlie Rose*, PBS, December 16, 1996, transcribed by the author.

40. "Woses Are Wed."

41. *New York Daily News*, Review of *Promenade*, James Davis, June 5, 1969.

42. *NYT*, "Theater: Wickedly Amusing 'Promenade,'" Clive Barnes, June 5, 1969.

43. *NYT*, "Hooray! He Gives Us Back Our Past," Walter Kerr, June 15, 1969. Marilyn Miller (1898–1936) was a popular star of sentimental Broadway musicals.

44. *NYT*, "Letters," July 6, 1969.

45. At the time of my interviews with Fredericks, the Music Circus website described Madeline as "a rather comic Magnolia." Ellie Koscheski, a spokesperson for the theater, confirmed that the copy was written by someone who did not see the production in 1969. Evidently the assumption was that if Madeline Kahn played something, it had to be funny.

46. *NYT*, "The Night: Sorry, It's an Eco-Thing, Show Thing, Hunk Thing," Bob Morris, October 9, 1994.

47. "Madeline's training is in the classical opera. She finds that music 'fulfilling, challenging, rewarding.' But Madeline is a Today girl who likes to be moved by the music she sings and the characters she plays. 'If I thought I had to do opera in a stilted way, I wouldn't do that, either.'" *Sacramento Union*, "Not Tradition Bound," Jackie Krug, August 4, 1969.

48. *Sacramento Union*, "'Remarkable' Musical: 'Show Boat' Ride Goes Beautifully," Richard Simon, August 6, 1969. The 5th Dimension's "Up, Up and Away" was a popular hit at the time.

49. Sacramento Music Circus, *Show Boat* program, courtesy of Ellie Koscheski, California Musical Theatre.

PART II

1. *NYT*, "The Funny Thing Is that They Are Still Feminine," Judy Klemesrud, January 14, 1970.

2. *Washington Post*, "A Beautiful Mimì," Paul Hume, March 7, 1970. Hume was rough on everybody, with the exception of Evelyn Mandac, who sang Mimì.

3. Met broadcast, January 3, 1985, cited in Part I.

4. Newspaper clipping, undated and unmarked, MK personal files.

5. Details on *Comedy Tonight* episodes, guest stars, and material can be found in TV listings. I relied on the *Kokomo (IN) Tribune* (July 5); the *Anderson (IN) Herald* (July 25); the *Anniston (AL) Star* (August 2); and the *Ludington (MI) Daily News* (August 7 and 21).

6. In act 2, Goldie lets her hair down and dresses like the family, in subdued colors and patches and tatters.

7. See *Boston Globe*, "'Two by Two' Lacks Real Sparkle," Kevin Kelly, Oct. 4, 1970. Kelly praises Willison as "sensational," adding that Madeline is merely "a cut below that." At the time of the review, she was still singing "Getting Married to a Person." Apart from Kaye and Copeland, Kelly lists the rest of the cast, describing them as "good, too."

8. *NYT*, "Stage: 'Two by Two'; Danny's the One," Clive Barnes, November 11, 1970.

9. *New York* magazine, "Divine Didactics," John Simon, November 23, 1970.

10. By coincidence, Joe Layton directed *Sherry*, the musical version of *The Man who Came to Dinner*, on Broadway in 1967. The experience didn't prepare him for Danny Kaye.

11. Photographs from the recording session for the cast album show Madeline wearing an especially large belt for support.

12. MK personal notebook.

13. "The Kaleidoscopic Madeline Kahn."

14. *Connoisseur*, "Madeline Kahn: A Talent Riddled with Self-Doubt," Linda Winer, January 1989.

15. *Charlie Rose*, December 16, 1996.

16. *Valentines & Vitriol*.

17. Ibid.

18. "Madeline Kahn: Maybe Now She'll Relax at Sardi's," Fran Weil. Undated clipping, no publication credited; found in MK personal files.

19. *Time*, "Popular Mechanics," Jay Cocks, April 10, 1972.

20. *NYT*, "What's Up, Doc?" Vincent Canby, March 10, 1972.

21. "The Kaleidoscopic Madeline Kahn."

22. Walter Willison was similarly "put on hold" for *Candide* and is the source for this background information.

23. Chapin, now the president and chief executive of the Rodgers & Hammerstein Organization, confirms the outlines of this story.

24. *Village Voice*, "Madeline Kahn: The Kook who Said 'Enough,'" Arthur Bell, June 14, 1973.

25. MK personal notebook.

26. "Woses Are Wed."

27. "The Kaleidoscopic Madeline Kahn."

28. Ibid.

29. *Valentines & Vitriol*.

30. NEA syndication service, "Madeline Kahn Looks Beyond Funny Roles," Dick Kleiner, March 31, 1975.

31. NEA syndication service, "Dick Kleiner's Showbeat," Dick Kleiner, December 4, 1972.

32. "Madeline Kahn: Maybe Now She'll Relax at Sardi's."

33. "The Kook who Said 'Enough.'"

34. "Woses Are Wed."

35. Ibid.

36. *New York* magazine, "Pleasure Trove," Judith Crist, May 21, 1973; *Time*, "Depression Diorama," Jay Cocks, May 28, 1973; "Maybe Now She'll Relax at Sardi's."

37. Eric Myers, *Uncle Mame: The Life of Patrick Dennis*, (St. Martin's Press, New York, 2000).

38. Richard Tyler Jordan, *But Darling, I'm Your Auntie Mame!* (Kensington Books, New York, 1998, 2004).

39. "The Kaleidoscopic Madeline Kahn."

40. *Valentines & Vitriol*.

41. Warren G. Harris, *Lucy and Desi: The Legendary Love Story of Television's Most Famous Couple* (Simon & Schuster, New York, 1991).

42. *Hollywood Reporter*, "Bea Arthur Quits 'Mame' Film After Role Disagreement," Radie Harris, December 22, 1972.

43. At the Golden Globe Awards in 1975, Arthur won the prize for best supporting actress in a motion picture for her work in *Mame*, beating Madeline, who was nominated for *Young Frankenstein*.

44. "The Kaleidoscopic Madeline Kahn."

45. The movie is sometimes referred to and marketed with its UK title, *The Hideaways*.

46. *Charlie Rose*, December 16, 1996. On a few occasions, Madeline alluded to her meeting with Brooks in the commissary, but their encounter made no lasting impression on him. In our interviews, he consistently said he didn't know her before her *Blazing Saddles* audition.

47. "Woses Are Wed." Ellipsis in the original.

48. "The Kaleidoscopic Madeline Kahn."

49. *NYT*, "Movie Review: 'Blazing Saddles,'" Vincent Canby, February 8, 1974.

50. Helen Epstein, *Joe Papp: An American Life* (Little Brown & Co., Boston, 1994).

51. Kenneth Turan and Joseph Papp, *Free for All: Joe Papp, the Public, and the Greatest Theater Story Ever Told* (Doubleday, New York, 2009). Bovasso preferred Jill Clayburgh, who auditioned for Chrissy and eventually married Rabe.

52. Ibid.

53. Ibid.

54. Ibid.

55. *NYT*, "Joseph Papp at the Zenith—Was It 'Boom' or Bust?" Patricia Bosworth, November 26, 1973.

56. *Free for All*.

57. *Time*, "Shallow Soul in Depth," T. E. Kalem, November 19, 1973.

58. *New Yorker*, *Boom Boom Room* review, Brendan Gill, November 19, 1973.

59. *NYT*, "'Boom Boom Room,'" Clive Barnes, November 9, 1973.

60. "Woses Are Wed."

61. *Washington Post*, "The Non-Perils of Playing Pauline: She's the Counterpoint on 'Cosby,'" Simi Horwitz, December 21, 1997.

62. WOR Radio, *Joe Franklin's Memory Lane*, interview with Madeline Kahn conducted by George Bettinger, circa 1997, courtesy of George Bettinger.

63. "Madeline Kahn Looks Beyond Funny Roles."

64. Gene Wilder, *Kiss Me Like a Stranger: My Search for Love and Art* (St. Martin's Press, New York, 2005). In correspondence with me, Wilder confirmed the recollections he shared in the book.

65. *Kiss Me Like a Stranger*.

66. Ibid.

67. Pauline Kael, *Reeling* (Little, Brown, Boston, 1977). The essays contained in the book originally appeared in the *New Yorker*.

68. David Black, *The Magic of Theater: Behind the Scenes with Today's Leading Actors* (Macmillan, New York, 1993).

69. *Newsweek*, "The Mad Mad Mel Brooks," Paul D. Zimmerman, February 17, 1975.

70. *The Paul Ryan Show*, undated, 1979. Found on YouTube and cited in *American Masters*, "Mel Brooks: Make a Noise," PBS, 2013.

71. *Washington Post*, "Madeline Kahn, On the Road Back to Broadway," Joe Brown, October 26, 1988.

72. "Madeline Kahn Looks Beyond Funny Roles."

73. Kreuger quotation from liner notes to the *At Long Last Love* soundtrack album, RCA recording ABL 2-0967.

74. Burt Reynolds, *My Life* (Hyperion, New York, 1994).

75. Not until Tom Hooper's adaptation of *Les Misérables* in 2012 would another big-screen musical be shot with live sound. Hooper's claim that his was the first film ever shot this way was either ignorant or fraudulent.

76. Reynolds, *My Life.*

77. Ibid.

78. Gould demonstrated his musical comedy skills in the *Saturday Night Live* episode in which Paula Kahn made her network television debut in 1976.

79. Pauline Kael, *Reeling.*

80. *NYT,* "'At Long Last Love' Evokes Past Films," Vincent Canby, March 7, 1975.

81. *Time,* "Playing Taps," Jay Cocks, March 31, 1975.

82. Ibid.

83. Kael, *Reeling.*

84. Madeline possessed drawing talent, though she didn't keep many samples of her work. The opening pages of her script for *Two by Two* are decorated with elaborate doodles, including her design for the Temple of the Golden Ram, topped off with curling horns.

85. Director's DVD commentary, *Sherlock Holmes' Smarter Brother,* 2006.

86. *NYT,* "Adroit 'Sherlock Holmes' Smarter Brother,'" Vincent Canby, December 15, 1975.

87. *Chicago Sun-Times,* "Gene Wilder," Roger Ebert, June 3, 1979.

88. Bruce Dern, *Things I've Said, But Probably Shouldn't Have: An Unrepentant Memoir* (with Christopher Fryer and Robert Crane; John Wiley & Sons, Hoboken, NJ, 2007).

89. Leibman won the Tony for his portrayal of another historical, closeted homosexual, Roy Cohn, in *Angels in America* in 1993. Both Leibman and Valentino deserved better than they got in *Won Ton Ton.*

90. *Things I've Said.*

91. MK personal notebook.

92. *NYT,* "Miss Kahn Lifts 'Won Ton Ton,'" Richard Eder, May 27, 1976.

93. *SNL*'s first music director, composer Howard Shore, describes the process by which he selected material for guest-hosts in Tom Shales and James Andrew Miller, *Live from New York: An Uncensored History of "Saturday Night Live" as Told by Its Stars, Writers & Guests* (Little, Brown, Boston, 2002).

94. Archive of American Television, Bucky Henry interview, February 26, 2009.

95. Though Radner later married Gene Wilder, she met him not through Madeline but on the set of *Hanky Panky* (1982). See *Kiss Me Like a Stranger.*

96. Madeline's copy of the *Carol Burnett* script contains an additional musical sketch, in which streetwalkers visit a used clothing store. The Jeanette MacDonald costume was later worn by Madeline's Upstairs co-star Dixie Carter in an episode of *Designing Women.*

97. *NYT,* "What Happens When the Scenery Tells Us a Lie," Walter Kerr, May 5, 1977.

98. *NYT,* "Language Alone Isn't Drama," Walter Kerr, March 6, 1977.

99. *NYT,* "'Marco Polo Sings a Solo,' a Play by John Guare, Opens at the Public," Clive Barnes, February 7, 1977.

100. *NYT,* "Song Pushes Song in 'She Loves Me,'" Richard Eder, March 30, 1977. Eder disliked both the material and the concert staging. His review of *She Loves Me* effectively doomed the rest of the concert series, Hayward-Jones says.

101. *Time,* "In Love with Love," T. E. Kalem, April 11, 1977.

102. Later, Whitlock appeared in *History of the World, Part I*, for which he painted the mattes that permitted Brooks to depict ancient Rome while shooting scenes "with a few sticks of furniture on the back lots of Universal," Brooks says. Whitlock's artwork is also featured in two films of particular interest to readers: *Willy Wonka and the Chocolate Factory* (1973), and *Mame* (1974).

103. *People*, "Picks and Pans," unsigned, January 23, 1978.

104. *NYT*, "Mel Brooks in 'High Anxiety,'" Vincent Canby, December 28, 1977.

105. "A Conversation with Neil Simon," DVD featurette produced and directed by Michael Gillis, *The Cheap Detective*, Columbia Pictures DVD, 2000.

106. *NYT*, "Simon's 'Cheap Detective': Everybody Revisited," Vincent Canby, June 23, 1978.

107. As of this writing, the Internet Movie Database still lists among Madeline's credits for 1977 a television production, *Once Upon a Brothers Grimm*. She is neither seen nor heard at any point in the program, though Teri Garr, Chita Rivera, and Cleavon Little participate.

108. Milholland was also an actor who worked with Ryan O'Neal in *So Fine* (1981). He reportedly based Oscar's character on the impresario David Belasco, author of the source play for Puccini's *Madama Butterfly*.

109. *NYT*, "A New Head of Stem for the Old 'Twentieth Century,'" Betty Comden and Adolph Green, February 9, 1978.

110. Ibid.

111. Eddie Shapiro, *Nothing Like A Dame: Conversations with the Great Women of Musical Theater* (Oxford University Press, New York, 2014). All quotations from Judy Kaye are derived from Shapiro's book; she declined an interview with me.

112. *Boston Globe*, "'Twentieth Century' Limited," Kevin Kelly, January 22, 1978.

113. *Time*, "Monorail," T. E. Kalem, March 6, 1978.

114. *NYT*, "Stage: 'On Twentieth Century,'" Richard Eder, February 20, 1978.

115. *NYT*, "Aboard the 'Twentieth Century'—Lots of Brio and a Few Bumps," Walter Kerr, February 26, 1978.

116. *New York*, "Charming Choo-Choo, Leaden Lulu," John Simon, March 6, 1978.

117. MK personal notebook.

118. Andy Propst, *You Fascinate Me So: The Life and Times of Cy Coleman* (Applause Books, New York, 2015).

119. MK personal notebook.

120. See Gould's obituary, *NYT*, "Dr. Wilbur J. Gould Dies at 74; Throat Surgeon to Famous Voices," Richard D. Lyons, February 6, 1994.

121. See Johnson's obituary, *NYT*, "Beverley Peck Johnson, 96, Voice Teacher," Anthony Tommasini, January 22, 2001.

122. Produced by the J. Walter Thompson agency, the television ad for *On the Twentieth Century* was one of the first for a Broadway show and extremely expensive, requiring construction of new sets that were destroyed after shooting ended. (This was less expensive than shooting on the real sets in the St. James, where stagehands would be paid overtime.) There was no question of reshooting for Judy Kaye, the ad's art director, Arthur Korant, says.

123. *Downstage Center*, American Theater Wing, interview with Cullum recorded December 28, 2007, found at http://americantheatrewing.org/downstagecenter/detail/john_cullum.

124. *People*, "'High Anxiety' Isn't Just a Film Title to Madeline Kahn, Newly Derailed on Broadway," Shaun Considine, May 15, 1978.

125. Kaye has won Tonys for her work as featured actress in the musicals *Phantom of the Opera* (1988, directed by Prince) and *Nice Work If You Can Get It* (2012). In the same category, she was also nominated for *Mamma Mia!* (2002).

126. Madeline weighed 117.5 lbs. when she left her apartment on Thursday, May 4, and must have been surprised to discover that she weighed 120 lbs. by the time she got to New Age, later that day. At the end of the first stay, her weight had dropped to 113 lbs. For those who aren't women, or actresses, or—more specifically—Madeline Kahn, the difference hardly seems worth troubling over.

127. This wasn't a problem when Madeline worked with Big Bird on *Sesame Street*, several years later.

PART III

1. *Washington Post*, "Madeline Kahn, On the Road Back to Broadway," Joe Brown, October 26, 1988.

2. *NYT*, "Screen: 'Simon' by Marshall Brickman," Vincent Canby, February 29, 1980.

3. Rosenberg went on to play a character based on Peter Bogdanovich in Cybill Shepherd's sitcom for Carsey-Werner in the 1990s.

4. Grant went on to play gay men in landmark productions: Joe Pitt in the original Broadway cast of *Angels in America*, and Russell on *thirtysomething*.

5. Henry already had co-directed *Heaven Can Wait* with Warren Beatty, in 1978, with a script by Beatty and Elaine May.

6. Rivers and Ullman in *American Masters*, "Mel Brooks: Make a Noise," PBS, 2013.

7. Comment from IMDb.com as of June 2013.

8. Kurt Vonnegut, foreword to *Slapstick, or Lonesome No More!* (paperback edition, Dial Press, New York, 1999).

9. *People*, "Madeline Kahn of Manhattan Is Now on a Santa Fe High and That Town's Blithest Spirit," Robert Goldstein, July 25, 1983.

10. *Santa Fe New Mexican*, "Festival Theater to Open June 29," June 17, 1981.

11. *Santa Fe New Mexican*, "Israeli Playwright's All-New 'Amerika' Debuts Monday," Benita Budd, August 1, 1982.

12. *Santa Fe New Mexican*, "'Amerika' and Footsbarn: 2 Theaters Centuries Apart," Benita Budd, August 8, 1982.

13. "Madeline Kahn of Manhattan Is Now on a Santa Fe High . . . ."

14. Associated Press, *Yellowbeard* review, Bob Thomas, found in the *Baytown (TX) Sun*, July 5, 1981.

15. Milligan in *Group Madness*, directed by Michael Mileham and Phillip Shuman, 1983.

16. Damski's recollections of *Yellowbeard* can be found on his blog for the *La Conner Weekly News*, published July 4, 11, and 18, 2012, and online at *If Mel Ran the Zoo*, http://www.ifmelranthezoo.com/?s=Yellowbeard.

17. "Madeline Kahn of Manhattan Is Now on a Santa Fe High . . . ."

18. *NYT*, "'Yellowbeard,' a 17th-Century Treasure Hunt," Lawrence Van Gelder, June 24, 1983.

19. "Mel Brooks: Make a Noise."

20. UPI, "Madeline Kahn Moves to Tube," found in *Logansport (IN) Pharos-Tribune*, July 31, 1983.

21. Carsey and Werner worked with Madeline on not one but two series. Both declined to be interviewed for this book. Background information and direct quotations (except where noted) are drawn from their joint interview with the Archive of American Television, from March 10, 2003, and from their website, carseywerner.com.

22. UPI, "High Points and Lows in ABC's Fall Show," Julianne Hastings, June 20, 1983.

23. *Washington Post*, "Oh No! 'Madeline'; ABC's Throwback to Comedy of the '50s," Tom Shales, September 27, 1983.

24. *Variety*, "TV Reviewed: 'Oh Madeline," review signed "Bok.," dated October 5, 1983. Earley and Rothenberg quotations from *TV Time Capsule*, "'Oh Madeline'? Oh Brother." Found at http://chrisbaker.typepad.com/tvtimecapsule/oh-madeline/. *People*, "Picks and Pans Review," unsigned, September 26, 1983.

25. UPI wire report, Kenneth R. Clark, July 30, 1983.

26. Ibid. See also Associated Press, "ABC Announces Fall Schedule," May 6, 1983; *Family Weekly* magazine, "Big-Screen Stars Turn to TV," Mark Goodman, September 25, 1983; *People* magazine, "Picks and Pans," September 26, 1983. Davis's health forced her to withdraw from *Hotel* after the pilot episode. Anne Baxter replaced her.

27. Associated Press, "Oh, Madeline: Kahn's New Series 'Defies Description,'" uncredited, found in *New Braunfels (TX) Herald-Zeitung*, October 23, 1983.

28. See *NYT*, *Périchole* review, Donal Henahan, October 31, 1983.

29. *NYT*, "Music Notes: From Film Comedy to Offenbach," Bernard Holland, October 2, 1983.

30. Interview with the Kalishes, Archive of American Television, part 4 of 4, December 21, 2012. Rocky Kalish did not work on *Oh Madeline* but witnessed from the sidelines.

31. Sloyan's and Giambalvo's representatives declined to respond to requests for an interview for this book. I was unable to find contact information for Jesse Welles.

32. UPI, "Censors, Not Ratings, Concern Comic Actress," uncredited writer, found in the *Salina (KS) Journal*, January 1, 1984.

33. Madeline's pride in engineering Ludlam's television debut can be detected in her biography in the playbill for *Born Yesterday* on Broadway. Nearly two years after his death, she cites this credit along with her Tony and Oscar nominations, and at greater length than she cites most of her best-known roles.

34. Kaufman, *Ridiculous!*

35. The scene is included in the complete episode found on the VHS copy in Madeline's personal collection.

36. Reynolds, *My Life*.

37. Best known for her films *Girlfriends* (1978) and *It's My Turn* (1980), Weill also has a long theater résumé and had staged Margulies's previous play, *Found a Peanut*, in 1984. *What's Wrong with This Picture?* found its way to Broadway in 1994, and in 1998, Margulies won the Pulitzer Prize for drama.

38. *Buzzfeed*, "'Something Terrible Has Happened Here': The Crazy Story of How 'Clue' Went from Forgotten Flop to Cult Triumph," Adam B. Vary, September 2, 2013. Found at http://www.buzzfeed.com/adambvary/something-terrible-has-happened-here-the-crazy-story-of-how#t1jd6z.

39. For more on Brennan's accident, see *People* magazine, April 22, 1985.

40. *Chicago Sun-Times, Clue* review, Roger Ebert, December 12, 1985.

41. *NYT*, "Screen: 'Clue,' from Game to Film," Janet Maslin, December 13, 1985.

42. "Madeline Kahn Steals the Show from the Rest of the Cast," *Altoona (PA) Mirror,* April 2, 1987; "The film's brief high points are those featuring the character of Gussie Mausheimer, whose voice is provided by Madeline Kahn repeating the Marlene Dietrich accent she used in *Blazing Saddles*, and Tiger, New York's only good cat [voiced by Dom DeLuise]," Vincent Canby, *NYT*, November 21, 1986. As for *My Little Pony*, Caryn James noted, "Madeline Kahn, Rhea Perlman, and Cloris Leachman bring some life to the clumsy witch daughters and their sinister mother," *NYT*, June 26, 1986.

43. We who have worked in television news refer to employees who conduct off-camera investigations as "producers," but the script for *Chameleon* doesn't go that far.

44. Draft letter of complaint, undated, found in MK personal files.

45. Both programs were broadcast on PBS, the Berlin on May 27, 1988, the Gershwin on November 27, 1987.

46. *NYT*, "How Madeline Kahn Works for Laughs," William H. Honan, January 29, 1989.

47. Ibid.

48. AADA speech.

49. *NYT*, "Stage View: Somebody Up There Likes Billie and Heidi," Walter Kerr, February 19, 1989. In the same essay, Kerr discusses Wendy Wasserstein's *The Heidi Chronicles*.

50. *Colorado Springs Gazette Telegraph*, "Kahn, Asner play to Comedic Perfection," Gilbert R. Johns, November 21, 1988.

51. *New Yorker*, "Yesterday Revisited," Mimi Kramer, February 13, 1989.

52. "On the Road Back to Broadway."

53. *Interview*, "Preview: Madeline Kahn," Hal Rubenstein, undated clipping from MK scrapbook.

54. Ibid.

55. "How Madeline Kahn Works for Laughs."

56. *Washington Post*, "'Born Yesterday': The Kahn Festival," David Richards, October 28, 1988.

57. "On the Road Back to Broadway."

58. Garson Kanin, *Born Yesterday* (Dramatists Play Service, New York, reissued 2002).

59. *Ryan's Hope* was also James Sloyan's best-known credit before *Oh Madeline*.

60. *Village Voice*, Bell column.

61. MK personal notebook.

PART IV

1. "Wasted here are the inimitable Madeline Kahn . . . ." *Los Angeles Times*, "Alan Alda's Talents Spread Too Thin in 'Betsy's Wedding,'" Sheila Benson, June 22, 1990.

2. Alda declined to be interviewed for this book.

3. *Toronto Star*, "Love Letters a Triumph in a Vacuum," Henry Mietkiewicz, June 21, 1990. A year later, Madeline performed *Love Letters* again, in Beverly Hills opposite Dabney Coleman.

4. *NYT*, "About Long Island: The Limelight Shines Brightly on the East Coast," Diane Ketcham, February 3, 1991.

5. Gleason confirms that, apart from Lemmon, the cast was not present for Madeline's scenes. The two actresses were friends, and Gleason is now married to *Marco Polo* co-star Chris Sarandon.

6. *Los Angeles Times*, "Lemmon Vehicle Seeks Laughs in the Streets," Chris Willman, February 29, 1992.

7. *Lucky Luke* was one of several Italian productions shooting in America at the time, when costs (outside Hollywood) were lower than in Europe. Hill is quoted in *NYT*, "In the U.S., Silenzio on the Set," Andy Meisler, August 2, 1992.

8. *Los Angeles Times*, "A Look Inside Vonnegut's 'Monkey House,'" John N. Goudas, February 21, 1993.

9. *Theater Week*, "Kahn's Way," Mervyn Rothstein, March 8, 1993.

10. Skipper is compiling an oral history of *Dolly*, containing interviews with virtually everyone who has ever worked on the show.

11. In fact, the amphitheater seats eleven thousand.

12. Clips of both performances can be found on YouTube.

13. Wendy Wasserstein, *The Sisters Rosensweig* (Harvest Books/Harcourt, San Diego, 1993).

14. Julie Salamon, *Wendy and the Lost Boys: The Uncommon Life of Wendy Wasserstein* (Penguin Press, New York, 2011).

15. Roy Harris, *Conversations in the Wings: Talking about Acting*.

16. *NYT*, "At Home with Madeline Kahn: Funny? Yes, but Someone's Got to Be," Michael Specter, April 8, 1993.

17. Wasserstein was the first woman to earn that double distinction in a single year.

18. "At Home with Madeline Kahn."

19. Wasserstein's script contains a lagniappe for Madeline, a malicious anecdote about Danny Kaye, told by Geoffrey while Gorgeous is onstage. Yes, Madeline laughed.

20. *Newsweek*, "You Gotta Have Heart," Jack Kroll, November 1, 1992; *Variety*, "The Sisters Rosensweig," Jeremy Gerard, October 23, 1992.

21. *NYT*, "Wasserstein: Comedy, Character, Reflection," Mel Gussow, October 23, 1992.

22. *Time*, "Reborn with Relevance," William A. Henry III, November 2, 1992.

23. "At Home With: Madeline Kahn."

24. Confusion about categories extended to Robert Klein, too. Although Mervyn is the principal male role in *Sisters Rosensweig*, he received a featured actor nomination at the Drama Desk Awards and lost to Spinella and Joe Mantello for *Angels in America* (David Marshall Grant was also nominated for his role in *Angels*). At the Outer Critics Circle Awards, *Angels* didn't compete that year, and there was no featured actor category, but with a nomination for best actor, Klein won.

25. *Conversations in the Wings*.

26. MK personal notebook.

27. Ibid.

28. Ibid.

29. Ibid.

30. *Entertainment Weekly*, "New York News," Ken Tucker, October 6, 1995; *NYT*, "Television Review: Mary, Mary, You're Turning Into Quite a Lou Grant," John J. O'Connor, September 28, 1995.

31. *San Francisco Chronicle*, "News Isn't Good for 'New York,'" John Carman, September 28, 1995.

32. *Washington Post*, "Moore Not Merrier in Gloomy 'N.Y. News,'" Tom Shales, September 28, 1995.

33. *Ogden (UT) Standard-Examiner*, *New York News* preview, Donald Porter, 1995. Found at http://theoccasionalcritic.blogspot.com/2012/11/mary-tyler-moore-new-york-news-1995.html.

34. MK personal notébook.

35. Because of the cancellation of *New York News*, guest appearances by Austin Pendleton, Julie Dretzin, and (in a three-episode arc) George C. Scott were never broadcast. Pendleton remembers no details about his time on the set.

36. *Live from New York*.

37. *San Francisco Chronicle*, "Stone's 'Nixon'—The Final Daze," Mick LaSalle, December 20, 1995. Joan Allen, star of Wasserstein's *Heidi Chronicles*, played Pat Nixon, earning an Oscar nomination, but LaSalle mentions her only in passing.

38. In case there's any doubt whose side we're on, Ivana Trump makes a cameo appearance.

39. *Variety*, "Ivana Trump's For Love Alone," Lisa D. Horowitz, January 5, 1996.

40. *Charlie Rose*, PBS, date unavailable, 1996, transcribed by the author. Cosby alludes to the pilot episode.

41. *NYT*, "New York Re-enters the Sitcom Universe, Wryly," Lawrie Mifflin, September 5, 1996.

42. *Washington Post*, "The Non-Perils of Playing Pauline; She's the Counterpoint on 'Cosby,'" Simi Horwitz, December 21, 1997.

43. See, for example, *Chicago Daily Herald*, "Cosby, Perlman take us back to the '70s," Ted Cox, September 16, 1996. Discussing *Cosby* and the Rhea Perlman sitcom *Pearl*, Cox wrote, "The written humor might be sparse, but Cosby himself seems to recognize that, so he takes up the slack in other ways. *Cosby* lets the star shine as a physical comedian; its best gags are slapstick. And when he and Kahn come up with a nice running joke about how they say goodbye to one another, it's icing on the cake."

44. "The Non-Perils of Playing Pauline."

45. Archive of American Television, interview with Phylicia Rashad, October 22, 2007, part 4 of 5. Rashad's representatives did not respond to requests for an interview. All quotations from her are drawn from the archive interview.

46. *Entertainment Weekly*, *Cosby* review, Ken Tucker, September 27, 1996.

47. *NYT*, "Dad's So Grumpy Now: The Cosby Persona Goes Into a New Phase of Life," John J. O'Connor, September 16, 1996.

48. Ted Barry letter to MK.

49. MK personal notebook.

50. See chapter 1, above.

51. See chapter 4, above.

52. See "The Butcher's Boy," collected in *Body, Boots & Britches: Folktales, Ballads and Speech from Country New York*, Harold William Thompson (Lippincott, 1939; reprinted by Syracuse University Press, 1979).

53. Meara appears briefly as Arthur's secretary in *Judy Berlin*, alongside Julie Kavner as a cafeteria worker.

54. Barrie had known Madeline socially for years. Her brother-in-law, Sheldon Harnick, wrote the lyrics to *She Loves Me*.

55. *Cosby*, "Loving Madeline," December 29, 1999.

56. Rashad, Archive of American Television interview.

EPILOGUE

1. "The following week, the *Globe* [a gossip magazine] quoted Hansbury 'sobbing' those exact words 'to friends.'" *Slate*, "Tabloids' 1999 Secrets Exposed!" Jennifer Mendelsohn (Eric's sister), December 31, 1999.

2. MK personal notebook.

3. See, for example, CNN interview with Chenoweth, December 7, 2011 (available at http://www.cnn.com/2011/12/07/world/cnnheroes-kristin-chenoweth/).

STAGE, SCREEN, AND TELEVISION
ROLES AND RECORDINGS

STAGE ROLES

Roles at Hofstra University include:

Judy O'Grady, *The Adding Machine* (Rice), Miriam Tulin, director, 1960.

Jenny (a servant), *The Contrast* (Tyler), 1960 or 1961.

Jacquenetta, *Love's Labour's Lost* (Shakespeare), Bernard Beckerman, director, 1961.

Hilda Miller, *Plain and Fancy* (Hague, Horwitt, Stein and Glickman), Gene Nye, director; Albert Tepper, music director, 1961.

Miss Adelaide, *Guys and Dolls* (Loesser), Albert Tepper, music director, 1962.

Soloist, *Requiem* (Mozart), Herbert Beattie, conductor, 1964. (Concert)

Chorus member, *Kiss Me, Kate* (Porter), John Fearnley and Billy Matthews, directors; Pembroke Davenport, conductor; Hanya Holm, choreographer; City Center, New York City, 1965.

Daisy Mae, *Li'l Abner* (DePaul, Mercer, Panama, Frank), mid-1960s, exact date and location unknown. An unmarked publicity photo showing Madeline and an unidentified actor can be found in her personal collection.

Various roles, *Just for Openers, Mixed Doubles, Below the Belt*, Upstairs at the Downstairs, New York City, Rod Warren, director, 1965–66.

Miss Whipple, *How Now, Dow Jones* (E. Bernstein, Leigh, Shulman), Arthur Penn and George Abbott, directors, Shubert Theatre, Boston, 1967.

Various roles, *Leonard Sillman's New Faces of 1968*, Leonard Sillman and Frank Wagner, directors, Booth Theatre, New York City, 1968.

Carol Melkett, *Black Comedy* (Shaffer), Martin Fried, director, Playhouse in the Park, Philadelphia, 1968.

Cunegonde, *Candide* (Bernstein, Wilbur, and Patinkin), Sheldon Patinkin, director; Maurice Peress, conductor, Philharmonic (Avery Fisher) Hall, New York City, 1968. (Concert staging.) Other appearances as Cunegonde include Corpus Christi and Philadelphia.

The Servant, *Promenade* (Carmines, Fornés), Lawrence Kornfeld, director, Promenade Theater, New York City, 1969.

Magnolia, *Show Boat* (Kern), Milton Lyon, conductor and director, Music Circus, Sacramento, 1969.

Musetta, *La Bohème* (Puccini), Maurice Peress, conductor, Washington Opera Society, 1970.

Goldie, *Two by Two* (Rodgers, Charnin, Stone), Joe Layton, director; Jay Blackton, conductor; Imperial Theatre, New York City, as well as tryouts in New Haven (Shubert Theatre) and Boston (Shubert Theatre), 1970–71.

Chrissy, *Boom Boom Room* (Rabe), Julie Bovasso and Joseph Papp, directors, Vivian Beaumont Theater, Lincoln Center, New York City, 1973. (Tony nomination, Drama Desk Award.)

Amalia Balash, *She Loves Me* (Bock, Harnick, Masteroff), John Bowab, director; Wally Harper, conductor; Town Hall, New York City, 1977. (Concert staging.)

Diane McBride, *Marco Polo Sings a Solo* (Guare), Mel Shapiro, director, Public Theater, New York City, 1977.

Lily Garland/Mildred Plotka, *On the Twentieth Century* (Coleman, Comden & Green), Harold Prince, director; Paul Gemignani, conductor; St. James Theatre, New York City, as well as tryouts in Boston (Colonial Theatre), 1978. (Tony nomination.)

Multiple roles, *Amerika* (Porat, Gronich), Robert Allan Ackerman, director, Festival Theater, Santa Fe, 1982.

Mme. Arcati, *Blithe Spirit* (Coward), Robert Allan Ackerman, director, Festival Theater, Santa Fe, 1983.

Shirley, *What's Wrong with This Picture?* (Margulies), Claudia Weill, director, Manhattan Theatre Club, New York City. (Workshop production.)

Billie Dawn, *Born Yesterday* (Kanin), Josephine Abady and John Tillinger, directors, 46th Street Theatre, New York City, 1989, as well as national tour prior to Broadway. (Tony nomination.)

Melissa Gardner, *Love Letters* (Gurney), John Tillinger, director, Winter Garden Theatre, Toronto, 1990; Canon Theater, Beverly Hills, CA, 1991.

Dolly Gallagher Levi, *Hello, Dolly!* (Herman, Stewart), Lee Roy Reams, director, touring production in Atlanta, St. Louis, and Kansas City, 1992.

Gorgeous Teitelbaum, *The Sisters Rosensweig* (Wasserstein), Daniel Sullivan, director, Vivian Beaumont Theater, Lincoln Center, and Ethel Barrymore Theater, New York City, 1992–93. (Tony Award, Drama Desk Award, Outer Critics Circle Award.)

Cora Hoover Hooper, *Anyone Can Whistle* (Sondheim, Laurents), Herbert Ross, director; Paul Gemignani, conductor, Carnegie Hall, New York City, 1995. (Concert staging.)

Helen Hobart, *Once in a Lifetime* (Kaufman & Hart), Michael Mayer, director, Roundabout Theatre Company, New York City, 1996. (Public reading.)

Kandall Kingsley, *Impossible Marriage* (Henley), Scott Ellis, director, Roundabout Theatre Company, New York City, 1996. (Workshop, closed reading.)

Gabrielle, the Madwoman of Montmartre, *Dear World* (Herman, Lawrence, Lee), Scott Ellis, director, Roundabout Theatre Company, New York City, 1998. (Public reading.)

SCREEN ROLES

Arthur's Wife, *A Song of Arthur, or How Arthur Changed His Tune and Solved a Weighty Problem*, David Hoffman, director, 1967.

Cousin Sigfrid, *De Düva* (The Dove), George Coe and Anthony Lover, directors, 1968.

Eunice Burns, *What's Up, Doc?*, Peter Bogdanovich, director, 1972. (Golden Globe nomination for most promising newcomer.)

Trixie Delight, *Paper Moon*, Peter Bogdanovich, director, 1973. (Academy Award and Golden Globe nominations for supporting actress.)

Schoolteacher, *From the Mixed-up Files of Mrs. Basil E. Frankweiler*, Fielder Cook, director, 1973.

Lili von Shtupp, *Blazing Saddles*, Mel Brooks, director, 1974. (Academy Award nomination for supporting actress.)

Elizabeth, *Young Frankenstein*, Mel Brooks, director, 1974. (Golden Globe and New York Film Critics nominations for supporting actress.)

Kitty O'Kelly, *At Long Last Love*, Peter Bogdanovich, director, 1975.

Jenny Hill, *The Adventure of Sherlock Holmes' Smarter Brother*, Gene Wilder, director, 1975.

Estie del Ruth, *Won Ton Ton, the Dog Who Saved Hollywood*, Michael Winner, director, 1976.

Victoria Brisbane, *High Anxiety*, Mel Brooks, director, 1977.

Mrs. Montenegro, *The Cheap Detective*, Robert Moore, director, 1978.

Woman in the El Sleezo Café, *The Muppet Movie*, James Frawley, director, 1979.

Cynthia Mallory, *Simon*, Marshall Brickman, director, 1980.

Bunny Weinberger, *Happy Birthday, Gemini*, Richard Benner, director, 1980.

Aunt Yochtabel (The Witch), *Wholly Moses!*, Gary Weis, director, 1980.

Constance Link, *First Family*, Buck Henry, director, 1980.

Empress Nympho, *History of the World, Part I*, Mel Brooks, director, 1981.

Eliza and Lutetia Swain, *Slapstick (Of Another Kind)*, Steven Paul, 1982–84.

Mrs. Yellowbeard, *Yellowbeard*, Mel Damski, director, 1983.

Caroline Howley, *City Heat*, Richard Benjamin, director, 1984.

Mrs. White, *Clue*, Jonathan Lynn, director, 1985.

Draggle, *My Little Pony: The Movie*, Michael Joens, director, 1986. (Voice only.)

Gussie Mausheimer, *An American Tail*, Don Bluth, director, 1986. (Voice only.)

Lola Hopper, *Betsy's Wedding*, Alan Alda, director, 1990.

Mrs. Muchnik, *Mixed Nuts*, Nora Ephron, director, 1994.

Martha Mitchell, *Nixon*, Oliver Stone, director, 1995. (Shared Screen Actors Guild Award for outstanding performance by a cast.)

Gypsy, *A Bug's Life*, John Lasseter and Andrew Stanton, directors, 1998. (Voice only.)

Alice Gold, *Judy Berlin*, Eric Mendelsohn, director, 1999.

NOTABLE TELEVISION ROLES

Various roles, *Comedy Tonight*, 1970.

Nurse Ruth Kelly, *Harvey*, Fielder Cook, director, 1972.

Doris Attinger, *Adam's Rib*, Peter H. Hunt, director, 1973.

Madeline Wayne, *Oh Madeline*, J. D. Lobue, director, 1983–84. (People's Choice Award for favorite female performer in a new TV program.)

Violet Kingsley, *Chameleon*, John Rich, director, 1986.

Ellie Coleman, *ABC Afterschool Specials*, "Wanted: The Perfect Guy," Catlin Adams, director, 1986. (Daytime Emmy Award.)

Lois Gullickson, *Mr. President*, various directors, 1987–88.

Pigeon Plumtree, *Avonlea*, "It's Just a Stage," René Bonnière, director, 1991.

Billie, *For Richer, for Poorer*, Jay Sandrich, director, 1992.

Esperanza, Queen of the Gypsies, *Lucky Luke*, "Midsummer in Daisy Town," Terence Hill, director, 1992.

Grace Anderson, *Kurt Vonnegut's Monkey House*, "More Stately Mansions," Brad Turner, director, 1993.

Nan Chase, *New York News*, various directors, 1995.

Sabrina, *Ivana Trump's For Love Alone*, Michael Lindsay-Hogg, director, 1996.

Sharon Semple, *Neil Simon's London Suite*, Jay Sandrich, director, 1996.

Pauline Fox, *Cosby*, various directors, 1996–99.

Notable guest appearances on:

The Carol Burnett Show, 1976.

Saturday Night Live, 1976, 1977, 1995.

The George Burns Special, 1976.

Klein Time, 1977.

The Muppet Show, 1977.

Sesame Street, 1978, 1983, 1987, 1988, 1993.

A Salute to American Imagination, 1978. (Marking the seventy-fifth anniversary of the Ford Motor Company, the program was written by Rod Warren of Upstairs at the Downstairs. As co-host, Madeline appeared with several notable colleagues, including Telly Savalas, Edward Asner, Imogene Coca, Sid Caesar, Neil Simon, and Johnny Mathis.)

Fridays, 1981.

All-Star Party for Burt Reynolds, 1984.

Comic Relief, 1986. (In this first benefit for the homeless, Madeline performed "I'm Tired.")

Celebrating Gershwin, 1987.

Irving Berlin's 100th Birthday Celebration, 1988.

Love Laughs, 1993. (Madeline sings "Das Chicago Song" and "Ain't Got No Home" in this program hosted by Teri Garr.)

Sondheim: A Celebration at Carnegie Hall, 1993.

NOTABLE RECORDINGS

Upstairs at the Downstairs: Just for Openers original cast album, 1965.

Upstairs at the Downstairs: Mixed Doubles/Below the Belt original cast album, 1966.

New Faces of 1968 original cast album, 1968.

Two by Two original cast album, 1970.

"I'm Only Thinking of Him," *Man of La Mancha* studio cast album, 1972.

At Long Last Love original soundtrack album, 1975.

"Steal Away Again," backup vocals, *Carole Bayer Sager*, 1977.

On the Twentieth Century original cast album, 1978.

"Sing After Me," *The Stars Come Out on Sesame Street*, 1979.

"Rumble, Rumble, Rumble," *Ben Bagley's Frank Loesser Revisited*, date unconfirmed.

"Lonesome No More" (Legrand, Vonnegut), unreleased, 1982.

"Getting Married Today," *Sondheim: A Celebration at Carnegie Hall*, 1993.

The Hungry Caterpillar, audiobook, 1994.

Anyone Can Whistle benefit cast album, 1995.

"Singin' in the Bathtub" (Cleary, Margidson, Washington) with "O Sole Mio" (di Capua, Capurro), duet with Johnny Cash, 1998.

Notable pirate recordings include *Candide* (1968), *She Loves Me* (1977), and *On the Twentieth Century* (1978); pirate video of *Hello, Dolly!* (1992).

Archival video of *The Sisters Rosensweig* (at the Mitzi Newhouse Theater, 1993) in the Theater on Film and Tape Archive at New York Public Library for the Performing Arts, Lincoln Center.

INDEX